UAW Politics in the Cold War Era

SUNY Series in
American Labor History

Robert Asher and
Charles Stephenson, Editors

UAW Politics in the Cold War Era

MARTIN HALPERN

State University of New York Press

All photos courtesy of the Archives of
Labor and Urban Affairs, Wayne State University.

Published by
State University of New York Press, Albany

© 1988   State University of New York

For more information, address State University of New York
Press, State University Plaza, Albany, N.Y., 12246

Library of Congress Cataloging in Publication Data

Halpern, Martin, 1945-
    UAW politics in the cold war era.

    (SUNY series in American labor history)
    Bibliography: p.
    Includes index.
    1. International Union, United Automobile, Aerospace,
and Agricultural Implement Workers of America—History.
2. Trade-unions and communism—United States—History—
Case studies.   I. Title.   II. Series.
HD6515.A82I574   1988   322'.2'0973   87-13890
ISBN 0-88706-671-2
ISBN 0-88706-672-0 (pbk.)

10   9   8   7   6   5   4   3   2   1

To My Mother, Helen Halpern,
and to the Memory of My Father,
Eli Sanford Halpern

Contents

Acknowledgements

I wish to acknowledge the help of librarians, archivists, and other staff of the following institutions: the Archives of Labor History and Urban Affairs, Wayne State University, especially Warner Pflug; the National Archives and Records Service, especially Patrick Garabedian; the General Archives Division; the Truman Library; the Michigan Historical Collections; the Wisconsin State Historical Society; the State of Michigan Archives; the Ford Motor Company archives; the Catholic University; the Columbia University Library; the Tamiment Library at New York University; the John F. Kennedy Library; the Chicago Historical Society; the Roosevelt University Archieves; the University of Michigan Library; the Michigan State University Library; the G. Flint Purdy Library, Wayne State University; and the Detroit Public Library.

I am greatly indebted to Professor Sidney Fine for the care with which he read the manuscript in its various stages, his stylistic suggestions, and his valuable substantive criticisms. With each new reading of the manuscript, Professor Fine raised fresh questions that helped me to reexamine my arguments and improve the work. If the result is not as balanced as it might be, it is more nearly so than it would have been without Professor Fine's counsel. I warmly thank Professor Robert Asher, co-editor of the SUNY series in American Labor History, whose expression of interest in the manuscript stimulated me to complete the revision of the work. I appreciate the encouragement Professor Asher offered and value his comments on the manuscript. Professors Gerald Linderman, Robin Jacoby, Thomas Weisskopf, Norman Markowitz, and Marilyn Young read all or part of the manuscript and provided useful advice. Professor John Barnard's and David Moore's criticisms of my paper on Coleman Young and the Wayne County CIO Council at the North American Labor History Conference helped me to recast the chapter on that topic included herein. I thank Christopher Johnson for sharing with me his soon to be published biography of Maurice Sugar.

I thank my colleagues at the Michigan Department of Public Health, particularly John Beasley, for their encouragement of my efforts to complete this work. Dennis Dodson aided me in the use of the University of Michigan computer system and provided me with advice on statistics. Janet Dodson provided me with assistance in word processing.

My parents, Eli and Helen Halpern, stimulated my initial interest in the labor and left wing movements, and provided me with the confidence that I could be both partisan and truthful. My wife, Helen Webb, and I hope that we can provide our children, Sheila and Leah, with the same confidence.

Introduction

In November 1947, the Reuther caucus defeated the Thomas-Addes-Leonard coalition at the UAW's eleventh convention and assumed complete control of the 800,000-member union. The Thomas-Addes-Leonard coalition, a popular front formation that accepted Communist participation, had been the majority group on the union's International Executive Board, but, with the loss of its base in union office, it went out of existence. The Reuther caucus, which united a variety of anti-Communist elements, succeeded in consolidating its power to such an extent that there has been no serious challange to its leadership since its victory. Within a few years of its triumph, moreover, the Reuther group largely succeeded in driving Communists and other left wingers from leadership roles even at the local union level.

The key event that led to the eventual elimination of the left-wing base from political life in the United States was the break up of the left-center coalition in the CIO. Thus, repression took its toll on UAW left wingers only after the Thomas-Addes-Leonard caucus, a left-center coalition, had been defeated and fell apart.

A number of scholars, including Bert Cochran and Harvey Levenstein, see little or no difference between the left-center alliance in the UAW and the Reuther right-center group. Both groups were, indeed, led by socially aware CIO trade unionists. The dominant fact about the caucuses, moreover, was that they were patronage machines built around national officers and regional directors. Through their staffs, these leaders provided services to local unions and opportunities for advancement to local officials. This reliance on staff members had increased significantly during World War II as the result of the expansion of the union's administrative apparatus to deal with wartime agencies of the federal government and the union's many war-related responsibilities. The differences between the two groups were nevertheless critical.

It is well known, of course, that the Reuther group included Socialists, social democrats, and members of the Association of Catholic Trade Unionists and excluded Communists, whereas the Addes group accepted Communist participation. The fact that the Addes group was willing to work with and was influenced by Communists and that the Reuther group was determined to oppose Communist activity in the union as illegitimate led to many differences between the caucuses.

The Reuther group was willing to accommodate itself to cold war priorities, whereas the Thomas-Addes-Leonard coalition resisted the new directions in United States foreign and domestic policy. Leaders of the Addes group were critical of the Truman administration in 1947, looked with favor on Henry Wallace, the chief critic of the administration's foreign policy, and opposed compliance with the required non-Communist affidavits and other provisions of the Taft-Hartley Act. Leaders of the Reuther caucus, on the other hand, withheld criticism of the president in 1947, were antagonistic to Wallace, and supported compliance with the Taft-Hartley Act.

Two influential writers on the UAW, Irving Howe and B. J. Widick, have contended that, whatever the political differences between the two auto union caucuses, Reuther won because he was more militant on economic issues than his opponents, as evidenced by his opposition to incentive pay during World War II, his willingness to consider modifying the wartime no-strike pledge, and his leadership of the GM strike after the war. The Reuther group used the incentive pay issue to make propaganda points during the postwar period, but, if the wartime questions had really been decisive, the Reuther caucus would have taken control at the tenth UAW convention in March 1946. As for the GM strike, although Reuther's approach caused a number of problems for the UAW, he did gain from the fact that he was the highly visible leader of the union's major reconversion strike. Reuther's success in increasing his personal strength enabled him to wrest the presidency from R. J. Thomas in 1946, but the Reuther caucus as a whole did not benefit and the Thomas-Addes-Leonard forces retained an executive board majority. During the 1946–1947 factional struggle, the two sides pursued essentially the same collective bargaining strategy in negotiations with the Big Three companies.

Until recently, most UAW scholars agreed with Walter Reuther's contention that he had won the battle against his opposition on the basis of legitimate trade union issues and not on the basis of name-calling or red-baiting. His opponents, on the other hand, saw red-baiting as the essential reason for his victory. "Name-calling" was not the sum total of the Reuther caucus campaign, but, in fact, his campaign was based, not on a positive program, but on negative issues connected with anti-Communism. His victory, however, did not stem from a rank-and-file rebellion against Communists or their allies. Rather, the pressures of the antilabor and anti-Communist campaigns caused many center elements in the union that had been relatively independent in factional terms and others who had been Addes supporters to line up with Reuther. Although the turning point in intraunion terms was the failure of an ill-conceived UAW merger with the left-wing FE that had been promoted by the Addes caucus, the underlying cause was the concurrent passage of the Taft-Hartley Act. The balance of power tipped to the Reuther side in mid-1947 as a significant number of centrist rank-and-filers and secondary leaders decided that the UAW would be subject to fewer attacks and would be better able to deal with antilabor forces if it were led by the Reuther group rather than the Thomas-Addes-Leonard coalition, which had Communist associations.

The shift of a section of the center to the Reuther group enabled it to win many local elections for delegates to the 1947 convention by small margins. It secured a two-to-one majority at the convention and won 18 of 22 seats on the union's executive board. Although its support at the local level was far less impressive than these margins suggest, the Reuther group was able to consolidate its hold on the leadership within a short time. The Thomas-Addes-Leonard coalition collapsed and disappeared because it lost its character as a patronage machine with its loss of national office and because cold war politics had undermined its strength with the union's center.

Following the decisive defeat of the Thomas-Addes-Leonard group in the UAW, the fortunes of the left-center trend in the trade union movement declined rapidly. Within a few weeks of the UAW convention, the new Murray-Reuther alliance in the CIO demanded that all sections of the industrial union movement oppose Henry Wallace's third party candidacy and endorse the Marshall Plan. Although Wallace's candidacy initially attracted the interest of many CIO center elements dissatisfied with Truman, as the cold war deepened and the campaign developed, support for him dwindled. Wallace's opponents within the liberal community, principally the CIO leadership and the Americans for Democratic Action, succeeded in labelling him as a "captive of the Communists." In the end, the Wallace voters mainly consisted of the left and its closest supporters. The left had become politically isolated.

Even before its isolation, opponents of the left attempted to oust its activists from any leadership role in the labor movement. With the left's isolation, the barrage from Congressional investigations, FBI antisubversive activity, company attacks, newspaper "exposés," and purge attempts by its union opponents became continuous. Before Senator Joseph McCarthy launched the anti-Communist campaign that became known as McCarthyism, the CIO expelled eleven left-wing unions on charges they were Communist dominated. The actions of liberal and right-wing anti-Communists succeeded in creating a wall against normal participation by Communists and their supporters in the body politic.

McCarthyism represented a new stage in the development of the domestic anti-Communist campaign. McCarthy attacked not only Communists but the New Deal itself. Although he did not succeed in convincing the majority that the New Deal was treasonous, he helped to shift the political spectrum significantly to the right. The war in Korea and the intensification of the domestic anti-Communist hysteria led by McCarthy brought about a deepening of the isolation of the left. The cold war consensus in foreign and domestic policy lasted for another one and one-half decades after McCarthy's downfall. The possibility that activists of the popular front period would rebuild a left-center alliance was not to be. The break up of the left-center trend of the 1935–1946 period was irreversible.

Although the cold war limited the progressive potential of the postwar period in a variety of ways, the Reuther administration, thanks to a booming economy and its own aggressiveness, was nevertheless able to win significant wage and fringe benefit gains for UAW members. The Reuther group consolidated its control of the union on the basis of real achievements, particularly in the collective bargaining arena. The UAW no longer supported popular front policies, but the elimination of such policies from the bounds of acceptable political discourse made the auto union's liberalism about as far to the left of the political spectrum as a major "respectable" organization could venture. The union movement, for a generation, had to function without the valuable catalyst of a grass roots radical movement.

Chapter One

The Automobile Industry
in the Postwar Era

As the result of the 1936–1937 Flint sit-down strike, the automobile workers captured the nation's imagination and played a leading role in the reshaping of the country's industrial, social, and political landscape. Workers in the automobile and other major industries had gained a say over their wages and working conditions, and their newly established unions had acquired an important role in politics and in the social life of the community. The corporations' acceptance of the new order of things was, at best, reluctant. They thought the new unions of the Committee for Industrial Organization (CIO) had acquired too much power and were too subject to radical, and especially, Communist, influence. Although almost all union leaders opposed a postwar corporate campaign for restrictive labor legislation, they were divided on the question of the Communist role in their unions. In the ensuing conflicts over labor power and Communist influence that helped to shape the direction of the labor movement in the postwar years, the automobile workers were again at center stage. The motor vehicle industry's economic importance helped to give the struggles of the United Automobile Workers (UAW) special significance.

The automobile industry occupied a central place in the United States economy in the postwar period. One in seven persons was employed in businesses dependent on the motor vehicle industry, including truck and bus drivers, those involved in the sale and servicing of automobiles, and workers engaged in the manufacture of automobiles, trucks, tires, and parts. Motor vehicle production had become the leading manufacturing industry by the end of the 1920s in terms of the value of its product. Although the automobile industry was hit hard by the depression, General Motors Corporation (GM), the leading manufacturing company, had reported a net income of $1.3 billion for the 1930s. The automobile industry had maintained its preeminence during World War II by converting to war production. The industry produced $29 billion in war products, about 20 percent of the total.[1]

Although automobile manufacturing was initiated at the turn of the century by many small firms, the industry had become dominated by the end of the 1920s by three large companies, General Motors, Ford, and Chrysler. The Big Three produced 85 percent of U. S. passenger cars during the 1946–1950 period. "Independent" firms such as Hudson, Nash-Kelvinator, Packard, and Studebaker produced the remaining vehicles. Although the independents' share of the market in the immediate postwar years was greater than in the years just before the war because of the pent-up demand for automobiles, the Big Three continued to dominate the industry.[2]

Control by a few firms extended from the assembly of finished vehicles to the manufacture of parts. Government data on economic concentration show that the four largest companies produced 56 percent of the $3.5 billion in value added by manufacturing in the motor vehicle and parts industry in 1947. By 1954, the top four firms accounted for 75 percent of value added by the industry. Fifty-nine percent of employees in the motor vehicle and parts industries worked for one of the four largest companies in 1950, a proportion that increased to 69 percent in 1954.[3]

In addition to producing many of their own parts, the Big Three often provided tools for their suppliers' production. In the event of an actual or threatened strike at a supplier firm, the Big Three company could withdraw its tools. Even when not dependent on GM, Ford, or Chrysler for capital, parts firms were in a subordinate position in the industry. The major share of the parts manufacturers' product had to be sold to one or another of the Big Three companies, whereas the latter generally had more than one supplier for each part or could choose to produce the item themselves. This situation enabled the Big Three to extract favorable terms from its suppliers. Ford, for example, paid Champion 6¢ for spark plugs that cost the public 22¢ to 29¢ as replacement parts.[4]

The Big Three also were able to control their relationships with their dealers. The basis of the dealers' business was the right to sell a particular brand of automobile, a right that could be revoked unilaterally by the manufacturer. The automobile producer could force the dealer to take unwanted cars and could dictate the terms of their financial arrangements. From the end of the war until the 1948–1949 recession, however, the dealers wanted all the cars the manufacturer could deliver. Throughout the years, the tendency of the manufacturers to take full advantage of their power over the dealers has been restrained somewhat by their need to have a "good and loyal dealer organization."[5]

The oligopolistic nature of the automobile industry allowed the Big Three, within limits, to set the prices for their products. As in other industries dominated by a few producers, prices in the automobile manufacturing industry were "administered." General Motors was the price leader, the other firms following its decisions. GM established a target profit rate of 20 percent and set its prices to reach this goal. Before the war, Ford Motor Company, a family-owned firm, had operated independently of GM and Chrysler with respect to prices and other matters. Henry Ford II, taking over from his grandfather in 1945, sought industry leadership on the price issue when he campaigned publicly against the extension of price control after the war. He then attempted to maintain Ford's low price reputation by cutting prices slightly on some models in January 1947. By the end of the year, however, Ford had more than eliminated its price cut and had followed GM's lead in increasing prices.[6]

The postwar price increases were substantial. The price of Ford's V-8 four-door sedan, for example, increased from a 1946 Office of Price Administration level of $885 to $1,546 in 1949. The demand for automobiles was so great, however, that a "gray" market developed for "used" new cars. The manufacturers did not raise prices as much as the market would have allowed because of the fear of "adverse reactions," such as antimonopoly moves by the federal government. The recession of 1948–1949 put an end to the excess demand for automobiles and the automobile gray market.[7]

Despite their price restraint, the auto companies' profits reached record levels in the postwar years. GM's 1947 reported net income of $288 million surpassed its 1928 high by $12 million. GM then realized new record profits in each of the next three years, $440 million in 1948, $656 million in 1949, and $834 million in 1950. GM's rate of profit on net worth also increased from 18.3 percent in 1947 to 35.0 percent in 1950. GM and the auto industry as a whole had a lower profit rate than other manufacturing corporations in 1946, a year of low automobile production. Between 1947 and 1950, however, the rate of profit for the automobile industry increased from 16.0 to 27.5 percent of net worth and ranged from 21 percent to 162 percent above the average for all manufacturing corporations.[8]

The reported record profits of GM and other auto firms give only a partial picture of the postwar profitability of the automobile industry. Dealers did especially well during these years of high demand, their rate of profit on net worth ranging from 15 percent to 38 percent between 1946 and 1950. When the salaries of officers of the dealerships are included, their profits ranged from 30 percent to 56 percent. Although in later years, the dealers' profits were about the same as those of other retailers, they were significantly above the norm in the immediate postwar years. The profitability of the industry also resulted in high salaries and bonuses for auto company executives. GM's president Charles E. Wilson, for example, received $586,100 in salary, bonus, and stock in 1949. Substantial GM profits also accrued to the company's unconsolidated subsidiary, General Motors Acceptance Corporation, which loaned funds to the purchasers of GM cars. Nor do reported auto industry income figures include unremitted profits from foreign operations, which were growing rapidly in this period. GM's consolidated foreign subsidiaries retained $90 million in profits in 1950, more than 50 percent of their net assets.[9]

Although lagging somewhat behind the industry average, Ford steadily increased its rate of profit in the five years after the war. Its profits were 22.5 percent on net worth in 1950. When Henry Ford II assumed the presidency of the company in 1945, the family-owned firm had to overcome crisis conditions brought on by poor management. The younger Ford brought in a group of GM executives, headed by Ernest Breech, who reorganized the company on the basis of GM management principles. Ford was no longer to be the maverick of the industry.[10]

The increase of automobile industry profits was based on the sharp rise in production and productivity in the postwar period. Value added by manufacture in the motor vehicle and equipment industry increased from $1.3 billion in 1939 to $3.8 billion in 1947 and $6.1 billion in 1950. When one takes account of the decline in the value of the dollar as measured by the Bureau of Labor Statistics' Consumer Price Index (CPI), the value added by manufacturing increased by approximately 80 percent between 1939 and 1947 and then by nearly 50 percent between 1947 and 1950. Productivity, as measured by the value added by manufacturing per hour of production work, also increased dramatically, rising (in 1950 dollars) from $3.16 in 1939 to $3.47 in 1947 and $4.56 in 1950. The annual rate of increase in productivity between 1947 and 1950 was nearly 10 percent. Although the automobile industry was not able to maintain this rate of increase in productivity after 1950, its performance remained well above the national average. Auto unionists often charged that the industry's increasing productivity was a product not only of technical improvements in machinery but of a "speed-up" of the workers.[11]

Although automobile workers were concerned about speed-up, they were able to increase both their money and real wages during the postwar years. Average weekly earnings increased from $32.91 in 1939 to $51.45 in 1947 and $73.25 in 1950. Real earnings (in 1950 dollars) increased from $56.91 in 1939 to $61.86 in 1947 and $73.25 in 1950. The relative increase in real wages between 1939 and 1947 was almost as great as the increase in productivity in that period. The 1947–1950 annual rate of increase in auto workers' real wages, however, was 5.8 percent, considerably less than the rate of increase in productivity. As a result of this disparity, the workers' share of the wealth produced by the industry declined. The proportion of the total value added by motor vehicle manufacturing which went to wages dropped from 48.9 percent in 1939 to 46.7 percent in 1947 and then to 40.0 percent in 1950. The growth of automobile workers' real wages was, nevertheless, an important achievement for the UAW.[12]

The UAW was quite successful in winning wage increases in the immediate postwar years, but the union was concerned about the implications of the huge expansion program of the industry. Union analysts noted that automobile companies were initiating a policy of geographic decentralization of the industry. Union leaders realized that the construction of modern plants in smaller cities removed from the Michigan center of the industry meant that workers in the older plants would face greater unemployment during hard times. The decline of the old industrial centers was well advanced by the 1970s, but UAW Local 600 took Ford Motor Company to court as early as 1952 in an unsuccessful attempt to stop the company from transferring jobs away from the huge River Rouge complex.[13]

The automobile industry was a powerful force in postwar politics, both nationally and in the localities in which the auto corporations operated. During the New Deal years, most auto industrialists, like the leaders of big business generally, opposed the Roosevelt administration. During World War II, however, leading figures from the auto industry, such as GM president William Knudsen, took important posts in the Roosevelt administration. The experience of World War II gave such auto executives as GM Chairman Alfred Sloan a new appreciation of the importance of a "close liaison between the Armed Forces and industry."[14] Confident of their power to influence the federal government, auto industry leaders and other business figures launched a major effort in the postwar period to convince Congress that the National Labor Relations (Wagner) Act was one-sided and that a balance had to be restored to labor relations. The business campaign, which culminated in the enactment of the Taft-Hartley Act, presented a major challenge to the UAW and the rest of the labor movement.

The UAW's internal life was affected both by the auto industry's political aggressiveness and by its economic vitality. The big business political campaign focused on the dangers of labor militancy and radicalism and intensified the conflict within the union between anti-Communists and those opposed to anti-Communism. The auto industry's highly favorable economic circumstances, on the other hand, meant that a well-led and strongly supported collective bargaining strategy could win significant wage and benefit concessions for union members. The group winning the union's factional war, which erupted with new force in 1946, could hope to consolidate its victory on the basis of an improvement in the standard of living of the auto union membership.

Chapter Two

The Auto Workers: From the Industry's Beginnings Through World War II

The first generation of auto industry workers was a heterogeneous group. Foreign-born workers made up about one-third of the wage earners in the industry's early decades (1900–1930), and second generation Americans probably made up an even larger proportion of the blue collar group. Although Black workers constituted only about 4 percent of all auto industry employees in 1930, they made up more than 10 percent of the labor force at two of the Ford Motor Company's huge Detroit area plants. There were also numerous Southern-born white workers in the automobile factories in the industry's early years. Women, who composed 7 percent of the industry's work force in 1930, were employed in large numbers in some areas of automobile manufacturing as well as in the clerical occupations that were relatively untouched by the unionization drive.[1]

Diverse in ethnic background, auto workers during the industry's initial years were alike in their lack of significant industrial skills. Most jobs in the industry required little or no prior training, and, apart from the small proportion of craft workers and former miners, few auto workers had been trade union members. Workers were attracted to the industry by relatively high hourly wages, but average annual wages were kept low by the frequency of unemployment experienced by auto workers at a time when there were no unemployment benefits.[2]

The speed-up was another problem facing early auto workers. The work of assembly line workers, who comprised about 15 percent of the work force, was especially difficult; they had no control over their work pace and felt constant pressure to keep up with the moving line. Since other operations in the plant fed into the assembly lines, the pressure to speedup was felt by many nonline workers as well.[3]

In their drive for production, the companies established personnel policies that were highly repressive. The average auto worker's hold on his or her job was uncertain. Many workers, particularly at the Ford Motor Company, had to pay bribes to obtain jobs. Both GM and Ford were reported to prohibit talking during work. Furthermore, the layoffs that were such a common feature of the auto workers' experience were not generally decided on the basis of seniority.

The determination of the auto manufacturers to keep the industry an "open shop," that is, to keep unions from representing their employees or having any say over wages and working conditions, increased the workers' feelings of insecurity. To ensure that the industry remained nonunion, auto companies employed hundreds of industrial spies to watch the workers and to report on organizational activity and on expressions of dissatisfaction with factory conditions. Although the bulk of the workers were not prounion before the New Deal, the companies' antiunion machinery added an element of fear to factory life that affected many employees.[4]

The principal union attempting to organize automobile workers before the New Deal was the Carriage, Wagon and Automobile Workers International Union (CWAW), an industrial union. Because of the CWAW's increasing membership among skilled workers, American Federation of Labor (AFL) craft unions demanded that the auto union, as an AFL affiliate, stop organizing in the auto industry. When the CWAW refused to abide by AFL convention decisions that it surrender its automobile workers, the Federation in 1918 suspended its affiliate. Continuing as an independent industrial union led by Socialists, the CWAW grew significantly during the World War I boom. It reached a peak membership of approximately 45,000 in 1920 and organized shop committees in several plants. Although able to secure some concessions on working conditions, particularly in small body shops, the CWAW did not win signed contracts even at the time of its peak strength. The severe postwar recession of 1920–1921 and the employers' open shop offensive led to wage cuts, unsuccessful strikes, and a drastic reduction in union membership and activity.[5]

When Communists after 1926 assumed the leadership of the auto union, known then as the Auto Workers Union (AWU), the organization gave prime emphasis to the abysmal working conditions facing production and other nonskilled workers. The AWU stressed the need for class solidarity and opposition to racial discrimination. It involved itself in a number of spontaneous strikes between 1926 and 1930, helping the strikers "to organize mass meetings, formulate demands, select strike committees, establish picket lines, write leaflets and obtain legal aid." Realizing that its forces were extremely limited, the AWU sought to encourage an organizing drive by the AFL, but the Federation chose not to act.[6]

The Communists were the principal force trying to organize auto workers in the 1920s. In addition to their activity in the AWU, Communists had shop units and shop papers of their own and reached a number of auto workers through activities in foreign language and ethnic cooperatives and through the ethnic press. Communists were also active in the Black community in such organizations as the League of Struggle for Negro Rights. At a time when the dominant trade unions in the United States were uninterested in the plight of the mass of the industrial workers, the AWU and the Communists acquainted numerous auto workers with the ideas of industrial unionism, militancy, radicalism, and socialism. The membership of the AWU remained very small, however, and the union was unable to win any contracts.[7]

Auto workers were major victims of the 1929 crash and the Great Depression that followed. Detroit was the hardest hit of the nation's largest cities, as layoffs mounted by the thousands. At the depths of the depression in the early months of 1933, 45 percent of the auto workers were out of work while the real income of those who were fortunate enough to retain their jobs was cut by 43 percent.[8]

The depression had a devastating effect on the workers' bargaining power, and few strikes were held between 1929 and 1933. Some auto workers, however, participated in the movement of the unemployed that developed in response to the depression. Led by Communists, Socialists, and other radicals, the Unemployed Councils, the Unemployed Leagues, and similar organizations gave the jobless a chance to fight evictions and to demonstrate and lobby for relief, unemployment compensation, and "work or wages." On March 7, 1932, 3,000 people gathered in Detroit for a march to the Ford Motor Company's River Rouge plant in nearby Dearborn to demand jobs. Dearborn city police attacked the demonstrators with tear gas, and the marchers fought back by throwing stones. At one point, the police and the Ford Motor Company's private guards fired their guns into the crowd, killing four people. Thousands participated in the funeral march to bury the dead in "the greatest demonstration the city had ever witnessed." Many automobile workers first joined the working-class movement during this period, and a number of UAW activists had their first organizational experience in an Unemployed Council or Unemployed League branch.[9]

As the depression hit bottom in early 1933, a series of strikes broke out in the auto industry. These were in large part spontaneous rebellions against the spiralling deterioration of wages and working conditions. Wages had been cut so deeply and working hours had been reduced to such an extent that many workers could not stand another pay cut without protesting. In many of these strikes, the workers turned to the Auto Workers Union for assistance. Other unions also developed in response to this upsurge of activity and militancy among auto workers. The growth of organization was given greater stimulus, however, by the change in the national political climate.

Franklin Roosevelt was inaugurated as president on March 4, 1933, after having defeated Herbert Hoover, who had done little to aid the millions of working people victimized by the depression. Under Roosevelt's leadership, the National Industrial Recovery Act (NIRA) was enacted into law in June 1933.

Although this legislation was primarily designed to help business lead the way out of the economic crisis, Section 7(a) of the act asserted that workers "had the right to organize and bargain collectively through representatives of their own choosing" and were to be free from employer interference with this right. Encouraged by the new legitimacy given trade unionism by the federal government, the AFL became active in the automobile and other mass production industries by chartering federal labor unions. The new legislation also stimulated the development of independent unions in the automobile industry. In addition, many automobile firms sponsored company unions, which the government's Automobile Labor Board (ALB) accepted as a legitimate form of organization under the NIRA. With thousands of workers enrolling in the AFL's automotive federal labor unions and the independent Mechanics Educational Society of America (MESA), the left-wing Auto Workers Union disbanded and most of its members joined these larger less radical organizations. For the Communists, this was a step toward the policy of the popular front adopted by the Communist International at its Seventh Congress in 1935.[10]

As the country's principal trade union center, the AFL attracted tens of thousands of auto workers seeking union representation. Because of craft union control of the Federation, the AFL's campaign in the auto industry was based on federal labor unions. Known as United Automobile Workers Federal Labor Unions, the auto locals were actually separate from one another, and each faced the prospect of having its members eventually divided among the AFL craft unions. Although the AFL's commitment to craft unionism remained unchanged, the Federation had moved away from a voluntarist, go-it-alone approach and was now depending on the government to aid it in organizing workers. AFL leaders and organizers, however, had little faith in action by the inexperienced and predominatly foreign stock auto unionists and so did their best to prevent strikes.[11]

The AFL's cautious policy had its biggest impact in Michigan: the Federation established its auto organizing headquarters in Detroit and closely supervised the federal locals in that state. Held back from taking militant action by AFL officials, Michigan auto workers found it difficult to counter the Big Three's well-financed antiunion campaign that included the establishment of company unions, the use of labor spies, and discriminatory dismissals of unionists.[12]

Michigan auto unionists also had to contend with the Black Legion, a Klan-like vigilante organization that included auto unionists among its enemies along with Communists, Blacks and Catholics. The Black Legion counted many Republican officeholders, police officers, fire fighters, and factory workers among its several thousand members. Even more influential than the Black Legion was the demagogic radio priest Father Charles Coughlin. From his parish in the Detroit suburb of Royal Oak, Coughlin broadcast attacks on bankers that won him an enormous national following in the early days of the depression. His location in Michigan gave him an opportunity to influence auto workers personally. Coughlin did not hesitate to oppose the AFL, and his National Union for Social Justice attracted some auto workers.[13]

Despite the many obstacles to unionism, membership in the AFL federal locals grew rapidly in the first few months of 1934 as enthusiasm for prospective strike action spread througout the auto industry, especially in GM's Flint plants. Although AFL officials had threatened to bring the auto workers out on strike, they really had no intention of doing so and hoped that the threat would bring White House action favorable to the union. President Roosevelt did indeed intervene in the dispute, but the settlement achieved under his auspices was a victory for the auto manufacturers because company unions were to have an equal right to participate in elections for employee bargaining committees chosen on the basis of proportional representation. The AFL's support of the president's settlement and the cancellation of strike action caused widespread disillusionment, with many union members dropping out of AFL locals.[14]

Although the AFL had cancelled industry wide strike action, a number of locals outside Michigan managed nevertheless to establish strong positions in their plants. Vigorous locals developed in auto plants in Kenosha, Racine, and Milwaukee, Wisconsin; South Bend, Indiana; and in Cleveland, Toledo, and Norwood, Ohio. All these federal locals gained their strength by pursuing a militant policy, and most had conducted strikes that had produced at least partial victories. In several cases, particularly in Cleveland and Toledo, radicals were active in leading and assisting strikes.[15]

Leaders of these strong UAW locals were critical of the AFL leadership in the auto industry because of its policy of avoiding strikes and its willingness to rely on government mediation to end those stoppages that did occur before the workers' principal demands were won. Some key local unions began pressing the AFL to give the auto workers an international union charter so that they could develop a coordinated plan to organize the industry. The Cleveland Auto Council, headed by the leftist Wyndham Mortimer, led this campaign, urging that the new international union should be an industrial union controlled by the rank and file. The leaders of the movement for an international union called themselves Progressives. The AFL acquiesced in the auto workers' demand only after containing another auto strike movement in the spring of 1935.[16]

Auto unionists were bitterly critical of the AFL leadership when they gathered at the founding convention of the International Union, United Automobile Workers of America in August 1935. The delegates represented some 26,000 dues paying members, of whom only about 4,000 were located in the key automotive state of Michigan. Although the auto unionists gained their union charter, the accomplishments of the convention fell far short of the delegates' demands. The delegates objected strongly to the limited jurisdiction granted them by the AFL Executive Council and to the appointment of the new union's officers and executive board members by AFL President William Green. The convention protested these decisions to the AFL Executive Council and then to the AFL convention, but it took another eight months before the auto workers gained autonomy for their young union.[17]

Although the 1935 AFL convention rejected the protests of the auto workers regarding the restrictions placed on their union, the UAW activists found powerful allies for their cause at the gathering. John L. Lewis, president of the United Mine Workers, led the effort to win convention approval for a campaign to organize the mass production industries on an industrial union basis. When the convention rejected the industrial union resolution, Lewis and other AFL leaders supporting industrial unionism decided to act independently and established the Committee for Industrial Organization to perform the job the dominant craft unionists had refused to sanction. Because of the pressure exerted by the CIO, the AFL agreed to end the auto workers' probationary period and to permit them to hold a convention in April 1936 to elect their own officers.[18]

The prospect of an autonomous auto workers' union backed by the CIO appealed to the independent unions that had secured a greater foothold in Michigan's auto plants than had the AFL. MESA, which was composed primarily of skilled tool and die makers, had established its presence in the automobile industry by a partially successful strike in the fall of 1933. Although MESA was more militant than the AFL, a Progressive caucus within the union led by Communists criticized its strike policies and advocated unity with production workers in an industrial union. Three of MESA's six Detroit locals were led by Progressives, and it was these locals that withdrew from MESA and affiliated with the UAW following the establishment of the UAW's autonomy.[19]

The other two independent unions that were to merge with the UAW had more conservative leaders. The Associated Automobile Workers of America (AAWA), founded in June 1934 by three Michigan AFL federal labor unions that had quit the AFL, was even less aggressive than the AFL in dealing with management. Some UAW activists considered it little different than a company union; several AAWA leaders had joined the Black Legion. The third major independent was the Automotive Industrial Workers Association (AIWA), which had developed out of the representation elections at the Chrysler plants organized by the (ALB). After failing to make progress in bargaining with Chrysler as a Works Council, ALB representatives decided to organize independently and established the AIWA in April 1935. Richard Frankensteen of the Dodge plant was elected president, and R. J. Thomas of the Chrysler Kercheval plant was chosen first vice president. Both later became top leaders of the UAW, Thomas as president and Frankensteen as vice president. In 1935, however, they and the AIWA were strongly influenced by Father Charles Coughlin. Even after two decades of involvement in the trade union movement, Thomas held to the belief that the right-wing radio priest had been "doing in those days a constructive job . . . of trying to give the workers some guidance."[20]

When the second convention of the UAW opened on April 27, 1936, in South Bend, Indiana, the union's total dues-paying membership was only about 20,000. Despite this organizational weakenss, the prospect of freeing themselves from the suffocating influence of the AFL and electing their own leadership, combined with the emergence of the CIO, gave the delegates cause for optimism. Representatives of MESA, AAWA, and AIWA were on hand to pledge their cooperation. The program adopted by the convention reflected the ideas developed by the Progressives in preconvention caucuses. The convention resolved to launch a campaign to organize the auto industry on the basis of industrial unionism, raise $250,000 to finance this effort, welcome the affiliation of the independent unions, and endorse the idea of a Farmer-Labor party. The delegates rejected a proposal to bar Communists from holding union office, but, in the closing moments of the convention, they did adopt a resolution condemning communism, nazism, and fascism. These contradictory actions were an indication of the fluid situation in the young organization. One UAW Progressive from Detroit, Frank Manfred, recalled: "When we were at that Convention, we were really scared. We did not know what was going to happen."

The delegates to the South Bend convention elected a leaderhip that was acceptable to the Progressives, although the majority of the officers and executive board members were not themselves members of the Progressive caucus. Of the sixteen officers and board members, only three were pro-AFL. Following the convention, the AIWA, AAWA, and three of MESA's Detroit locals joined the UAW. Frankensteen of the AIWA received the seat on the executive board set aside by the convention for a representative of the independents. Confirmation of the UAW's new direction came two months after the close of the convention when the auto workers' union formally affiliated with the CIO. Suspension and then expulsion from the AFL followed the UAW action, but the auto unionists were not unhappy with putting the AFL era behind them.[21]

With the CIO's financial and organizational support, the UAW began a major organizing drive. This campaign was given great stimulus by the landslide reelection of President Franklin Roosevelt against strong big business and conservative opposition on November 3, 1936. Just two weeks after the election, the first UAW sit-down strike took place at the South Bend plant of the Bendix Products Corporation. Two days after the UAW achieved a partial victory there, UAW local 155, one of the former MESA locals, initiated a sit-down at the Midland Steel Products plant on the east side of Detroit. When the Midland strike resulted in what the UAW called "the most significant union victory in the history of the automobile industry in Detroit," several new sit-downs occurred in Detroit in December 1936. The most important of these was the victorious sit-down that the West Side Local conducted against Kelsey Hayes. These successful strikes not only led to substantial increases in UAW membership in the plants in which they occurred but gave the UAW needed experience to wage its sit-down strike against the leading producer in the industry, General Motors.[22]

The victorious prosecution of the General Motors strike of 1936–1937 was the key event in the organization of the UAW and, in fact, of the entire CIO. The 44-day sit-down strike, centered in Flint, captured the imagination of the nation. When the UAW won recognition from the leading automobile corporation, the very symbol of American big business, a great wave of organization was unleashed throughout American industry. In the months following the February 11, 1937, settlement of the GM strike, the UAW won recognition at Chrysler and at many smaller auto firms. Only Ford continued to resist recognition of the UAW, despite strikes that occurred at outlying company plants. Union membership increased from a few thousand in April 1936 to 350,000 by the date of the third annual covention in August 1937.

The UAW's victories resulted, first, from the unity and militancy of thousands of rank and file auto workers. Ignoring many differences of race, nationality, religion, and political belief that separated them, auto workers united to force the automobile corporations to recognize their right to a say in their working conditions. Auto workers had learned from experience that they could not rely on mediation or presidential support to solve their problems, and so they resisted efforts to end their strikes before victory had been won. Aiding the grass roots movement of the auto workers were the women's auxiliaries composed of workers' wives, daughters, and friends, and the "women's emergency brigades," AFL unions, and community organizations sympathetic to the UAW cause.[23]

Crucial to these 1937 gains was the development of a leadership able and willing to pursue a militant strategy. The UAW leadership that emerged from the struggle against the AFL's conservative policy included representatives of local unions that had been militant and had waged strikes despite the AFL's antistrike policy. In addition to adopting the radical sit-down tactic, UAW organizers made use of mass strike committees, strike newspapers, sound trucks, mass picketing, rallies, and parades. They encouraged participation by the foreign-born, women, and Black workers and appealed to broad community and labor circles to support the factory workers' struggle for dignity. Instead of being intimidated by employer charges of illegality and by injunctions, the union leadership counterattacked by portraying GM and other manufacturers as labor law violators and by exposing company control of local officials. Communists and Socialists were prominent among the leaders of the 1936–1937 strikes, but some with less radical views, such as Homer Martin and Richard Frankensteen, also played key roles. The CIO's aid was also a necessary factor in the UAW's successful drive: the Lewis-led movement helped the auto workers to sustain their struggle against General Motors at a time when the fledgling union's resources were miniscule compared to those of GM.[24]

Equally necessary to the UAW victory was the favorable political climate in which the auto workers undertook to strike GM and other firms. Hearings held by the LA Follette Civil Liberties Committee focused public attention on violations of the rights of union members by GM and other employers. Most important, the UAW and CIO, as they sought to win union recognition from the corporations, received assistance from the Roosevelt and Murphy administrations. In sharp contrast with the policies of almost all of their predecessors in major labor conflicts, Roosevelt and Murphy pressured the manufacturers to negotiate settlements with representatives of their employees. To be sure, these Democratic executives also applied pressure on union leaders to evacuate the plants, which, they averred, were occupied in violation of the law. Nevertheless, in the key GM dispute, Roosevelt and Murphy refrained from publicly criticizing the union, refused to use force to remove the sit-downers, and continued to pressure GM. As a result, the economic pressure of the sit-down strike finally forced GM to abandon its adherence to the open shop and to agree to offer the UAW limited union recognition.[25]

The union's principal gains in its first contracts were improved working conditions and a voice in determining these conditions. Although the UAW in most agreements did not win acceptance of its shop steward system, auto managements nevertheless agreed to recognize a shop committee of union represantatives. Management continued to make the final decision on questions of work standards, but the workers now had a say, and their voice was strengthened by the grievance procedure. Although the GM agreement provided that the parties could mutually agree to refer unsettled grievances to an impartial umpire, the union retained the right to strike once the grievance procedure had been exhausted.[26] In these early days of auto industry labor relations, only days or weeks were required for a grievance to work its way through the procedure, not the months or years about which auto workers were later to complain.[27]

The UAW's victory in the GM strike and the recognition that followed led to "pay raises . . . , the acceleration of the shift to hourly rates, the retiming of jobs, the reinstatement of discharged workers, the preparation of seniority lists available to union representatives, and the [adjustment of] hundreds of minor grievances . . . ." As one Flint worker, not a strike supporter, declared: "The inhuman high speed is *no more*. We now have a voice, and have slowed up the speed of the line. And [we] are now treated as human beings, and not as part of the machinery." In the space of a few short months, the UAW had not only established new, contractual relations with most auto manufacturers but had also won a place for itself in the hearts of thousands of auto workers.[28]

Most of these new union members saw themselves in a new light as a result of the labor upheaval of 1937. They had a new confidence in their strength as members of a broad social movement. Henry Kraus, the editor of the UAW newspaper during the Flint strike, described how deeply committed to the union large numbers of workers had become: "One could no longer imagine that these people would ever be able to live without the union again. It had become the very center of their existence."[29]

Consolidation of the UAW's immense collective bargaining gains involved some difficulties; the UAW still had to contend with continuing management resistance to unionization of the industry. The union not only had to eliminate vestiges of the company unions in order to confirm its place in the factories; it also faced the task of bargaining on the shop floor with supervisors trained according to open shop principles. In asserting their new rights, local unions and rank-and-file workers conducted hundreds of strikes, including "quickie" sit-down strikes not authorized by the international leadership. Because the UAW had established itself as a militant, enthusiastic, grass roots movement, it was probably inevitable that the consolidation of the union at the local level would be accompanied by unauthorized strikes. During this period of consolidation, a factional conflict erupted within the UAW, a conflict that continued for two years and threatened to destroy the union. The principal figure in its initiation and continuation was Homer Martin.[30]

Martin was one of the conservative unionists who had allied with the Progressives to win autonomy for the UAW in 1936. He was a former Baptist preacher who had worked briefly at the Kansas City GM plant and had become a leading figure in the UAW local. Martin was appointed vice president of the UAW by William Green at the August 1935 UAW convention but soon after began to oppose Francis Dillon, the AFL organizer whom Green had designated as president of the union. Martin was admired for his oratorical abilities, and the fact that he held an office higher than that of any other UAW member put him in position to succeed Dillon. Although elected president by auto worker delegates without opposition in April 1936, Martin lacked any real knowledge of trade unionism, had no administrative abilities, and was personally unstable.

Martin's shortcomings took on added significance because the political situation within both the UAW and the CIO was volatile. The rapid growth of the UAW and the political diversity and inexperience of its membership made its future unpredictable. Some CIO leaders, moreover, hoped for reconciliation with the AFL even though the federation had attacked the industrial union movement during the 1937 strike wave. Most prominent among these CIO leaders was David Dubinsky, president of the International Ladies Garment

Workers Union (ILGWU). On Dubinsky's recommendation, Martin began to rely on Jay Lovestone, head of the Communist Party (Opposition), for advice and help in strengthening his position within the UAW. Lovestone, the former General Secretary of the Communist party, had been expelled from that organization for "right-wing deviationism" in 1929. By the time Homer Martin was introduced to Lovestone, the latter's principal political passion was opposition to the Communist party.[31]

Shortly after the sit-downs, Martin and his supporters in the UAW organized the so-called Progressive caucus with the aim of ousting Wyndham Mortimer and other leftists from office. Although Martin enjoyed the support of a majority of the union's executive board, most members of the old Progressive group responded to the Martin caucus by joining to form the Unity caucus. The two caucuses agreed on many issues, but the Martin group emphasized strengthening the authority of the president and eliminating unauthorized strikes, whereas the Unity caucus stressed such matters as enlarging the power of the shop stewards and ensuring the membership's right to vote on strikes. In contrast to the Martin group, the Unity caucus, which included leaders of the General Motors strike, Communists, and Socialists, did not seek to remove its rivals from office. Reflecting some years later on the situation at the August 1937 convention, Mortimer reasoned: "Had a whole slate been run, I am not too sure what the results would have been . . . . Because there had been such a new influx of members and we were also trying to digest the Coughlin Union, and this Greer outfit had joined in, so that you were not too sure where it would go."

A split in the UAW was averted at the 1937 convention only by the delegates' acceptance of the advice of John L. Lewis to retain the union's existing officers and to create two new vice-presidencies for Frankensteen and Thomas, both Martin supporters. Although Martin thereby increased his majority on the union's executive board, he was unable to secure passage of his principal proposals for union centralization. Also, the Unity group retained a strong base in several local unions.[32]

UAW members who hoped that the convention compromise would keep the organization united were soon disappointed. Following the convention, Martin replaced key organizers who had built the union and had led several of the 1936–1937 strikes with more conservative auto workers and with nonauto workers who were members of Lovestone's group. Although Martin at first emphasized the need for union discipline and accused other UAW leaders of encouraging unauthorized strikes, he increasingly resorted to red-baiting his union rivals. The UAW president's policies, however, were drawing increasing opposition from secondary union leaders.[33]

Martin's negotiation of an inferior contract with General Motors, his harsh criticism of local strikes, and his suspension of local union newspapers alienated many UAW members. The Unity caucus as a consequence won most of the important local union elections in March 1938. Martin's response to his deteriorating political position was to suspend five fellow UAW officers, a drastic action that caused the CIO to bring its weight to bear against what it viewed as Martin's destructive factionalism. In the ensuing struggle for control of the union, Martin was opposed by the majority of the UAW executive board and by most secondary union leaders. After it was learned that Martin was attempting to negotiate a back-door agreement with the Ford Motor Company, the UAW split into two rival organizations.[34]

Aided by the CIO, which became the Congress of Industrial Organizations in November 1938, most of the UAW's executive board and secondary leaders reorganized the union at a special convention in Cleveland in March 1939. Whereas about 90,000 workers were represented at this UAW-CIO convention, Martin's group, which moved toward affiliation with the AFL, spoke for about 17,000 auto workers at its convention, which was held in Detroit a few weeks prior to the UAW-CIO gathering. The UAW-CIO faced the tasks of rebuilding its dues-paying membership and regaining collective bargaining arrangements that had been broken at the instigation of the auto companies in the midst of the union split. Through strike actions and National Labor Relations Board (NLRB) elections the UAW-CIO proved that it had the backing of the decisive majority of the rank and file. By the August 1940 convention, the UAW-CIO's dues-paying membership was 294,000 and the union had contracts covering 412,000 workers, while the 1940 membership of the UAW-AFL was only 19,000.[35]

Unfortunately for the UAW-CIO, factionalism was not at an end. Although the Martin faction had passed from the scene, other political tendencies in the union came into conflict. During the period of consolidation following the sit-down strikes, the various political groups within the union took on a more coherent form. Among the principal tendencies were the Commuist-led left-wing, the Socialist group led by Walter Reuther, the conservative Association of Catholic Trade Unionists (ACTU), and a group of miscellaneous New Deal progressives. Although caucus alignments often shifted, two main coalitions emerged: the left-progressive and Socialist-ACTU blocs.

The left progressive or left center coalition that included Secretary-Treasurer George Addes, Vice President Richard Frankensteen, and the Communists was sometimes called the "left wing," but the left-wing designation more properly refers to the radical element within that coalition. Communists were the largest single element in the left-wing, but this group also included other radicals who were active in such organizations as the National Negro Congress, the Civil Rights Federation, and the Workers Alliance. The left wingers believed in the class struggle, saw the importance of interracial unity, gave priority to the struggle against fascism, opposed anticommunism, sympathized with the Soviet

Union, and were generally socialist-minded. Not all who believed in socialism, however, were part of the Communist-led left wing. A number of non-Communist socialist organizations opposed the Communists, the left-wing trend they led, and the broader left-progressive coalition.[36]

The Socialist party was the most significant of the socialist groups in the auto union, but it was smaller than the Communist party. Although several Socialist party members had worked in a united front with Communists in 1936 and 1937, most of these Socialists had by 1938 come into conflict with Communists. The Socialists opposed the Communists' strategy of a popular front against war and fascism, and it was their foreign policy disagreements that disrupted Communist-Socialist cooperation early in 1938. Whereas the Communists supported United States participation in collective security arrangements aimed at curbing fascist aggression, the Socialists gave prime emphasis to keeping the United States out of war and regarded the Communists' proposals as "prowar." On the national political level, Socialists began working with isolationists while in the UAW they sought an alliance with Homer Martin and the Lovenstonites. Although Martin and the Lovenstonites were also opposed to collective security, their trade union policies and purges of opponents prevented the development of a stable coalition with the Socialists.[37]

Unable to form an alliance with Martin, the Socialists established a distinct caucus within the UAW in 1938–1939. Its principal figure was executive board member Walter Reuther, who had emerged into prominence as a leader of the 1936–1937 strikes. Although Reuther had dropped his membership in the Socialist party in 1938, his approach was informed by his Socialist background, and several of his coworkers in the new group were members of the Socialist party. The Reuther group also included some non-Socialist adherents attracted by its posture as a middle-of-the-road alternative to Martin and his opponents, but it was a relatively minor force in the union at the 1939 UAW convention.[38]

The clearly dominent force within the UAW at the Cleveland convention was the coalition of left and "center" or "progressive" trade unionists. The bulk of the union's leaders and the rank and file were "progressive"—New Deal Democratic in political outlook. New Deal Democrats like Frankensteen and Addes had cooperated with the left in 1936 and 1937 in building the union, as had the Socialists. Although at first divided over Martin's policies, the center elements overwhelmingly turned against the UAW president when the destructiveness of his policies became clear. The center forces then worked with the left to defeat Martin and to rebuild the union. As Arthur Case, elected to the UAW executive board from Flint in 1939, recalled: "Communists . . . helped to do the job . . . we were getting help wherever we could get it at that time. We did not care greatly about a man's politics." These progressive auto workers, in fact, had few disagreements with the left on immediate political issues.[39]

After the signing of the Nazi-Soviet Non-Aggression Pact in August and the start of World War II in September 1939, UAW Communists became isolated because of their opposition to the Roosevelt administration's foreign and domestic policies. Although the Communists continued their support of Roosevelt in the first weeks of the war, they declared in February 1940 that his administration "had taken the road of reaction and war" and had scrapped progressive social legislation. They opposed the administration's anti-Soviet line, the policy of aid to Britain, and the defense build up. These views, however, were not shared by their progressive allies within the UAW. Although center leaders at first withheld support from the defense program and emphasized their opposition to United States intervention in the war, to the draft, and to threats against civil liberties, they usually avoided direct attacks on the administration. Unlike the Communists, UAW leaders like Addes saw the principal danger to New Deal reforms as stemming from conservative forces outside the administration. After France's June 1940 fall, most UAW progressives voiced support for the defense program.[40]

The Socialist party, for its part, continued to adhere to an anti-interventionist position, but it did not face the strong political attack launched against supporters of the Soviet Union by both interventionists and isolationists. Some Socialists and others in the Reuther caucus were anti-interventionist, but Reuther personally worked closely with Sidney Hillman, the leading labor official in the Roosevelt administration's defense program. Reuther also cooperated with UAW President R. J. Thomas, who had achieved the top union office at the 1939 convention as a result of the urging of Hillman and Philip Murray of the CIO. With the European war the central American political issue of 1940–1941, the Reuther group, which was united on the basis of opposition to Communists, became a powerful force within the UAW.[41]

The Reuther supporters showed their antagonism to the Communist-led left-wing when they designated their group as the "right-wing." Most participants in the Reuther group, to be sure, were to the left of the center of the American political spectrum. In UAW terms, however, the Reuther group was a center-right coalition. The center included New Deal Democrats like Richard Leonard. The right-wing was composed of the consistent anti-Communists, including Reuther, other Socialists and former Socialists, members of the Association of Catholic Trade Unionists, and business unionists like Richard Gosser.

The conservative Association of Catholic Trade Unionists was an important element in the Reuther group. The first local chapters of the ACTU had been established in 1937 and 1938 out of Catholic concern over Communist influence in the CIO. The ACTU had the official support of the Catholic hierarchy, and priests acted as advisers to local groups. The organization's stated aim was "to foster sound trade unionism along Christian lines, so that the labor movement may be effective toward the establishment of a Christian social order . . . " This new "social order" was to be based on capital-labor partnership in the form of industry councils. Within the UAW, the ACTU directed its efforts to opposing communism; it formed local union "conferences" as "permanent counter-minorities" to the Communist party. Its hostility to communism led the ACTU to ally itself with the Socialist-oriented Reuther group, with which it otherwise had numerous ideological differences.[42]

The Addes-Frankensteen-left caucus, dominant at the 1939 UAW convention, split on war-related issues. At the 1940 UAW convention, Addes and Frankensteen spoke in favor of an anti-Soviet resolution. Although both declared that they were opposed to any purges, neither took a position on the constitutional amendment offered at the convention to bar from local office any person who was a member of an organization declared illegal by the United States government. Although a substantial minority vote was cast against the latter proposal, delegate support for the left wing's opposition to the anti-Soviet resolution and to a UAW endorsement of Roosevelt's reelection was confined to less than 10 percent of those present. The Reuther group strengthened its position on the UAW's executive body as a result of the convention's elections so that the Addes-Frankensteen and Reuther groups became relatively equal in strength.[43]

Although the 1940 convention had supported some anticommunist resolutions, its decisions taken as a whole did not indicate a decisive shift toward conservatism. A major emphasis at the convention was the need to organize the unorganized, with the focus on the Ford Motor Company and on the burgeoning aircraft industry. Having won new and improved contracts at GM, Chrysler, Briggs, and other firms, the UAW sought new fields to conquer. The long-delayed drive on Ford was at last undertaken in earnest.[44]

The Ford drive centered on the huge River Rouge complex in Dearborn. The union not only had to overcome the fear that the Service Department's goons and spy machine had instilled in Ford workers but had to contend with Ford's attempt to divide the workers along racial lines. Approximately 12,000 Black workers, 15 percent of the work force, were employed at the River Rouge complex, making the company by far the largest employer of Black labor in the Detroit area. Ford sought to exercise a controlling interest in the Black community by backing Black ministers financially, by developing ties with other Black community leaders, and by building its own Republican political machine in the community. The company sought through these relationships to use Black workers against the union.[45]

In its campaign to organize Ford, the UAW was able to draw on the assistance of a large number of strong local unions in the Detroit area. It also had the support of numerous workers inside the giant River Rouge plant who had participated in various union and progressive political campaigns in the area and the aid as well of a few thousand fired Ford workers eager, at last, to put the union label on the autocratic Ford Company and to return to their jobs. Such community organizations as the National Negro Congress and the Civil Rights Federation and such individuals as State Senator Charles Diggs and State Representative Reverend Horace White, the two leading Black elected officials in Michigan, also assisted the union's Ford drive. The union faced a tense situation when the company hired many Black youths before and during the April 1941 strike, hoping to use them against the UAW. The union responded by strengthening its ties with the Black community, with many Black union members playing key roles in this regard. Unity and discipline were achieved, a race riot was prevented, and Ford, in the end, was forced to accept the union.[46]

The UAW's organizing campaign in the aircraft industry was not as solidly rooted as that at Ford. That rapidly growing industry was concentrated in the West, far from the centers of UAW strength. The auto union, however, enjoyed the strong support of the national CIO, and it was able to win a number of aircraft contracts. Because of intraunion differences, however, it was unable to achieve the dominance in the industry that Wyndham Mortimer, the aircraft industry campaign's director, had anticipated. Frankensteen, the head of the UAW's aircraft department, consulting with both CIO leaders and Roosevelt administration defense officials, denounced as Communist-inspired a strike at North American Aviation that occurred while the dispute was before the National Defense Mediation Board. President Roosevelt ordered a federal takeover of the plant, a leading producer of fighter planes, and sent in troops to break the strike. Although the UAW was able to gain an improved contract at North American Aviation and to increase its membership in the industry, the federal strikebreaking contained the rank-and-file upsurge in the industry and caused great concern throughout the labor movement. In the end, the weakening of the UAW drive meant that the auto union had to share jurisdiction of the industry with the AFL-affiliated International Association of Machinists.[47]

When the UAW met in its sixth convention in August 1941, the union's membership was at a new height, 556,132. Despite the significant growth achieved and the new stability that characterized the union's position, the convention was the scene of sharp factional divisions. Although the convention opened after the Nazi attack on the Soviet Union and the beginning of a rapprochement between the governments of the United States and the U.S.S.R., there were more expressions of opposition to communism than at any previous UAW convention. The delegates approved by a two-to-one margin a Reuther-backed constitutional amendment to bar members of Communist, Nazi, or fascist organizations from holding union office. In the wake of the North American strike, Frankensteen reversed his previous opposition to purges and supported the anticommunist amendment. Although opposed to the amendment, Addes, too, abandoned his earlier antagonism to purges and, in a manuever aimed at Reuther, supported an amendment that would have excluded Socialists as well as Communists, Nazis, and Fascists from union office. Some left and center delegates spoke out against both amendments as restrictions on union democracy. The "Communist" issue had thus split the Addes-Frankensteen-left alliance into three groups, but the delegates nevertheless rebuffed the Reuther caucus on some issues and voted to retain in office Addes and most others of his group.[48]

Although the balance between the two union caucuses remained essentially the same following the 1941 convention, a perceptible shift occurred in the stance of the delegates to the 1941 UAW convention as compared with those present at the 1940 convention. Concern for the protection of rank-and-file rights was evident at the both conventions, but in 1941 the preservation of the union's relationship with the White House was given equal priority. The hostile reactions of the administration, Congress, and the press to the 1941 strike wave helped to create a climate favorable to the adoption of extreme anticommunist measures. The union membership no doubt supported the actions of the convention because of antipathy to communism and a belief that the UAW had to accommodate itself to the demands of the larger American society.[49]

National issues became an even more overriding concern of the union at the end of 1941 than at the time of the convention. The Japanese attack on Pearl Harbor put an end to an era in UAW history. Auto workers, like most other Americans, had wanted to avoid participation in the war that was engulfing the rest of the world; but once events had brought the United States actively onto the Allied side in the conflict, the overwhelming majority of auto workers and all major political tendencies in the union fully supported the war.[50]

Even before Pearl Harbor, the union leadership had pressed insistently for rapid conversion of the automobile industry to war production, labor participation with management in planning the transition to a war footing, and layoff bonuses and retraining for displaced workers. Although the UAW's conversion proposals, such as a plan for "500 planes a day" popularized by Walter Reuther, were not accepted, they helped to focus public attention on industry's slowness in shifting from automobile to war production. After Pearl Harbor, UAW leaders strengthened the cooperative relationships they had previously established with defense officials. Winning the war was now the union's principal objective. It concentrated on helping to produce for victory, supporting to this end the establishment of labor-management committees as part of the government's War Production Drive. In addition, the union called for a program of "Victory through Equality of Sacrifice" by all sections of American society. Although the union's leaders were committed to the protection of the interests and rights of union members, they agreed in April 1942 to the first material homefront sacrifice, the suspension of payment for the war's duration of double time for weekend work.[51]

The UAW's participation in the war effort was multifaceted. It supported war bond drives and scrap drives. UAW officials participated in numerous government agencies, including the War Production Board, the War Manpower Commission, the Office of Price Administration (OPA), and the War Labor Board (WLB). The union supported community war chests, war relief organizations, and civil defense. It showed special concern for programs to support members of the armed services.[52]

The most publicized aspect of the UAW's wartime program was its no-strike pledge. A national labor-management conference convened shortly after Pearl Harbor led to no-strike and no-lockout pledges and to the establishment of a tripartite War Labor Board with power to issue binding orders in cases referred to it. The board gained the authority to order contract clauses containing improvements in union security, a power conflicting with management's demand that the status quo be frozen for the war's duration.

The labor movement's victory on the union security question was understandable because the full employment brought by the war had placed the unions in a position to go on the economic offensive. Under the circumstances, the no-strike pledge of the unions was much more of a concession than was management's no-lockout pledge. The leaders of the UAW and most other unions were willing to make the sacrifice because of their desire to support the war effort and because they were concerned that a conservative Congress would enact repressive antilabor legislation to curb wartime strikes.[53]

Although the War Labor Board gained more authority than management wished, the labor movement found the board a mixed blessing. On the positive side, WLB decisions enhanced union security in the auto industry by ordering maintenance-of-union-membership provisions at General Motors, Briggs, and several other auto companies. Thanks to WLB assistance and the expansion of war production, UAW membership grew from 605,212 in December 1941 to a wartime peak of 1,242,569 in March 1945. On the other hand, the WLB's Little Steel Formula prevented wage increases from exceeding 15 percent of the January 1941 figure. Although this formula was theoretically designed to enable workers to keep even with inflation, auto workers' hourly wages did not in fact keep pace with increases in the cost of living. Furthermore, workers were often dissatisfied with the slowness of WLB consideration of shop grievances that the union had been unable to resolve in direct negotiations with management.[54]

The UAW leadership's efforts to change an unfair wage policy did not prevent rank-and-file dissatisfaction with inflation and other aspects of life on the home front from expressing itself in strike action. Although few auto strikes occurred in 1942, a large number of unauthorized stoppages took place in 1943 and 1944. The major causes of these strikes were unsettled grievances, especially those concerning working conditions, and disciplinary actions by management. The strikes did not reflect opposition to the war effort; they were responses to specific grievances and the manner in which domestic policies were impinging on workers. War workers had to work long hours under difficult conditions, but they received insufficient help in dealing with the many problems created by the war emergency. Workers who migrated to war centers often had great difficulty finding housing. Child-care facilities were insufficient to meet the needs of women flocking to jobs in war plants. Whereas wage increases lagged behind price increases, workers saw business people making few sacrifices. Furthermore, sacrifices for the war effort may not have seemed quite so critical by 1943 since the threat of an Axis victory had become remote.[55]

The outbreak of strikes in many auto plants in 1943 was accompanied by renewed factionalism within the UAW. The sharp intraunion conflicts of 1941 had come to an end with the United States's entry into the war. In 1942, the union leadership had united around the program of "Victory through Equality of Sacrifice," and, at the 1942 UAW Convention, Addes had nominated Reuther for office and Reuther had returned the compliment. The end of two years' isolation for UAW left wingers was indicated when the two major factions joined in the passage of a resolution calling for the opening of a second front. Unity, however, came to an end in 1943 as the result of conflict on such issues as incentive pay, retention of the no-strike pledge, and relations with the WLB. Thomas, Addes, Frankensteen, and the left gave priority to the need for victory in the war. Reuther, on the other hand, gave priority to the immediate economic interests of the auto workers. Both sides, to be sure, believed in the need for victory and in the need for protecting the rank and file, but the difference in emphasis led to very sharp conflicts.[56]

The first major factional conflict in 1943 developed around the issue of incentive pay. Addes, Frankensteen, and the Communists advocated incentive pay both as a means of helping to increase war production and as a device to increase wages frozen by the Little Steel Formula. The Communists were its most vociferous advocates. Most local union leaders, however, were not persuaded by the assertion that the proposed new incentive pay systems would be radically different from the individual and group piecework systems traditionally opposed by the union. UAW area conferences, the 1943 Michigan CIO convention, and the 1943 UAW convention all rejected the incentive pay concept. Reuther was outspoken in his opposition to inentive pay proposals, and many leaders and delegates to the 1943 UAW convention not aligned with the Reuther caucus joined with him on this issue.[57]

The increasing number of unauthorized strikes and the attempts by UAW officers to end them made the union's no-strike pledge a factional issue. The majority of the leadership supported continuation of the pledge, both because they supported the war and because they believed that revocation of the pledge would weaken the union politically. Congress had passed the antistrike Smith-

Connally Act in June 1943, and union leaders feared even more repressive legislation. They thus tried to persuade striking members to return to work, but they did not generally "crack down" on the strike leaders.

A number of secondary union leaders favored more militant action than the top leadership did, some of them wishing to show their dissatisfaction with the government's economic policies. Opposition to the no-strike pledge became a key objective of the Rank and File Caucus, some of whose leaders were Trotskyite opponents of the war. Although Reuther personally attempted to straddle the issue, some of his caucus activists were among the opponents of the pledge.[58]

A motion to rescind the no-strike pledge at the 1944 UAW convention received 37 percent of the vote, two-thirds of the support coming from delegates who backed Reuther's reelection. Reuther's own proposal to abandon the pledge only in nonwar plants received even fewer votes then the proposal to rescind, while the resolution to reaffirm the pledge fell just short of a majority. Opponents of the pledge won convention backing for a referendum on this issue, but the delegates voted to reaffirm the pledge in the interim.

The referendum idea eventually backfired on its initiators. Most UAW board members (including Reuther) and secondary leaders advocated retention of the pledge, and it secured a two-to-one majority in a vote of about one-quarter of the membership. Although the unsuccessful battle to rescind the pledge had weakened Reuther's political position at the 1944 convention, the conflict did not strengthen the position of Reuther's opponents. Most UAW activists supported the reaffirmation of the pledge because it was the sensible political thing to do to preserve the union's position, but they were not enthusiastic about the commitment. They did not agree with the Communists' very sharp condemnation of wartime strikes because they were aware of the conditions that had provoked those incidents. Many union activists, to be sure, had themselves participtaed in brief work stoppages.[59]

The factional alignments during 1943–1945 were similar to those of 1939–1941. Frankensteen returned to his alliance with Addes, while the Communists formed a distinct group but generally supported Addes and Frankensteen. The Reuther caucus continued to bring together such diverse elements as Socialists, Trotskyites, and the ACTU. President Thomas, who had worked closely with Reuther during the 1939–1941 period, and Richard Leonard, Ford Department director and a former leader of the Reuther caucus, attempted to found an independent group during the war, but this caucus was not able to compete successfully with the two principal factions.[60]

Although the alliances were similar to those of the pre-Pearl Harbor era, the policy orientations of the two major factions were almost the reverse of what they had been in the earlier period. Whereas in 1940 and 1941, the Communists had been critical of the defense buildup, Addes had been cautious and Reuther enthusiastic, Communists were now the most ardent supporters of a "win the war" program, Addes gave victory in the war the highest priority, and Reuther, while supporting the war effort, advocated modifying or threatening to cancel the no-strike pledge and favored pulling out of the WLB and other government agencies whose policies were unsatisfactory to the UAW. In 1940, the Communists pushed for independent political action and opposed a third term for President Roosevelt. In 1943 and 1944, Reuther supporters organized the Michigan Commonwealth Federation, an independent party, and advocated no more than a qualified endorsement of Roosevelt's reelection. Addes, Frankensteen, and the Communists were less conditional in their support of the president and opposed a third party effort as premature and harmful to Roosevelt.[61]

The explanation for these wartime policy changes lies in the opposed political outlooks of the contending groups. For the left, the war had been transformed from an imperialist war to a people's antifascist war. Similarly, Addes and the forces associated with him became more enthusiastic about the war because the United States was directly involved and American soldiers were fighting and dying. Reuther, too, increased his support because of American involvement, but by 1943 he was becoming concerned about the postwar situation. Like other anticommunists, Reuther believed that Americans should not abandon their opposition to Communism just because the United States was allied with the Soviet Union in the war against the Axis. He was not motivated so much by opposition to specific Communist proposals or actions during the war as by a general anticommunist stance that predated the war. His enthusiasm for the war was kept in check by the fact that he did not like the United States's Soviet ally. He was, therefore, ready to take advantage of opportunities to support policies that might help to enhance his position withing the union or weaken that of his adversaries.[62]

Anticommunism was a feature of the wartime factional conflict as it had been in the earlier period. During the 1943 convention, Reuther partisans had attacked Addes and Frankensteen as the "boys who take their orders / straight from the office of Joe Stalin . . . " Anticommunism had less of an impact during than before the war, however, because of the U. S.–Soviet alliance and the strong support of American Communists for the Roosevelt administration and the war effort. Leonard Woodcock, a leader of the Reuther caucus, recalled that "when the war broke out, the communists got ultra-patriotic and Russia became quite popular. Being anticommunist was sometimes a very misunderstood role, very misunderstood."[63]

Despite factional controversies, the UAW's growth during the war was spectacular. Of the hundreds of thousands of workers entering the auto and allied industries for the first time, a large proportion were women and Blacks. The number of women UAW members increased from about 5 to 25 percent of the total membership, and the proportion of Black workers grew from 4 to 10 percent. This new membership compelled the union to confront the problem of discrimintion on the job and in the community. Dual seniority systems, unequal pay for equal work, and friction among union members were some of the problems that the UAW had to address.[64]

Although the union's policy declarations were supportive of equality, its actions did not always measure up to its pronouncements. Important gains were made in achieving "equal pay for equal work" for women workers, but dual male/female seniority systems and the pattern of distinct male and female job categories remained largely intact. Black workers gained access to new and better paying job classifications, but many jobs were still reserved for "whites only." The UAW leadership effectively ended numerous "hate strikes" directed against the upgrading of Black workers by groups of mostly skilled white workers, and the union also established a Fair Practices Committee to combat discrimination and support the President's Committee on Fair Employment Practices (FEPC), but proposals to elect a Black worker to the union's executive board were defeated. Furthermore, the 1943 Detroit "race riot" indicated that sharp tensions existed between Blacks and whites in the automobile city and that Blacks were victimized by poor housing and mistreatment by police. Advances had been made in the struggle against racism, but racial discrimination was to plague the UAW in the postwar era.[65]

The membership of the union in 1944 and 1945 was comprised about equally of those who had joined the union during the initial organizational period and those who had joined after Pearl Harbor. Having entered the UAW at a time when gains resulted from the alliance between union leadership and government, the new members by and large lacked the militancy and progressive political outlook that had characterized the initial wave of union members. The wartime militancy that manifested itself in unauthorized stoppages was in fact narrowly based. Although the Rank and File Caucus attempted to connect this militancy with independent political action through the formation of such organizations as the Michigan Commonwealth Federation, the influence of the caucus was very circumscribed. The major UAW political action was the campaign of the CIO Political Action Committee (PAC) in behalf of the reelection of Roosevelt. This was a vigorous movement, but it lacked the transforming power of such events as the Flint sit-down and the 1941 Ford strike. Those actions had not only changed the everyday reality that workers experienced but had enabled them to gain a new sense of their own power. Roosevelt, Murphy, and other New Deal officials had aided labor in the organizational upsurge between 1936 and 1941, but the workers involved were confident that it was their own activity that had been decisive. Between 1942 and 1945, however, this relationship seemed reversed, with the administration playing the decisive role and union labor only a supporting part. Union leaders served on various governemnt boards, participated in community campaigns, and mounted political activities in behalf of the commander-in-chief. The auto workers entered the postwar period with a strengthened organization, but its power had yet to be fully tested.[66]

The conservative big business drive was to provide the test for the UAW, a test not only for the union as such but for its two principal factions. Once again, the political issues confronting the country and the union changed as the United States shifted from an alliance with the Soviet Union to cold war confrontation. The position of the caucuses underwent another change, the Reuther caucus accommodating itself to the new national direction and the left-center group adopting a more oppositional stance. Before the pressures of postwar conservatism and cold war anticommunism exacerbated UAW factionalism, however, the union faced the problem of reconversion to civilian production in a relatively united manner.

Chapter Three

The UAW and Reconversion

Early on the morning of August 14, 1945, radio reports announced Japan's acceptance of Allied surrender terms. Many Detroiters immediately began to celebrate the end of World War II, crowding downtown in such numbers that stores were forced to close. Having heard rumors of peace before, workers in the war plants waited until President Harry S. Truman, at 7:00 p.m., announced United State's approval of the Japanese surrender statement and orders to Allied forces to suspend offensive operations. Workers then left the factories by the thousands and poured downtown to join the tumultuous and happy throngs. There was much hugging, kissing, and drinking as the city enjoyed the greatest festivities in its history.[1] There was good cause to celebrate the final defeat of the Axis drive for world supremacy. Not since the Civil War had the nation faced such a difficult struggle.

Auto workers had contributed to the victory over fascism on both the battle front and the production front. Two hundred and fifty thousand members of the UAW served in the armed forces, while auto workers at home produced some $29 billion worth of military hardware for the Allied forces, working long hours under difficult conditions. Although the enthusiasm of the victory celebrations was real, auto workers could not help but feel anxiety about the future since they knew that the mass unemployment of the Great Depression was ended only by the defense and war boom. Workers knew also that past war booms had been followed by postwar busts. Would depression-level unemployment return? Would there be a union-busting drive like the one following World War I?[2]

A new era was already beginning in both domestic and international affairs as World War II came to a close. On August 14, the UAW International Executive Board announced the end of the union's wartime no-strike pledge. Although the union declared that the revocation of the pledge would not bring an immediate rash of strikes, a period of sharpened labor conflict clearly lay ahead. The years of overtime hours, accumulated grievances, and wartime inflation stimulated a militancy among workers that was no longer restrained by the need for national unity against the foreign foe. Internationally, the nuclear age began when the United States dropped atomic bombs on two major Japanese cities on August 6 and 9, causing more then 200,000 civilian casualties by explosions, fires, and atomic radiation. Commenting on the development of nuclear weapons, Donald Montgomery, the UAW's Consumer Counsel, declared that the bomb was "an instrument to make war impossible. [We must] end war or face the certainty of international suicide," he maintained. Growing differences between the Soviet Union and its Western allies, however, made many Americans doubtful about the prospects for creating a lasting peace.[3]

As the United States prepared for reconversion to civilian production, the membership of the labor movement was the greatest in American history, having increased from 8,944,000 to 14,796,000 between 1940 and 1945. The unions hoped the transition to a peacetime economy would bring full employment and a new level of social security. Labor leaders wanted to move forward to an expanded New Deal, based on the concept of the Economic Bill of Rights outlined by President Roosevelt in January 1944.[4]

Conservative big business circles had their own plans for the reconversion period. Like organized labor, big business had been strengthened by World War II. Cost-plus contracts brought to the biggest corporations the highest profits in history. After-tax profits increased from an annual average of $3.9 billion during the 1936 to 1939 period to more then $9.4 billion during the 1941 to 1945 period. Corporate figures like General Motors's William S. Knudsen took leading positions in the federal government, and the plethora of new government agencies controlling the billions in government expenditures were generally run by business executives. The leading economic and political roles taken by business figures during the war helped the corporations to overcome much of the negative reputation they had acquired during the depression. The wartime experience of big business executives in the federal government led to a changed conservative approach: instead of the narrow opposition to federal government programs characteristic of the New Deal period, business leaders now favored federal responsibility in managing the nation's economy; instead of relying on their own private efforts and on the judicial system, conservative business people now wished to use the federal government to weaken the unions.[5]

The employer drive to secure the enactment of legislation restricting trade union rights was already well underway during the war. A number of antilabor laws were passed, particularly in the states.[6] The central goal of the National Association of Manufacturers and other employer groups, however, was replacing federal legislation offering aid and protection to labor organizations with legislation severly limiting labor's activities. With the end of the war approaching, the Automotive Council for War Production, an association of automotive employers, demanded that Congress enact a "modern" labor policy that would decentralize unions by preventing them from representing workers of separate employers, outlaw union political activity, and penalize unions that struck before exhausting grievance procedures. Looking back on this drive for antilabor legislation, President Truman wrote William Green in 1952 that he had little doubt "that a definite plot was hatched at the close of the war to smash or at least to cripple, our trade union movement in a period of postwar reaction. The conspiracy was developed by a little group of politicians working with representatives of our most reactionary employers . . . "[7]

This antilabor offensive received strong backing in the commercial press, which sensationalized almost every strike. Wartime strikes, according to the newspapers, undermined the war effort; postwar strikes delayed reconversion of the consumer-goods industries to civilian production. The antilabor campaign received a warm reception in a Congress dominated by Southern Democrats and conservative Republicans. From April 1945 through June 1947, when the Taft-Hartley Act finally became law, one or another extreme antiunion proposal was under serious consideration in the Congress.[8]

A second major objective of big business groups was the ending of wartime price controls. Firms in many industries delayed production and distribution of goods in an effort to pressure the federal government to abolish price controls. Corporate propagandists then blamed the shortages about which the public was complaining on price controls and on strikes. Business representatives insisted as well that any wage increases for workers would require price increases. Such corporate propaganda had a significant impact although polls showed that public opinion continued to favor government controls to hold the line on prices. The first major breach in the price wall was a $5 per ton increase in steel prices granted by President Truman to the steel companies in February 1946. Ignoring OPA's objections, Truman authorized the price increase to encourage the steel companies to settle an industrywide strike of the United Steelworkers (USW) for higher wages. Thereafter, one powerful industry after another followed steel in gaining price increases. The OPA's authority was further weakened by new legislation that removed from the agency's jurisdiction supervision of most food prices and relaxed controls on other products. By November 1946, meaningful price controls had all but been abandoned. The government's CPI increased by 18 percent between February and December 1946.[9].

Business also gained from Congress and the Roosevelt and Truman administrations the enactment of specific measures to aid it in the transition to peacetime production. Under the tax laws, corporations received as compensation for postwar reductions in profits below average prewar income millions in refunds on excess profits taxes paid during the war. In the end, the federal government—and thus nonbusiness taxpayers—absorbed about 85 percent of the major corporations' reconversion costs. Fortified by this guarantee against any significant reduction in profits, big business was in a favorable position to resist the contractual demands of the trade unions.[10]

While the big business offensive unfolded rapidly on the political, ideological and economic fronts, labor's offensive was slow to develop. The unions sought immediate help to cushion working people against the impact of reconversion and also such major reforms as full employment legislation, national health insurance, expanded public housing, an improved minimum wage, and a permanent fair employment practices commission.[11] The unions were much stronger organizationally than ever before in American history, but they were ill-prepared ideologically and politically to meet the problems of the postwar world. Their own internal weaknesses and a balance of political forces already tipped against them stalled labor's postwar offensive almost as it began.

World War II had brought substantial changes in the outlook of the American labor movement. In the 1930s, the philosophy of the labor movement, particularly that of the CIO, was shaped by the struggles for jobs and relief, the stormy battles for union recognition, the uphill fight to establish the broad new social programs of the New Deal, and the campaign against the world threat of fascism. The CIO was militant and socially and politically active. Many workers and union leaders were radical and class conscious. Of course, the CIO included many old-line labor leaders and conservative workers, but the dominant tone of the 1930s was a militant progressivism. World War II significantly altered this spirit. Four years of full employment, national unity focusing on the war effort, and government participation in union contract negotiations all weakened labor radicalism. Ideas of "class peace" became widespread during the war and were advocated for a time even by many CIO left wingers. Labor leaders were caught up in joint production committees, labor-management luncheons, and trips to Washington. Union officials devoted themselves to the skillful preparation of briefs for submission to the WLB. A rank-and-file-based militancy seemed less important; expertise and good contacts seemed more important. As Jack White, a left winger at GM's Ternstedt plant in Detroit, recalled it, "we had production committees, we had in-plant feeding committees, I was so bogged down with this bullshit that I was glad to go in the service and be divested of it." Despite this weakening of labor radicalism, the intraunion factionalism endemic in the UAW and other CIO unions continued.[12]

Millions of new workers, moreover, had joined the unions during the war without the radicalizing experience of the labor struggles of the 1930s, and many of them came from segments of the population previously underrepresented in the CIO—women, ex-farmers, Southerners, and Blacks. Coming to union membership during a period of relative labor peace, these new groups were not welded into a unified whole with the veterans of the 1930s, and tensions between various groups of workers ran high. The many changes in the experience, outlook, and composition of workers and union leaders meant that labor's independent political strength by no means matched its organizational strength.[13]

Although not as enmeshed in the Democratic party as it would later become, the labor movement during Roosevelt's final months in office had relied on his leadership to win the support of public opinion and the Congress for progressive legislation. What might have happened had Roosevelt lived to complete his fourth term is impossible to say, but it was evident by the close of World War II that New Dealers were becoming less and less important in the Democratic party.

Harry Truman, who succeeded Roosevelt in April 1945, was more of a Democratic party man than a New Dealer. In the summer of 1945, UAW President R. J. Thomas noted a "rightward deviation" in Truman's appointments that would "certainly make it easy for him to swing sharply to the right if he should choose to do so." Truman did propose on September 6, 1945, a 21-point progressive domestic program that embodied many of labor's goals, but he did not fight for it and settled for many compromises unacceptable to labor. The president also opposed Congressional liberals who sought a stong full employment bill, and he undermined the power of the FEPC, thus aiding its eventual elimination in 1946. Truman further separated himself from labor by proposing restrictive labor legislation. Also, although Truman spoke out in favor of wage increases, he refused to put the power of his office behind a specific substantial increase in workers' pay. Most important, Truman gave priority to a policy of "getting tough with Russia." He was then, at best, a vacillating ally of the labor movement in 1945-1946. He was not the leader of the progressive coalition that, for better or worse, the trade unions had come to rely on in the president during the Roosevelt administrations. The conservative coalition in Congress was thus able to block the passage of any significant social reform legislation during the 79th Congress (1945-1946). The labor movement, for so long politically reliant on the White House, was unable to mount an independent campaign for a progressive program.[14]

The CIO's own political apparatus, the Political Action Committee, had functioned most successfully when linked to President Roosevelt in his 1944 re-election campaign. The PAC was not very active between elections, however, and did not function especially well in the 1946 Congressional elections. Political mobilization of labor's ranks for jobs, housing, and health care legislation was sporadic at best. The CIO organized large-scale campaigns of lobbying, letter writing, and mass demonstrations on only two, essentially defensive, issues: retention of price controls and opposition to restrictive labor legislation. The labor movement failed to mobilize its forces to secure its broader political objectives.[15]

UAW President Thomas and other CIO leaders joined Soviet, British, and other trade unionists from Allied countries in forming the World Federation of Trade Unionists (WFTU). CIO leaders spoke out for peace and postwar cooperation between the United States, the Soviet Union, and Great Britain, but they did not regard this eventually decisive question as a matter of high priority. They were cautious about moving too far in opposition to a hardening United States foreign policy.[16]

The PAC did conduct a major campaign to elect UAW Vice President Richard Frankensteen mayor of Detroit in the fall of 1945. It spent more then $100,000 and organized 500 precincts in a vast effort to secure his election. Frankensteen led in the August primary with 41 percent of the vote, whereas incumbent Mayor Edward Jeffries could muster only 34 percent. In the final round of the nonpartisan balloting in November, however, a huge anti-CIO campaign allowed Jeffries to gain reelection by 275,000 to 217,000 votes. Two of three CIO-backed Common Council candidates were also defeated, including the progressive Black minister, Reverend Charles Hill.[17]

One cause of Frankensteen's defeat was the old division between the CIO and the AFL, which endorsed Jeffries. Another factor was an antilabor scare campaign waged by business and the three Detroit daily newspapers, the *Free Press*, the *News*, and the *Times*. "The rival goon squads," the *Free Press* charged, "will move from the industrial belt into the City Hall." Although this coalition had defeated the UAW eight years before when Labor's Non-Partisan League ran a "Labor Slate" for mayor and Common Council, CIO leaders pointed to the electoral progress organized labor had made since 1937: the mayoral vote for the CIO candidate had increased from 154,000 to 217,000 and from 37 percent to 44 percent of the total vote. One reason for this improvement was that Frankensteen ran a broad "people's" rather than a narrow "labor" campaign like that of 1937. The strong Black vote for Frankensteen of approximately 65,000 was responsible for most of the increase over the vote for the 1937 Labor Slate, which had lacked major Black support. The solid support of Frankensteen in the Black community (an estimated 90 percent of the total Black vote) represented an important political advance for the labor movement. Frankensteen, however, gained a smaller share of the white vote than had the 1937 labor candidate despite the fact that the 1945 Detroit CIO membership of 350,000 to 400,000 was nearly double 1937 membership in the city. The nonpartisan form of Detroit city elections makes it possible to view these contests as tests of the UAW's and CIO's independent political strength.[18] Thus, the failure to secure increases in electoral support for a UAW-CIO candidate in Detroit corresponding to the union's membership strength was a sign of the political problems facing the CIO movement.

Frankensteen's platform included a call for jobs, improved mass transit and recreational facilities, public works, and labor peace. The forces backing Jeffries opposed integrated housing and public housing, and his backers whipped up fears that, if Frankensteen were elected, Blacks would "invade" white neighborhoods and destroy property values. The theme of a reactionary whispering campaign was: "No kidding, if Frankensteen gets elected, the niggers will just take over Detroit."[19]

The expansion of war production had attracted thousands of Black workers to Detroit. Although the city's Black population had increased from 151,000 to 213,000 between 1940 and 1944, there was a net gain of less than 3,000 new housing units for Black residents. Most Black newcomers thus had to move into old buildings, including "stores, stables, attics, basements, and other improvised buildings considered totally uninhabitable in 1940." Both the city government and the real estate interests insisted that any new housing for Blacks would have to be located in the already overcrowded ghetto. The housing situation and police brutality were the main causes of the Detroit race riot of June 1943. After the riot, Jeffries issued a "white paper" condemning Black leaders, militant organizations, and the Black press. Employing racist tactics, he then defeated a UAW-backed candidate in the 1943 election and followed the same approach in the 1945 campaign, only on a bigger scale.[20]

Frightened by the racist campaign waged by his opposition, Frankensteen failed to come out in support of integrated housing. He also made concessions to red-baiting and anti-Semitism, but his retreat on these issues did not slow the reactionary campaign. Jeffries's backers, indeed, tried to undermine Frankensteen among his own supporters by using UAW factionalism against him and by attacking him in the Black and Jewish communities as an advocate of racism and anti-Semitism![21]

The hate campaign, especially its racism, prevented Frankensteen from significantly increasing his share of the vote beyond the percentage he had received in the primary. Frankensteen had been expected to pick up the second round vote of the other major anti-Jeffries candidate, but this failed to materialize. An analysis of the election results reveals that Frankensteen had 61 percent of the vote in Polish working-class neighborhoods, 45 percent in Irish neighborhoods, 75 percent in Italian neighborhoods, and 45 percent in the poorest native-born white neighborhoods, in which large numbers of Southerners resided. These percentages were significantly below the normal Democratic party votes in these neighborhoods. The nonpartisan electoral system generally results in a reduced vote for pro-labor and pro-minority candidates, in part because of an increase in the influence of daily newspapers and middle class civic reform organizations in such elections. Taking advantage of the nonpartisan ballot, conservative forces successfully played on ideological weaknesses and fears of Detroit workers to prevent the CIO from establishing a local beachhead from which to push forward in the battle for progressive domestic reform.[22]

The political problems for the UAW disclosed by the Frankensteen campaign came on top of economic difficulties resulting from the end of the war, a massive cutoff of military orders, and wholesale layoffs of auto workers. In Detroit alone, auto employment, already down 100,000 from the wartime peak on August 14, 1945, was slashed another 160,000 by mid-September. There was no rush by the auto companies to return to civilian production. Having already almost secured the maximum net profit allowable for 1945, the corporations sought to use a slow reconversion to pressure the OPA to grant price increases. Only 70,000 cars were produced in 1945, instead of 200,000 projected several months before the end of the war. Before the start of the General Motors strike in late November 1945, auto industry employment of production workers was 32 percent below the wartime peak.[23]

Whereas auto production workers had been earning $55 and $60 per week during the war, jobless workers just after the end of the war received an average of $21 and a maximum of $28 per week in unemployment benefits in Michigan and less than $20 per week in most other states. Unemployed workers, especially women and Blacks, were threatened with the loss of even these meager benefits if they did not agree to take any available low-paying job. In Michigan, the Unemployment Compensation Commission allowed a worker only four weeks to seek work in his or her customary occupation, after which offers of other work were "deemed suitable" Workers who had learned new skills and won corresponding increases in wage rates during the war were thus forced to return to a low-wage labor pool.[24]

Because of the high unemployment, management made greater demands on employed workers, and working conditions worsened. Disciplinary actions by management provoked unauthorized work stoppages. These strikes were headlined in the daily press, which blamed the unions for the slow reconversion.[25]

Workers who kept their jobs during the reconversion process also faced financial difficulties. Many were downgraded to less skilled jobs with a corresponding reduction in hourly pay, and their work hours were reduced to forty or less per week. The years of working many overtime hours during the war had been very hard on auto workers, but overtime pay had helped them to keep up with inflation. The combination of reduced hours and lower wages due to downgrading meant a cut of nearly 25 percent in weekly income from the wartime levels for auto production workers who managed to retain their jobs. The average weekly earnings of auto production workers had dropped in the last months of 1945 to about $44.60, approximately the level of late 1941. Prices, in the meantime, had risen 17.5 percent according to the government's CPI. Labor leaders, moreover, protested that the actual increase in prices for working-class consumers was twice as great as the increase in the CPI.[26]

Black and women workers faced special problems during reconversion because the auto companies sought to return to prewar employment patterns by sharply limiting opportunities for these two groups. Officially, Charles E.

Wilson, president of General Motors, and other top business representatives joined leading union officials in voting at Truman's November 1945 Labor-Management Conference "to urge on all elements of labor and management the broad democratic spirit of tolerance and equality of economic opportunity in respect to race, sex, color, religion, age, national origin or ancestry in determining who are employed and who are admitted to labor union membership." A wide gap existed, however, between this expression of support for "tolerance and equality" and management's actual employment policies. The attitude of a segment of Michigan industry toward Black workers was voiced by the chair of the Detroit Committee for Economic Development, William H. Leininger, at an interracial conference in June 1945. "The Negro," he declared, was "racially more of an individualist that the white" and was therefore unsuited for work in mass production industries where there would be too few postwar jobs for all who wanted to work. Leininger recommended that Blacks should return to jobs in garages, filling stations, and the service trades. In line with this racist attitude, such auto plants as the Ford Rouge, Chevrolet Gear and Axle, and Dodge Main filed orders with the United State Employment Services (USES) for white workers only. Black workers who already had seniority in the auto industry were not called back to work in line with their seniority or, when recalled, were placed on prewar foundry and janitorial jobs.[27]

The federal government reduced its support of equal employment opportunity during the reconversion period. The USES abandoned its wartime policy of refusing to process discriminatory employment orders. Even before the war ended, Congress had drastically cut funding for the FEPC. President Truman further undermined the power of the FEPC by cancelling a committee directive ordering the Capitol Transit Company of Washington, D.C., to cease discriminatory practices against Blacks. One of the committee's two Black members, Charles Houston, resigned in protest, charging that "the failure of the Government to enforce democratic practices and to protect minorities in its own capital makes its expressed concern for national minorities abroad somewhat specious, and its interference in the domestic affairs of other countries very premature." Killed by Congress in 1946, the FEPC observed in its final report: "The wartime gains of Negro, Mexican-American and Jewish workers are being lost through an unchecked revival of discriminatory practices."[28]

The UAW opposed the increased discrimination against Black workers. The UAW leadership had vigorously supported President Roosevelt's 1941 Executive Order establishing the FEPC. President Thomas and other UAW officials firmly put an end to "hate strikes" designed to prevent employment of Blacks in jobs from which they had previously been excluded. In 1944, the UAW executive board set up a Fair Practices Committee. Under the leadership of Executive Director George Crockett, the committee worked closely with the FEPC, dealt with complaints of discrimination within the union, established ties with minority group organizations, and conducted a union educational campaign. The committee's educational programs were popular with many locals. The strength of the committee's activities was due in part to the growth in the number of Black workers in the industry and the increasing political weight Black unionists carried within the UAW. Although far from establishing full equality within the union, the Fair Practices Committee was able to keep a watchful eye out for the possibility of discriminatory mass layoffs of Black workers, to call attention to discriminatory hiring and recall policies, and to urge locals strictly to protect Black workers' rights.[29]

The employment of Black workers in the auto industry accelerated throughout the war, increasing from 4 percent of the total number of auto workers in 1940 to 10 percent at war's end, but the trend of a continuously increasing Black share of total auto industry employment came to an end during reconversion. The proportion of Black workers placed in auto industry jobs through USES declined from 15.5 percent in the last half of 1944 to 10.5 percent after V-J Day. Black employment thus remained at about 10 percent of total auto industry employment. The position of Blacks in the industry did undergo a qualitive deterioration, however, because Black workers were more often downgraded into less skilled jobs than were white workers with the same seniority. Although the vigilance of the Fair Practices Committee helped prevent massive discriminatory layoffs of Blacks, the union was unable to check this relative decline in the status of Black workers.[30]

Women workers, too, were unable to maintain the position they had achieved in the relatively high-paying auto industry during the war. Although government and union surveys showed that most women war workers wanted to keep their jobs, the proportion of women employed as auto production workers dropped from a wartime peak of 25.8 percent in November 1943 to 8-10 percent after V-J Day. Black women were the hardest hit, their numbers dropping from 3 percent to 0.5 percent of all production workers. One cause of this decline was the low seniority of women workers, most of whom did not gain their jobs in the industry until 1942 or 1943, but a key factor in the disproportionate loss of jobs suffered by women was a systematic drive by industry to reduce female employment. Employers made use of numerous contract provisions that allowed them to discriminate against women. Also, in violation of union contracts, many companies arbitrarily laid off, fired, or refused to recall women workers because they were overweight, had varicose veins, were unable to perform the most difficult job in the plant, and similar contrivances.[31]

The UAW's response to the discriminatory drive against women was inconsistent. Women union members and their supporters suceeded in getting strong resolutions passed at UAW conventions that put the union on record in opposition to the campaign to exclude women from the industry and

President Thomas officially urged locals strictly to protect women's seniority rights. Some locals did succeed in stopping some of the discriminatory layoffs and firings, but the UAW leadership and membership continued to approve contracts with such discriminatory clauses as separate male and female seniority lists. Sections of the union's leadership and rank and file actively supported the drive to oust women from the plants. Many workers feared that there would be a postwar shortage of jobs and that the large scale employment of women would reduce the number of good jobs available to men, particularly returning veterans. Given this climate, the protest actions of women union members were limited in their impact. The majority of women workers were forced to return to the low-paying jobs they held before the war. Few realized that reducing women to a low-wage pool dragged down the conditions and wages of all workers.[32]

To avoid the complicated ideological questions associated with women's place in American society, the union adopted a "sex-blind" policy that required women members to reject "special privilege" for their sex. This approach denied the reality of the many sex-based discriminatory obstacles facing women and weakened those activities the union did conduct against discrimination. Women auto workers thus found that their special problems were largely ignored by the union, and the UAW itself missed the opportunity to enlist the full and active participation of its more than 300,000 women members in the reconversion wage struggles.[33]

The drive to push women out of the plants succeeded in part because women had not been employed in the auto industry long enough to establish a significant political position for themselves within the UAW. Often new to trade unionism, burdened by the responsibility for housework and child care, women had little time to participate in union activities. They achieved far less representation in local office, as convention delegates, and on the international staff than their numbers warranted. Only a handful of women were staff members, and women constituted only one to two percent of the delegates at international conventions in 1944 and 1946. A woman was not elected as a member of the International Executive Board until 1962. The UAW's experience contrasts with that of the United Electrical Workers (UE), where women were a significant part of the industry before the war and 40 percent of the union membership in 1944. The UE reported in 1943 it had 18 women local presidents and 46 women on the international staff and noted that 35 percent of its national full-time organizers were women. The first woman was elected to the UE executive board in 1944. Although UE women were far from achieving equal representation in office, they had a base of political power within their union that UAW women lacked. As members of a left-led union, they did not have to contend with the argument that women had to avoid seeking "special privilege" at all costs.[34]

Reconversion brought many changes in the lives of both men and women war workers, but even greater changes occurred in the lives of returning veterans. Of all Americans, G.I.s made the greatest sacrifice in World War II. The shift from the war front to the job front was not always an easy transition. Aid to returning veterans, however, was immensely popular politically, the veterans being the only nonbusiness group to receive reconversion help from Congress. Even the most conservative members of Congress believed themselves obliged to support aid for veterans. The G.I. Bill of Rights, enacted into law in 1944, provided veterans with mustering out pay, reemployment rights, unemployment compensation, hospitalization and medical care, and education and home loan benefits.[35]

With the war's end, a "bring the boys home" campaign by the public and the G.I.s themselves brought about a much more rapid demobilization of troops than the government had planned. A total of 9,000,000 veterans had returned home by the end of 1946. More than 200,000 of these ex-G.I.s had seniority rights in the auto industry, and many more hoped to secure auto industry jobs. As it turned out, they received a high percentage of the new auto industry jobs that became available. By the last quarter of 1946, veterans constituted 59 percent of new auto industry workers hired through the United States Employment Service as contrasted with 36 percent of new hires in all nonagricultural jobs. Black veterans, however, were denied equal access to these new auto jobs by overt discrimination.[36]

Business attempted to compete with unions for the loyalty of the returning veterans. Some conservative forces, moreover, sought to turn veterans against the labor movement. The Ford Motor Company gave newly hired veterans at its Highland Park plant day-long orientation sessions in which the UAW was attacked for blocking a "fine" seniority plan for veterans. During the 1945-1946 strike at General Motors, that corporation made some unsuccessful attempts to use veterans against the union.[37]

When in 1944 Selective Service Director General Lewis Hershey issued an interpretation of veterans' reemployment rights that gave ex-G.I.s "super-seniority" over all other workers, the labor movement saw this as an attempt to undermine the entire seniority system. The UAW and other unions favored, instead, reemployment of veterans on the basis of their accrued seniority, with time spent in the service counting as if the worker had remained on the job. Despite some tension between veterans and nonveterans, the need for solidarity in the great wage struggles of 1945-1946 proved decisive, and contingents of veterans became a regular feature of union picket lines and rallies. In May 1946, the United States Supreme Court upheld labor's contention that Congressional enactment of reemployment rights for veterans was not intended to "sweep aside the seniority system."[38]

It was on the economic front that industrial workers put up their big fight against the corporation-controlled reconversion. Preferring a test of strength, employers rebuffed attempts by labor leaders to reach a compromise on the wage issue that would avoid strikes during reconversion. Commenting on the authorized stoppages provoked by management's disciplinary actions in the weeks following V-J Day, *Automotive and Aviation Industries* declared, "The industry has known for a long time that sooner or later it must stand on its fundamental right to manage if full and efficient production is to be attained." The automobile workers accepted the corporate challenge, as 320,000 General Motors workers joined more than 4,000,000 workers form other industries in strikes to regain wartime take-home pay and to maintain the strength of their unions.[39]

Chapter Four

The General Motors Strike:
The UAW Jumps the Gun

With the relaxation of wartime controls, the UAW launched a campaign to win a general wage increase, focusing its energies on negotiations with the General Motors Corporation. To make up for the decline in workers' take-home pay, the union demanded a 30 percent increase in wages (or 33.5¢ per hour for the average GM worker). After negotiations failed, 180,000 workers shut down the huge General Motors empire on November 21, 1945. They were joined by another 140,000 GM workers who were on layoffs at the time of the strike.[1] The strike continued for a longer period than any previous UAW strike, lasting through the long winter months and ending only after 113 days.

The GM strike was part of the big 1945-1946 strike wave, the largest in United States history. The wave crested in 1946 when 4,600,000 workers struck and 116,000,000 workdays were lost, four times as many work days lost to strikes as in 1937, the year of the sit-downs.[2] The 1945–1946 strikes resulted in a general wage increase of 18.5¢ per hour for workers in the major mass production industries. The wage hike did not compensate fully for the postwar decline in take-home pay, but it was the largest general wage increase in the history of the CIO to that time. The corporations were compelled to grant a larger wage increase than they wished and were unable to weaken the newly strengthened organizations of their workers. Some corporations did obtain concessions, however, on their demands for "company security" from unauthorized stoppages and guarantees of employee productivity. The corporations, moreover, advanced toward their goals of eliminating price control and passing restrictive labor legislation. Under strong business pressure, long-standing ties between the CIO and the Democratic administration were broken during the 1945–1946 shutdowns.

On August 16, 1945, two days after accepting Japan's surrender, President Truman announced a reconversion wage policy that permitted management and labor to agree on wage increases provided no price increases resulted therefrom. This policy was promulgated as Executive Order 9599 on August 18. On that same day Walter Reuther, director of the UAW's General Motors

Department, sent a letter to GM President Wilson demanding an immediate 30 percent increase in wages "to cushion the economy against the awful impact of wholesale contract terminations." Citing the vast financial resources at the disposal of the corporation, Reuther asserted the union's view that a 30 percent wage increase could be granted without increasing prices. The coupling of the demand for a wage increase with a demand that GM not increase its prices—a crucial feature of the UAW-GM dispute—was based on the newly announced government wage policy, with which, Reuther declared, the UAW was "in hearty accord." The tying of the UAW GM Department's negotiating stance to Truman's August wage-price policy proved in the end to be a serious mistake.[3]

Reuther justified the demand for a wage increase without a price increase by insisting that wages should be based on a corporation's "ability to pay." He contended that General Motors could meet the UAW's demand and still earn high profits without increasing its prices. The "ability to pay" issue became the focus of public controversy. GM refused to discuss the issues between itself and the UAW in terms of its ability to pay, insisting that the company's prices and profits were none of the union's business. Although GM claimed its ability to pay was not a legitimate issue, the corporation inconsistently charged that the union's demands were inflationary: the company could pay increased wages only by raising prices.[4]

Reuther's focus on General Motors's excellent financial position and its ability to increase wages substantially without raising prices captured public attention and put the corporation on the defensive. Reuther's call for GM to "open the books" to prove its claims that the UAW demands were unreasonable also improved the UAW's public position, but the "ability to pay" and "open the books" slogans also had some negative consequences for the union. General Motors was able to mobilize support on the issue of the right of a business to manage its own affairs, and the abstract issue of ability to pay became the key issue in the dispute instead of the need of workers to maintain their take-home pay. As a result, Reuther faced a number of difficult problems and questions. What would become of the union's demand for industrywide negotiations and standards if the individual company's ability to pay were taken into account? What was to be done in 1945–1946 with regard to a company like Ford, which was financially troubled? What would happen in a depression? Were workers' wages to be reduced then because of a reduced employer ability to pay? Reuther's answers to these questions varied in their effectiveness. What is important is that the ability-to-pay principle was confusing and divisive. It was, indeed, a principle generally used by employers in their fight against wage increases.[5]

The UAW itself, as a matter of fact, did not employ the ability-to-pay theme in negotiations with Ford and Chrysler. President Thomas called instead for presenting the union's case in human terms. "We should emphasize," he declared, "that cuts in take-home pay mean less food, less clothing, less medical care, less opportunities for education—and above all . . . a cut in income for all other American workers and farmers and professional people." At the same time, Thomas urged that the union cite labor's record in fighting inflation and denounce industry for seeking inflationary price increases. Reuther did not ignore the concrete problems of workers and, like Thomas, saw increased purchasing power for workers as essential to prosperity, but his insistence on the ability-to-pay principle got the union bogged down in abstract arguments.[6]

Reuther's approach to bargaining stemmed from his reformist ideological outlook. He spoke out during the GM negotiations for a properly balanced relationship among wages, prices, and profits. Reuther believed that capitalism should be reformed to provide a balanced, full-employment, depression-free economy, with production, productivity, and real wages all increasing simultaneously. This would result in prosperity for workers, the middle class, and business people. Reuther told GM officials during the 1945–1946 negotiations that he wanted "to help you people save this thing called free enterprise." Although he favored eventual public control of utilities, railroads, and such monopolistic industries as aluminum and magnesium, he, like other UAW leaders, supported private ownership of the auto industry. The UAW vice president even declared that he wished GM to be the "most prosperous company in this industry." His aim was "to raise collective bargaining above the Law of the Jungle." General Motors, however, was unmoved by Reuther's plea for reform, seeing in his approach a "socialistic" attempt by labor to gain control of management and destroy "free enterprise."[7]

The UAW executive board formally adopted the demand for a 30 percent wage increase as the "blanket demand" on all auto companies at its first postwar meeting in September 1945. At the same time, the board agreed on what became known as the "one-at-a-time strategy." President Thomas opened the board's discussion of wage strategy by reporting on numerous requests by locals for strike authorization. In Thomas's view, management was attempting to provoke strikes, and workers were "falling into the trap." The Detroit press was attacking the union for "irresponsibility" because of an unauthorized strike at Kelsey-Hayes which, the newspapers charged, was causing thousands of layoffs at other plants. Restrictive labor legislation was under consideration in Congress, and Thomas was concerned that "if the present unruly condition" were permitted to increase, "the Union will be destroyed." He therefore called on board members to help in restoring peace and order in the union and to participate in Truman's upcoming Labor-Management Conference. At the same time, however, members of the wartime Rank and File Caucus, factional opponents of the union leadership, picketed outside the board meeting, demanding support for the Kelsey-Hayes strike and an immediate convention to replace the union's leadership. Although the picketers represented a section of the Reuther caucus, Reuther himself offered a "positive program" to the board as an answer to the chaotic conditions described by Thomas.[8]

The essence of Reuther's proposal was the one-at-a-time strategy, Reuther contending that all the union's resources should be concentrated on one company as a test case. In Reuther's opinion, General Motors was the logical target because of its financial position and dominant role in the industry. Reuther reported that an excellent brief had been prepared supporting the demand that General Motors increase wages by 30 percent. To exert maximum economic pressure on General Motors, he asserted, the union had to exercise control over its membership so that production in the firms of GM's competitors continued without interruption. The Reuther strategy was based on the theory that the competitive rush for postwar markets would force the target corporation to meet the union's demands. The union executives resolved to adopt the one-at-a-time strategy. The target corporation, the board decided, should be one "which we think is strategic in terms of its economic position in the industry on policy matters." Strikes that strengthened the position of the target company were not be authorized.[9]

In adopting the on-at-a-time strategy in September 1945, the UAW Executive Board did not decide to launch an immediate strike. Reuther had told the board that the proper time to push the wage demand was when reconversion was complete and "the corporations are ready to go to town." Although Reuther and other UAW officials expressed this position to the press, the media emphasized the strike threat facing the industry. The press focus was partly a result of the union decision to file petitions with the NLRB for the conduct of strike ballots since the War Labor Disputes Act required 30 days' notice and a membership vote before a strike could take place. The crisis atmosphere was intensified, however, because Reuther, without authorization, told the press and a conference of GM workers that General Motors would be the target. According to one press account, Reuther predicted that the strike would occur "before the snow flies" if the 30 percent demand were not met. Thomas and other UAW officials then told the media that the target company had not yet been selected and the union was not seeking an immediate strike. Although the board was leaning toward GM as the target company in September, the official decision to strike GM rather than Ford or Chrysler was made only on the eve of the GM shutdown in November.[10]

An early indication that the auto corporations would not allow themselves to be divided came when Ford announced the layoff of 50,000 workers only two hours after Reuther stated that GM would be the union's target. General Motors, for its part, was slow in responding to the UAW's demands, rejecting them only on October 2. Five days before the union's scheduled strike vote, GM offered at 5 to 8 percent wage increase, coupled with a provocative proposal that the union join with the corporation in calling for a revision of the

Wage and Hours Act to increase the standard work week from 40 hours to 45 hours. Reuther charged that "General Motors wants a strike. It is baiting labor; it is baiting the Government; it is planning to use its vast economic power to coerce Congress."[11]

The hard line adopted by General Motors was similar to that taken by other major corporations. United States Steel refused to negotiate on wages with the United Steelworkers unless the OPA promised price compensation. The corporations' position was enhanced by legislation that guaranteed excess profits tax refunds for losses suffered during reconversion. GM and other large companies had particularly little incentive to produce in 1945 since the wartime taxation rate of 85.5 percent on excess profits remained in effect and GM had already earned close to the maximum possible profit for the year. On November 8, Truman signed legislation repealing the excess profits tax and lowering the general tax rate as of January 1, 1946.[12]

CIO leaders were agreed that strikes soon after V-J Day would be premature in most industries. Under CIO President Philip Murray's leadership, officials of the major CIO unions began meeting in early fall to coordinate the drive for higher wages and agreed on a $100,000 publicity campaign. Although Bert Cochran's study questions the existence of a "CIO strategy," the organization's leaders in fact planned on pressuring the Truman administration for action on the wage issue and conducting coordinated strikes after January 1, 1946, if a successful resolution of the wage conflict had not been achieved.[13]

Murray outlined his approach to the problem of a national wage policy in a report to the CIO executive board meeting of November 1–2, 1945. "The employers," Murray declared, "are engaged in a national sit-down strike, they are engaged in a national price fight . . . . The Government has been without any affirmative wage policy, the result being that there is a considerable amount of misunderstanding and confusion as to what the final attitude of the Government is going to be . . . ." If the administration had any wage policy, Murray said, it was one of "going into collective bargaining," but he charged that collective bargaining had "for all practical purposes broken down in almost every industry" because of the employers' sit-down strike. Murray pointed to strike votes being taken by the UAW, UE, and the Steelworkers and stated that he was "hopeful that settlement of a satisfactory nature can be effectuated without resort to strike." The key factor, in Murray's view, was the response of the Truman administration, which was "bound to be extremely anxious to have something done at the earliest possible date to avert the possiblity of the kind of disaster that might result in the event strikes of this magnitude should occur in our country."[14]

Several CIO board members expressed great concern about the need for unity and coordination of action of all affiliated unions in the difficult situation facing the CIO. Aware of the possibility of the UAW's going its own way, Sidney Hillman, president of the Amalgamated Clothing Workers, emphasized the necessity of cohesion and expressed the hope that "one or another [union] does not step out of what is general policy." Van Bittner of the Steelworkers warned against one union's "jumping out into the forefront" declaring, "the bigger the Union, if you fall, the harder you fall, and one union falling in the CIO under these circumstances may mean the interruption of the whole plan and policy as enunciated by President Murray in this resolution." Although Murray's resolution did not in itself embody the "plan," Bittner was calling for all to follow Murray's leadership. In reply, R. J. Thomas said that he agreed with Murray's approach, but he complained that the auto companies were "trying to get our people in a frame of mind" to "shut down the plants" and seemed to be succeeding.[15]

Newspaper accounts reveal further details of the CIO strategy that were not recorded in the CIO Executive Board's official minutes. According to a December New York Times story, "The CIO apparently hoped to avoid a strike anywhere, but if one came the plan was to have it in steel first, because cutting off that basic production material would bring tremendous pressure for a quick settlement." The Detroit Free Press reported that the CIO plan called for delaying strike action in steel "until this coming January when reconversion would be fairly well along." Similar accounts appeared in the Daily Worker.[16]

The UAW, however, diverged from general CIO policy and launched its strike against General Motors on November 21, 1945. The timing of the strike was such that the union was unable to exert economic pressure on the corporation during the first six weeks of the stoppage: GM received $34,415,207 in excess profits tax refunds as compensation for the losses it incurred in the last quarter of 1945 with the result that its 1945 net income of $188,268,115 exceeded its 1944 income even though production was much less in the later year. Why did the UAW strike GM when the corporation had little incentive to produce and nearly one-half of GM workers were on layoff? UAW President Thomas cited management provocation and rank-and-file readiness to strike when he spoke before the CIO executive board. These factors were important, but they also existed in other industries.[17] It was not only these factors but UAW factionalism and the UAW's hopes that the Big Three auto companies could be divided that brought about the premature strike at GM.

Walter Reuther was the architect of the UAW's strike strategy. Despite his stated opposition to acting before reconversion was completed, Reuther in fact pushed for an early strike. He hoped to establish himself as the militant leader of the reconversion wage battle as a preliminary step to a run for the UAW presidency. During the war, Reuther had partially identified himself with the movement to repeal the no-strike pledge. Now he partially identified himself with rank-and-file militancy expressing itself in unauthorized strikes and requests by dozens of locals for authorized strikes. Reuther reported to the UAW board one week after the GM strike had begun that "the Strategy Committee had authorized the General Motors strike realizing it had but one alternative: that if it did not sanction the strike at this date, it would be faced with a wave of unauthorized strikes, walkouts, etc., in the industry throughout the country." Leo Fenster, one of the left-wing leaders of Fisher Body Local 45 in Cleveland remarked, "I don't know who was going to walk out since we were all on layoff." On the other hand, Charles Beckman, left-wing president of Local 45 and a member of the GM national negotiating committee, agreed with Reuther's position. George Addes, national leader of the left-center coalition, recalled, "we reached a point where we had to do something . . . We weren't prepared to accept a decision from the CIO." Although Reuther's intraunion opponents constituted a majority on the six person Strategy Committee, they were both influenced by his ideas and hesitant to oppose militancy and thus weaken their position within the union. They took no action to prohibit the premature strike action. They may have feared that the Reuther caucus would make their leader's prediction come true by fomenting local walkouts if the GM strike were not authorized.[18]

A comparison of the situation in the UAW with that in the electrical and steel unions demonstrates the importance of auto union factionalism. The UE channeled rank-and-file militancy into the building of broad local coalitions for jobs, increased unemployment compensation, and union rights. Some UE local strikes occurred, but industrywide strike action was delayed despite company provocations. The steel industry also witnessed numerous local strikes, but steel union leaders did not call a premature industrywide strike. The factional situation in the UAW prevented that union from following a similar course.[19]

Despite early evidence that the auto companies were united, union leaders continued to hope that the family-owned Ford company, long the industry maverick, could be split from General Motors. The press speculated that 28-year-old Henry Ford II, the company's new chairman, was a "statesman" who would come to terms with labor. The *New York Times* reported in November, on the "highest authority," that union leaders had had a secret meeting with Henry Ford II and expected to conclude an agreement with the company, but Ford declared on November 15 that it was not the proper time to talk about wage increases. The company, instead, launched an offensive against the union on the issue of company security.[20]

Ford, the only one of the Big Three with a union shop and checkoff, demanded that in exchange for these concessions the union should protect the management against work stoppages and losses of production. The company proposed 31 contract changes, including clauses requiring: (1) union responsibility for increased productivity and prevention of work stoppages; (2) union reimbursement of the company for damages suffered as a result of strikes or other interferences with production while a contract was in effect; (3) union payment for union committeemembers, whose number should be greatly reduced; (4) seniority to be a secondary factor in demotions and certain layoffs; (5) employee initiation of grievances by first presenting them verbally to foremen; and (6) a CIO commitment to refrain from organizing employees in excluded categories, such as inspectors and production clerks. Ford's position was consistent with the general antilabor offensive launched after the war by various employer associations. The Chrysler Corporation also demanded increased company security and an end to the system of arbitrating grievances, thus completing the united front of the auto industry Big Three.[21]

UAW Ford Department Director Richard Leonard attacked the Ford company's statement as a "union busting, irresponsible, and strike-provoking document . . . . The only interpretation we can put on the statement," he said, "is that the company is anxious to provide a strike."[22] The union's inability to split the Big Three before striking GM was an indication that the one-at-a-time strategy would fail. The UAW nevertheless continued on the course of early strike action based on the notion that GM would be pressured by the continued operation of the other auto firms.

Despite the theoretical economic advantage the UAW was offering the other companies, Ford and Chrysler were in no hurry to seek to undermine GM's share of the automotive market, especially in the high tax year of 1945. Complicating production—and the one-at-a-time strategy—further was the interdependence of the auto industry. General Motors was the biggest customer for many parts companies and a big supplier of parts to other auto firms. Layoffs thus spread in the industry as a result of the GM strike and a strike of flat glass companies, and auto production remained in low gear throughout the GM strike. GM's competitors had produced only 298,000 cars by March 15, 1946, compared to General Motors's 30,000. Although GM suffered losses during the final phase of the strike, it did not face the kind of competitive crisis the one-at-a-time strategy predicted. GM's position within the auto industry remained secure.[23]

Although divided on strategy and tactics, leaders of the steel, auto, and electrical unions were united in seeking the Truman administration's support for the CIO's wage demands. CIO leaders hoped and expected that support from the administration would serve as a counterweight to conservative Congressional backing for the corporations. The actual development of the Democratic administration's policy, however, greatly disappointed the CIO. Despite some actions by the administration favorable to organized labor, an open break developed between these two former allies by the end of 1945. The CIO found that, although it could pressure the Truman administration, it could not rely on it for support.[24]

Truman's initial postwar labor policy, as we have seen, permitted voluntary wage increases that did not result in price increases, but the WLB had to
pass on wage increases requiring price relief. The president called for voluntary compliance with WLB orders and renewal of the wartime no-strike,
no-lockout pledges during the transition to a peacetime economy. Economic
Stabilization Director William Davis and OPA Director Chester Bowles
attempted to combine a reconversion no-strike pledge with a 10 percent wage
increase, but Secretary of Labor Lewis Schwellenbach and Truman did not
support the initiative. Truman believed that he had already secured a no-strike
commitment from top labor leaders, although neither the CIO nor the AFL
had made any such promise.[25]

In early September, as the CIO wage drive was just getting underway,
Davis asserted that wages should be increased 40 to 50 percent over the next
five years without an increase in prices. Truman promptly repudiated the
statement and dismissed Davis. The president on September 6 submitted to
Congress a program of domestic reform embodying most of labor's legislative
goals, but he did not advocate wage increases, saying only that he opposed
drastic wage cuts.[26]

The administration was forced to act on the wage issue when in late
September a strike spread through most of the oil industry in support of
demands by the CIO Oil Workers for a 30 percent wage increase. With oil supplies at a critical level, Schwellenbach requested that management and labor
agree to a 15 percent wage increase and a forty-hour week for oil workers pending
negotiations or federal arbitration. When management rejected this proposal,
Truman, acting under his war powers, seized the companies. Although it was
management that had refused the administration compromise, the president
used the power of his office to compel the oil workers to return to work at the
old wage rates. Truman appointed a fact-finding board, which did not make
its non-binding determination until January 12, 1946, on the eve of the steel,
electrical, and packinghouse strikes.[27]

The Truman administration's support for some of the economic demands
of the business community had the effect of strengthening the employers in
their struggle with labor. The administration, as noted, supported the repeal
of the excess profits tax as of January 1, 1946, as well as a continuation of the
refund provision of the 1942 tax law. These measures received Congressional
approval whereas administration proposals that would have strengthened labor's
economic position, such as improved unemployment compensation, did not
pass. The administration did not support the efforts of Montana Senator James
Murray, chairperson of the Senate Committee on Education and Labor, to
amend the tax law so as to deny refunds to corporations that refused to bargain
in good faith. Unions and many pro-labor members of Congress believed, as
Senator Murray stated: "If corporations are to engage in union busting, they

should be required to do so at their own expense." The Truman administration did not adopt this pro-labor position.[28]

CIO President Philip Murray attempted to influence administration wage policy as a member of the Reconversion Advisory Board. As a result of an initiative by Murray, the staff of the Office of War Mobilization and Reconversion (OWMR) prepared a report analyzing the relative economic positions of business and labor in the light of governmental policies which concluded that industry in general could raise wages 24 percent without increasing prices and that the more profitable companies could pay even more than this. Murray considered the OWMR report "perhaps the best break that labor ever got from Government at any time in its history." Although Reconversion Director John Snyder prevented the report from being released as an official document, it was leaked to the press at the end of October and received wide publicity helpful to the CIO's cause.[29]

Some other federal agencies also gave important political support to labor's wage drive. Secretary of Commerce Henry A. Wallace released a report prepared by his department supporting increases in auto industry wages of 15 percent by 1946 and 25 percent by 1947 within the existing price structure. Just before the start of the General Motors strike, the OPA published the list of new auto price ceilings: Chrysler and Ford prices were raised only 1 or 2 percent, and GM prices were lowered. The OPA rebuffed the auto companies' demands for large price hikes, demands that had predated the wage negotiations.[30]

Truman himself finally spoke out in favor of wage increases on October 30, some two and one-half months after his first revision of wartime wage-price policy. The president declared in a nationwide radio address that wage increases were "imperative—to cushion the shock to our workers, to sustain adequate purchasing power, and to raise the national income . . . . industry as a whole can afford substantial wage increases without raising prices." Although wages should rise, Truman said, there would have to be a drop in take-home pay because of the reduced work week. "But the Nation," he declared, "cannot afford to have that drop [be] too drastic."[31]

Although the CIO Executive Board called on industry to comply with the president's mandate, CIO officials were somewhat disappointed that Truman had not advocated a specific wage increase figure. They also thought that the portions of the president's address that pleased them would have had a much greater impact had the speech come two months earlier. Murray told the CIO board that, although Truman had not agreed to use the material prepared by the OWMR staff, the president's address was "not a bad speech . . . . perhaps it was about as far as the President could be expected to go under existing circumstances." Murray reported to the board that he and other CIO representatives had told Truman at a November 1 meeting "that we had no substantial disagreements with him about his attitude on the wage issue." Murray and other CIO leaders were quite dissatisfied, however, with Executive Order 9651, the modification of wage-price policy that accompanied Truman's October 30 address.[32]

Although Executive Order 9599 of August 18, 1945, remained in effect, the new order defined the criteria under which wage increases that might result in price increases could be approved by the government. Increases could be granted when needed to raise straight-time hourly wages to match the increase in the cost of living between January 1941 and September 1945, to correct inequities between plants in the same locality and industry, or to recruit workers for industries crucial to reconversion. Employers could apply for immediate price relief when granting wage increases that met these criteria. If the employer's request for immediate price relief were denied or if a firm granted a wage increase without seeking price compensation, OPA was directed to consider requests for price relief after a six-month test period. Administration officials acknowledged that few wage increases could be granted under the new criteria. Stabilization Administrator John Collett conceded that the increase in straight-time hourly wages had exceeded the 30 percent rise in the cost of living index in the majority of industries.[33]

Business opinion was divided regarding the new wage-price policy. The *Journal of Commerce* expressed satisfaction that the president had not advocated a specific percentage increase in wages. George Romney, head of the Automobile Manufactures Association, declared: "The President has done the country a great service in keeping the wage policy within essential principles of our competitive enterprise." United States Steel was unmoved by the president's address, however, and continued to refuse to bargain unless the OPA promised price increases to match wage increases. General Motors, on the other hand, improved its wage offer to a 10 percent cost-of-living increase, tying its proposal to provisions in Executive Order 9651 for compensating price increases. The UAW rejected this proposal, Reuther characterizing it as "an attempt to bribe General Motors workers with the wooden nickels of inflation. You put a dime in one pocket and take 15¢ out of the other pocket."[34]

The UAW formulated its collective bargaining policy on the basis of Executive Order 9599 and Truman's stated support for substantial wage increases within the existing price structure. GM, for its part, based its position on a different aspect of Truman's wage-price policy, the details outlined in Executive Order 9651. Truman was, of course, well aware that his advocacy of higher wages was contradicted by narrowly constructed administrative regulations. Fearing inflation, Truman chose to follow Chester Bowles's recommendation of a rigid hold-the-line policy, despite the warning of Secretary of Labor Schwellenbach that "unless there be [*sic*] a relaxation of controls there can be no appreciable increase in basic wage rates, and a failure to increase basic wage rates would result in such widespread industrial strife as to stall our economy and threaten its collapse."[35] Neither the auto nor the steel conflict was brought closer to a solution as a result of the administration's slight shift in policy.

As the date for the Labor-Management Conference drew near, the president expressed concern that labor strife might impair the world role of the United States. When Truman opened the conference on November 5, 1945, he failed to mention the need for immediate wage increases. In fact, he told the conference, "if we get the production that we need, the production which our resources and industrial skill make possible, the present problem of wages and prices will be easier to solve." Truman saw the key task of the conference as the development of a mechanism to prevent industrial disputes from interfering with reconversion. If collective bargaining failed, the president declared, the parties should rely on impartial machinery that based itself on proven facts and realities. The CIO, for its part, placed emphasis at the conference on the problem underlying the existing disputes—the need for substantial wage increases. It attempted to get a resolution passed supporting the president's earlier call for "imperative" and "substantial" wage increases, but representatives of management, John L. Lewis, and the AFL all opposed this as contrary to "free enterprise." The labor representatives were united, however, in rejecting the fact-finding approach to solving disputes suggested in Truman's opening speech and formally proposed by management representatives. Although the acceptance of the legitimacy of collective bargaining by management representatives at the 1945 conference was a step beyond the refusal to grant such recognition at a post-World War I labor-management meeting, the conferees were unable to agree on any solution to the threatening labor disputes.[36]

Hoping that it would receive some assistance from the NLRB, the UAW on November 8 formally filed an unfair labor practices complaint against GM. The UAW charged, among other things, that GM had refused to discuss its ability to pay while pleading financial inability to pay and seeking to discourage membership and activity in the union. The NLRB, however, did not immediately act on the UAW complaint.[37]

As the Labor-Management Conference was drawing to a close, Reuther proposed to GM that the dispute be arbitrated, with records of the corporation to be opened to the arbitrator and the ability of the corporation to pay the 30 percent increase without a price increase as the sole issue to be resolved. General Motors rejected this proposal, and so the GM workers struck on November 21. The main concern of the White House, which was reportedly neutral regarding the merits of the dispute, was the resumption of negotiations. Inside the cabinet, Secretary Schwellenbach declared that he had changed his mind and was now convinced that the administration had to step into the labor situation in a decisive way. He complained that both GM and the union were being recalcitrant.[38]

Despite the sharp conflicts between GM and the UAW at the bargaining table and in the media that preceded the strike, the UAW began its walkout with little strike machinery in readiness. In the first days of the strike, no mass picketing occurred at most plants. At the Fisher Body plant in Cleveland, almost everyone was on layoff until the Monday before the strike when management called in a few thousand workers. "There was nothing for them to do," Leo Fenster recalled, "but by calling them in . . . . [the company] took them off unemployment compensation . . . . It was the most ridiculous time to call a strike." Similarly, the official history of the Guide Lamp local in Anderson notes that the strike was "unexpected by most of the membership"; it seemed an "unpropitious time for a strike." Both locals, nevertheless, strongly supported the strike. Although many workers "felt it wasn't the right time to strike," Fenster recalled, "emotionally, they really wanted to strike . . . . The participation of the membership was fantastic." Local 45 members picketed in large numbers and collected food and money for strike relief at plant gates throughout northeast Ohio. So much food was collected that the local had to rent a warehouse.[39] By the beginning of the second week the pro-labor *Federated Press* reported "strong, spirited turnouts" on the Detroit area picket lines. The UAW permitted union members to work who were needed to maintain the powerhouses and other equipment required to prevent damage to machinery in the company's plants. In a concession to rank-and-file militancy, the Strike Strategy Committee, composed of the union's four officers and the directors of the Ford and Chrysler Departments, gave local unions the option of barring office and supervisory workers from company plants. Most locals prevented the white collar force from entering the plants, but the Strategy Committee thought this a mistake and did not prevent office workers at GM's main headquarters from going to work.[40]

General Motors continued its hard-line stance, declaring that it would not negotiate unless "illegal" picketing were ended, the union receded from its "unreasonable" wage demand, and the union abandoned its "attempt to negotiate wages on the basis of our past profits, assumed future profits, and our selling prices . . . . " The UAW replied to GM's ultimatum by filing with the NLRB a supplementary unfair labor practice charge against the company. As for the union's picketing tactics, UAW officials sought a commitment from the corporation that employees entering the plants would not be required to do the work of striking union members. GM refused to agree and, instead, sought injunctions in a number of cities against the UAW's militant picketing. In Detroit, GM failed to obtain injunctions as Police Commissioner John F. Ballenger indicated that his department was "enforcing the peaceful picketing law—with judgement." A senior Detroit police inspector commented that "the worst thing I've noticed was one picket using vulgar language." In some locations, injunctions were issued limiting pickets to five at each gate, and in other places police broke through the picket lines to escort white collar employees into work. The Strike Strategy Committee now urged, but did not order, that locals permit the entry of office and supervisory employees because they "cannot build automobiles" and "the effort required to bar them now will merely dissipate energy which may be sorely needed later on." Picket line incidents tapered off as 1945 drew to a close.[41]

During these early, difficult weeks of the strike, GM workers received considerable support from other trade unionists. Shortly after the strike began, 3,000 Ford River Rouge workers marched to GM's Cadillac plant to join the picket line. In December the Steelworkers donated $100,000 to the GM strikers even though the steel union was planning its own strike. The CIO established a broadly representative strike support committee whose first task was to aid the GM strikers. Some 6,000 unionists in New York marched around the General Motors Building in a demonstration organized by the CIO. Various CIO unions contributed money, food, clothing, and Christmas toys to the strikers and their families. Philip Murray and other CIO leaders assisted the striking GM workers despite their serious reservations regarding UAW strategy. CIO unions were the main base of support for the GM workers in the first phase of the strike, but support from AFL and independent unions and from the general public also began to develop, particularly in locations with large numbers of GM workers. After reading the transcript of the UAW-GM negotiations at the union's invitation in early December, a 15-member committee of nationally prominent individuals concluded that the UAW approach was "statesmanlike."[42]

In implementing its one-at-a-time strategy, the UAW encountered serious difficulties. On November 30, while the company was still refusing to meet with the UAW to negotiate its demands, GM President Wilson offered to reopen parts plants to produce for GM's competitors. *Business Week* interpreted the GM offer as a public relations move and an attempt to get "one bloc of workers or another . . . riled by the union leaders' decision." GM's tactic succeeded: the union released a letter in Thomas's name welcoming the company's "generous" offer but predicting that only one or two operations would be involved. The *Detroit Free Press* headlined the UAW reply and reported that dozens of plants would be reopened. A storm of opposition immediately erupted within the union; many local union strike committees sent telegrams of protest to Thomas. The UAW president, who had been in Washington when the letter to GM was released in his name, "exploded" upon seeing the headlines when he returned to Detroit.[43]

At first, Thomas criticized erroneous interpretations placed upon his letter, contending that the international officers were only seeking to determine which GM-produced parts were needed to keep competitor firms working. The decision to return, he said, would be left to the strikers. To shift attention from the internal union controversy, Thomas wired the United States Attorney General demanding an investigation of GM's monopoly position in the industry on the grounds that Wilson's offer to reopen some plants implied that they were needed for the operation of other companies in the industry. Thomas later disavowed the letter sent to GM over his signature. Although the daily press reported the fact that the UAW reply had been sent out by a Thomas assistant after Reuther had reviewed it, Reuther asserted he had disagreed with the letter. The incident generated sharp conflict among top UAW leaders. Thomas, appearing to be an ineffectual leader, was no doubt weakened by the dispute.[44] In the end, the letter did not lead to the reopening of any auto plants.

On December 3, 1945, Truman presented to the Congress his bombshell fact-finding proposal even though the concept had earlier been rejected by the unions. His proposal called for the creation of fact-finding boards to deal with strikes of national importance. While a board was meeting there was to be a 30-day cooling off period that could be extended. The fact-finding board would have the power of subpoena, but its findings would not be binding. While Congress deliberated on the bill, Truman announced that he would appoint fact-finding boards for the General Motors and steel disputes that would not, however, possess subpoena power. He called on the steel workers to delay strike action and on the GM workers to return to work.[45]

Truman's message was opposed by all sections of the labor movement. The CIO's criticism was the most harsh, with Murray delivering a national radio address in which he denounced Truman's proposal and pledged a nationwide mobilization to defeat it and all other antilabor measures. While welcoming the focusing of public attention on the facts involved in labor disputes, Murray indicted Truman for ignoring industry's failure to bargain. The CIO president accused Truman of pursuing a "policy of continuous appeasement of American industry." The president's proposal, Murray declared, was laying the groundwork for legislation "to ultimately destroy labor union organizations . . . . It can be but the first step for ever more savage legislative repression . . . . "[46]

UAW leaders joined in the attack on Truman. Thomas charged that GM's Wilson had met privately with Truman while UAW leaders had had no such opportunity to meet with the president. Wilson, Thomas also charged, had recommended to Truman the abridgement of the right to strike. "Where does the right to strike go?" the UAW president asked. Why was a board not appointed 100 days earlier? Thomas pointed out that GM workers had waited 97-days before striking. Vice President Reuther said that Truman had "bum advisers" and had made a "clean break with the labor policies" of Franklin Roosevelt. Both Reuther and Secretary-Treasurer George Addes declared that if they were GM workers, they would vote no on Truman's request to return to work. Addes sent telegrams to all UAW locals calling on them to fight the Truman program.[47]

Management's reaction to Truman's fact-finding proposal was positive but not enthusiastic. Ira Mosher, president of the National Association of Manufacturers (NAM), remarked that Truman's program was a step in the right direction and pointed out that the NAM had recommended fact finding during the 1937 GM sit-down strike. Although employers welcomed Truman's proposed restriction on the right to strike, management representatives cautiously voiced some specific disagreements with Truman's approach. Management did not wish to permit fact-finding boards to make recommendations and opposed the idea of giving a fact-finding board subpoena power over company records. According to Truman's proposal, company records would be used by the fact-finding boards in making a determination of facts but were to be kept confidential. GM contested this aspect of the president's plan not only because it was fighting the ability-to-pay concept but also because it opposed increased government interference in management's business. GM and the NAM thought that the regulation of labor, not of management, was required to establish what they characterized as "equality under the law" between employers and unions.[48]

Truman delayed the appointment of the auto and steel fact-finding boards, hoping that the impact of his message to Congress would force the disputants to compromise their differences. On December 5, the Office of Economic Stabilization issued new regulations putting Truman's Executive Order 9651 into effect. These regulations strengthened GM's negotiating stance, which was based on adherence to the specifics of the executive order and the linking of wage increases to price increases. The regulations provided that companies could base applications for price increases on wage raises granted to meet a 33 percent increase in the cost of living since January 1941. The 33 percent figure derived from the increase in the CPI plus a 3 percent upward correction recommended by a special presidential committee. Reacting to the new regulations, General Motors on December 6 slightly improved its wage offer from the pre-strike proposal of 10 percent (the equivalent of about 11¢) to 13.5¢—12¢ for a cost of living increase and 1.5¢ to cover inequities.[49]

The presidential request to return to work and the new wage-price regulations did not persuade the UAW to accept GM's terms and abandon its strike. On December 8, a conference of GM workers unanimously rejected both the company offer and Truman's back-to-work appeal. The union chose to fight rather than to cave in to the pressure being exerted by the administration.[50]

Although the union continued the strike at GM, UAW leaders reacted to the president's message by initiating a significant policy change in the Ford negotiations. They concluded that Ford, despite its recent attack on the union, could be detached from the industry's united front. In pursuit of this goal, the UAW's Ford Department director, Richard Leonard, presented a proposal to the company on December 10. In response to a company demand that the union be fined $5 per day for each worker involved in an unauthorized strike, the union proposed that the actual participants in stoppages be fined. The penalty would be $3 per day for the first such stoppage and $5 per day for the second. Leaders of unauthorized walkouts would be subject to discharge under the union plan. Similar penalties were to be invoked against management personnel guilty of provoking a stoppage.[51]

Leonard's proposal represented a major departure in union policy. When Ford had earlier issued its demand for increased company security, Leonard had responded: "There is a very simple way to avoid work stoppages. That is to stop provoking them. Every work stoppage in Ford plants has been provoked by the unfair practices of management." This new approach, a reaction to growing antilabor sentiment, was approved by Thomas, Addes, and Reuther and reportedly had Murray's support. Union leaders hoped by this proposal to achieve a breakthrough in the Ford negotiations and, at the same time, to frustrate the developing legislative attack on unionism.[52]

Although the UAW's company security proposal was well received in press and governmental circles, it was sharply criticized by many union rank and filers and secondary leaders, who continued to emphasize management's role in causing unauthorized stoppages. Management, they insisted, failed to resolve grievances promptly and thus provoked the workers. Critics of the Leonard proposal thought that "the problem of dealing with persons who violate union policy is not one for the company or an umpire to settle. It is an internal union problem." Corporate and legislative attacks on unionism, they contended, would be fueled, not slowed, by company security proposals. The Detroit and Flint GM strike committees denounced the union's offer as "a stab in the back" and "a treacherous blow" to the GM strike.[53]

On the same day that Leonard offered his "union responsibility" proposal, GM cancelled its contract with the UAW and declared that a guarantee of union responsibility for uninterrupted production must be a feature of any new agreement. Despite the Leonard proposal, the union was unable to conclude an agreement with Ford. Although Ford officials called the union's company security proposal a hopeful step, the company preferred its own proposed contract terms. The company offered the union a conditional 15¢ (12.4 percent) wage increase to go into effect only when production reached 80,000 vehicles per month and to remain in effect for two years thereafter. The company terms also included the elimination of unauthorized stoppages, the maintenance of management prerogatives, and reduction in the number of union committeemembers. In rejecting the Ford offer, the union asserted that the wage increase was insufficient and a two-year wage freeze unacceptable. The union did not reject company terms regarding management prerogatives, unauthorized strikes, or reduction in the number of committeemembers. The continued willingness of top UAW leaders to make major concessions to management demands remained a source of division in the union.[54]

Lack of unity was a problem not only within the UAW but between the UAW and other CIO unions. Although the UAW's sister CIO unions were the strongest supporters of the GM strikers both financially and politically, neither the Electrical Workers nor the Steel Workers allowed their bargaining strategy to be determined by the UAW's one-at-a-time approach. Probably because of Reuther's hostility to the Communist-led UE, its proposal for joint UAW-UE negotiations with GM was not accepted by the UAW; and the UE did not join the UAW strike by halting work at GM's electrical plants. The UE continued to plan for simultaneous negotiations with all the electrical companies and to coordinate its efforts with those of the steel union.[55] On December 11, the Steelworkers set a strike date of January 14, 1946. UAW president Thomas said that he had had no advance indication of the steel union's strategy, and one UAW leader was reported to ask: "What in the world is their strategy?" The *New York Times* stated that high UAW sources saw the steel union's plan as a blow to the UAW. The auto union leaders continued to adhere to the one-at-a-time concept and feared that a steel strike, which would cut the flow of steel to auto plants, would remove competitive pressure from GM.[56]

Because the negotiations that followed in the wake of his fact-finding message to Congress had failed to end the GM strike, Truman announced the appointment of the GM fact-finding board on December 14. The members of the board were Lloyd Garrison, chairperson of the WLB; Judge Walter Stacey of the North Carolina Supreme Court; and Milton Eisenhower, president of Kansas State College. At the end of the month, Truman also appointed a steel fact-finding board. No serious negotiations had yet taken place between the Steel Workers and the steel companies.[57]

GM representative Walter Gordon Merritt declared at the fact-finding board's first session on December 20 that GM would not submit the issue of prices and profits to the board because Congress had delegated responsibility for these questions to the OPA. Merritt reiterated the corporation's conception of national wage policy, with standards determined by such tests as inequities, substandard rates, and maladjustments, and argued that the UAW was attempting to secure a repudiation of that policy. As the first day of the hearing was about to end, the White House released a statement quoting the president as saying that ability to pay was one of the relevant factors in determining wage increases and that fact-finding boards should have authority to examine the employers' books, without those records being made public.[58]

In a policy declaration on December 21, the GM fact-finding board, consistent with the president's statement of the preceding day, stated that ability to pay was a relevant factor in the dispute but was not the only or the controlling factor. The board announced that, in examining the issues, it would be governed by the wage-price policies announced by the president in executive orders and addresses and by the stabilization administrator in administering the Price

Control Act of October 2, 1942. If it recommended wage increases above the amount that could be approved for price purposes under Executive Order 9651, the board declared that it would state whether the increase could be absorbed by GM, but it would not assume OPA's function. Although the board postponed consideration of the issue of examining the corporation's books, it said it would nevertheless "require" certain information from the parties. Finally, the board called on GM and the UAW to renew collective bargaining and to take into account the latest policy statements by the president and the board itself.[59]

Some business representatives, including Mosher of the NAM, sharply attacked Truman for his advocacy of ability to pay in the midst of the dispute over this issue between GM and the UAW. Opposition to Truman's approach, however, was not unanimous in business circles. *Business Week* pointed out that not all companies shared GM's brilliant prospects—Western Union, for example, had recently pleaded inability to pay even a modest wage increase—and therefore believed that a company's financial situation was a relevant factor in negotiations. The business magazine noted, however, that business people were united in opposing exposure of company records to fact-finding boards.[60]

The GM fact-finding board resumed its hearings on December 28 after collective bargaining had once again failed to resolve the auto dispute. GM, however, now announced that it was withdrawing from the proceedings. The company repeated its view that what it was facing in the strike was "a broad attack on American industry and free enterprise." The UAW-GM dispute, the corporation maintained, was a matter of "ideology and national policy which really belongs to Congress." GM stated that it would provide the board with information on wage rates, take-home pay, and the cost of living only if assured that the scope of the board's investigation would be limited to these questions. Criticizing GM's decision to withhold information, the fact-finding board pointed out that ability to pay had been a factor in previous arbitration and WLB cases, including a GM case. Although GM opposed federal intervention with the old conservative, individualist rhetoric, GM's fight was not against federal intervention as such but rather against intervention that might aid labor.[61]

GM's strategy for dealing with administration policy was to rely on the conservative coalition in Congress, which is why the corporation kept referring to the authority of Congress.[62] As 1945 drew to a close, the CIO and the Truman administration were not as far apart as they had been following the president's fact-finding address. Although the administration continued to seek and the CIO continued to oppose the president's proposed fact-finding legislation, Truman's backing of the UAW position before the GM fact-finding board provided the union with some needed assistance. Action aiding the UAW helped the CIO, too, despite the organization's unhappiness with UAW strategy. The CIO prepared to launch its *economic* offensive as 1946 dawned, with strikes planned for the steel, electrical, and packinghouse industries on January 14, 15, and 16, respectively.

Chapter Five

The General Motors Strike:
The Long Stoppage is Won

On January 3, 1946, a new Detroit-based, auto industry-connected organization, the Society of Sentinels, announced its program for America through one-half-page newspaper advertisements. The Sentinels called for repeal of the Wagner, Social Security, and the Wage and Hour Acts. "We . . . have gotten off the main highway of economic freedom and constitutional government," the Sentinels claimed. The vice chair of the Society of Sentinels was Stephen DuBrul, General Motors's chief economist and a member of the company's negotiating team. The UAW's Thomas denounced the Sentinels as a fascist group. Pointing to the militaristic-sounding name, Thomas said: "I suppose they didn't quite have the nerve to go the whole way and call themselves the Army of Vigilantes." While the Sentinels sought to recruit members, DuBrul remained active in the negotiations between GM and the UAW. [1]

GM invited representatives of the steel, electrical, and packinghouse companies, all of them facing strikes, to a secret conference at the Waldorf Astoria in New York City on January 9. When later questioned at an NLRB hearing about the aims of this meeting, GM President Wilson claimed that no agreement had been reached by the participants. However, " . . . it's too bad," Wilson arrogantly declared, that "that group of men can't make some decisions for the country right now."[2]

The Truman administration now became more actively involved in labor affairs as it attempted to head off the threatened strikes, particularly in the critical steel industry. Although the president mildly criticized GM in early January for failing to cooperate with his fact-finding board, administration officials were simultaneously encouraging United States Steel to negotiate with the steel union by promising the company a $4 per ton price increase, $1.50 more than OPA thought justified. On January 10, United States Steel offered the union a 15¢ increase, and the union at the same time reduced its demand from 25¢ to 20¢. That same day President Truman made public and gave his endorsement to the recommendations of the GM fact-finding board. The board recommended a 19.5¢ wage increase (17.4 percent); reinstatement of the old contract while work resumed and noneconomic issues were negotiated; and production without interruption aiming at new levels of production and efficiency. In addition to these formal recommendations, the board stated that it did not believe the proposed wage increase necessitated a price increase. In endorsing the fact-finding report, Truman made no comment on the price question. Following release of the GM report, the Steelworkers reduced their wage demand to 19.5¢, but steel company negotiators refused to move beyond 15¢. When the steel talks deadlocked on January 11, Truman asked that bargaining be resumed at the White House. Both sides agreed to the president's request.[3]

The UAW's immediate reaction to the GM fact-finding report was largely favorable. Although critical of the board's failure to support the union's 30 percent wage demand, Reuther focused on the price question. The board report, he announced, was "a complete endorsement of the union's position and represents a historic step in the fight to establish a full production, full employment, full consumption economy." By standing firm, the UAW vice president maintained, GM workers had "won a smashing victory for themselves and the American consumers on the price front." Reuther's victory claim proved premature, for on January 11 General Motors rejected the fact-finding board's recommendations. Ignoring the board's comments on the price question, the company called the 19.5¢ wage proposal unjustified. In addition, GM declared its firm opposition to reinstatement of the old contract on the grounds that many of its clauses had been ordered by the WLB and were unacceptable to the company under peacetime conditions.[4]

General Motors' rejection of the fact-finding report and the impasse in the steel negotiations greatly troubled Murray. In a message to the CIO Shipbuilders' convention on January 11, he declared that the unions faced a "showdown" and that the next 48 hours would be the most crucial in the history of the labor movement.[5]

Negotiators for the Steelworkers and the United States Steel Corporation conferred with administration officials and President Truman at the White House on January 12. United States Steel President Benjamin Fairless indicated that he would seek steel industry support for the union's proposal of a 19.5¢ wage increase. At Truman's request, Steelworkers President Murray, in turn, agreed to a one-week postponement of the steel strike. The negotiators agreed to return to the White House on January 16, and Truman indicated publicly that he expected a settlement at that time. Murray had earlier refused to delay the strike, but he now went along with Truman because the president had involved himself in the negotiations and because Murray was hoping that the chief executive would support the union's wage demand. Although agreeing to postpone the strike, Murray complained to Henry Wallace about the pro-steel industry outlook of top Truman advisors and the "raw deal" the union was getting from the administration.[6]

The UAW's General Motors conference formally accepted the fact-finding board's report on January 13, with the proviso that local union issues had to be satisfactorily resolved as part of any overall settlement. In a message to President Truman, the union stated that the GM fact-finding report represented both a victory over inflation and a victory for the administration's policies. The union declared, however, that it was up to the president to get GM to accept the recommendations of his fact-finding panel. If the corporation did not accept the board's recommendations within one week, the union stated, it would insist upon its original demands. The GM workers' conference asked the union's Strike Strategy Committee to increase economic pressure on GM by stopping work on the company's orders at tool and die shops.[7]

On the day of the UAW's GM conference, the NLRB, acting on complaints filed by the UAW in November 1945, finally issued a complaint against GM for failing to bargain in good faith. The board set January 28 as the date for a hearing on the charges. Issued shortly after the fact-finding board's report and GM's rejection of the board's recommendations, the NLRB complaint was anticlimactic and had little impact.[8] NLRB chairperson Paul Herzog later admitted to a Senate committee that prompt action by the agency might have swung public opinion to the union "and perhaps aided in reaching a settlement."[9] Herzog stated, however, that the government should not handle cases like a "three ring circus"; the involvement of the NLRB when other federal agencies were handling the dispute, he declared, "would have confused the public."[10]

The NLRB's Detroit office had recommended the issuance of a complaint against General Motors as early as November 23, but Herzog, after consulting with administration officials, had decided to delay action. The NLRB chairperson, in fact, timed the issuance of the refusal-to-bargain complaint to meet the wishes of the president. Herzog took "full responsibility" for the decision to give precedence to Truman administration policy rather than the enforcement of the Wagner Act.[11]

Despite his support for the fact-finding concept, Truman turned aside the UAW appeal that he pressure GM into accepting the fact-finding board's recommendations. Commenting on GM's action, the president on January 15 simply stated that the corporation had not seemed to take much interest in the report, but he hoped it would do so at a later date.[12]

The focus of the Truman administration was on steel, but it did not ignore the other industries that also faced strikes. With seizure of the telephone industry imminent, the administration on January 13 persuaded the independent Telephone Federation to postpone the spreading general strike in that industry. Two days later, however, the CIO began its offensive with a strike of 200,000 electrical workers against General Electric, Westinghouse, and General Motors. The electrical firms refused the UE's offer to remain at work in return for company agreement to go along with the outcome of the White House steel negotiations. On January 16, some 190,000 members of the CIO Packinghouse Workers and 70,000 members of the AFL Butcher Workmen shut down most of the meat packing industry. A last-minute appeal by Secretary of Labor Schwellenbach, speaking on behalf of President Truman, for a delay in the meat strike received a positive response from the AFL union's leaders but was rejected by the CIO union's leaders.[13]

When the steel negotiators reconvened at the White House on January 16, Fairless once again refused to improve on the company's offer of a 15¢ increase. The American Iron and Steel Institute, the industry association, had not only rejected the administration-supported settlement of 19.5¢, but also was holding out for a price increase even larger than the promised $4 per ton. Equally important, the industry saw an opportunity to weaken the union. Truman put his presidential prestige on the line on Janaury 17 by privately proposing a compromise agreement of 18.5¢. The steel union leaders accepted Truman's proposal, an action that no doubt had the short-run effect of weakening the UAW's fight with General Motors.[14]

The GM fact-finding board's recommendation of 19.5¢ was now eclipsed by Truman's 18.5¢ compromise, and Murray supplanted Reuther as the leader of the CIO wage drive. The CIO president, actually, had no choice but to accept Truman's proposal if he were to defend the interests of the CIO as a whole. Truman undoubtedly would have declared "a plague on both your houses" had Murray spurned the president's offer, weakening the CIO's position with the general public and making successful prosecution of the CIO strikes more difficult.

The steel industrialists, for their part, chose to defy the president and reject his compromise. The broad political aims motivating the steel industry's action were revealed in a speech by Republic Steel head Charles M. White to 1,000 business leaders brought together by the National Industrial Conference Board on January 17. White called for replacing the Wagner Act with legislation that would penalize "unions and strikers for felonies or mass picketing" and subject labor to antitrust and extortion laws. On the immediate issue confronting the country, White declared: "If Government can't hold the situation in line, industry has got to do it. Industry is rallying to do the job which the elected representatives of the people seemingly don't have the courage to do."[15] Organized labor had to be stopped, and the manufacturers were proposing to do the job!

Truman went public with his compromise offer of 18.5¢ (or 17.1 percent) on January 18 while reiterating his support for the GM fact-finding board's recommendation of 19.5¢ (or 17.4 percent). Both proposals were fair, the president said. "I still hope," he stated, "and on behalf of the great mass of American citizens, strongly urge, that my suggestion of settlement be adopted by the

United States Steel Corporation." Truman was to repeat this exhortation after the steel strike began, but he shrank from the decisive action of seizing the vital industry and putting into effect his recommendation for a wage increase.[16]

In Murray's view, the actions of General Motors and the steel industry made clear who was responsible for the existing industrial strife and the resulting delay in reconversion. Both the Steelworkers and the Auto Workers had cited the "national interest" in agreeing to compromise proposals, but the steel industry, Philip Murray charged, "damns the President of the United States and the American Government." American big business, he asserted, was involved in an

> evil conspiracy . . . to exact unconditional surrender of the American people and the United States Government . . . . American industry, fattened with war profits, guaranteed a high level of profits through special tax rebates under laws written at their behest, have [*sic*] deliberately set out to provoke strikes and economic chaos, and hijack the American people through uncontrolled profits and inflation . . . .

Murray called for full support for President Truman "in the struggle which lies ahead to maintain true collective bargaining and protect our free democratic institutions" from industry attack.[17]

Although Murray called for the public to back Truman's position in the steel conflict, CIO unions did not give the president unconditional support. Thus, when the Truman administration seized the meat industry on January 26, the CIO Packinghouse Workers refused to return to work until they had extracted a commitment from the Secretary of Agriculture that the fact-finding board's recommendations would be put into effect.[18]

The CIO offensive achieved its first victories at three major companies seeking to escape the shutdown of their plants. On January 26, Ford and Chrysler reached wage agreements with the UAW. The new Chrysler-UAW contract provided for an 18.5¢ wage increase (or 16.7 percent). The UAW and Ford agreed to an 18¢ increase (or 15.1 percent), although final contract terms and the effective date of the wage increase still remained to be decided. Ford, at the same time, stated that it would not request an upward adjustment in prices. On January 27, the Radio Corporation of America (RCA), the one major electrical company not struck by the UE, agreed to give its workers an 18¢ raise.[19] The Ford, Chrysler, and RCA agreements were based on the standard established by Murray's acceptance of Truman's 18.5¢ proposal for steel. Although these settlements made it more difficult for the UAW to win the 19.5¢ it was seeking from General Motors, the net effect of the agreements was to aid the GM workers because its two principal competitors had agreed to raise wages by 4.5¢ and 5¢ more than the leading auto firm had proposed. The fact, furthermore, that three major industrial corporations essentially agreed to meet Truman's compromise proposal for steel strengthened the efforts of the Steelworkers and the CIO in general to establish 18.5¢ as the pattern wage increase.

The Ford and Chrysler agreements were important victories in the UAW's wage battle, but they also represented backward steps on the issue of company security. The Ford-UAW announcement was accompanied by the statement: "Details connected with fair, efficient and uninterrupted production will become effective not later than February." The UAW and Chrysler jointly stated that "the union recognizes the importance of company security against unauthorized strikes and the need for productivity on the part of the employees." The terms of the new Chrysler contract required the union to cease processing grievances of workers guilty of leading an unauthorized strike. In addition, the umpire in such cases could only decide the guilt or innocence of the accused; he could no longer modify the penalty in the light of extenuating circumstances. A further concession by the union came in the form of a company-union letter stating that high productivity was in the interest of both parties and that both sides desired to restore prewar productivity. This letter was not part of the contract submitted to the rank and file for ratification, and, following the settlement, union members began to complain that supervisors were increasing production rates and were claiming that the union had agreed to the speed-up.[20]

The Ford contract, finally signed by company and union officials on February 26, went much further than the Chrysler contract in embodying company demands for "security." Although the company withdrew its demand to penalize the union financially for unauthorized strikes, the contract stated that this issue could be renegotiated if unauthorized strikes were not reduced to a "negligible minimum." According to the terms of the "union responsibility" clause, workers guilty of instigating, fomenting, leading, or even "actively supporting" an illegal strike were subject to discharge. As in the Chrysler contract, the union could not file a grievance if its investigation substantiated the company claim. Likewise, the umpire could modify the penalty imposed by the company if he or she found the worker guilty of involvement in an unauthorized stoppage only if he or she determined that the accused worker's activity had been limited to "participating" in the walkout instead of "actively supporting" or leading it. The worker could be suspended for two weeks for a first offense and discharged for a second offense.[21]

The new Ford contract also contained a tough management prerogatives clause providing that a worker failing to meet production standards was subject to discipline or discharge. Workers who participated in efforts to limit production faced a similar fate. Related to these provisions strengthening the company's power in the plant was a change in the nature of union representation. Under the old Ford contract, union committeemembers were permitted to leave their jobs to handle grievances, but under the new contract a smaller number of committeemembers were to work as full-time union representatives. This change pointed in the direction of a separation of plant union officials from the rank and file and the building of a union bureaucracy. This was certainly a retreat from the goal of progressive unionists in the 1930s, namely, a steward for every supervisor. There were sharp debates among Ford workers regarding the company security provisions in the new contract that led the union's Ford Council to instruct the bargainers to renegotiate the clauses on promotions and productivity. The contract was finally ratified late in May, however, without any change having been made in its provisions.[22]

Despite the agreements between the UAW and Ford and Chrysler, the auto union was unable to make progress in the GM negotiations. As hardships resulting from the long strike multiplied for GM workers, trade union and community support for the strike increased. Not only did CIO unions accelerate the collection of money, food, and clothing, but Eleanor Roosevelt, Henry Morgenthau, Jr., and other prominent individuals formed a Citizens' Committee to Aid the Families of General Motors Strikers. Some AFL unions also began to raise funds to help the GM workers. At the end of January, 41 members of Congress called on GM and United States Steel to accept President Truman's proposed strike settlements.[23]

Although the union declared that economic force was the only language GM understood, its efforts to increase the pressure on the company were limited. The union leadership authorized UAW tool and die shop workers in the Detroit area to stop work on dies for GM's 1947 model but refused to accede to the demand of several local and citywide strike committees for a shutdown of GM's powerhouses. The International Executive Board's position was that this action would delay GM employees' return to work because repairs would have to be made on damaged machinery. More important than the failure of the union to shut down the powerhouses was the general decline in rank-and-file participation in the strike following the confrontations on the issue of barring the white collar force. Union members did turn out at the plant gates in large numbers in response to newspaper reports of individuals attempting to start blue collar back-to-work movements at a few plants, but the union generally maintained only token picket lines. The General Motors strike was thus the first of a new type of strike—the stay-at-home strike. Because the corporation was not attempting to operate the factories with scabs, advocates of the stay-at-home strike argued that it was not necessary to picket the plant gates with more than a few workers.[24]

In the steel strike, which began on January 21, a tendency to follow a stay-at-home approach was also seen. On a tour of the strike fronts for the *Daily Worker*, the old Industrial Workers of the World (IWW) and then-Communist leader Elizabeth Gurley Flynn discovered a new type of strike activity that she characterized as "chicken coop picketing." At one steel plant, Gurley Flynn found picketers housed in shacks made out of chicken coops purchased at Sears and containing glass windows and a small stove. Flynn commented:

> It's cozy and warm this chicken coop picketing. The companies were very charming about it. Wood, coal, lumber, even hot coffee, were offered and accepted in various places. But has the capitalist leopard changed his spots so completely from Lawrence in 1912, Steel in 1919, Ludlow in 1914?
>
> . . . some of a new younger generation are wondering: "Is this what dad called a strike? There's nothing to it!" So they are lulled into a false security.
>
> It isn't their fault. Orders from above were: no mass picketing, no mass meetings, and in some instances, to hold off appeals for relief . . . .
>
> Strikes were certainly very different in former days. Mass picketing in various languages, bulletins, daily strike committee meetings, women's meetings, yes, even children's meetings were all features of a good strike.[25]

Although the 1946 strikes represented a transition from the old-fashioned strike to the new-fashioned, stay-at-home, wait-it-out strike, there were mass picket lines, demonstrations, and a mobilization of broad, communitywide support for the strikers in some localities. Jack White, a left-wing worker at GM's Ternstedt plant in Detroit, returned home from the U. S. Navy two days before Christmas to find "a few people sitting around" at the union office. Ignoring the advice to "take a rest" because "nobody was going through the gate," White "rounded up all the troops" and organized a welfare commit-tee. "In a short time," he recalled, "we had almost a thousand pickets and were paying them $5 a week plus feeding them . . . ." The Ternstedt welfare com-mittee solicited donations from churches, and when left-wing personalities like Zero Mostel came to town they appeared at cocktail parties and other events to raise money for the strikers. Picket lines were kept up around the clock and Ternstedt began "infecting" other GM plants in Detroit with its approach. In Anderson, Indiana, a Republican mayor appointed two GM strikers to the City Council. In several cities there were community general strikes to back up hard-pressed unions.[26]

The shift toward the stay-at-home strike was a sign that CIO leaders, although ready to take decisive national strike action, still hoped that the peaceful labor relations of the war period would return. Although important differences were evident among them on other issues, Murray, Thomas, Addes, and Reuther all agreed to keep the conflict within carefully circumscribed limits. "We could actually tell our people to go fishing and the strike would be just as effective," Thomas told a Senate committee. When Henry Ford II spoke out for "human engineering" on January 9, 1946, George Addes praised him as a "great industrial statesman," and UAW spokespeople said that Ford had stolen a page from Reuther's book. Among other things, the new head of the Ford Motor Company called for strengthening the position of labor leaders so that they could "help in solving the human equation in mass-production . . . and accept the social obligations that go with leadership."[27]

Although the left-led UE united with Murray's Steelworkers in making demands on the corporations and began its own strike just six days before the steel union's, the UE's *conduct* of the strike contrasted sharply with the Murray approach. Not only did the UE engage in mass picketing at struck plants, but it prevented research and most clerical and supervisory employees from entering General Electric facilities. Only those who were given passes by the UE were permitted inside. GE agreed that it would not try to operate the plants during the shutdown.[28]

Despite the limitations imposed by the strike leadership, the 1945–1946 strike wave was a tremendous historic upheaval. On February 15, 1946, the CIO won a victory in the decisive steel industry when the companies agreed to the 18.5¢ wage increase that they had previously rejected. The steel union had met the test sought by industry and won the battle on the key issue of wages. The steel victory established the pattern that other unions would try to match.[29]

Although the steel union had won the battle on the central issue of wages, the steel industry gained a $5 per ton price increase from the Truman administration. This was $1 more than the president had been ready to grant before the strike and $2.50 more than OPA chief Bowles thought justified. The new wage-price policy announced by Truman on February 14 permitted wage increases in specific industries and geographical areas if required to conform to the general postwar wage pattern. Companies could now use wage increases to secure immediate price adjustments from the OPA. This brought to an end the policy of allowing wage increases to be reflected in prices only after a careful examination of costs and prewar profits or after a six-month test period. Although Truman declared that the steel price increase was only a "bulge" in the price line, it was really the beginning of the end of price control. "From this point on," according to the official history of the OPA, "a really firm price policy was in fact no longer possible, either administratively or politically."[30]

The Truman administration and the corporations were directly responsible for the undermining of price control, but the AFL's leadership charged that Murray and the CIO leadership had also contributed by pushing their wage demands too aggressively. Reuther supporters, on the other hand, intimated that Murray and other CIO leaders were partly responsible for inflation because they had failed to fight hard enough for price control.[31] The CIO wage drive was, in fact, neither a direct nor an indirect cause of the subversion of the hold-the-line price policy. The balance of forces was such that business was bound to succeed in defeating price control.

Murray was undoubtedly right in putting the emphasis on the wage question. If Murray had adopted the Reuther approach and given the main weight to the price issue, he would have turned the conflict into a political one: the primary issue would have been a CIO demand for the Truman administration to establish and adhere to a progressive wage-price policy. A concentration of CIO resources on challenging the administration would have weakened the pressure on industry. Furthermore, it seems unlikely that Truman would have supported the 18.5¢ increase if Murray had insisted that the wage rise not be accompanied by any change in administration price policy. Under these circumstances, the CIO campaign for substantial wage increases would have been jeopardized. Far from ignoring the price issue, Murray continued to oppose the "hijacking of prices to the point where the public suffers." Murray told a Senate committee that a $4 per ton increase in steel prices would provide an $84 million profit for the steel companies over and above any possible increase in labor costs. Murray, however, did not make his disagreement with the administration on the price question an obstacle to agreement on the wage issue. Following the strikes, the CIO organized a major political campaign to keep price controls in effect.[32]

The Truman administration's abandonment of its hold-the-line price policy undermined Reuther's advocacy of "a wage increase without a price increase." Although the UAW now emphasized GM's arrogant rejection of the fact-finding board's wage recommendation, the UAW vice president nonetheless declared that the main issue in the labor disputes was prices and not wages. Reuther wired Truman on February 2 to declare that the General Motors fight is "your fight" and "demands your immediate and militant support," but Truman continued to focus his attention on the steel negotiatons, to ignore Reuther's price stance, and to refuse to put any additional pressure on GM.

In the meantime, the aggressive and well-timed action of the steel, electrical, and packinghouse workers forced new concessions from management on the wage issue. A side effect of the other CIO strikes was the intensification of the factional struggle in the UAW because the January strikes, by disrupting the supply of materials to GM's competitors, threatened not only Reuther's one-at-a-time strategy but his plan for winning the presidency of the auto workers' union. The broad, national CIO struggle, directed by Murray, denied Reuther the role of hero of the postwar economic struggle that he may have been seeking for himself.[33]

Intraunion dissension had developed early in January when some UAW leftists began to push for the extension of the GM strike to other auto corporations. In the second week of January, Reuther criticized both Murray and electrical union leaders in internal UAW meetings. The criticism grew in intensity and sharpness as the steel negotiations reached a successful conclusion while the GM negotiations remained deadlocked. After the conclusion of the basic steel negotiations, GM's president, Charles Wilson, told UAW negotiators that the General Motors fact-finding board had lowered its recommendation from 24 percent to 17.5 percent at the instigation of Philip Murray. Wilson claimed that the CIO president had said a settlement of the steel dispute would not be possible if the higher figure were adopted by the board. Murray denied the charge, but it was spread throughout the UAW by Reuther partisans. Reuther and his supporters were also critical of Murray's position on the price question.[34]

Although the rumors and charges against Murray were, by and large, not broadcast publicly, UAW officials openly attacked the UE for its February 9 agreement with GM calling for an 18.5¢ wage increase. Thomas, Reuther, and the UAW negotiating committee blasted UE leaders for weakening the UAW's fight for the 19.5¢ recommended by the fact finders. Addes, too, was critical of the UE, though privately. The auto union leaders claimed that UE had agreed to strike GM when the UAW did and had also agreed not to conclude a separate settlement with the corporation. UE officials replied that they had made no such commitments and that the UAW had declined their proposals for joint negotiations. The UAW charges against UE were essentially false. The UE was being made a scapegoat for the UAW's own failure in negotiations with GM. The steel union had weeks before reduced its demand to 18.5¢, and the UAW had itself settled for 18¢ and 18.5¢ with Ford and Chrysler. The partial truth in the UAW charges was that a lack of coordination between the two unions existed. This is one reason why Thomas and Addes joined in the criticism of UE: they had participated in the conduct of the long GM strike and believed that the UE should have coordinated its actions with those of the UAW. In view of the UAW's pursuit of its own independent strategy, that UE leaders were principally concerned with solving their own problems in the electrical industry, where Westinghouse and General Electric were the biggest firms, is hardly surprising. Winning the pattern 18.5¢ from General Motors put pressure on the two biggest electrical firms. The UE, from its point of view, had no reason to strike GM early and no reason to hold out longer for a penny above the steel pattern.[35]

On February 12, GM offered the UAW an 18.5¢ wage increase and proposed an immediate return to work while a new contract was being negotiated. The old contract was to be renewed in the interim except for those provisions that had been ordered by the WLB. The new contract, GM contended, should include provisions to ensure the company "uninterrupted and efficient production." The company also proposed a dues checkoff in place of the WLB-ordered maintenance-of-membership provision in the old contract. The UAW's negotiating team rejected the GM offer since it fell "far short of the recommendations of the President and his fact-finding board." The union also declared that local issues had to be settled before it could accept a final agreement to end the strike. Citing 19 contract clauses that would be removed or weakened if GM's proposal were accepted, the union charged that it would be left with an "emasculated contract that would leave the union in a helpless bargaining position." The UAW reiterated its support for the fact-finding board's recommendation of 19.5¢ and reinstatement in full of the cancelled contract. Walter Reuther declared that General Motors was "thumbing its nose" at the president of the United States.[36]

In the course of negotiations during the next several days, GM agreed to the inclusion of several of the WLB-ordered clauses, and there were as a result optimistic reports that a settlement was near. Reuther, however, corrected this impression in a February 17 telegram to UAW locals indicating that disagreements continued over union security, wages, and seniority in promotions and transfers. Referring specifically to the latter issue, Reuther told reporters: "I want our locals to understand that it is this important part of the contract which is the stumbling block, rather than a mere 1¢ difference over wages."[37]

The union soon agreed to the corporation's proposal to substitute a dues checkoff system for the maintenance-of-membership provision in the old contract, and GM yielded on 16 of 19 WLB-ordered clauses. When Wilson outlined the corporation's position to UAW negotiators on February 28, stating, "Gentlemen, this is our last offer. Take it or leave it," outstanding issues included the 1¢ difference on wages, seniority in promotions and transfers, and local issues at the majority of plants. Union officers presented the corporation's proposal to the conference of GM-UAW delegates without a formal recommendation. Although the strike was already 14 weeks old, the conference unanimously rejected the company's offer, declaring once again that it did not meet the terms of the fact-finding board's recommendations. The local union leaders were especially concerned about the many unresolved local issues, and they wanted a settlement that could be recommended by the top union leadership as a significant victory of the long and difficult strike. With the union's convention now only three weeks away, factional considerations also played a part in the conference proceedings. The conference passed an implicitly pro-Reuther resolution to "remain 100 percent in support of the international GM strike policy and leadership." Influenced by the Reutherite criticism of Philip Murray, the delegates also formally urged the CIO president to call a meeting of the CIO Executive Board "to consolidate a policy of pressure"on General Motors.[38]

Harry W. Anderson of GM responded to the union's rejection of the company's "last offer" by accusing union officials of deliberately prolonging the strike because of union politics. Union officials, Anderson charged, did not want to jeopardize their political futures at the upcoming union convention. He maintained that the union was delaying a settlement to secure the additional 1¢ and because of a difference with the company regarding the contract clause covering transfers. The GM conference, still in session, blasted the corporation for attempting to "create a division in our ranks" and asserted that every decision in the GM negotiations since the UAW executive board meeting in September had been unanimous. The union renewed its prestrike proposal for binding arbitration on the remaining issues, suggesting now that President Truman appoint the single arbitrator. GM, however, refused once again to agree to arbitration. Instead, the corporation proposed that union members be given the opportunity to vote on the company's final offer. GM made public a list of the contract clauses to which it had agreed.[38]

In rejecting GM's call for a vote by the striking GM workers, UAW President Thomas charged that the corporation's proposal was "an unwarranted interference in the affairs of a democratic union and . . . probably an infraction of the National Labor Relations Act." Thomas, however, agreed with the corporation's assessment that the differences between the two sides were not very great. In contrast, Reuther insisted that GM was trying to minimize important differences between the company and union on wages, basic contract matters, and local working conditions. The union therefore countered GM's call for a membership vote on its offer with a proposal that the strikers be permitted to express their preferences as between the positions of the company and the union. This proposal was summarily rejected by GM.[39]

Despite Reuther's denials, the key obstacle to the settlement of the national negotiations was the 1¢ wage difference. The promotion-and-transfer clause was an important matter, but the union kept it on the table primarily as a bargaining chip. Why was General Motors so adamant in its opposition to giving the extra penny? The union's negotiating committee, accusing the company of trying to play union politics, asserted that GM wanted to "put an end to the union's advocacy of higher wages without price increases or turn out of office the union leadership which advocates that kind of economic thinking." This charge does not stand up to close examination. It was not so much that GM wanted to defeat Reuther personally as that it did not want to suffer defeat in the long strike. GM had fought against the UAW's ability-to-pay concept by arguing that it was an unsound notion that would require the successful corporation to pay more than the average company. Thomas, on the other hand, pointed out that GM would not be paying more than the going rate if it agreed to the 19.5¢ because its prestrike wage rates were lower than those of its competitors. GM officials, however, did not want to give in now and agree to a larger hike than the pattern increase of 18.5¢ because it believed that payment of that extra 1¢ would have constituted a *special defeat* for the corporation. General Motors, therefore, was willing to continue the shutdown even though it was by this time anxious to get back into production.[40]

The UAW, for its part, was adamant about the penny primarily because Walter Reuther was seeking a *special victory* above and beyond other CIO victories in order to justify the length of the strike and enhance his personal prestige. Other top UAW officials feared that they would be attacked by Reuther if they moved to settle the strike. With the union's convention scheduled to open on March 23, factional considerations were uppermost in the minds of UAW leaders. No official wanted to be accused of being responsible for a less than satisfactory settlement. Rank-and-file GM workers remained solid in their support of the strike. For the rank and file, the desire for unity and the concern about local issues were more important than factional politics.[41]

By the weekend of the March 1–2 UAW-GM conference, the strike was 14 weeks old and was having a serious economic impact in communities dependent on the auto industry. Much support for the UAW's renewed proposal for arbitration was seen, and pressure mounted on the White House to intervene in the dispute. City councils in Detroit, Cleveland, Saginaw, and other auto industry towns called on President Truman to act; the *Washington Post* editorially accused GM of turning the strike into a lockout; Senator James Murray declared that some members of his Committee on Education and Labor thought GM was trying to break the union; and Chester Bowles, now serving as head of the Office of Economic Stabilization, was reportedly urging Truman to summon the negotiators to Washington.[42]

Resisting these pressures, Truman refused to help the UAW during the last phase of the strike. He told reporters on March 8 that he still favored the GM fact-finding board's recommendations but would not agree to the Detroit City Council's request that he intervene in the dispute. Truman apparently resented Reuther's pressure more than he appreciated the UAW vice president's continuing support of administration policy. Truman complained to reporters that it was "too bad that the people who do the right thing can't get just as much publicity as those who are running for headlines to settle things in the newspapers." Labor and management had come to agreements in the rubber and telephone industries with much less "ballyhoo," Truman said. The UAW had won increased support from some circles with its offer of arbitration, but the Truman administration denied the union its assistance. The union also failed to receive the help of the NLRB after the agency's initial, long-delayed, issuance of a refusal to bargain complaint against GM. Thomas protested that the board, by adjourning hearings on the UAW-GM case on March 6, was aligning itself with the corporation. The NLRB did not, in the end, find GM guilty of any of several unfair labor practices violations charged by the UAW.[43]

The presidents of 17 Detroit area UAW locals, claiming they represented 235,000 union members, formally launched a drive on March 9 to "draft" Reuther to run for president of the international union. Although the GM strike was still unsettled, the committee issued a well-publicized statement hailing Reuther's accomplishments in the dispute and alleging that he would have achieved "even greater victories" if other unions and union leaders had supported him. Despite the factional implications of the latter charge, the Reuther for President Committee insisted that its aim was to end factionalism in the union and to unite the leadership. Asserting that it was composed of representatives of both the "so-called 'Reuther' and 'Addes' group[s]," the committee charged that R. J. Thomas had maintained himself in office "only by fostering rivalry between Reuther and Addes." As proof of its antifactional purpose, the Reuther for President Committee announced its support for the reelection of George Addes as secretary-treasurer of the union. Leaders of the Reuther caucus evidently decided to forget their wartime attack on Addes as one of the "boys who take their orders/Straight from the office of Joe Stalin."

The Reuther for President Committee was, unsurprisingly, composed largely of members of the Reuther caucus. Putting aside its traditional fight with the Addes-left coalition, the Reuther caucus focused its attack on the "independent" Thomas. As the Reuther for President Committee saw it, the "overwhelming rank-and-file sentiment . . . demands a change to efficient and effective administration and an end to disunity in the top leadership." Committee representatives contended that support for Reuther was such that he would not have to divert attention from the GM strike to campaign for the union presidency. Merely accepting the draft, they claimed, would ensure his election.[44]

To aid his campaign for the UAW presidency, Reuther sought to make a deal with Addes. "We ought to get together," he told Addes. "We're the people who have the power in the union. We ought to forget the Thomases, the Leonards." Reuther proposed to Addes that they both run for president and the winner then support the other for secretary-treasurer. Reuther's representatives argued that the union could have a really powerful leadership under such an arrangement, without caucuses of infighting. Addes listened to the Reuther offers, but, without criticizing Reuther, he announced to a caucus meeting of his supporters on March 21 that he would support both Thomas and Reuther for reelection to their existing positons. "I wasn't interested," Addes recalled, "in . . . a deal to leave people out who had contributed to the union. I felt that Thomas had done a decent job and . . . needed an opportunity to work in a postwar period."[45]

Thomas was unable to muster the kind of support for his campaign to retain the presidency that the Reuther for President Committee was able to marshal in Reuther's behalf. Thomas's own base of support was narrower than Reuther's. The UAW president's ability to maintain his position had depended on the continuation of a balance of power between the two main union blocs. On March 10, Thomas, abandoning his traditional stance as a nonfactional president, struck back at the Reuther partisans at a closed meeting of the UAW Ford Council. "Why isn't the GM strike being settled?" he asked. Referring to the fact that Reuther was then at a meeting at Thomas's home local, Chrysler

Local 7, the UAW president charged, "At the moment I am talking here, members of the GM staff are at a caucus of my own local union trying to get my job." The news media were quick to pick up Thomas's criticism of Reuther. To counter the support this gave to GM's charge that union politics was delaying settlement of the strike, Addes arranged for the release on March 11 of a joint statement signed by Thomas, Reuther, and himself which declared that the three leaders were "unanimous in all action now being taken" in negotiations. The release reiterated that all union decisions in the strike had been unanimous.[46]

The closing weeks of the strike saw factionalism manifest itself even in the collection of relief funds. Reuther, as leader of the GM strike, sought to have such funds sent to his office or to committees controlled by his supporters. Addes, as the union's secretary-treasurer, complained when the Reuther-allied treasurer of the Michigan State CIO Council sent relief money to the Michigan Citizens' Committee to Aid the Families of General Motors Strikers rather than to the UAW itself. For Reuther, holding the funds in his own hands enhanced his position as the leader of the strike and his ability to argue for the continuation of the strike.[47]

The bulk of the funds to aid the GM strikers came from nonstriking UAW members and from other CIO unions. Left-wing locals and international unions were particularly active in sending aid. At the end of January 1946, a new strike committee, the United Labor Committee to Aid the UAW-GM Strikers, was formed in New York. Union officials sponsoring the new committee were primarily anticommunist liberals and Social Democrats of both the CIO and AFL. Among AFL union presidents on the committee were David Dubinsky of the ILGWU, Max Zaritsky of the Millinery Workers, Sal Hoffman of the Upholsterers, and A. Philip Randolph of the Sleeping Car Porters. Reuther attended a rally of the New York-based committee on February 25 at which time tens of thousands of dollars were collected to support the strike, a reported $75,000 coming from the ILGWU alone. As if to counter the political impact of these funds on the UAW presidential race, Thomas requested and received $100,000 from the CIO's Amalgamated Clothing Workers to aid the strike in its closing days.[48]

The money contributed by Dubinsky and the ILGWU became a source of controversy within both the UAW and the CIO. Dubinsky had recently returned to the AFL Executive Council and had urged that individual CIO unions restore "labor unity" by leaving the newer federation and affiliating with the AFL. He had also supported the now discredited Homer Martin during the 1938–1939 factional crisis in the UAW, a fact that aroused concern among many in the auto union about his purpose in aiding the strike. The Dubinsky-supported paper, the *New Leader,* was now praising Reuther and attacking CIO President Murray for giving GM workers a "stab in the back." The *Daily Worker,*

R. J. Thomas, and Philip Murray all charged that Dubinsky was trying to split the CIO. "There is Dubinsky money being sent into our union to aid anti-CIO forces," Thomas told the UAW Ford Council. Murray was quoted as saying that "the moneybags of John L. Lewis and David Dubinsky are open to anybody who will help split the CIO." Dubinsky later acknowledged his union's intervention in the UAW's internal politics, saying "our locals did help Reuther financially and [in] every other way." Dubinsky also conceded that a key ILGWU official had made the rounds of UAW locals, pledging funds to them so that they could send pro-Reuther delegates to the UAW convention.[49]

The Thomas-Addes-Reuther joint statement of March 11 proclaiming unity on moves "being taken" in negotiations indicated that UAW leaders were ready to shift their bargaining position. The public revelation of the union's factional dispute had apparently undermined Reuther's ability to keep up the fight for the extra penny. At 9:30 p.m. on March 12, the UAW and General Motors began what proved to be the final negotiating session. The negotiators worked through the night and concluded the agreement at 2:30 p.m. on March 13, just ten days before the scheduled opening of the UAW convention. A GM official later recalled that Reuther "stormed out" of the final bargaining session. Thomas's recollection was that "all night long Walter insisted he wanted to go home, to leave the negotiations." Whatever his private feelings, Reuther fully supported the agreement on March 13 and, more important, was in command of the UAW's public position.[50]

The union's initial official statement on negotiations took the form of another joint Thomas-Addes-Reuther declaration but essentially reflected Reuther's views. The statement claimed that the settlement was superior to the terms recommended by Truman's fact-finding panel. Gains from an agreement to correct wage inequities coupled with the 18.5¢ across the board wage increase, it was asserted, would bring the total wage raise to 19.5¢. The provision for a dues checkoff, according to the statement, was "a long step forward towards the union shop," and the clause on transfers was "a tremendous step forward" in the recognition of the principle of seniority. According to the UAW, GM had been forced to abandon its company security demand "in the face of the excellent war production record of the General Motors workers and the good faith they have shown in carrying out their collective bargaining agreement." The union statement gave special emphasis to the price issue, alleging that GM workers had "fought and won their price battle," prevented the company from increasing prices, and helped the federal government to avoid runaway inflation. On the question of local issues, the union announced that GM had "acquiesced to the Union demand that it instruct its local managements to proceed immediately with negotiations on local demands with a view to settling them satisfactorily *before* ratification meetings are held."[51]

The UAW's GM conference met to consider the new agreement on March 15. In advocating the contract before the conference, Reuther outlined his views on the forces at work in the strike and the broad significance of the struggle. He alleged that the steel strike "weakened our position" and that the UE settlement was "Treason and Double-Cross." He spoke of division in the labor movement on the price question, portraying some as saying, "Get Wages [and] to Hell with prices." Reuther, on the other hand, praised the support that he had received from top UAW officers, especially George Addes. Among the important results of the strike, Reuther cited the placing of American labor on the offensive and breaking the back of the big business antilabor drive; setting the pattern for the highest wage increases in the history of American labor; raising new basic concepts regarding the wage-price issue; smashing GM's campaign to force a union retreat; and winning substantial contract gains such as on transfers. Reuther's presentation to the GM conference, while clearly claiming victory, was a more sober assessment of the contract than that contained in the union's official statement and was an attempt to put the agreement in its political context.[52]

The GM conference voted overwhelmingly to approve the agreement and sent it to the locals for ratification. Although the union delegates supported the contract, they shifted the union's approach on the settlement of local issues: local unions were to vote on the national contract even if local issues remained outstanding. The conference decided that some locals could continue strikes on plant issues while other locals returned to work. The delegates resolved that striking locals should have the full support of the international.[53]

The UAW's GM locals voted heavily in favor of the new contract. A majority of locals having approved the national agreement, the union advised GM on March 19 that the contract had been ratified. Many local unions, however, had voted to remain on strike until local issues had been resolved. GM attacked the international union for allowing local strikes, charging that the UAW was unilaterally changing the terms of the agreement. Unless the local strikes were ended, the company threatened that it would not reopen any of its plants. Reuther denied GM's allegation and asserted that there had been no misunderstanding; GM, he asserted, knew that the local issues had to be settled. In Atlantic City for a preconvention board meeting, R. J. Thomas was pressed by reporters for a response to GM's new ultimatum. He responded that the international was on record as supporting the locals' efforts to win their demands. Having allowed Reuther a free hand in the ratification process, Thomas expressed his annoyance: "It's Reuther's baby," he said, "let him handle it." The international executive board affirmed its support of the striking locals on March 21. Reuther sounded a conciliatory note, however, predicting that all but two or three of the local disagreements would be settled within three days. Some local leaders were displeased with this prediction because it put pressure on the locals.[54]

Two days before the UAW presidential balloting, General Motors announced a reversal of its policy of continuing the shutdown until all locals had ended their strikes. Harry Anderson said that Reuther had assured him that locals that had not yet signified a readiness to return to work would do so promptly. GM's policy change was probably timed to signal that the company was not opposed to Reuther's election as UAW president. In any event, two local strikes dragged on for another six to seven weeks after the national settlement.[55]

The sharpest local disputes centered on the demand of ten local unions for a shift from an incentive to an hourly pay system. Winning this demand was made more difficult by the national agreement, which continued to require that any such change in pay systems "must be made on a sound and equitable basis which does not increase average production costs, and which provides for maintaining efficiency of the plant." Because productivity is generally higher under a piecework system, this clause made it difficult for the locals concerned to change to an hourly system of pay. The Cleveland Fisher Body strike against the incentive pay system did not end until May 12, the settlement in this plant providing that jobs would be shifted from piece rate to day rate when the 1941 efficiency level had been reached. Leaders of the left-wing Fisher Body local later complained that "Fisher Body workers . . . were left in the lurch for two months after they had been led to believe by continued assurances that 'nobody would go back until everybody went back' and the piece rate problem was solved."[56]

The piecework clause was only one of several areas in which the national contract fell short of union goals. The union's March 13 victory statement exaggerated the merits of the newly negotiated contract. The agreement to increase wages 18.5¢ was, of course, an important success for the union, but the UAW did not win the extra 1¢ that it had sought from GM. The agreement to correct wage inequities did not provide for the setting aside of a specific sum of money to deal with this problem, as the UAW had demanded and as had been provided in the 1940 contract. It instead gave local managements authority to adjust intraplant wage rates; if the local union were dissatisfied with the adjustment, it could appeal to the international union, which might then seek redress from top management. Because the union had originally proposed a 1¢ per hour fund to deal with intraplant inequities, that something less was actually won is clear. Reuther supporters later acknowledged that the union did not win the extra penny.[57]

The question of transfers had been the second major difference delaying an agreement during the final few weeks of the strike. Despite the union claim of a "tremendous" victory on this issue, the clause on transfers was something less than a significant improvement, if an improvement at all. The 1942 agreement gave GM sole authority on transfers; but, under the 1945 WLB-ordered clause, whereas temporary transfers remained a management prerogative, permanent transfers were to be determined by local seniority agreements. The new contract gave workers capable of performing a job in their department preference over new hires but not over fellow employees with less seniority. The new clause on transfers was superior to that in the 1942 agreement and to GM's publicized proposal of March 2, but it was a backward step compared with the recognition of the seniority principle in the 1945 contract. Reuther's trumpeting of this clause as a triumph for seniority resulted in several grievances that were processed to the umpire. The union lost all of them.[58]

The claim that the union had won a big gain in union security was also exaggerated. The 1946 dues checkoff clause provided that the union was to collect the initiation fee and the first month's dues from the new employee and that the corporation thereafter would deduct the dues from the unionized worker's pay check and remit the sum to the union. The new dues checkoff clause, like the maintenance-of-membership provision in the old contract, provided for a brief grace period during which members could drop out of the union. The maintenance-of-membership provision ordered by the WLB in 1942 was, however, superior to the new dues checkoff agreement from the standpoint of union security. Under the WLB clause, employees who did not quit the union during a 15-day grace period were required to maintain their membership during the life of the agreement as a *condition of employment.* This degree of acceptance of the union was not reflected in the 1946 contract because the dues checkoff was stated to be merely for the "convenience" of the union. The UAW thus took a step backward, not a "long step forward," on the issue of union security in 1946. Reuther admitted to the UAW executive board that main-tenance-of-membership "would have been preferable." At one point, Reuther made the more limited claim that the dues checkoff was an advance in terms of GM's "voluntary" recognition of the union. This was a more accurate assess-ment: the dues checkoff was "voluntary" in the sense that it was agreed to through collective bargaining, whereas the maintenance-of-membership clause had been imposed on GM by the government during the war.[59]

The 1946 agreement included a new clause on vacation pay. Under the old formula, workers received a bonus of 40 or more hours of pay in lieu of a vacation, with the pay per hour based on seniority. The new formula provided that workers were to receive 2 percent (or more) of their 1945 gross pay, which Reuther claimed was a major victory that would net GM workers $5 million. Although many war workers did better under the new plan than the old, most veterans received little or no vacation pay under the new formula. This denial of vacation pay to veterans was a cause of protest demonstrations later in 1946. The next GM contract returned to the old principle.[60]

Although both Chrysler and Ford had secured concessions from the UAW on the issue of company security clauses, no new company security clauses were added to the GM contract in 1946 despite the company's demand for such provisions. The GM contract, however, was from the company's viewpoint about as satisfactory on this issue as the contracts of its competitors. The GM agreement contained a clause barring strikes, sit-downs, stay-ins, slowdowns, "or any curtailment of work or restrictions of production or interference with production" until the bargaining process was completed; the corporation had the right to discipline employees who violated this clause. Workers so disciplined received expedited arbitration if they were laid off for a least two weeks or terminated, but the umpire was not empowered to award back pay in such cases. Related contract language gave GM the sole responsibility to hire, promote, discharge, or discipline for cause and to maintain discipline and efficiency of its employees. GM's contractually guaranteed management prerogatives were very substantial, but the fact that no new company security clauses were added to the 1946 agreement was of some importance to the UAW.[61]

There was, of course, no provision in the new GM contract restricting the company's right to increase prices. Reuther's claim that the union had achieved victory in its price battle was not justified by the facts. Auto manufacturers were granted three price increases in the three months following the conclusion of the GM strike; the general CPI rose by 12 percent during the six months between March 15, 1946, and September 15, 1946. The most intense political battles on the issue of price control and inflation came in the months following the strike.[62]

A new feature of the UAW-GM agreement was the provision that the contract would run for two years. This was a longer-term contract than those previously agreed on by GM and the UAW. There was, however, a provision in the contract permitting the parties to reopen discussion on wages after a year; the parties were to resolve the matter within a two-and-one-half-month period. The UAW's contract with Chrysler provided for the reopening of wage negotiations on 60 days' notice, giving the union a greater ability to respond to the inflationary pressures than the GM contract permitted. In most respects, the GM contract was comparable to other major UAW contracts of the time. The wage gain at GM was equal to or slightly better than that secured by the union at other major corporations, but the GM wage scale remained a few cents below that in effect at Ford. On the issues of company and union security, the union avoided making concessions to GM but was itself forced to take a backward step with the removal of a maintenance-of-membership clause. At Ford and Chrysler, on the other hand, the union made concessions to management demands for company security while maintaining the status quo on union security.[63]

The loss of maintenance-of-membership at GM caused the UAW to fall behind the Steelworkers and the Electrical Workers in the area of union security. In 1945, more than 50 percent of auto, steel, and electrical workers were covered by contracts with maintenance-of-membership provisions, but in 1946 only 10 percent of the auto workers were covered by such provisions, whereas coverage for steel and electrical workers remained above 50 percent.[64]

The GM contract was inferior to other major UAW contracts with regard to the issue of nondiscrimination on the basis of "race, color, or creed." The UAW maintained old or negotiated new nondiscrimination clauses at Ford, Chrysler, Briggs, and Bendix; the Bendix agreement was the most effective in this regard because it prohibited discrimination in hiring as well as in the administration of the contract. No clause barring racial discrimination was included in the GM contract despite the focus of the UAW'S Fair Practices Committee and the Detroit Black newspaper, the *Michigan Chronicle*, on GM's discriminatory practices. Although George Crockett, executive secretary of the union's Fair Practices Committee, delineated the discriminatory effects of the noninterchangeable occupational group seniority system, this system was not altered by the contract. Crockett and George Addes, the chairperson of the committee, succeeded, however, in persuading GM to write a letter stating that it pursued a nondiscriminatory policy, but UAW negotiators did not press the issue nor did Reuther publicize the matter.[65]

Despite many obstacles and difficulties and the shortcomings of some of the contract provisions, the GM strike was still, in many ways, a victory for the UAW.[66] The union had survived a long and complicated struggle, proving once again that it was a vital institution. The thousands of union members who had joined the union during the war and the returning veterans remained loyal to the union despite the hardships of nearly four months without a pay check. The 18.5¢ wage increase was nearly twice the largest increase the UAW had previously won (10¢).[67]

Under Walter Reuther's leadership, the UAW strengthened its ties with national liberal leaders during the GM strike, and the support of liberal forces helped the UAW and the CIO to win their wage victories. Although the Truman administration eventually adopted a stance that contributed to the CIO victory, union leaders were unhappy with the administration's vacillating policy. The CIO's dissatisfaction with Truman was not confined to the wage-price question. Denied presidential leadership, the CIO had been unable to secure the Congressional enactment of any of the domestic reform legislation that it favored. The CIO's policy of relying on a Democratic president no longer appeard to be viable. Third-party talk increased during the GM strike; left, center, and right CIO leaders all spoke of the need for more independent political action. Developing a new political strategy proved, however, to be a complicated and difficult task. The CIO, to be sure, had to respond not only to a shift to the right in the White House but to the changing balance of political forces in the country and a growing conservative offensive.[68]

The GM strike strengthened Walter Reuther's position within the UAW. Although it might be said that the UAW won the strike despite Reuther's leadership, he was still *the* leader of that important struggle. Even if many GM workers were unhappy with some of Reuther's tactics during the strike, he had, at the very least, provided some kind of leadership. R. J. Thomas had been president of the UAW for more than seven years, but the GM strike showed him to be a less effective leader than Reuther. George Addes, the leader of the left-center caucus and the only other official in a position to seek the presidency, had decided to continue his past policy of working with Thomas.[69]

Reuther's position within the UAW was enhanced by the fact that the media treated him as the union's principal leader. This was due in part to a skillful use of publicity by Reuther and his staff. An additional factor was Reuther's stance as an outspoken opponent of Communists in the labor movement. The extensive and sympathetic coverage of Reuther's activities by the conservative Luce publications—*Time, Life,* and *Fortune*—was probably due primarily to the UAW vice president's anticommunism.[70]

Although Reuther's personal standing in the union had been enhanced by the strike, the strength of his caucus within the union had not changed significantly. Reuther had gained in influence because auto workers were impressed with his leadership abilities rather than because they necessarily agreed with his ideology and program. The ideological and political currents in the locals had not altered in any significant way as a result of the GM strike. Union activists unaffiliated with either of the two major union caucuses might favor Reuther because of his role in the GM strike but still support local and regional officials from the Addes caucus whom they knew to be effective. Reuther's leadership of the GM strike, however, helped to make his caucus more cohesive and stimulated it to perfect its organizational activities.

Despite a reduction in membership and a difficult strike at GM, the UAW had managed to maintain its position in the auto industry during the reconversion period. The union had been relatively successful in reconversion collective bargaining and relatively unsuccessful in reconversion politics. With the completion of the first round of postwar wage negotiations, the UAW's attention shifted to the political arena. Here, the pressure from antiunion social forces was even greater than in the economic field. The general antilabor drive intensified after the strike wave receded, and the increased antilabor pressure on the UAW accentuated differences within the union. Factional conflict, which erupted toward the end of the GM strike, became the focal point of union concern between 1946 and 1947.

Chapter Six

The Faction Fight Begins: The 1946 UAW Convention and its Aftermath

On March 23, 1946, the tenth convention of the UAW-CIO opened in Atlantic City, New Jersey. The nearly 1,900 delegates present came from about 650 local unions and represented more than 800,000 members. The contest for the union's presidency between incumbent R. J. Thomas and Vice President Walter Reuther dominated the attention of the delegates. The well-publicized "draft Reuther" campaign had begun several weeks before the convention. Then, just two days before the convention's opening, Reuther's representatives passed the word to the newspapers that anticommunism would be Reuther's battle cry. "Reuther to Fight UAW Reds," the *Detroit Free Press* proclaimed in a banner headline. The *Free Press* cited the declaration of an unnamed "unimpeachable" source close to Reuther that the challenger would run on an anticommunist platform and would show that Thomas adhered to the Communist party line; if victorious, Reuther would institute a "union-wide purge of Communists." Although Thomas had rejected Communist support at earlier UAW conventions when he had faced no serious opposition, he now indicated that he would not reject Communist support. "I would even accept support from a Reuther-type Socialist," Thomas joked in an attempt to get off the "red" hot spot and put Reuther on it.[1]

In his opening report to the convention, Thomas attacked Reuther indirectly. He charged that David Dubinsky of the AFL-affiliated ILGWU was once again interfering in the UAW as he had when Homer Martin was president. Dubinsky's purpose, Thomas charged, was to bring the UAW into the AFL, thereby undermining the CIO. The clear implication was that Reuther was an instrument of Dubinsky's anti-CIO plans. At a press conference on the second day of the convention, Thomas went public with his criticisms of Reuther's handling of the GM strike. He charged that Reuther had picked GM as the target "on his own hook" and that the strike had been called six weeks too early and lasted four weeks too long. Thomas also criticized the ability-to-pay and open-the-books concepts, asserting that they had hurt the union's position in the Ford negotiations. When questioned by reporters about Thomas's comments, Reuther defended his handling of the strike and its timing. Calling Thomas a liar, he charged that the UAW president, despite his denial, had actually signed a letter to GM's President Wilson responding positively to a proposal to reopen GM parts plants. Reuther protested that the ability-to-pay idea had not been aimed at small companies and that the open-the-books slogan had been a "maneuver" to get GM over a barrel. The *Washington Post* and the *Detroit Free Press* attacked Reuther for the "manuever" phrase, stating that it showed the union's whole approach in the GM strike had been meretricious.[2]

The charges and countercharges of the Reuther and Thomas camps captured media attention and undoubtedly hurt the union, but they probably had little impact on the delegates. Familiar with last-minute election propaganda, the auto workers responded with skepticism. The Reuther caucus, in fact, dropped the anticommunist theme and instead concentrated on such issues as wages, prices, civil liberties, consumer cooperatives, and political action. The Addes-Thomas forces were slower to recognize the limited impact of negative-sounding campaign literature and continued to stress the anti-Reuther theme. The principal reason for this approach was that Reuther had gained the political initiative, and his opponents felt themselves compelled to respond to his moves. The terms of the debate were set by Reuther's proposals, ideas, and actions.[3]

One charge of the Addes-Thomas group had the potential to disrupt the Reuther drive for the UAW presidency: that Reuther was against CIO policy in general and against CIO President Murray in particular. The enormous popular response of the UAW delegates to Murray's appearance at the convention testified to the danger to the Reuther candidacy if his opponents could stigmatize him as an anti-CIO candidate. Aware of this danger, Reuther, ignoring the fact that Thomas had not appointed him one of Murray's escorts on the convention floor, pushed his way to Murray's side and accompanied him to the podium. Murray's address to the convention was not one to comfort Reuther, however. Without mentioning those responsible by name, Murray reviewed the rumors about his conduct during the GM strike that had been circulated by the Reuther partisans and disputed them one by one. Murray denied that there had been an agreement not to strike steel. He responded to charges that he had not aided the GM strike by pointing out that the United Steelworkers, of which Murray was president, had contributed $100,000 to the UAW and that UAW officials had understood that the USW was prepared to drain its treasury in the auto workers' behalf. Murray informed the delegates, moreover, that he had offered to participate in the strike negotiations. He reserved his harshest criticism for the "company rumors" that he had induced the GM fact-finding board to reduce its wage recommendation from 24 percent to 19.5¢. This, he charged, was "a diabolical, detestable lie, manufactured out of whole cloth by a high officer of the General Motors Corporation and circulated throughout the Union for the purpose of creating division among CIO workers."

Murray made an implied attack on David Dubinsky for seeking to undermine and destroy the CIO. The delegates applauded the CIO president's strong declaration that efforts to split the CIO would not succeed: "I don't give a damn," he asserted, "who those people are in New York, they can't do it, they are not going to do it; whether they are alleged leaders of the American Federation of Labor makes no difference—they are not going to do it!"

Citing the World Federation of Trade Unions as a "movement [that] is going to be a potent force for peace . . . ," Murray praised Thomas's role in the development of the world body. Murray also credited Thomas (along with Addes and "others") for assisting in the fight at the Labor-Management Conference against the Chamber of Commerce, the NAM, and AFL leaders Green and Lewis. Concluding his speech, Murray thanked each of the UAW's officers but declared that Thomas was "that great big guy for whom I have a distinct fondness."[4]

Murray received a trememdous ovation from the auto worker delegates. As a Reuther supporter observed: "Murray made a very impressive speech . . . the Reuther faction was down in the mouth because they had figured the Murray speech had taken the fence riders and the weak delegates to Thomas . . . ." After the Murray talk, however, the Reutherites presented a resolution challenging Thomas to debate the issues with his opponent. Thomas supporters asserted that this was a trick, but a large number of undecided delegates apparently thought the proposal made sense. Although Addes, who was then chairing the convention, ruled that the debate resolution fell short of the two-thirds majority needed to change the convention's agenda, the proposal had the support of more than one-half the convention. The impact of Murray's speech was not totally dissipated, but some delegates no doubt thought that Thomas's charges against Reuther must have been exaggerated if he were not willing to make them in a face-to-face debate with his opponent.[5]

The contest between Thomas and Reuther was a conflict between two contrasting personalities. Edwin Lahey, a journalist who admired Reuther, saw the challenger as "energetic, ambitious and opportunistic." Reuther was not a drinker nor did he play cards or dice, and Lahey thought that he lacked "human warmth." "Reuther," Lahey wrote, "has none of the charm of fallible men who go through life committing indiscretions and deviating from the path of moral righteousness." Lahey believed that Reuther's power lay "in his remarkable technical competence, the brilliance of his public relations, his genius for making simple presentations of complex economic issues, and above all his increasing diligence in the art of building political fences." The left-wing CIO journalist Len DeCaux wrote that "Reuther registered as smart, to the point of intellectual, as able and determined, but otherwise as too self-centered and calculating to please." Although Reuther may have lacked warmth, he did make the effort to speak to delegates personally, and this impressed many.[6]

Thomas, more personable than Reuther, was a "big, burly man, tough and with a good sense of humor."[7] Unlike Reuther, he knew how to relax, play poker, and have a drink with the "guys." Thomas had become UAW president as a result of CIO intervention, not because he was a leader popular with a controlling section of the union. Although he had retained the position as a compromise figure between the two major factions, he did grow with the job. He became a good speaker and worked well with government officials during the war. He showed courage in tackling the issue of racism within the union and the community. Thomas was, nevertheless, called "bumbling" by friend and foe alike. During the GM strike, he twice found himself criticized for tactless statements harmful to the strike. He lacked the energy and efficiency of Reuther. Addes later characterized Thomas as "wishy-washy." He was clearly a less dynamic figure than Reuther.[8]

There is no doubt that the personality factor was an important feature of the contest. "I could not help him [Thomas]," Addes recalled, "as my support disliked him more than they disliked Reuther . . . . Several of my own people said that they'd vote for Reuther over Thomas." Although the Addes supporters did, in the main, vote for Thomas, Addes's remark indicated a degree of disaffection within the ranks of the Addes caucus.[9]

Sharp differences of personality were not matched by equally clear differences on issues. Reuther and Thomas and their respective caucuses agreed on many fundamental objectives of trade unionism and on many specific issues. Both caucuses supported resolutions calling for the expulsion of fascist Argentina and Spain from the United Nations, the enactment of a national health care program, a permanent federal fair employment practices committee, and child-care legislation. Both groups advocated equal pay for equal work, regardless of race or sex, and full employment and housing legislation.[10]

The Reuther and Thomas forces did diverge on some important questions. The Thomas-Addes program, taking issue with Reuther's approach in the GM strike, called for setting wages in accord with the needs of the workers and the nation, not on the basis of corporate "arithmetic." The Reuther policy statement regarding wages avoided mention of the wage principles Reuther had advanced in the GM strike and instead called for industrywide bargaining and a guaranteed annual wage. On the question of civil liberties, the Reuther program proposed nondiscrimination on the basis of race, religion, sex, and national origin but did not mention political affiliation. The Thomas-Addes program, however, opposed "Congressional witch-hunts against racial, national, or political minorities." It also called for support of permanent fair employment practices and antipoll tax legislation, neither of which was mentioned in the Reuther program. On the other hand, the Reuther group advocated cooperatives, calling for joint action with farm organizations and consumer cooperatives to advance "the principle of democratic social ownership." In addition, the Reuther group supported political action to "build [the] base of a new progressive party." The Thomas-Addes program did not mention cooperatives, but it paid greater attention to the existing political situation than did the Reuther program, supporting action by the CIO-PAC to force the Truman administration onto a "path of progress" and to prepare the way "if necessary" for independent labor political action. The Thomas-Addes program also called on the UAW to fight for "the guarantee of peace in a democratic world" and backed the WFTU as the "world's best instrument for a peaceful and democratic future." The Reuther program contained no mention of the fight for peace or the WFTU.[11]

Although the *Nation*, a leading liberal magazine, saw Reuther as more politically aware than Thomas, the Addes-Thomas program was to the left of the Reuther program in its greater emphasis on such "progressive" political issues as the fight for peace and the struggles against racism and witchhunting.[12] Despite their generally more progressive position, however, the leaders of the Addes-Thomas caucus did not join their left-wing allies in supporting a proposal for Black representation on the union's executive board. The discusssion of this recommendation produced the convention's only significant debate on a political issue.

The controversy over Black representation developed during the discussion of a proposed constitutional amendment to convert the Fair Practices Committee (appointed by the union's executive board in 1944) into a department and make it a permanent part of the union's structure. The amendment, as approved, required each local to establish a fair employment practices committee and to contribute funds to finance the new department. The director of the department was to be appointed by the president. A minority report called for the election by the convention of an International Executive Board member who would be the director of the Fair Practices and Anti-Discrimination Department. The minority report was presented by Shelton Tappes, a Black leader from Ford Local 600, and was supported by John Orr, a white progressive, also from Local 600. The other seven members of the constitution committee, including five Thomas supporters, backed by majority report.

The supporters of the minority report argued that their proposal would make electing a Black to membership on the Executive Board possible, whereas "under the presently operated type of political caucusing . . . it is practically an impossiblity." Electing a Black to top leadership, the minority argued, would be an important step in the fight for equality for Blacks in the union and in the community. Speakers for the majority criticized the minority proposal as reverse racism and argued that, if it were adopted, other groups would soon be demanding seats on the board. Ben Garrison, who later went on to nominate R. J. Thomas for president, declared that he was against having a "director on the basis of lines adopted by the Soviet Union . . . [and against] a commissar over any particular segment of our membership." Another Thomas supporter said: "I urge everybody here to make it understood once and for all that no minority political party is going to dictate to this convention what it wants . . . ." Communists were, to be sure, prominent in supporting the minority report. Most Thomas and Addes supporters, however, apparently joined Reuther partisans in voting against the minority report.[13]

The debate at the 1946 UAW convention on the fair practices question differed markedly from that at the 1943 convention, when similiar proposals were before the delegates. In the earlier convention, top UAW leaders had addressed the issue; both Thomas and Reuther had spoken in favor of a majority report for a minorities department with an appointed director. On that occasion, Addes and Frankensteen had taken the floor on behalf of a minority report that provided for the election of the director of the department as an at-large member of the Executive Board with a single vote. (Other board members had one vote for each 1,000 dues-paying members in their regions.) The convention, however, had voted down both the majority and minority reports. In 1946, by contrast, top UAW leaders did not directly participate in the debate on the issue.

In both conventions, opponents of the proposal to make the director of the new department an elected member of the board used the "reverse Jim Crow" argument. In the 1946 convention, however, several opponents of the minority report—all Thomas supporters—raised the question of communism in the course of their remarks. By contrast, the proposal had not been attacked as Communist-inspired on the floor of the 1943 convention even though Communist leader Nat Ganley had presented the minority report. Clearly, the developing cold war climate was having its effect on many union activists and not just on Reuther supporters.[14]

Given the fact that the two Reuther partisans and the majority of Thomas supporters on the constitution committee opposed the minority report, it is not surprising that the proposal for Black representation on the board went down to defeat. The majority report for the creation of a Fair Practices and Anti-Discrimination Department carried the convention, however, even though it was a stronger proposal than the failed 1943 motion. George Crockett, director of the old Fair Practices Committee, had feared that the introduction of the idea of Black representation on the board would arouse "latent animosities" and defeat the proposal for a permanent status for the committee. The vigorous activities of the Fair Practices Committee under Crockett's leadership had, however, laid the foundation for a permanent antidiscrimination department within the UAW.[15]

Most issues of factional import were not debated at the 1946 convention in the detailed manner in which the fair practices question was discussed. Although foreign policy and political action issues were eventually to divide the UAW, resolutions on these questions did not reach the convention floor. The majority and minority reports of the resolutions committee on these issues and the speeches of leading UAW officials at the convention nevertheless indicate the beginnings of the split that would become fully manifest only in 1948. In his opening address to the convention, R. J. Thomas was critical of the unfolding cold war, accusing the "reactionary press" of "doing everything it possibly can to tear us asunder, we who worked together during the war, to again bring on another war." In addition, Thomas voiced strong support for both the United Nations and the WFTU.[16]

That the foreign policy approach of Walter Reuther and his caucus differed somewhat from that of Thomas can be seen in the majority report of the convention resolutions committee, which was chaired by Victor Reuther and had a pro-Reuther majority. The foreign policy resolution drafted by Victor Reuther criticized the United States, Great Britain, and the Soviet Union for "deliberately circumventing" the United Nations and for apparently preferring the "old imperialist, war inciting methods of power politics and military alliances." Furthermore, the Reuther resolution praised and criticized specific actions of the Big Three powers. On the historic speech at Westminister College by Winston Churchill, delivered just three weeks before the UAW convention, the Reuther resolution declared: "We join with all peace-loving people throughout the world in denouncing the recent speech of Winston Churchill calling for an American-British military alliance against Soviet Russia." Finally, the majority resolution did not stress the importance of the World Federation of Trade Unions in the struggle for peace but instead merely called for the adoption of the resolution's principles by the WFTU. The Reuther resolution, written at a critical point in the development of the cold war, supported liberal values in international relations and asserted UAW independence of the foreign policies of each of the Big Three powers.[17]

A minority report of the resolutions committee, drafted by Roy England of the Canadian Ford local and supported by the Communist leader Nat Ganley, called for opposition to "war mongering" and proposed that the United States, Britain, and the Soviet Union iron out their differences and cooperate in peace as they had during the war. The minority resolution also supported the United Nations and sharply criticized Churchill's recent speech, citing James Roosevelt's call for "every peace-loving man and woman in the world to stand up now and repudiate the words, the schemes and the political allies of the

Honorable Winston Churchill." The minority resolution, moreover, advocated a conference to settle peacefully the differences between the United States, Great Britain, and the Soviet Union. Concentrating on the single question of Big Three unity, the minority resolution attacked Churchill but avoided direct criticism of any of the three major powers. Addressing the most critical foreign policy problem, the minority saw conservative circles in the West as the main enemies of peace and sought a real world solution to the push toward the cold war. The Reuther resolution, on the other hand, took a detailed position on numerous foreign policy questions and viewed each of the Big Three powers as imperialist.[18]

The resolutions committee also drafted majority and minority reports on the question of political action. The Reuther-backed majority resolution supported eventual formation of "a new political party of labor, farmers, progressive middle class people, consumers, and members of minority, racial and religious groups." Ganley took a similar position in a resolution that was also sharply critical of President Truman for "capitulating on issue after issue to the camp of reaction." Victor Reuther's first draft of a resolution on political action, in contrast, declared only: "Even the President himself has found it impossible to persuade the present legislators who control Congress to enact laws keyed to the needs of human reconversion." The final wording of the Reuther-supported majority resolution stated that Truman "has been unwilling in many instances and found it impossible in other instances" to persuade the legislators. Another important difference between the majority and the Ganley resolutions was that the former ignored the approaching 1946 elections whereas the latter called for support of the CIO-PAC and of candidates "pledged to the domestic policies and foreign policies of the late Franklin D. Roosevelt." The Ganley resolution also called for the encouragement of independent and third party candidates where neither major party candidate had an acceptable program or record. The principal difference between the Reuther and Ganley approaches was that the Ganley resolution envisioned immediate organization of independent political activity against the Truman administration, whereas the Reuther resolution favored independent political activity without a defined antagonism to the Truman administration.[19]

The Reutherites' cautious approach to Truman was seen in Walter Reuther's statement following his election to the UAW presidency that he would withhold comment on the national administration "for the time being." Thomas and Addes, like Ganley, were critical of Truman. In his speech to the convention, Thomas characterized Truman's conduct during the GM strike as "weak" and "spineless." Addes was even more critical of Truman.[20]

A second difference between the Reuther and Ganley positions on political action was the specific support for the PAC in the Ganley resolution and the absence of such a reference in the Reuther resolution. This difference was highlighted when a reporter asked the new UAW president if he would accord uncritical loyalty to PAC as Thomas had; Reuther replied that he would provide "intelligent loyalty." This lack of enthusiasm for the PAC by the Reuther caucus was nothing new. During and immediately after the war, the Reutherites had been lukewarm or hostile to the PAC, with many Reuther supporters participating in the independent Michigan Commonwealth Federation.[21]

Given the militancy of the Reuther caucus in criticizing the Roosevelt administration during World War II, why was it so cautious in voicing hostility to the Truman administration? Both in foreign policy and in political action, the Reuther group hoped to maintain a middle-of-the-road position. Reutherites wanted to separate themselves from the left-wing attacks on the Truman administration's policies, foreign and domestic. They saw themselves stationed in the middle of the road between the country's right-wing conservatives and its Communist-oriented left wing.[22] As the cold war deepened, those relatively subtle and unpublicized differences on foreign policy and political action became more pronounced.

The issues of wage-price policy and of company security were other questions of comparative importance to the union that did not reach the convention floor. The action of the resolutions committee indicates that the Reuther approach on wage-price policy was not fully accepted even by Reuther supporters. Victor Reuther's initial draft declared that "employers' prices, profits and ability to pay higher wages are at all times matters of legitimate concern to organized labor." This statement was dropped from the second draft proposed by Reuther and approved by the committee. The approved version declared that wages whould be paid out of "high profits of full production" but had nothing to say about "increasing wages without increasing prices." On the question of inflation, Reuther's first draft opposed "profiteering and price raising practices" without advocating governmental price controls. The second draft, however, favored a strong price control policy. Like the critics of Reuther's GM strike policy, the pro-Reuther delegates on the convention's resolutions committe saw politics, not collective bargaining, as the best arena in which to fight to hold down prices.[23]

A resolution entitled "So-Called Company Security" proposed by Nat Ganley called for union security in the form of the union shop and dues checkoff. "We stand opposed, and will struggle to prevent or eliminate," it declared, "any and all types of penalty systems which the corporations have falsely labeled 'Company Security' because these penalty systems weaken the union and undermine peaceful collective bargaining relations." This resolution was not approved by the committee, which did not otherwise address the questions of union security or company security, pivotal issues in management's postwar offensive. The delegates thus did not have the opportunity to assess the backward steps the union took in negotiations with the Big Three auto companies.[24]

The Reuther group's approach to issues at the convention indicated that its anticommunism was moderated by its need to remain within the orbit of CIO policy, which at this stage was critical of the turn toward cold war. It is noteworthy that the Reuther caucus at this time refrained from engaging in the sharp anticommunist attacks it had conducted on the floor of some previous conventions. Anticommunist comments were, as a matter of fact, offered by delegates supporting each of the two factions. Reuther's 1946 victory was in no sense a victory for cold war, anticommunist tactics.[25]

The stance of the Reuther caucus during the 1946 convention was influenced by two contrary pulls. On the one hand, it wanted to be on the opposite side of the fence from the Communists. Anticommunism had been the basis for the formation of the Reuther coalition in the late 1930s, and it remained operative in 1946 as the foundation for the group's unity. In the national CIO, however, Communists and those close to the Communist party had helped develop and implement policy through their active roles in the CIO national office and in the leadership of about a dozen CIO unions.[26] In the wake of the successful CIO wage offensive conducted under Murray's leadership, declarations of support for CIO policy were popular with the rank and file. Taking pot shots at CIO policy was not as acceptable in the UAW as it had been during the war.

The minutes of the convention's resolutions committee indicate that the pro-Reuther majority defeated a resolution supporting what CIO publicists called Murray's "three-point program" and substituted a resolution focusing on one of the points, the organization of the South. Paul Silver, a Thomas supporter who proposed the pro-Murray resolution, indicated that he would submit a minority report. This did not prove necessary, however, as Victor Reuther, the committee's chairperson, eventually submitted the pro-Murray resolution. Perhaps the desire to appear supportive of CIO policy had caused the Reutherites on the committee to change their position. At any rate, the delegates approved the resolution, which called for resisting attacks on price control, opposing "sinister legislative proposals pending in Congress," and organizing the unorganized, including a $100,000 UAW contribution to the CIO Southern organizing drive. The enthusiastic response to Murray's appearance at the convention demonstrated the strong attraction of both CIO policy and Murray personally.[27]

Like the Reuther group, the Thomas group also was pulled two ways but in a different manner. Thomas had been associated with Murray personally since Murray and Hillman, supported by Communist party leader Earl Browder, had persuaded UAW leaders to accept Thomas as the new presidential choice. Thomas had no reservations about CIO policy, even if Communists were participating in its formulation. Thomas viewed CIO policy as a progressive trade union policy, which it was. He, along with Addes and many other officials, met with Communist party representatives to discuss policy questions facing the trade union movement. Nevertheless, Thomas wanted to avoid being tarred with the Communist brush. He was aware of the negative impact charges of association with Communists had in the press and in emotional election campaigns. In the past, Thomas had always publicly distanced himself from Communists, rejecting Communist party "endorsement" of his candidacy for president and declaring, for example, in response to charges of Communist influence in a UAW strike, "You boys notice that nobody is calling me a Communist, don't you?" In joining with the Addes caucus, however, Thomas drew closer to the Communists.[28]

Thomas sought to undercut the accusation of Communist ties by bringing into the coalition with Addes union elements experienced in the tactics of anticommunism. Although the Reuther caucus refrained from raising the communist issue during most of the convention, it is nonetheless doubtful that aligning with anti-Communist party individuals helped the Thomas-Addes coalition. One of these anticommunist allies, Ben Garrison, was selected to make the nominating speech for Thomas. In the course of a weak presentation, Garrison said of Thomas, "Ofttimes I have disagreed with him on his tolerant attitude toward certain groups in our Union. Ofttimes I have vigorously opposed him on Union issues." With friends like that, Thomas did not need any enemies! As the *Daily Worker* observed, putting such individuals as Garrison forward as spokespersons only "served to confuse delegates" and "created doubt in the minds of many."[29]

The Addes-Thomas forces had not formulated a program prior to the convention and they came into the convention as two distinct groups. Rumors of a Reuther-Addes coalition had been widespread in the weeks before the convention and had dissipated only on March 21 when Addes announced to a caucus of his supporters that he would back the reelection of Thomas and other officers. This announcement did not end the long-standing division between the Addes and Thomas groups.[30] Thomas had prided himself on being a non-factional president, an independent without a caucus. During the period from 1939 to 1943, he had actually been closer to the Reuther group than to the Addes group.[31]

Thomas had personal as well as political grounds for diverging from his alliance with Reuther. After Thomas was elected to the UAW presidency in 1939, he appointed Reuther to the key post of GM Department Director. Reuther was strongly supported by Philip Murray, who became CIO president in the fall of 1940, a time of relative Communist isolation in the CIO. When the United States became allied with the Soviet Union during World War II, the CIO leadership renewed friendly relations with the Communists. Reuther, in contrast to Thomas and Murray, did not have the responsiblity of leading his own union or a union federation containing Communist-led unions. Reuther's role was that of a leader of a faction; perserving the integrity of this faction meant persevering in his anticomunism. This also led Reuther into independent actions hostile to CIO policy. As a result, Thomas increasingly found himself in conflict with Reuther on policy grounds. Thomas had helped to build up Reuther's strength, but it became obvious to Thomas that Reuther would use his power to seek the UAW presidency for himself.[32]

Richard Leonard, director of the Ford Department, also split with Reuther. As the number two person in the Reuther group, he had run against Addes for secretary-treasurer in 1941 and in 1943, falling short by only a few votes in the latter year. According to Leonard Woodcock, a leader of the Reuther caucus, Leonard began to think that he should be the top person in the right-wing group. Leonard thought that the caucus was serving only as a personal vehicle for Reuther, Woodcock recalled. Thomas, Leonard, and a few other leaders attempted to establish a third force in the union during the 1944 convention. Failing to achieve major caucus status, however, the Thomas-Leonard group reacted to the threat posed by Reuther's presidential candidacy by merging its strength with that of the Addes caucus.[33]

Reuther was elected president over Thomas by the narrow margin of 114 votes out of 8,761 cast. One major source of Reuther's strength was the General Motors locals; they provided him with 1,045 votes, which constituted 66 percent of the votes of GM delegates and nearly one-quarter of Reuther's total of 4437.6 votes. Delegates from Region 1C, covering the General Motors centers of Flint and Lansing, gave Reuther 60 percent of their votes, a substantial improvement over the 41 percent they had given him in his 1944 race against Richard Frankensteen for the vice presidency. Although Reuther's leadership in the GM strike was no doubt a factor in securing for him a large vote among GM delegates, the role of the strike in solidifying his support among GM workers should not be exaggerated. Reuther could count on support from the GM workers by virtue of his position as director of the General Motors Department. In his 1944 vice presidential race, Reuther had received 67 percent of the votes of the GM delegates even though he lost the contest by more than 900 votes.[34]

Reuther drew new strength in a few areas that enabled him to win the UAW presidency in 1946. In comparison with 1944, Reuther improved his relative vote total in nine regions, but his vote decreased in seven regions. Reuther made his most substantial gains in Region 9A, one of two regions covering the northeastern United States. He received only 10 percent of Region 9A votes in 1944 but 47 percent in 1946. He gained in excess of 500 votes from this region as compared to 1944. The Region 9A director, Charles Kerrigan, was a Reuther ally in 1946, and his staff campaigned for Reuther. An important factor in the shift in Region 9A was the retirement of Richard Frankensteen as UAW vice president. As director of the Aircraft Department, Frankensteen had enjoyed a significant influence in the region, which had a large number of aircraft plants. Frankensteen's popularity had declined, however, following his failure to win the Detroit mayoral election in the fall. He had been devoting less and less time to union duties, and in the winter newspapers had run a cartoon of Frankensteen sunning himself in Florida while General Motors workers picketed in the snow. His decision to leave the union (he soon took a management job) added to the negative reaction toward him; booing greeted his appearance at the convention. Although he was a supporter of the Thomas-Addes forces, Frankensteen's ability to influence the delegates was slight because he could no longer provide services to the local unions or international staff jobs. As Frankensteen himself recalled, " . . . I was not able to deliver my strength. While I was there I was there to protect them, too. But when I was out, they did not want to be on the 'outs' with Walter, who was going to be a powerhouse, so they switched over. I could not deliver that strength."[35]

Reuther also increased his strength considerably in Region 1, which encompassed Detroit's east side. This was the UAW's largest region, with 1680 convention votes in 1946. Reuther received about 40 percent of the vote in 1944 and 51 percent in 1946, gaining about 430 votes in the process. Reuther's advance in this highly political and factionalized region was a personal success and was not shared by the candidates running for the vice presidencies with his support. Only 24 percent of the vote from Detroit's east side went in a bloc to the three right-wing candidates. Another 19 percent of the region's votes were cast by delegates voting for two of the three Reuther-backed candidates. Reuther gained, then, among the large group of split-ticket voters in Region 1.

The rapid decline in aircraft production after the war brought about a substantial reduction in employment and union membership in plants in the industry. Delegates from aircraft plants represented about 220,000 workers at the 1944 UAW convention but only 150,000 at the 1946 convention. Even the latter figure was considerably higher than the actual membership because a number of local unions from plants that were closed or closing were still able to send full contingents of delegates based on previously paid-up membership. Union funding for the aircraft division had declined by more than 80 percent between 1944 and 1946, while funding for the union's departments and regions remained relatively stable. Frankensteen's aircraft division had been the largest single component of the union during the war, receiving one-third of the funding going to all the regions and more than six times as much as the GM Department received at the war's peak. In the six months preceding the 1946 convention, the aircraft division received only 70 percent as much financial support as the GM Department. At the convention, Reuther received slightly more than one-third of the votes of the reduced aircraft workers' group, about the same proportion that he had received in 1944. The decline in the voting strength of the aircraft locals, however, provided Reuther with a relative gain of more than 300 votes.[36]

Reuther's presidential victory in 1946 was not due to any broad shift in delegate allegiance to him or his caucus. Reuther benefited rather from the decline of the aircraft industry and the departure of its director. He also made some gains as an individual leader among delegates not strongly allied with either caucus. Although Reuther's victory was primarily a personal one, it was nonetheless of historic importance. For the first time in seven years, a leader of one of the union's two major caucuses had sought the union's highest office. Given the serious threat to his position, Thomas abandoned his independent position and merged his modest strength with the other major caucus. The traditional balance between the two groups was thereby disrupted, and the prospect of factional warfare for control of the union loomed.

Following Reuther's close victory over Thomas in the presidential balloting, the two sides maneuvered for victory in the vice presidential contests. Reuther and several regional directors met with CIO representative Allan Haywood to make know their opposition to the suggestion that Thomas be a candidate for a vice presidency. Perhaps because of this pressure, the CIO offered Thomas a job. According to the *New York Times*, however, several Reuther delegates called upon Thomas and urged him to run. Both caucuses had internal disputes over their vice presidential nominees. The steering committee of the Reuther caucus selected Richard Gosser and Jack Livingston as the group's candidates, but an ACTU leader reported that when Melvin Bishop supporters "raised hell," Reuther negotiated a "last minute deal" for Bishop to run in the first vice presidential contest. Disagreement also was reported within the Thomas-Addes caucus over the selection of Thomas over Leonard for the first vice presidential position. Both were nominated for the post, but Thomas received the endorsement of the caucus; Leonard ran only to draw anti-Thomas votes away from Bishop. Thomas received the highest vote of the convention, 4,474 votes to 3,913 for Bishop and 200 for Leonard.[37]

Thomas received 151 more votes for vice president than he had received for president. Bishop's total, on the other hand, was 524 votes below that cast for Reuther on the first ballot. Thomas gained some votes from both Addes and Reuther supporters who wanted to see him in a top leadership post other than the presidency. The unpopularity of Bishop, however, was the most significant factor accounting for Thomas's victory. This was reflected not only in the low vote for Bishop but in the fact that two-thirds of the relative gain in Thomas's vote came in Region 1, where Bishop was a regional director. Bishop, a former member of the Addes caucus, had become highly unpopular in his region, especially with Briggs Local 212 and Hudson Local 154, for alleged collaboration with management in the firing of militants. Local 212 had called for an investigation of Bishop for alleged involvement in the beatings of Local 212 members. Carl Haessler recalled that Bishop was "a pretty rough customer." Shortly before the convention a UAW international representative picketed UAW headquarters, charging Bishop with beating him in his office. Bishop replied that the accusation was the beginning of the campaign of John Anderson, president of Local 155 and a well-known Communist, for regional director.[38]

Leonard, director of the Ford Department, won the second vice presidential race by a mere 42 votes more than John Livingston, the director of Region 5, which covered an area from southern Illinois to New Mexico. The voting patterns in this contest were similar to those in the presidential race. Leonard, however, ran substantially better than Thomas had in the presidential race in the two Detroit regions, making a relative gain of 580 votes. As might have been expected, a substantial share of Leonard's gain in the Detroit area came from the Ford plants; his relative improvement among Ford delegates nationwide was about 325 votes. Leonard also showed a net gain of 125 votes from Chrysler plants on Detroit's east side. Leonard had been president of a Chrysler local and also had served as a regional director in Detroit.[39]

Although he lost the election, Livingston showed greater strength than Reuther in some areas. In GM plants, Livingston received 175 more votes than Reuther had received. Livingston had worked at the GM plant in St. Louis and had served as chairperson of his local strike committee during the 1936–1937 recognition strike. Between 1939 and 1942, Livingston functioned as vice chairperson and then chairperson of the national negotiating committee for GM. These positions gave him support among GM workers that was not available to Reuther. Livingston also improved his vote in comparison with Reuther's in the aircraft plants, gaining about 280 more votes than Reuther received. He gained nearly 200 votes in Region 9A. Livingston's gains in the latter region and in the aircraft plants were due primarily to the switch from Thomas to Livingston of all 122 votes of Local 669, the Wright Aeronautical plant in Patterson, New Jersey. This switch came amidst charges of gangster pressure on the local union.[40]

The results of the three contested ballots showed that those voting for the Thomas-Addes-Leonard candidates on all three roll calls constituted the largest group in the convention. A total of 3,530 votes went to the straight Addes-Thomas-Leonard ticket, about 7 percent more than the 3,290 votes cast for the straight Reuther ticket. Delegates voting for two of three Addes-backed candidates cast 850 votes, compared with 982 votes cast by those voting for two of three Reuther-supported hopefuls. Split-ticket voters cast the majority of their votes for Reuther in the presidential race (58 percent), Thomas in the first vice presidential contest (52 percent), and Livingston in the second vice presidential race (51 percent). Although the Reuther caucus lost the two vice presidential contests, the voting patterns showed that Reuther's ability to appeal to the uncommitted was an important asset.[41]

The Addes-Thomas-Leonard coalition followed up its triumphs in the two vice-presidential races with victories in nine of 18 regional director contests. The Reuther caucus won eight regional directorships, and one seat went to an independent who leaned toward the Addes group. In these contests for regional director, all incumbents seeking reelection were returned to office. William Stevenson, a Leonard ally, was elected as one of Detroit's two west side regional directors in place of Leonard. Emil Mazey, a Socialist aligned with the Reuther caucus, was elected in Melvin Bishop's place as one of Detroit's two east side regional directors, even though he had not yet returned home from the armed forces.

The regional directorship was an important source of power in the union. Local unions not only depended on the regional office for a variety of services, but the latter also provided local officers opportunities for advancement. Although the votes for regional director were not recorded in 1946, the roll calls for the three contested offices indicate regional voting patterns. In nearly every region, a majority of the delegates voted a straight ticket in line with the affiliation of the regional director. The most notable exception was Michigan's Flint-Lansing region, where the majority of delegates voted for all three Reuther candidates even though the regional director was a supporter of the Addes-Thomas caucus. This reflected the influence of Reuther's role as leader of the GM section of the union, which was concentrated in the region, and the traditional independence of the strong Flint locals.[42]

The directors of collective bargaining departments, like the regional directors, brought strength to the caucuses with which they were affiliated because of the services they could provide to local unions and because they could promote local leaders to staff positions. Although the collective bargaining department and the regional offices were the two most important sources of factional strength for each of the two caucuses, ideological groups in strong locals represented sources of strength that were relatively independent of the power of higher officials. In his campaign for the office of secretary-treasurer against Addes in 1943, Ford Department Director Richard Leonard received only a minority of votes of the Ford delegates because of the strong left-wing presence in the largest Ford group, Local 600. In 1946, the ACTU brought some additional backing to the Reuther group as did the Communists to the Thomas-Addes-Leonard group. The power of ideological groups and strong locals in Detroit counteracted the influence of patronage and accounted for the closeness of the contests for office in the two largest UAW regions.[43]

The weighted voting strength of the Thomas-Addes-Leonard-aligned regional directors in April 1946, came to 330 as compared to 264 for the Reuther-aligned directors. Counting the votes of the four officers, the result was 510 votes for the Addes group compared to 324 votes for the Reuther group and 60 votes for an independent. The distribution of voting strength, at least on the surface, gave the anti-Reuther group a larger majority than it had previously enjoyed. Reuther's drive for the presidency had intensified factional rivalries. Several regional directors who had worked with Reuther in the past now shifted to the Addes-Thomas-Leonard coalition. They saw in Reuther's accession to the presidency the danger that the union would become dominated by a single individual with a consequent reduction in their power as regional directors. With Reuther people preparing to run against them in their areas, Addes recalled, "they had to come into some force that would give them the support."[44]

In his victory speech to the convention, Reuther assured the delegates that he would cooperate closely with the CIO. " . . . as long as I am the President of this great organization," he declared, "it will be a source of strength to President Murray and the CIO." The new UAW president also stressed the need to establish unity within the auto workers union itself. Speaking to the leader of the left-center caucus, Reuther said, "I want to say to George Addes, who I think will be elected your Secretary-Treasurer, that I extend my hand to him and together we will stand united." At the next convention, Reuther pledged, there would not be "two pieces of Union, but . . . one organization united from the top to the very bottom." According to Reuther critic Carl Haessler, "Reuther conducted himself in . . . a virtually flawless manner in the chair . . . . He made unity his watchword . . . . Reuther by offering unity seemed to the uncommitted to offer peace to the UAW . . . [to] shape it into a weapon not only for trade union ends but for labor political ends . . . ."[45]

Upon his unanimous election as secretary-treasurer, Addes responded positively but with some ambivalence to Reuther's offer of unity. "I hope and pray," Addes declared,

> That our newly elected President will carry out the policies and pronouncements he made after his election . . . because with those policies and pronouncements I am convinced (in my own mind) that those differences, those bickerings that go on in Local Unions as well as in convention will be minimized and . . . we can unite our forces . . . . I believe if we are both sincere—and I am in my remarks, and I believe he is, too—we can build a tremendous Union . . . .[46]

Addes's hesitation was an indication that he was uncertain that unity with Reuther was really possible. Haessler observed that "Addes had the greatest distaste for Reuther personally," and this may have caused the irresolution in his remarks. Addes conceded more to Reuther than he might have, however, on the question of unity when he voiced the opinion that if both Reuther and he were sincere, "we can establish the most progressive policies that the Union has ever been able to operate under heretofore." Following the convention, Addes again remarked that there were prospects for greater internal unity in the UAW than ever before. These statements made clear the view, expressed by Addes years after leaving union office, that there really were no issues involved in the factional conflict, only personalities and rivalry for office. "Walter and I got along, when business was at hand," Addes recalled. "We generally saw eye to eye." The implication was that both sides were progressive and that Reuther was an advanced progressive. The left wingers in the Addes-Thomas coalition could not have disagreed more. They instead shared the view expressed by the *Daily Worker* that "the chief source of UAW factionalism has always been Reuther's opposition to, or reservations upon CIO policy and Murray's leadership." Addes was, of course, aware of those policy differences, but he may have regarded the policy differences as stemming from the factionalism rather than the other way around.[47]

Reuther soon made clear that his conception of unity did not include all UAW members. At a press conference following the convention, he said that he would seek to mobilize 90 percent of the membership around the top leadership, "thereby isolating the 10 percent which has outside loyalties." After Reuther stated, in response to a question, that the Communist party was such an outside group, the correspondent for the *Daily Worker* asked him about the Socialists and Trotskyites. Reuther responded that no "outside" group, "whether Communist, Trotskyite or Socialist" would dictate to the UAW. Although he included Socialists in his list of outside groups, he acknowledged that he had been a Socialist party member for about one year and that one of the candidates he supported, Emil Mazey, might be a Socialist. Denying any "witch-hunting" intention, Reuther nevertheless affirmed, "We are interested . . . in trying to break up and isolate a small disciplined minority." Reuther thereby made clear his intention to use anticommunism to fight the left wing of the Addes-Thomas-Leonard coalition.[48]

Reuther's anticommunist pronouncement at the end of the convention was welcomed by the *Detroit Free Press*. "If Reuther does live up to his pledge to war against the Communist elements," it editorialized, "he will be doing his union a service." *Detroit Labor Trends*, a periodical that kept management abreast of union developments, also expressed appreciation for Reuther's pronouncement. "Dissidents," it commented, "will be dropped overboard where possible—a factor which, if it works may improve the outlook for discipline in the shops." Newspaper and magazine praise for Reuther's approach was to be a continuing feature of the UAW factional battle between the tenth and eleventh UAW conventions.[49]

The 1946 UAW convention helped create the preconditions for a factional struggle that would lead to a turning point in the history of the union. In the wake of Reuther's drive for the presidency, officials and staff members who had only been peripherally involved in caucus politics now lined up more fully with one caucus or the other. With the ouster of Thomas from the presidency, the buffer between the two caucuses was removed. This development, combined with the pressure of the antilabor drive, brought about an intense struggle for control of the union.

Both sides had substantial administrative powers and support among secondary leaders and the rank and file, who became very active in the battle. During this warfare, the anticommunism of the Reuther caucus, which was relatively dormant at the tenth convention, became increasingly important. Developments in the cold war increased domestic anticommunism, and the passage of the Taft-Hartley Act would put the Thomas-Addes-Leonard coalition, which advocated a popular front, at a disadvantage in the intraunion battle. In the early skirmishes, however, each side had opportunities to present itself as the group with the better program for the union.

The first International Executive Board meeting following the tenth UAW convention opened on April 16, 1946. Many major questions not decided by the convention, such as wage-price policy, political action, and foreign policy were left for the board to decide. George Addes presented a comprehensive program to the board that had been agreed to by his caucus before the meeting. In the view of the Communists, "non-Communist progressive forces" had for the first time taken the initiative away from Reuther on overall program and policies.[50]

The initial draft of the program had actually been prepared by Communists and had then been modified by the leaders of the Addes-Thomas-Leonard coalition. Walter Reuther had not seen the program before it was presented to the board, and he was consequently miffed. After defeating a motion to table the proposal until Reuther could prepare a statement, the board approved the Addes program by a vote of 14 to seven. Reuther told the press that he thought some of the items in the program were "very wrong," particularly the statement on foreign policy and "another making Red-baiting along with Catholic, Protestant, Negro, and Jew baiting a cardinal sin." Within a few days, Reuther drafted an alternative policy statement expressing his own point of view on the questions on which the board had acted.[51]

The Addes and Reuther programs were quite similar in a number of respects. Although leaders of both caucuses had negotiated the union's contracts with the Big Three automakers, both programs contained either explicit or implicit criticism of those contracts, reflecting questions raised by left-wing and rank-and-file union members. Both programs supported union security and opposed company security.

Despite his initial criticism of the board's statement on foreign policy, Reuther adopted a similar position in his program. The board majority called for the unity of the United States, the Soviet Union, and Great Britain, supported the WFTU, and attacked the "Winston Churchills and William Randolph Hearsts" who were trying to divide the United Nations. Reuther also explicitly urged support for the unity of the Big Three. The new UAW president adopted as his own the foreign policy statement of the CIO-PAC issued just before the UAW board meeting: "We repudiate all efforts calculated to weaken or destroy friendship and close collaboration among the Big Three. We reject proposals for American participation in any bloc or alliance which is inimical to their unity." Those who "seek to use the great power of America to win world domination for themselves," the statement proclaimed, "must be isolated and defeated."

In his wide-ranging program, Reuther refrained from the sharp criticism of the Big Three powers his brother Victor had voiced in the convention's resolutions committee. Just one week prior to the board meeting, Walter Reuther and the members of his caucus had boycotted a banquet for Philip Murray in Detroit. The resulting negative publicity tended to undermine Reuther's attempt to appear as a CIO supporter and a force for unity in the UAW.[52] Reuther chose, therefore, to align himself with the CIO position on international relations rather than strike a discordant note. That he decided to "subscribe wholeheartedly" to the CIO-PAC policy statement rather than put in his own words a similar anti-cold war sentiment is significant. Within 18 months he was to speak favorably of Truman's foreign policy.

Both the board majority and Reuther supported independent political action by labor. The board majority proposed that the union "work toward the eventual formation of a broad third party based on the thinking and interests of millions of the labor, farmer, progressive and other people of our nation." Although cautioning against a premature and narrow third party effort, the board program attacked President Truman and his administration for "yielding and capitulating on issue after issue to the forces of reaction." Reuther's approach to the formation of a third party was identical to that of the board majority, but the UAW president avoided criticizing Truman. Reuther, however, stressed the need to fight for the "domestic and international policies championed by the late President Roosevelt."

The board program emphasized the importance of the 1946 elections, pledging to give full support to candidates of the major parties who backed Roosevelt's policies and encouraging the entry of independent candidates into the race where the major party candidates were unacceptable. Furthermore, the board program reaffirmed its support for the CIO-PAC against the efforts of "the forces of reaction . . . [and] also certain groupings posing as progressives" trying to "undermine" the PAC and damage the CIO-allied National Citizens PAC. The latter statement was an implied slap at such Reuther-allied groups as the Michigan Commonwealth Federation. The Reuther program mentioned neither the upcoming elections nor the need to support PAC. The long-term third party strategies of the two programs were quite similar, but the board majority, unlike Reuther, evidenced a concern for immediate political activity and a willingness to break with the Truman administration.

The differences between the two programs were quite marked in the field of wage-price policy. The board program asserted that wage increases should be obtained from technological advances and profits rather than from higher prices. Reuther, of course, agreed that wage increases should not generally be reflected in price increases, but his program stated that price increases would be necessary in some industries and some parts of industries that could not "otherwise raise their wages to a decent level." The board majority emphasized that "higher wages did not result from any so-called partnership of industry and labor" but "had to be fought for and won." The Reuther program looked forward to a future in which higher real wages for UAW members would be obtained primarily out of the efficiency of improved technological processes and out of the economies that flow from the steady operation of industry at a high level output. Reuther did not supplement this "progress through technology" concept with the idea that wage increases should come out of profits. Although believing that wage increases should be taken out of profits, the board majority affirmed its support for the right of capital to a fair return on its investment. Despite this assertion of support for capitalism, the board majority's statement, on balance, supported a "struggle" approach to obtaining higher wages while the Reuther approach envisioned higher wages as resulting from the operation of a balanced, technologically advancing economy.

Both the board program and Reuther's program supported price control and asserted that the UAW would have to reopen wage negotiations if price controls were eliminated. The board program, however, in a comment directed at Reuther, declared that the illusion that the union already had fought and won the price battle and had prevented a price increase in GM products had to be abandoned. The board, in setting forth its price policy, also criticized several other Reuther concepts. It opposed showing any concern with whether the corporations were protected in maintaining their high profit levels. Reuther, it will be recalled, declared during the GM strike that he wished that company to be the "most prosperous" one in the automobile industry. The corporations, the board asserted, were adequately capable of protecting their own profit levels without any help from labor representatives. The board also opposed a proposal to allow prices to rise and fall on a seasonal basis that had been advocated by Reuther and a proposal for an up-and-down wage escalator, tied to the cost of living, that was being pushed by Trotskyite supporters of Reuther.[53] In another implicit attack on Reuther, the board criticized the lack of a coordinated CIO wage strategy in the GM strike. For the first time since the end of the war, the Addes-Thomas forces aggressively challenged Reuther's leadership in the economic arena.

The sharpest contrast between the two programs concerned communism and red-baiting. The board majority based its position on the article of the UAW constitution that stated it be a union objective "to unite in one organization, regardless of religion, race, creed, color, political affiliation or nationality all employees under the jurisdiciton of the International Union." The board majority declared, "the constitutional rights of our membership to belong to our union regardless of religion, race, creed, color, political affiliation or nationality shall be fully protected from all forms of Catholic-baiting, Protestant-baiting, Negro-baiting and Red-baiting." The Reuther program, on the other hand, called for the enforcement of the section of the constitution adopted in 1941 that called for barring from union office those associated with "Communist, Nazi or fascist" organizations that owed their "allegiance to any government other than the United States or Canada."[54] To bring this constitutional dead letter to life, Reuther said, "We must . . . be vigilant to protect the union against those whose loyalties to groups outside the union and to foreign powers causes [sic] them to take positions and from time to time shift positions on union issues, without regard for the welfare of either the union, its members, or our country." The board program ignored the section of the union's constitution cited by Reuther, and he in turn ignored the constitutional statement of purpose that was the basis for the board's position against red-baiting.

The Communists, for their part, contended that Reuther knew that the anticommunist clause did not apply to any member of the Communist party since, they maintained, that their party owed no allegiance to any foreign government. They insisted that the Supreme Court had so held in the *Schneiderman* case, which was not precisely accurate.[55] This unsuccessful attempt by the United States government to denaturalize a leading Communist had taken place when the United States and Soviet governments were comrades-in-arms. As cold-war hostility between the United States and the Soviet Union intensified, an anticommunist climate like that which had led to the adoption of the UAW's constitutional amendment developed once again. The board's position in favor of the democratic rights of the membership and against divisive red-baiting stopped short of advocating the removal of the anticommunist clause from the UAW constitution and the right of Communists to hold union office. As a result, the semilegal status within the union of the Communist allies of Addes, Thomas, and Leonard gave Reuther an effective weapon against his opponents. The Addes-Thomas-Leonard coalition remained on the defensive on the communist issue.

The board had enacted a new policy, but it still had to select the personnel to help carry out the program. Also, the Thomas-Addes-Leonard coalition had to contend with the fact that Reuther was now president of the union. In his position as president, Reuther gained important powers. He had the authority both to assign tasks to other officers and board members and to withdraw the assignments. If he withdrew an assignment, however, the board could overturn the decision. Pending the approval of the board, the president also had the power to appoint international representatives and technical and professional staff other than in the office of the secretary-treasurer. Reuther was in a position to split the Thomas-Addes-Leonard coalition by bargaining and making deals.[56]

When staff assignments were discussed at the April board meeting, Reuther asserted that he had no intention of conducting a purge. He had already made clear, however, that he wanted to remove from the union's staff anyone whom he considered a Communist. Equally important was his desire to appoint to key positions those who would support his policies and his caucus. In the bargaining over appointments, Reuther concentrated on those positions that permitted the incumbent to exercise political and ideological influence on the membership. He succeeded in getting board approval for his selection of directors of the Publication, Education, and Fair Practices Departments as well as two of four staff members in the UAW's Washington office. The other politically sensitive positions went to Vice President Leonard, whom Reuther appointed head of the Political Action Department and to whom the other two Washington staff members were assigned.[57]

The members of the Thomas-Addes-Leonard caucus were divided in their response to Reuther's appointments. Leonard voted to confirm Reuther's appointment of his brother Victor as head of the Education Department as did three regional directors associated with the Thomas-Addes-Leonard caucus. Victor Reuther was approved for the position by a weighted vote of 473 to 361; 12 board members supported the selection, and nine opposed it. Thomas objected that the appointment was "factional," and Addes believed it was "unwise . . . to appoint in the Education Department or any other . . . one whose philosophies and ideologies have not been in the past in line with the policy of the International Union . . . ." Addes was referring to the fact that Victor had espoused positions during the war that were contrary to UAW policy but which his brother Walter, as a top union official, had refrained from adopting.[58]

In the discussion concerning the appointment of director of the Fair Practices Department, Reuther indicated his desire to appoint Addes, who had been the chairperson of the old Fair Practices Committee, to the board committee responsible for supervising the department. Addes, however, did not want to serve on such a committee if the authority of the committee chairperson were to be divided with that of the director of the department. Contradicting his long-standing opposition to so-called reverse discrimination, Reuther rejected a suggestion to appoint Addes director by declaring that he felt obligated to appoint a Black unionist to the post because of the constitutional change approved at the convention. Although establishing the Fair Practices Department did not require appointing a Black director, Reuther was certainly right that Blacks and other union members concerned with antidiscrimination activity expected a Black to be appointed to the new position. After the board considered establishing a women's division within the Fair Practices Department, Reuther shifted ground again and appointed himself director and William Oliver, a Black international representative on Leonard's staff whom Reuther characterized as nonpartisan, codirector. A woman codirector was to be appointed later.[59]

The Fair Practices Department appointments were narrowly approved by a weighted vote of 392.5 to 374, with 11 board members in favor and eight opposed. In this ballot, Reuther picked up the votes of two members of the opposing caucus who had voted against him on the Education Department appointment. Only Addes, Thomas, and three regional director voted against Reuther on both the Education and Fair Practices directorships. Although the Addes forces had won a victory on the union's basic statement of policy, Reuther capitalized on divisions among his opponents to gain the upper hand in the selection of personnel to implement union policy. The control of such key political positions as Education Director gave Reutherites access to many local union leaders and the opportunity to influence thousands of rank-and-file activists ideologically.[60]

In the months following the first postconvention board meeting, the quesiton of staff appointments remained a controversial matter. Officers and board members of both caucuses accused their opponents of dismissing staff members aligned with the rival caucus. Although Addes caucus members dismissed some members of their staffs, it was Reuther as president who was in a position to seek the removal of staff members assigned to other officers and board members, except those on Addes's staff. Moreover, Reuther had the weapon of anticommunism to use against staff members aligned with the Thomas-Addes-Leonard caucus. The "Communist" charge could and sometimes did cause some officers and board members to hesitate in defending their own staff members. On the other hand, when the union had to reduce expenditures in the summer of 1946, the board majority approved a plan that resulted in a somewhat greater layoff rate for Reuther-aligned staff members than for those aligned with the Addes caucus.[61]

Shortly after the April board meeting, Maurice Sugar, UAW General Counsel and left-wing leader of the Addes caucus, warned that failure to defend the members of their own staffs would be fatal to the board majority. Reuther "is out to eliminate the generals by destroying their colonels and majors and captains and lieutenants," Sugar warned. "To the extent that he gets a foothold in the membership who now constitute his opposition, he will have vantage points to move farther and farther." It was necessary to stop Reuther's purge at the beginning or all was lost. "How could these appointees, or anyone else for that matter," he argued,

> be expected to support them in future, when those very officers, after being elected as a result of the loyalty and work of these appointees, turn their backs on them? . . . those leaders . . . will only have themselves to blame when they see defections from the ranks of their supporters and find that those who fought loyally for them throughout the years quit them in disgust because they have been betrayed and deserted.

Although board members aligned with the Thomas-Addes-Leonard caucus did not abandon their staffs, some loyal supporters received unfair treatment. The board, for example, failed to restore the left-wing William Levitt to his Educational Director position upon his return from the armed forces despite his seniority.[62] The contest between the two caucuses, however, was to be determined by their relative strength among the union's membership. Political, economic, and union issues would all influence rank-and-file thinking about the emerging battle for control of the auto workers' union.

Chapter Seven

Characteristics of the Two
UAW Caucuses and Trends

The principal support for each of the two UAW caucuses came through the organizational base its leaders had developed by administering a collective bargaining department or one of the other international union departments or by serving as regional directors. Both groups were patronage machines, coalitions of officeholders who provided staff services to local unions and advancement opportunities to local officials.

As John Barnard remarked, the union's political structure resembled a feudal regime more than a two-party system.[1] At the top of the structure were the officers and regional directors, each of whom had an independent power base. This was especially true of regional directors because they were elected by convention delegates in their regions. Directors of the departments were appointed by the president with the board's approval. Directors of the collective bargaining departments, in particular, acquired independent political strength because, like the regional directors, they provided services to the local unions. If they provided satisfactory service to the locals, the regional directors and collective bargaining department heads could generally count on support from the local unions. Regional and department staff members devoted considerable time to garnering support in the local unions. These staff members usually came from one of the strong locals in the region or department and retained personal links with their local unions. A loyal, skilled, and politically well-connected staff was a board member's most important source of strength. Board members sometimes interceded with companies to gain favors for friends and offered its supporters such minor perquisites as appointment to convention committees. An extra week or two out of the plant to attend a convention out of town was a nice break from the drudgery, noise, and dirt of normal work routine.

Incumbent board members had a considerable advantage in the UAW's political structure. Given their independent strength, board members could extract favors by offering to bring their voting bloc behind one or another candidate for the officer positions which were elected by the convention as a whole.

It is not surprising, then, that there was a good deal of shifting back and forth between the two major UAW caucuses. Arnold Atwood and Joseph Mattson, for example, were in the Reuther caucus in the early 1940s but joined the Thomas-Addes-Leonard group in 1946–1947.[2]

Despite the shifting nature of the UAW's alliances, two principal factions emerged in the auto union by the end of the 1930s. Although contesting for offices was the principal purpose of the caucuses, each developed a distinct outlook. The philosophy of the two groups derived from the views of their leading personalities and the orientations of the organized political groups which participated in them.

The influence of the philosophy of an individual personality was especially marked in the caucus led by Walter Reuther. The right-wing caucus for a time called itself the Reuther-Leonard caucus when Richard Leonard came close to defeating George Addes for secretary-treasurer.[3] By the end of the war, however, Walter Reuther was the single leader, the "star" of the right-wing caucus. Born in 1907 in Wheeling, West Virginia, Reuther was a second generation American whose parents were immigrants from Germany and Lutherans. Reuther's father, Valentine, was active in the labor and Socialist movements. Valentine Reuther served for a time as president of the Ohio Valley Trades and Labor Assembly, ran as a Socialist for a seat in the state legislature, and campaigned for Eugene Debs for president. When Walter was 11 years old, Valentine took Walter and his younger brother, Victor, to visit Debs in a West Virginia federal prison where the Socialist leader was imprisoned for his opposition to World War I. An important feature of the Reuthers' family life was the regular Sunday debates which the four boys engaged in under their father's direction.[4] "Walter . . . became a powerful, self-assured speaker, with inexhaustible verbal energy and an effortless capacity to weave ideas and facts into a persuasive message."[5]

Walter early proved himself to be talented at work as well as verbally proficient. He moved to Detroit in 1927 and by 1929 was die room supervisor at the Ford Motor Company's new River Rouge plant. While working the afternoon shift, Walter completed high school and began taking classes at Detroit City College. He also started to save and invest money. When Victor joined him in Detroit, the two joined the Socialist party and became active on picket lines and in student Socialist work. After Walter was laid off from Ford, he and Victor embarked in 1933 on a European journey which featured a period working at the Gorki auto plant in the Soviet Union. Upon returning to the United States in the fall of 1935, Reuther's outlook was pro-Soviet. When he began working in the fledgling UAW early in 1936, he was a member of the Socialist party and a friend of the Communist party.[6]

Although he was new to UAW activism, the absence of well-known union figures in Detroit, Reuther's speaking ability, and the support he received from the union's left wing led to Reuther's election as a member of the union's executive board at the 1936 South Bend convention. With his brothers Victor and Roy, Walter worked alongside Communists Wyndham Mortimer and Bob Travis, with other non-Communist leftists like Stanley Nowak, and with nonradical trade unionists like Richard Frankensteen in the early difficult struggles to establish the UAW in the auto industry. The three Reuther brothers were part of a small group of Socialist party members active in the UAW. There also were members of other radical noncommunist groups active in the UAW, but, in the struggles of 1936–1937, the Socialists and Communists within the UAW worked well together. Differences on domestic and foreign policy issues between the Socialist and Communist parties and the decision of the Communist group within the UAW not to support Victor in two contests for state CIO office in 1938 and 1939 led to a permanent break between the Reuthers and the Communist party.[7]

Although ideological differences between the Socialist and Communist parties were a factor in Walter Reuther's shift from a pro-communist to an anticommunist position, he also had his differences with the Socialist party. As a leader of the UAW, Reuther endorsed and worked to reelect Frank Murphy as governor of Michigan even though the Socialist party fielded its own candidate in the election. Believing that he would have a greater opportunity to bring about change as a leader of the UAW and CIO than as a Socialist, he dropped his membership in the party in 1939. The parting was a friendly one, however. While his period of cooperation with the Communist party was brief, Reuther had been brought up in the Socialist party and maintained a social democratic outlook. He believed that the major social problems had economic roots and that capitalism was in need of radical reform. A politically aware and active union movement, Reuther believed, could help prompt the kind of government action needed to deal with the problems of capitalism. As the postwar period began, he expressed the hope that new national policies could "remedy the central flaw of our economy, wiping out the fitful succession of boom and bust, feast and famine, and providing stable mass distribution of the goods and services made available by mass production."[8]

Reuther was not only an articulate advocate of a social democratic viewpoint, he was also hard working and ambitious. "He worked hard like a horse," Stanley Nowak recalled in characterizing Reuther as a "workaholic."[9] Reuther attracted a cadre of like-minded social democrats. Although some of Reuther's coworkers were still members of the Socialist party, most joined with him in the belief that the party was too narrow; they considered the UAW a better organizational vehicle to achieve change. They sought to infuse the UAW with social democratic thinking and believed that an industrial union led by far-sighted leaders would a play crucial role in bringing about the fundamental reform of capitalism that they advocated.[10]

One major source of Reuther's support was the ACTU. During the early part of the century, when Socialists contended for leadership in the AFL, the Militia of Christ for Social Service was a lay Catholic organization supporting the more conservative AFL leaders. The ACTU's apprehension about the Communists' role in the CIO was similar to the earlier organization's anxiety about the Socialists. Although opposed to Socialist ideology and to Socialist activity in the political arena, the ACTU regarded Communism and Socialism as qualitatively different movements. "These people," Detroit ACTU said of the Socialists in 1943, "differ materially from the Communists in that they are democrats, they have principles, and they lack the intrinsically evil character of the CP [Communist Party]." The friendliness of this comment stemmed from the fact that the Socialists were opposing the Communists. ACTU's active cooperation with Reuther began once he opposed the Communists in the late 1930s.[11]

Although anticommunism was ACTU's central interest, it provided its members with a more liberal labor philsophy than that of the earlier Militia of Christ, which had opposed minimum wages, eight-hour legislation, industrial unionism, and independent political action by labor. Like its predecessor, ACTU had official backing from the Catholic Church but church policy had changed substantially. The Conference of American Bishops in 1919 endorsed public housing, minimum wage, social security, and other measures of state intervention in social and economic life. ACTU, for its part, supported industrial unions, the guaranteed annual wage, credit unions, consumer cooperatives, and labor unity. It declared its opposition to all forms of racial discrimination. "Individual members are urged to refrain from the use of terms of racial opprobrium or terms which are offensive to racial groups," an ACTU policy statement explained. ACTU members should "make good-humored protest when such terms are used in their presence."[12]

As far as the CIO was concerned, ACTU was relatively conservative. During the war in Spain, ACTU supported Franco against the Republic. In discussing the use of the strike weapon, ACTU declared that specific conditions had to be met before a union embarked on a work stoppage: Grievances must be intolerable; peaceful methods of settlement must have been exhausted; reasonable prospects must exist for success; and incidental injury to third parties must be kept to minimum. This approach led the ACTU to support some of the provisions of the Taft-Hartley Act, such as the ban on secondary boycotts, even while it criticized the legislation. The ACTU was particularly conservative on the issue of women's equality. It held that women should be discouraged from working and during the war opposed the "promotion of nursery schools designed to lure mothers of small children into war plants."[13]

During the war, ACTU's activity decreased, but it continued its opposition to Communists in internal union controversies just as it combated leftists in general in the political arena. When the war ended, ACTU activity increased. It supported Reuther's approach in the GM strike, both because of its long association with him and because it saw the GM strike program as similar to Catholic concepts of the just price and the just wage. As the Detroit chapter of the ACTU saw it, "Reuther policies have been constantly in harmony with the principles laid down in the Papal Encyclicals." The ACTU hoped that labor and industry would cooperate in planning the economy and in establishing a just social order.[14]

The Catholic hierarchy supported the ACTU and priests were active in the leadership of the organization as well as in teaching labor schools for the organization. Membership was open to practising Catholic unionists, with the chaplain or spiritual director deciding on all religious questions. The chaplain, who was appointed by the archbishop, also served on the executive board, and he or any priest designated by him was an ex-officio member of all committees. The chaplain obtained a report from the parish priest on new members. Labor schools presented instruction in Catholic labor philosophy, public speaking, and parliamentary procedure. Nationally, 100 ACTU labor schools were graduating 7,500 students in 1948. Furthermore, social and religious activities such as retreats, nocturnal adoration meetings, communion breakfasts, and special masses drew more participants than the chapters' secular activities.[15]

In internal UAW matters, support for Reuther, the ideological leader of anticommunism in the UAW, was the touchstone of ACTU policy. Before the 1946 convention, the ACTU had sought "to heal the rift" between Thomas and Leonard on the one hand and Reuther on the other, all of whom had had ACTU support. When these efforts to restore anticommunist unity failed, the ACTU abandoned Thomas and Leonard while maintaining its alliance with Reuther. Through its labor schools, its weekly newspaper, and its caucuses, the Detroit ACTU, with a 1946 membership of 1,000, provided the Reuther caucus with considerable support. It provided some support to the Reuther caucus at times in Milwaukee, Saginaw, Michigan, and North Tarrytown, New York. Although the ACTU did not dominate the Reuther caucus, as some of its critics asserted, it did add a strong element of conservatism to the Reuther-led coalition.[16]

The Trotskyites were another ideological group that sided with Reuther at the UAW convention. Some individuals the *Daily Worker* characterized as Trotskyites had been supporters of the Thomas-Leonard attempt to form a third force group in 1944 and had played a prominent role in the Thomas group in 1946. The principal Trotskyite organizations, however, supported Reuther. Both the Socialist Workers' party and the Workers' party thus supported the GM strike program and saw in it "revolutionary implications." They backed Reuther as the most progressive UAW leader and shared his antagonism to the Communist party. Their membership among auto workers was, however, quite small.[17]

The Communists were the principal organized ideological group within the Thomas-Addes-Leonard coalition. Between 2,000 and 3,000 Communists were members of the UAW at the time of the 1946 convention. Probably an equally large number of union activists were non-Communist left-wing members influenced by the Communist party. This group, in the main, also participated in the Addes caucus. The Communists were active in the Thomas-Addes-Leonard caucus at the 1946 UAW convention. Although the Communists had long been allied with the Addes group, they had since 1940 operated separately from that caucus at union conventions. In 1940 and 1941, the Communists had had important disagreements with the Addes group on war-related issues. In 1943 and 1944, the Communists had functioned as a distinct group, opposed wartime factionalism, and appealed for unity for the sake of the war effort. The Communists during the war had wavered between attacking the Reuther caucus and hoping that they might come to agreement with members of the caucus, if not with Reuther personally. After the Communists in 1945 repudiated the leadership of their General Secretary, Earl Browder, they were no longer reluctant to participate directly in the Addes caucus. They sought to develop unity around a pro-CIO policy and emphasized the issues arising from the GM strike and the company security question. The Communists saw themselves as part of the "progressive coalition" and believed that they "won substantial support and brought sizable blocks [*sic*] of votes for the progressives [at the convention]." Although merging into a single caucus behind Addes, Thomas, and Leonard, the Communists did take a stance independent of the Thomas-Addes coalition in advocating the election of a Black leader to the International Executive Board.[18]

Communist advocacy of Black participation in the top leadership of the UAW and the historic role of Communists and their associated left-wing allies in championing the fight against discrimination on the job and in the community helped influence a large majority of Black delegates to support the Thomas-Addes candidates. Prominent in the Reuther caucus, on the other hand, was the Toledo Regional Director Richard Gosser, who had come under harsh criticism for his anti-Black bias. Reuther's trade union abilities and his "innate sense of theoretical justice in all interracial matters" were impressive, according to George Crockett, but the "the perpetual question that constantly bobs up when Negroes in UAW talk about union politics is 'Why is it the great majority of the prejudiced elements in UAW are Reuther's most vociferous supporters?' "[19]

Blacks appraised the records of Thomas and Reuther quite differently. At the 1943 UAW convention, Thomas and Leonard, it is true, had joined Reuther in opposing the effort to elect a Black to the UAW board, using the reverse racism argument to defeat the proposal. Thomas, however, had been outspoken in opposing strikes against Black upgrading, had supported expansion of housing for Blacks despite racist attacks, and had put forward a program to deal with the causes of the 1943 Detroit race riot. According to August Meier and Elliot Rudwick, Thomas was "quite clearly sensitized to the concerns of a thoroughly aroused Negro community, emerged as black Detroit's most vigorous white supporter."[20] Crockett credited all four UAW officers with supporting the establishment of the union's Fair Practices Committee, but he thought it was "an open secret" that the committee had survived only because of the active support from Thomas and its chairperson, Secretary-Treasurer Addes. Addes had supported the elevation of a Black worker to the Executive Board in 1943 and had advocated increased hiring of Blacks on the staffs of the regional directors. Leonard was in agreement with Addes on the hiring of Black staff members, but Reuther, Gosser, Reuther's vice presidential candidate Jack Livingston, and one other Reuther allied regional director helped to defeat the Fair Practices Committee's recommendation of such a hiring policy.[21] That the vast majority of Black delegates supported Thomas for president and vice president and preferred Leonard to Livingston for the second vice-presidential slot is hardly surprising.

Gloster Current, the executive secretary of the Detroit National Association for the Advancement of Colored People (NAACP), differed with most Black delegates at the convention in his support of Reuther. Current believed that the new UAW president's approach to fair practices was based on sound economic thinking, "not an emotional approach with drum-beating, such as we experienced, perhaps, during Thomas's administration." Current agreed with Reuther that adoption of fair practices to benefit minorities could not be achieved until there was full employment; both believed "special privilege" could not help minorities. Responding to this defense of Reuther's opposition to what today is called affirmative action, Crockett declared, "What Negro UAW members want is not 'special privilege' for them but less 'special privilege' for others." Black union members, Crockett believed, wanted an end to racial discrimination in hiring for international and regional staff and clerical positions.[22]

The Communists and their left allies favored the maintenance of a popular front coalition to fight for an expanded New Deal and for peace in the world based on the unity of the Big Three powers. The Communist-led left saw the CIO as the principal force in such a coalition and was therefore committed to the preservation of an alliance with centrists like Murray, Thomas, and Addes. The Communists believed that Reuther, on the other hand represented a danger to the CIO as well as to the Communists because his social democratic ideology enabled him to challenge the CIO's popular front policies with proposals that might sound radical but, in the Communists' view, were misleading. The Communists brought to the Thomas-Addes-Leonard coalition an emphasis on political action. They believed that it was necessary to oppose Reuther, but they asserted that the fight should be conducted on a political and ideological basis, not on a basis of factional "wheeling and dealing."[23] Criticism of an individual can turn into a fight over personality rather than issues, however, and this tended to happen as the factional controversy developed. When the controversy did become personalized, the anti-Reuther forces lost rather than gained ground.

Thomas, Addes, and Leonard, of course, were neither Communists nor leftists. It has been argued that they were old-style traditional unionists, whereas Reuther was a more socially conscious leader. Reuther's Socialist background certainly made him more comfortable with radical ideas than were the leaders of the Thomas-Addes group. Moreover, Reuther, using such vehicles as the *New York Times,* gave great attention to the presentation of his views on issues of national import to the broadest possible audiences. Addes, Thomas, and Leonard, to be sure, shared a trade unionist philosophy, but the type of trade unionism they espoused was not traditional business unionism but the unionism of the CIO. Stressing the primacy of the union's economic purpose and the need for union responsibility, Addes recalled that the UAW "politically stood for . . . policies that would help the downtrodden . . . the minority groups." CIO unionism in 1946 was a social unionism strongly influenced by the thinking of the left.[24]

The left-center group in the UAW consisted of three elements: Communist party members, non-Communist leftists, and New Deal progressives. The Communist party members and the non-Communist leftists believed in the class struggle and socialism and were sympathetic to the Soviet Union. Although not members of the Communist party, the non-Communist leftists generally viewed the Communist party in a positive light. The New Deal progressives, on the other hand, believed in a militant approach to trade union action but not in class struggle and regarded the Communists and other left-wing members as trade unionists who made a positive contribution to the union. Those who adhered to the broad left-center trend came to view attacks on and criticism of Communists as divisive red-baiting. Attacks on the CIO and UAW as Communist-dominated had come from members of Congress like Martin Dies, the Hearst newspaper chain, and discredited union officials such as Homer Martin. Their own experience led the left-center unionists to regard accusations against the Communists as nonsensical. The difference between the red-baiting hurricane that began in 1946 and previous storms was that the existence of the cold war meant that the tempest would be unrelenting for many a year.

Were members of the left-center trend culturally or ethnically different from members of the Reuther caucus or from union members generally? Several recent studies have highlighted the importance of ethnically based communities to the organization of the CIO. This was particularly true of Detroit.[25] The left was composed, in the main, of two distinctive elements: (1) first generation immigrants such as members of the old language federations that had been an essential element of the left wing of the Socialist party and of the Communist party at its founding, and (2) second generation immigrants and Blacks who were young adults when the depression hit the United States and joined in the radical upsurge against that calamity. Thinking of these two groups in his local, Harold Christoffel, long-time leader of the left-wing Allis-Chalmers local in Milwaukee, observed: There were "a lot of immigrants" among the older people, people from Germany and Slavic countries, who "had a background of . . . worker solidarity." The younger people, he said, were "depression children" and "the government policy was unionism." Each group had distinctive strengths and weaknesses. Whereas the first generation group had been working in factories and shops for a number of years, the work experience of Blacks and second generation immigrants was generally more fragmentary. This group included both children of working-class families and of middle-class families who found their business or professional aspirations thwarted by the economy's depressed state. Whether children of middle-class or working-class families, member of the second group tended to have more education and more possibilities for upward mobility than was true of members of the first group. If members of the second group had a less stable position within the working class, they were also more active in the union and more attuned to the popular front politics and thinking of the left-center coalition. Jack White recalled the reaction of one "old language comrade" on the floor of a union meeting to his proposal to raise relief funds by going to the churches. "You're just like all the rest," the man said. "You ain't going to get nothing out of those Jesus screamers."[26]

Members of certain ethnic groups were more likely to be supporters of the left-center trend than were union members in general. Most Black union activists in the Detroit area were left-wingers and Blacks generally supported the left-center caucus. At Ford Local 600, in addition to its strong base among the large number of Black workers, the left was particularly strong among Armenians, Rumanians, Hungarians, and South Slavs "functioning in ma[n]y ways as the legitimate political organization for a large part of the community."[27] In describing the sources of strength for the left leadership in the Cleveland Fisher Body Local 45, Leo Fenster noted that the plant was in a Slovenian neighborhood and that about one-third of the union membership was Slovenian. The major organizations in the Slovenian community, such as its fraternal organization, were pro-socialist, Fenster recalled, and the "general view" among the Slovenians, was "that socialism was a thing that would come."[28] Theirs was a vision of a socialist transformation of society, not simply a reformed capitalism led by a British-style labor party. An analysis of the names of a sample of about 1,000 delegates attending UAW and Michigan CIO conventions between 1946 and 1948 showed that the left-center caucus drew a greater proportion of its votes from those with Eastern European, Italian, and Greek names. The Reuther caucus drew more of its strength than the left-center group from among those with British, German, Dutch, and French names.[29]

Activists in the left-center caucus were participants in, or were influenced by left-wing, cultural life. They often read left-wing newspapers such as the *Daily Worker,* the *Glos Ludowy,* and other left-wing ethnic papers. Cultural activities included forums, dances, sports activities, youth activities, plays, and so forth. Activities of this sort gave these unionists a different frame of reference, a different set of norms from that of the society at large. They were able to develop their own concept of what "loyalty to America" meant. They believed in an Americanism that was open to all races and ethnic groups living in the United States and that was not hostile to other nations and cultures. Appeals to national chauvinism and jingoism were less influential among them than among union members generally. Many left-center supporters were themselves members of groups that had been subjected to racial and ethnic discrimination and others had developed a strong commitment to opposing such discrimination.

The cold war assault on the left-center trend came at a time when both lives of auto workers and the communities in which they lived were undergoing rapid change. The war and reconversion had caused significant changes in the work forces at factories and in neighborhood residential patterns as well. Old community, social, and political ties were weakened as a result of these developments. Many left progressives had served in the armed forces during World War II and faced the same problems of readjustment as did other veterans. At the same time, union activists assumed the same kinds of new responsibilities as did other Americans as the postwar baby boom began. The sharp changes in the Communist party's policy and leadership, moreover, led to the disorientation of some.[30] As a result, although the left-center trend was a significant force in the UAW and in auto union towns as the postwar period began, it was entering a new battlefield in some disarray. Those who were ready to jump into the fray were often able to convince fellow union members of the validity of the popular front approach and retain or regain their base of support. There were many others who, while retaining the old values, at first stood on the sidelines.

Whereas the vitality of the left-center trend was based on the accumulation of experience in oppositional struggles, the strength of the right-wing trend was continuously renewed by the influence of the conservative forces of society. Unless they were children of participants or supporters of the left-center trend or came under the personal influence of left-progressive activists, new union members were likely to be influenced by the newspapers' hostility to communism in labor's ranks. The novel *Between the Hills and the Seas,* by K. B. Gilden, describes the reaction to the developing cold war by the rank and file in a local union led by a coalition of progressives and Communists: " . . . workers were falling back under the daily onslaught of headlines and radio," Gilden wrote, "Bomb Moscow, Canadian Red Spy Ring Revealed. A . . . defense contract with the Atomic Energy Commission jeopardized by certain suspect elements in the union . . . "[31] The rapid unfolding of foreign policy conflicts between the United States and the Soviet Union and the increasing attacks on domestic communism brought new activists into the Reuther group. Certainly, all union members were faced with the same personal concerns of readjusting to the new postwar realities that caused some disarray in the ranks of the left-center forces. The influence of the dominant institutions of society and external events, however, stimulated a modest growth of the right-wing forces. Anticommunism and national political issues assumed major importance as the two union caucuses sought to strengthen or at least preserve their positions within the UAW.

Chapter Eight

The Politics of Auto Union Factionalism: Anti-Communism and the Erosion of the Popular Front on the National Level

Apart from the 1939–1941 interlude, the popular front approach had been the dominant one in both the UAW and the national CIO since 1936. Left-wing unionists were particularly active in the political sphere and played a key leadership role in the CIO-PAC. The left-center alliance in the CIO, however, had become accustomed to supporting President Roosevelt's policy of maintaining a course a little to the left of center. President Truman's inconsistent approach to issues of concern to labor led him to offer less resistance than his predecessor had to the conservative offensive that was already underway during Roosevelt's tenure. The supporters of the popular front approach were thus weakened by the loss of a charismatic leader with a large national following and his replacement by a president who vacillated between antagonizing and assisting labor and progressive groups. Given this state of affairs, the left-progressive forces had difficulty in developing a focused campaign to further its political and electoral objectives. At the same time, the anticommunist tendency within the CIO responded to the intensification of anticommunism and anti-Sovietism in national politics by concentrating its energy on an internal battle against its left-wing opponents.

The one political issue on which the UAW succeeded in mobilizing its membership during 1946 was inflation. Both union caucuses strongly opposed the rapid rise in prices that had followed the expiration of price control on June 30, 1946. The union organized widespread protest actions, including a "buyers' strike," mass rallies, and work stoppages. The *New York Times* reported UAW rallies on July 16, 1946, of 50,000 in Detroit, 3,000 in Chicago, 3,000 in Toledo, and 2,000 in Cleveland. In Detroit, 20,000 to 30,000 Chrysler workers left work early that day, as did 40,000 Cleveland auto workers. Reuther and Leonard spoke at the huge Detroit protest. Truman, who had contributed to undermining price control by his actions, was of little help in this battle. Congress restored price control but only in a very weakened form, and, by November, effective price control was at an end.[1]

For several months before the November 1946 election, left-wing and progressive leaders sought to launch an offensive to stem the conservative tide. In April 1946, a broad coalition of leftists, progressives, and liberals held a Win the Peace Conference, but no national organization developed from this meeting. At the end of September, 300 delegates attended a Conference of Progressives in Chicago sponsored by the CIO-PAC and its close political allies, the National Citizens Political Action Committee [NC-PAC] and the Independent Citizens Committee of the Arts, Sciences and Professions [ICC-ASP]. Signers of the conference call included Philip Murray, James Patton, president of the National Farmers Union, Walter White of the NAACP, and former Roosevelt cabinet members Harold Ickes and Henry Morgenthau, Jr. The resolutions adopted by the conference endorsed a series of progressive domestic programs and "a swift return to the progressive global thinking of Franklin Roosevelt," including, first of all, the restoration of "mutual trust among the great powers." The foreign policy resolution did not, however, condemn the "get tough with Russia" policy because of Murray's strong objections. In addressing the conference, Murray departed from his text to insist that "there is no more damn business for an American Communist meddling in our business than there is for any American meddling in the Russian Trade Union Movement."[2]

Murray's anticommunist outburst at the Conference of Progressives did not bode well for the future of a united front policy. When the conference's Continuations Committee met in October, Murray, however, chose to emphasize his belief in the conference's potential. "We expect this movement," he asserted, "to expand and become in due course the most powerful liberal and progressive organization brought together in the history of the country." At a postelection meeting, however, the Continuations Committee refused to support George Addes's proposal for the development of ward and precinct organizations. According to UE president Albert Fitzgerald, after this final meeting of the Conference or Progressives group,

> Murray said . . . these people don't represent anybody. Only he (Murray) had a following; the others were star gazing. Right then, he predicted that things were going to get pretty tough; that relations between the United States and the Soviet Union were worsening and people in the labor movement were going to have to get solidly behind the Truman administration . . . Then he said that others were going to have to mend their ways and stop following the Communist party line.

Murray's opposition to further development of the Conference of Progressives group effectively killed the organization.[3]

Murray was in a crucial position because the CIO was the key organization for any progressive offensive against the turn to the right in domestic and foreign policy. The CIO had about 6,000,000 members, whereas the ICC-ASP had 10,000; the NC-PAC, 18,000; the National Farmers Union, 145,000 dues paying heads of families; and the NAACP, 535,000. The failure of the Conference of Progressives to establish a permanent organization meant that the best hope for the formation of a national left-progressive coalition with a mass trade union base had been lost.[4]

In a sense, then, one person, Philip Murray, had prevented the development of a united counterattack against the conservative drive. That a single individual had the power to decide on the course of action of the whole CIO resulted in part from the origin of the CIO as a coalition of established, bureaucratically run unions. More important, a significant section of the CIO leadership thought that popular front coalitions had lost their usefulness. Given the developing hostility between the United States and the Soviet Union and the growth of domestic anticommunism, these leaders believed that the CIO had to rid itself of Communist influence. This was a renewal of the effort begun in the late 1930s that had reached a peak in 1941 before being interrupted by the wartime alliance between the United States and the Soviet Union. With the end of the war, the breakdown of the unity of the Big Three, and the initiation of another anticommunist campaign by the political right, the opponents of the left within the CIO renewed their campaign to purge the left.[5]

In January 1946, the ACTU launched a successful campaign in the Shipbuilding Workers Union against Communists and their allies in the international and in local unions. Shipbuilders president John Green and the Workers' party, a Trotskyite group, supported this effort. Within the Steelworkers, anticommunist leaders aligned with the ACTU began a campaign to have that union's convention condemn communism and ban Communists from serving as officers. When the steel union's convention took place in May 1946, Murray opposed a purge, but he won unanimous convention endorsement for his declaration that "this union will not tolerate efforts by outsiders—individuals, organizations, or groups—whether they be Communist, Socialist or any other group to infiltrate, dictate or meddle in our affairs." Left-wing delegates voted for the resolution in the hope that maintenance of unity in support of an overall progressive policy would stem the right-wing drive and prevent the division of the union and the initiation of a purge. Following the Steelworkers convention, however, the union's newspaper began regular publication of anticommunist articles.[6]

The increasing division in the labor and progressive movements was one of many factors contributing to a disastrous defeat for the Democratic party, progressives, and the CIO in the November 1946 elections. The Republican party won control of both houses of Congress, and many progressives backed by the CIO went down to defeat. In Michigan, the Republicans succeeded in electing 95 out of 100 state representatives and even won a majority of the vote in Wayne County (which includes Detroit). Although a discernible shift to the Republicans occurred among some sections of the electorate, the main reason for the GOP victory was the low turnout of Democratic voters. UAW leaders saw the vote as one against the party in power rather than against the New Deal. "The few Congressmen who compaigned on a real New Deal program," UAW political action director Leonard complained, "had to apologize or ignore the head of their party, President Truman. They had to explain the disgraceful failures of Truman and his Administration." It was also true, however, that the Republicans had made gains among the electorate by campaigning against the CIO-PAC and left-wing Democrats as "Communists."[7]

The poor record of the Truman administration and the Democrats in Congress made it difficult for the union leadership to mobilize the rank and file. How much enthusiasm, after all, could a union activist develop for Democrats endorsed by the CIO-PAC when only 12 Democrats had voted in the House of Representatives against Truman's bill to draft railroad strikers? CIO-PAC-endorsed candidates were also handicapped because the PAC and the CIO unions were late in developing ward and precinct organizations to get out their vote.[8]

Late in the 1946 campaign in Michigan and a few other states, the PAC sponsored successful mass rallies at which former Vice President Henry Wallace was the featured speaker. Wallace, the most prominent progressive figure in American political life, had been fired from the cabinet by Truman in September because of his differences with the administration's cold war foreign policy. Although the Democratic leadership had agreed to Wallace's campaign swing, Leonard lamented that "the big wigs" of the Democratic party demanded that Wallace refrain from criticizing Michigan's Republican Senator Arthur H. Vandenberg because he was a Truman ally in the development of a bipartisan cold war foreign policy. The Michigan Democratic party, as a consequence, ran only a token candidate against Vandenberg.[9]

Other problems plagued the 1946 campaign. Old Guard Democrats did not exert themselves in the campaign because they were resentful of left-wing influence in the party. Many top AFL leaders supported the Republicans, and left-wingers charged that Michigan CIO President August Scholle sabotaged the PAC effort by attempting to steer labor support to the Republican gubernatorial candidate, Kim Sigler. Scholle had indeed opposed endorsing Sigler's Democratic opponent, former Governor Murray Van Wagoner, and the *Michigan CIO News* gave little attention to Van Wagoner's candidacy. In Milwaukee, Wisconsin, the PAC backed candidate for Congress, Fur Workers' leader Eddie Bobrowicz, defeated a conservative Democratic incumbent in the primary but lost the general election by a few thousand votes when the defeated incumbent ran an independent campaign against him. Seeking election during the course of the UAW's difficult battle against the Allis-Chalmers Company,

Bobrowicz was subjected to a tremendous red-baiting campaign by the city's newspapers and the Republican party. Bobrowicz, a left-wing Democrat and liberal Wisconsin Democrats also had to contend with the opposition of the Socialists, who were critical of their support for cooperation with the Soviet Union. In sum, the Republicans were on the offensive on the issues of shortages and communism. The Democrats had failed to implement the progressive program presented to Congress by Truman at the end of the war and were divided.[10]

The decisive setback for labor and the progressives in the November election proved to be a turning point in the anticommunist campaign within the CIO. At the eighth annual CIO convention, just two weeks after the election, Murray demanded left-right unity on a policy statement dealing with the communist issue. The convention adopted a resolution that declared, "We . . . resent and reject efforts of the Communist party or other political parties and their adherents to interfere in the affairs of the CIO." Left-wing leaders helped prepare the statement, and left-wing delegates voted for it in an effort once again to maintain unified support for progressive domestic and foreign policies and to prevent the kind of division and purges that, they feared, would lead to the destruction of the CIO. Murray, indeed, assured the delegates that he wanted no purges, and some right-wingers expressed grave disappointment with Murray's stance on the communist issue. Other convention decisions providing for tight national control over state and local CIO bodies and restricting official support for non-CIO groups to a narrowly circumscribed list of endorsed organizations proved to be the basis for a systematic effort to eliminate left-wing control of several CIO bodies and to break long-standing ties between the CIO and many popular front organizations, such as the National Negro Congress. The possibility was thereby eliminated that the CIO would serve as the base for a united grass roots coalition for policies of cooperation with the Soviet Union abroad and an expanded New Deal at home.[11]

Although the convention affirmed support for a policy of Big Three unity and endorsed other progressive foreign and domestic policy positions, the espousal of anticommunism and the organizational decisions to tighten top-level control of subsidiary bodies were of greater significance in the long run. The CIO left-wing still sought to preserve its alliance with Murray on policy issues, but his lieutenants began acting in concert with the CIO's anticommunist factions to purge the left. The coalition between Murray and the left in the national CIO was now effectively at an end. Despite resolutions supported by the left and occasional gestures to left-wing leaders by the Murray forces, the latter had shifted from an alliance with the left to an alliance with the right. This put the Addes-Thomas-Leonard caucus in the UAW in a difficult position. One of the chief sources of its strength had been its close relationship with Murray, who had led a coalition in the CIO similar to that which Addes, Thomas, Leonard and the Communists sought to preserve in the UAW. Murray's anticommunist stance and his sponsorship of the "resent and reject" resolution aided Reuther ideologically. The CIO president was not opposed to Addes, Thomas, or Leonard as leaders of the UAW but the actions of his assistants in city and state CIO councils undermined the strength of their left-wing allies and enhanced the power of the Reuther forces.

In the wake of the November 1946 electoral defeat for the Democratic party and the CIO, a variety of liberal and progressive groups sought new forms for political action. Although the preelection Conference of Progressives had not led to the development of a new mass political action organization, two of the principal conference organizations, the NC-PAC and the ICC-ASP decided to merge. Composed primarily of middle-class progressives, they acted with only limited support from the CIO-PAC, with which they were closely allied. Although Philip Murray, CIO-PAC head Jack Kroll, and rail union leader A. F. Whitney were named vice chairpersons of the new organization, the Progressive Citizens of America [PCA], only Whitney participated in the group's founding conference on the last weekend of 1946. The major figure associated with the new movement, although not formally a member, was Henry Wallace, the featured speaker at the founding meeting. Charging that the Democratic administration had abandoned the Roosevelt program in domestic and foreign affairs, the PCA signalled its intention to consider the formation of a third party. The new organization sought to unite all progressives who agreed with its objectives, "regardless of race, creed, color, national origin or political affiliation."[12]

One week after the founding conference of the PCA, the rival Americans for Democratic Action [ADA] held its organizing meeting. The gathering was initiated by the Union for Democratic Action [UDA], an anticommunist liberal group that was considerably smaller than the NC-PAC and the ICC-ASP. The ADA, like the PCA, called for an expanded New Deal and the protection of civil liberties. Whereas the PCA associated itself with Wallace's criticism of the Truman administration's foreign policy, the ADA indicated its support for "the general framework of present American foreign policy" and, specifically, for the "American plan for international control of atomic energy." The ADA also came down on the opposite side of the PCA on the question of left-progressive unity, rejecting "any association with Communists or sympathizers with communism in the United States." Its leaders believed that liberal organizations in the past had failed to win wider acceptance of their views because these groups too often had been influenced by Communists and their sympathizers. A strong and vital liberal movement, ADA leaders thought, could be built only by excluding Communists. ADA enjoyed the support of such prominent New Deal figures as Eleanor Roosevelt, Leon Henderson, Wilson Wyatt, and Chester Bowles. Labor participants included such top officials of CIO and AFL unions as Walter Reuther, Emil Rieve, James Carey, Allan Haywood, Samuel Wolchok, John Green, Willard Townsend, David Dubinsky, and Hugo Ernst.[13]

The strong participation of leading CIO officials in the founding ADA meeting was another indication that the November 1946 CIO convention had not contained the drive to bar Communists from the organization. The principal thrust of the ADA was to purge the liberal movement of Communist influence. Despite Murray's stated opposition to witch-hunting, the CIO convention resolution to "resent and reject . . . interference" by the Communist party or other political parties had only stimulated the movement to exclude Communists.

The ADA's stance constituted a tentative move away from the compromise position of the CIO convention regarding foreign policy. Like the ADA statement, the CIO resolution on foreign policy contained no explicit criticism of the Truman administration and endorsed the United States's plan for the control of atomic energy, but the CIO plank also called for terminating the stockpiling of atomic weapons, severing diplomatic relations with fascist Spain and Argentina, demilitarizing Germany and Japan, and ending intervention by the United States and other governments in the affairs of China. The CIO resolution especially emphasized the need for unity among the Big Three powers: "Our great war President, the resolution stated, "recognized that friendship and unity could flow from understanding, negotiation and agreement and not from maneuver and pressure and denunciation on the part of any of the Big Three . . . We reject all proposals for American participation in any bloc or alliance which would destroy the unity of the Big Three." The ADA approach to foreign policy contained none of the implicit criticism of the Truman administration voiced by the CIO.[14] On the other hand, the PCA's charge that the administration had abandoned Roosevelt's policies made plain what was implied in the CIO statement.

Despite the differences between CIO and ADA policies, Murray initially sanctioned the participation of CIO officials in the group and sent a representative to the founding meeting. When UDA leader James Loeb consulted Murray about the ADA's formation, Murray expressed support for the ADA's objectives but was "quite vague," Loeb complained, about "the method of achieving the objectives." In fact, Murray was unhappy with the extensive publicity about division in the liberal movement and the CIO that accompanied the establishment of the PCA and the ADA. In March, the CIO board, at Murray's suggestion, recommended that CIO leaders participate in neither the PCA nor the ADA. Murray withdrew as a vice chairperson of the PCA, and Reuther stopped participating in the ADA for the time being.[15]

The ADA responded to a CIO appeal for liberal unity by charging that it was "based on the theory that unity with Communists is possible." The implication was clear: the ADA not only rejected association with Communists but association with anyone (namely the popular front oriented forces in the PCA) who associated with Communists! Although Murray clearly did not favor the PCA's movement in the direction of a third party, he could not at this early date condemn the group as Communist in view of the long association between the CIO and the two principal organizations involved in forming the PCA. Murray himself, indeed, had been on the board of the NC-PAC.[16]

The ADA's formation represented the beginning of organized cold war liberalism. At this early stage, however, even the ADA's support for a cold war foreign policy was quite tentative. Reuther, for example, refrained from speaking out in support of Truman and against Wallace on foreign policy issues. Reuther, to be sure, readily attacked Communists in the labor and progressive movements, but anti-Sovietism was not a high priority for the UAW president in early 1947. Support for a program of "understanding, negotiations, and agreement" remained strong in liberal circles and the labor movement, and Reuther chose not to challenge it.[17]

Reuther's sponsorship of the ADA was his first public step away from the progressive, pro-Big Three unity position he had adopted shortly after being elected UAW president. He had, however, chosen that stance primarily for tactical reasons. His aim had been to follow a middle-of-the-road position and not to side with any of the great powers or with either the right or left in American political life. At least on the surface, this middle-of-the-road position was the one assumed by Henry Wallace. The former vice president told the PCA founding conference:

> As American progressives we are not interested in any fight between the Russian haters and the Russophiles . . . We shall not allow the attacks of the enemy to stampede us into foolish red-baiting. Nor shall we allow those who owe their primary allegiance to some foreign power to determine our course . . . We progressives believe that the United States can eliminate the excesses of the business cycle without danger to peace or to the essential freedoms.[18]

The ideological outlooks of Reuther and Wallace were indeed quite similar. Both believed in reforming capitalism to make it more progressive.

Neither Wallace nor Reuther was able to adhere to the middle-of-the-road position each had originally adopted. Wallace's principal concern was foreign policy, and he believed the Truman administration was taking a dangerously wrong path and squandering an opportunity to establish a lasting peace. In acting on this view, Wallace found himself allied with left-wing critics of the president. Reuther's principal concern was his struggle with the Thomas-Addes-Leonard coalition for control of the UAW. Attacking communism was a useful weapon in this internal union struggle because it put Reuther's opponents on the defensive and united his supporters. Because Reuther had long employed both anticommunism and anti-Sovietism in his battles inside the UAW, his move to the right as the middle-of-the-road position eroded is hardly surprising. At first, however, the UAW president refrained from speaking on the issues because statements praising the unpopular Truman's foreign policy course would not have contributed to unifying his caucus.[19]

Third party sentiment spread rapidly within the UAW because of Truman's unpopularity with the rank and file and with secondary leaders of both union caucuses. Many local unions passed resolutions calling for a new labor-based party. The second largest local in GM, Chevrolet Local 659 in Flint, established a Labor Party Committee with an elected organizer in each of 49 districts. Given sentiments of this sort at the local level, Reuther's caution in expressing support for Truman is understandable.[20]

Although Reuther stopped participating in the ADA, his initial affiliation with the organization in itself constituted a significant shift in his position. He now refrained from criticizing Truman even on domestic issues and from voicing support for the eventual formation of third party. Although the ADA was not enamored of Truman in 1947, its purpose was to attack and isolate the left and to build a strong liberal center. If it attacked any part of Truman's policy, it feared, this would only strengthen his left-wing critics in the labor movement and those progressives in the Democratic party who were thinking of bolting to a third party. The ADA represented a coalition of union officials (Socialists, social democrats, and liberals) concerned with opposing Communists and their allies in the labor movement and former New Deal officials interested in establishing liberal control of the Democratic party. On the issue of remaining within the Democratic party, Reuther and the ADA were in complete agreement with Murray, who had consistently voiced his opposition to a third party.[21]

The ADA's commitment to cold-war policies became evident in March 1947 when Truman initiated new "get tough" policies on the foreign and domestic fronts. The president, in proclaiming what became known as the Truman Doctrine, called for the United States to provide military and economic assistance to the governments of Greece and Turkey to enable them to resist "attempted subjugation by armed minorities or by outside pressures." Truman justified sustaining the right-wing regimes by the use of a "domino theory": other nations would also be engulfed by "totalitarianism" if Greece and Turkey were allowed to fall. In announcing the new policy, Truman bypassed the United Nations. Less than two weeks after the declaration of the Truman Doctrine, the president issued an executive order establishing a loyalty program for all 2,000,000 federal workers. Every employee of the federal government was to be investigated. Those workers found by a loyalty board to be members of or sympathetic to organizations or movements designated by the attorney general as "totalitarian, fascist, communist or subversive" were to be fired. The accused employee had no right to face his or her accusers. Truman's launching of policies of anticommunism at home and messianic anti-Sovietism in foreign affairs led to an intensification of the anticommunist political climate in the United States. The ADA supported the Truman Doctrine and endorsed the aims of the loyalty program while criticizing it on procedural grounds. The PCA condemned both policies.[22]

As Truman initiated his new policies, communism and red-baiting emerged as central issues in the UAW. At an unofficial "unity" meeting in Louisville during the UAW board's March deliberations, Reuther expressed his concern about the use of anticommunism against the labor movement. He proposed to George Addes that the two caucuses compose their factional dispute and "have a solid front" against the antilabor forces. The four officers should keep their positions, Reuther suggested, and the two sides would discuss the regional directorships. The Reutherites insisted, however, on adherence "without qualification to the policy of completely isolating members of the Communist Party, and other groups subservient to any foreign government, from leadership in the International and local unions." Recalling this off-the-record meeting, board member Percy Llewellyn remarked on Reuther's warning about Congressional investigations of communism. "A lot of your friends are going to get hurt and possibly some of my friends," Reuther admonished, according to Llewellyn. Regarding Reuther's characterization of the danger of association with Communists as self-serving, the Addes group did not accept the UAW president's offer. The Addes forces thought unity against anti-communism was the proper course. If they went along with Reuther on this issue, they understood that they would have alienated a key part of their coalition. Although some CIO leaders like Michael Quill and Joseph Curran broke their alliances with Communists in this period, for Addes and Thomas this path would have meant playing second fiddle to Reuther rather than establishing control in their own right, as Quill and Curran succeeded in doing.[23]

Thomas refused even to attend the "unity" meeting, believing he had Reuther "beat" and would regain his presidency. Throughout the period between the tenth and eleventh UAW conventions, Thomas looked for opportunities to attack Reuther and project himself as an alternative leader of the union. When Thomas publicly attacked Reuther's role in the Allis-Chalmers strike, the UAW received widespread negative publicity. Thomas's aggressive attacks on Reuther led many rank-and-file workers to perceive the Thomas-Addes-Leonard caucus as disruptive. Addes thought it was in "bad taste" to "publicly condemn a president of your union regardless of where he fits with you." He told Thomas and Leonard that he would "break from the group" if any more attacks of that kind were issued. Future statements about Reuther, Addes insisted, had to be approved by all three officers.[24]

A few days after the failure of the "unity" meeting and one day after Truman issued his loyalty order, the *New York Times* reported that Walter Reuther was embarking on a "personal drive" against leftist influence in the UAW. At the UAW's Louisville board meeting, Reuther proposed that the board terminate the services of UAW Washington representative, Irving Richter, on the grounds that he supported communism. Reuther asserted that the purge of Richter was a necessary act of self-defense for the UAW. "Now let's not hide against the charge that we can start a witch-hunt," Reuther said. "Boy, believe you me if the Communist Party guys hide behind that, if they get any power, God help any labor leader. They will be mowed down . . . we must recognize we are going to protect ourselves against any sort of attack." Although Reuther was right that antilabor forces were using the issue of communism against the labor movement, he himself was a leader, not an opponent, of the witch-hunt. Unpersuaded by Reuther's arguments, Reuther's opponents on the board refused to follow his recommendation concerning Richter.[25]

The differing approaches of the UAW factions to the antilabor witch-hunters became apparent a few days later when Michigan's Republican Governor Kim Sigler testified before the House Un-American Activities Committee [HUAC]. Sigler told the committee that there were more than 15,000 Communists controlling certain unions in Michigan. He labelled Thomas, Addes, and Leonard as "captives of the Communist Party" and characterized the struggle within the UAW as one between Communists and "good, loyal, American citizens." Ignoring Sigler's support for his faction, Reuther condemned the governor's testimony, asserting that reactionary forces were "resorting to the traditional Red scare" because they had not solved the problems of the people. Reuther, however, took the opportunity to do some red-baiting himself, restating the CIO's opposition to "Communist interference" and claiming, absurdly, that Communists would benefit from the attack made upon them and their allies by the Republican Governor. " . . . Sigler has performed a valuable service to the Communists. They will be quick to seize upon the opportunity this attack affords them of hiding behind the genuinely liberal and progressive forces in the labor movement." As Roger Keeran has observed, "Reuther's liberal anticommunism accepted without question the premise that the Communists represented a relentless, diabolical, and totalitarian force that had to be opposed . . . " There was no liberalism in the approach of the Reuther-allied ACTU, which praised Sigler for "exposing a lot of Communist monkey business."[26]

Addes, Thomas, and Leonard branded Sigler's charge against them as a "deliberate falsehood" designed to weaken the UAW on the eve of wage negotiations. In a radio address Addes, in behalf of himself and the two UAW vice presidents, blasted Sigler as a puppet of the auto companies who had not done "a single constructive thing for the people of Michigan since he took office." Addes asserted that the governor's attempt to divide the workers would "boomerang" because the people were "fed up with the use of the Red-baiting techniques to smear every legitimate aspiration of the common people." Taking the opportunity to make a factional point, Addes pointed out that "Sigler seems to like some labor leaders and he dislikes certain other labor leaders . . . Frankly, we would consider it a deep insult to our integrity and our honesty as leaders of the auto workers' union if the men in control of the auto companies—through their puppet—would bestow upon us the very dubious honor of their favor." Addes also noted in his *United Automobile Worker* column that the "witch-hunt . . . unfortunately is being ably aided and abetted by members of our union."[27]

Reuther raised the communist question once again at the April board meeting. The issue this time was Reuther's interpretation of Article 10, Section 8, of the UAW constitution, which barred from union office members associated with organizations "such as the Communist . . . which owes its allegiance to any government other than the United States or Canada . . . " Holding that this section applied to members of the Communist party, the UAW president argued that the party owed its allegiance to the Soviet Union. He cited the report of the Royal Commission of Canada on Soviet spy charges in support of his position. Only one board member, Detroit West Side Co-Director Percy Llewellyn, took issue with Reuther on this question and inaccurately contended that the Supreme Court had ruled in the *Schneiderman* case that the Communist party was not subservient to a foreign power. Despite this comment, Llewellyn joined the rest of the board in voting that Section 8 applied to the Communist party. After it made this decision, the board took up Reuther's proposal that the disqualification should be automatic where there was no question of fact but that trials should be held in other instances. The Reuther enforcement proposal provided for a review by the international of cases in which a local union had failed to remove a known "Communist" as requested by a member. With most board members voting along caucus lines, Reuther's proposal to abrogate the right to trial under certain circumstances was defeated by a 14 to eight vote.[28]

More than the matter of formal rights was involved in the dispute over the enforcement of Article 10, Section 8. In practical terms, the Reuther proposal for automatic removal would have led to the elimination of many more "Communists" than had been true in the past. The provision for an appeal to the international contained in Reuther's recommendation would have given anticommunists in local unions a means to challenge the right to hold office of Communist officials who were popular with their locals. The effect of this procedure would have been to centralize more power in the hands of the international and to open the door to a unionwide purge of Communists by the international. Although the Thomas-Addes-Leonard caucus later raised these issues, they opposed Reuther's proposal at this stage primarily on the issue of the right to a trial.[29]

It is not surprising that the Addes forces agreed with Reuther that the constitutional clause in question applied to the Communist party. Reuther opponents on the board could not dispute his argument that the Communist party was one of the organizations convention delegates were aiming at when they had added that section to the constitution in 1941. Although it might have been possible to vote that the clause did not apply to Communists on the grounds that the Communist party did not "owe its allegiance" to any government other than that of the United States or Canada, board members so voting would have been open to the charge that they were attempting to overturn a convention mandate on a technicality. The Addes-Thomas-Leonard caucus leaders had not succumbed to the "anti-Communist orthodoxy" of the day; they had been trapped rather by their failure to have opposed the anticommunist clause before the cold war set in.[30]

In its establishment of a political test for union officeholding, Section 8 of Article 10 of the UAW constitution was undemocratic by its very nature. The clause had been adopted just after the end of the period of the Nazi-Soviet pact, which was accompanied by a great deal of anticommunism and anti-Sovietism in the United States. Thomas and Leonard had favored the amendment, and Addes had supported an alternative that would have added Socialists to the list of those to be barred from office. As potent as the "foreign agent" charge was in 1941, it was doubly so in 1947, when the Soviet Union was being depicted by United States policy makers as a direct threat to United States interests. Thomas, Addes, and Leonard had all moved away from the anticommunist positions they had espoused in 1941. During the war, they had developed more favorable attitudes toward the Soviet Union and had worked with U.S. Communists to some degree. They did not, however, advocate removing the anticommunist clause. Perhaps they were satisfied with the fact that when they joined in united fronts with Communists, the latter usually occupied second-class positions in the coalition. The Communists and other left-wingers themselves campaigned only sporadically to remove the provision and win the right for Communists to participate equally in the UAW. In the end, the anticommunist clause in the UAW constitution became a weapon of the right wing not only against the Communists but against the entire left-center coalition.[31]

Chapter Nine

The Politics of Auto Union Factionalism: The Michigan CIO in the Cold War Era

In their discussions of the postwar defeat of the left in the United Automobile Workers (UAW), Bert Cochran and Harvey A. Levenstein depart from some of the early judgments of Irving Howe and B. J. Widick, but they agree with the idea that the left wing undermined its own position before the cold war began. Cochran and Levenstein both cite the Reuther group's victory at the June 1946 Michigan CIO convention as evidence that the balance had shifted to the right wing shortly after Walter Reuther's election to the UAW presidency and argue that the Addes-Thomas group was an opportunistic vote-getting alliance rather than the expression of a trend of thinking among the union membership that resisted the new orthodoxy of the cold war. An examination of the postwar factional conflict in the Michigan CIO shows, however, that the left-center coalition maintained its strength longer than is generally supposed and, moreover, represented a left-influenced trend of thought among the union membership on questions of domestic anticommunism, foreign policy, political action, and Black representation in union leadership.[1]

During the period that the battle for control of the UAW was raging, the importance of Michigan to the UAW and of the UAW to the Michigan CIO made the state CIO conventions mini-UAW conventions; auto workers cast more than 80 percent of the convention's votes. The Michigan CIO gatherings were unlike the UAW conventions, however, in paying far greater attention to political matters. The state CIO represented the general interests of the industrial union movement; politics was the organization's principal concern, and the more politically minded union activists sought election as delegates.

The June 1946 Michigan CIO convention served as an early test of strength of the two UAW caucuses. Heading the pro-Reuther Michigan CIO slate were the incumbent president and secretary-treasurer, August (Gus) Scholle and Barney Hopkins. Scholle also served as CIO Regional Director. The opposition slate was led by two centrists, Glen Sigman, an assistant regional director for Philip Murray's Steelworkers, and W. G. Grant, a past president of Ford

Local 600. Although both slates could boast candidates for president who had ties to Murray, the popular president of the national CIO, the Scholle-Hopkins slate had the advantages of incumbency. In a closely divided convention, control of the convention machinery was very important.[2]

In the view of the pro-Reuther ACTU's *Wage Earner*, the convention contest was "a grand no-holds-barred struggle over practically nothing," because there was "a complete dearth of real issues" betweeen the two sides.[3] Although the policy differences between the two caucuses were not as sharp as they had been in some past conventions, the two groups held contrary views on communism and red-baiting, and there were indications of the future split on such other cold war-connected issues as foreign policy and political action.

Anticommunism was not the major convention theme it was to become in subsequent years, but the attitude toward communism nevertheless constituted an important area of disagreement between the two factions. The pro-Scholle group put out a flyer focusing on the "switches" of the Communist party. Scholle picked up a Reuther theme of establishing unity by isolating the left wing, asserting that "all that stands between us and the unity we must have is a noisy minority of professional trouble-makers." With Reuther's attempts to discharge some left-wing UAW staff members clearly in mind, Glen Sigman declared his opposition to "the type of unity whereby people go out and drive out of the ranks of the CIO people who oppose them on program and policy." Instead, Sigman favored "the type of unity whereby regardless of race, creed, color, or political belief you will have the right to free speech in any convention."[4]

At this early point in the cold war, most Reuther supporters took a dovish foreign policy stance and generally avoided anti-Sovietism. In their report to the convention, Scholle and Hopkins declared: "Hiroshima and Nagasaki were a signal to the world that men must learn to live together or suffer complete annihilation . . . . " This dovish foreign policy stance stemmed in part from a continuation of the wartime mood and in part from the Reuther caucus's desire to avoid straying too far from the position of Murray and the national CIO, which then strongly supported unity of the Big Three powers.[5]

The continuing hostility to the Soviet Union of some Reutherites became apparent, however, when a left-wing delegate proposed a resolution critical of Great Britain's policy in India. In a speech to the convention, an Indian trade union leader had outlined the oppressive conditions in his country and appealed for support for a planned nationwide railway strike against the government. Arguing that the British Labor Party government was moving "to grant India freedom," Roy Reuther threw the convention into an uproar when he angrily attacked the resolution as "a very clever political one" because it ignored the "areas dominated by the Soviet Union." Two other prominent Reutherites, Horace Sheffield and Emil Mazey, agreed with the condemnation of British policy, however, and the convention, in the end, adopted the resolution.[6]

In addition to expressing peace sentiments and opposing "imperialism," the Sigman-Grant caucus denounced the emerging cold war policies of the United States. "We repudiate," it asserted, "all efforts calculated to weaken or destroy the friendship and close collaboration of Great Britain, the Soviet Union and the United States within the United Nations." The Sigman-Grant group condemned Truman along with Michigan Senator Vandenberg and William Randolph Hearst as "enemies and betrayers of the policies of Franklin D. Roosevelt" who were leading the United States to "new patterns of fascism . . . and the destruction of humanity in a worldwide atomic war."[7]

Although highly critical of Truman, the Sigman-Grant supporters did not propose an immediate break with the Democratic party. Instead, they advocated endorsing progressive candidates of both parties, encouraging independent candidates, and eventually forming a third party. Less critical of Truman, Scholle and Hopkins argued that labor could not afford to divert its political energies into efforts to organize a third party in an election year, but they acknowledged that such a party might be needed in the near future. The administration-appointed resolutions committee, however, proposed immediate preparation of the groundwork for a new party. The resolution, which was approved by the convention, called on officers, executive board members, and local union officials to participate in conferences regarding the third-party question and authorized the state organization "to make substantial financial contributions" to such efforts. The ranks of both union caucuses were very hostile to the Truman administration and favored a search for a political alternative, but the Scholle administration thought that the resolution violated national CIO policy and refused to implement it.[8]

Although the statements of the two caucuses on political action sounded similar, the Sigman-Grant supporters disapproved of the Scholle administration's implementation of policy and of its role in state politics. The Sigman-Grant group criticized Michigan CIO participation in a banquet for Republican Harold Stassen and Scholle's advocacy of an early endorsement of Detroit Mayor Edward Jeffries's bid for reelection in 1945 despite the sharp opposition to the incumbent in the Black community. George Crockett rebuked Scholle for "playing hide-and-go-seek" with the CIO's policy of nondiscrimination; and he charged that Scholle had "engineered" lily-white slates of PAC-endorsed candidates at the 1944 and 1946 PAC conventions. Crockett asserted that Scholle had given his backing to a Black candidate in 1946 only after Black workers made a fight on the issue. A group of CIO veterans complained that, while CIO veterans were meeting in the state capital to develop a program to present to the state legislature, the city's newspapers "headlined August Scholle's disapproval on their front pages." The dissatisfaction with Scholle's leadership was real and went beyond factional considerations.[9]

In the contest for office, the Reuther forces had the substantial advantage of exercising control over the state administration of the CIO. The right wing set the tone of the convention, appointed the committees, and generally had its proposals presented for consideration to the delegates. Because the administration, in contrast to the UAW leadership, refused to appoint members of the rival caucus to any convention committee, there were no minority reports.[10]

A favorable factor for the left-center group was the apparent split between Reuther and CIO president Murray. The two, as we have seen, had differed sharply on the timing and conduct of the previous winter's General Motors and steel strikes. Prior to that disagreement, Murray had usually supported Reuther in his UAW factional battles, but the CIO president had shown his distinct preference for Thomas over Reuther at the recent UAW convention. Although Murray did not give formal backing to Sigman's candidacy, it is unlikely that the steel union representative would have entered the campaign without Murray's approval.[11]

The anti-Scholle forces constituted a broad coalition, but caucusing during the convention revealed weaknesses in the coalition's solidarity. Although the Sigman-Grant group took a forthright position against red-baiting in its platform statement and on the floor of the convention, it was less successful in dealing with this question behind the scenes. Alex Waislew, a rubber worker from the small town of Jackson who was nominated for vice president on the Sigman-Grant slate, vividly remembered his first experience with big city factional politics. The Reutherites, Wasilew recalled, "were using slur tactics by whispering we were Communist-led . . . and we are dupes or followers or pinkos . . . We never used this term in Jackson, . . . this is something we read in the paper." The attack was focused on the election of John Anderson to head the Sigman caucus and the placing of three leftists, including Communist party leader Nat Ganley, on the caucus's slate of 17 vice presidential candidates. Anderson and Ganley were publicly known Communists and leaders of UAW Local 155, one of Detroit's larger local unions. Wasilew looked upon the challenged left wingers as trade unionists "fresh from the old depression time . . . where communism was the only shining light because everybody else including the government turned their backs on working people." Some members of the Sigman caucus, however, such as Douglas Fraser of DeSoto Local 227, thought Communists were "very, very detrimental to the caucus." For their part, recalled Fur Union leader Harold Shapiro, the leftists "were adamant" in holding that they "had something to contribute" to the coalition and "could not be excluded."[12]

Because of their anticommunism, 26 percent of UAW delegates supporting the Sigman-Grant slate failed to vote for one or more of the three left-wing candidates even though they supported all the other candidates on the ticket.

Ganley's vote was about 22 percent lower than the median vote for the slate, and the vote totals for two other left-wing candidates were 7 percent lower than the median.[13]

The pro-Reuther forces won a decisive victory in the convention balloting. Scholle defeated Sigman by a vote of 2,297 to 1,868, and Hopkins won by a slightly larger margin. All 17 vice presidential candidates on the right-wing slate were also elected. Most of the officers of the state council had been right wingers before the 1946 convention; their retention of control was a significant success because the officers and staff of the council were to play an active role in the UAW's political in-fighting. It is inaccurate, however, to conclude, as Bert Cochran does, that the convention's results constituted a "decided shift to Reuther."[14] At the UAW convention in March, Reuther had received 55 percent of the votes of delegates from Michigan, whereas Scholle received 58 percent of the votes of UAW delegates, a small improvement for the Reuther forces.[15]

Scholle's gain stemmed from his group's control of the state CIO apparatus and of the convention machinery. As the convention opened, a Sigman supporter charged: "You have some fellers here who went around the state, and it was a question of who had the biggest suitcase and picked up the loose credentials and brought them down here." A number of locals were, in fact, represented by pro-Reuther delegates who were not members of those locals. The left-center group also objected to the seating of delegates from "blue sky" locals such as UAW Local 50, which had represented workers at the long-closed Ford bomber plant but had lost a bid at the UAW convention to be accorded jurisdiction over the new Kaiser-Frazer plant at Willow Run. The credentials committee appointed by the right-wing state CIO administration proposed the seating of all these delegates. The acceptance of the committee's report by the narrow vote of 358 to 354 kept the convention under right-wing control.[16]

Scholle's narrow victory on the credentials dispute enabled him to roll up substantial majorities among UAW delegates from the smaller locals and from locals outside the major manufacturing companies. More than 80 percent of Scholle's plurality in the UAW delegate voting came from locals representing fewer than 3,000 members but having about one-third of the convention's total vote. Whereas Reuther had received essentially the same share of the votes from UAW locals of all sizes, Scholle acquired 46 percent of the votes of auto locals with five thousand or more members but 71 percent of the ballots of UAW locals with fewer than 5,000 members. Similarly, whereas Reuther had received about the same share of the votes of delegates from large and small companies, Scholle received 50 percent of the votes of delegates from the Big Three auto companies and the independent manufacturers but 67 percent of the votes of delegates from other plants. Judging by the 1946 Michigan CIO convention vote, the Reuther caucus was far from achieving decisive control of the auto workers' union at the local level.

In the wake of their group's convention defeat, Addes and Leonard held a caucus meeting with a number of Detroit area local union presidents. Recalling the meeting, Doug Fraser remarked that Addes and Leonard "made a political decision that they were being badly hurt by the Communist party and the argument went there, let's just divorce ourselves from the Communist party and say you no longer belong . . . in our caucus." When front page stories in the *Detroit News* and *Detroit Times* reporting the meeting praised Addes and Leonard for a planned "red purge," both officials denied any such intention. In his column in the UAW newspaper, Addes reaffirmed his opposition to red-baiting, purges, and the restriction of Communists to second-class citizenship status in the union. He, nevertheless, held that formulation of policy should be the "sole prerogative" of those whose "first loyalty" was to the UAW and CIO and asserted that members of the "Socialist Party, Communist Party, ACTU, Trotskyite Party and others . . . often times" put loyalty to their party first. Although Addes's position was an undemocratic denial of the right of all members to full and equal participation in the union, it was also a far cry from the Reuther approach of characterizing Communists as agents of the Soviet Union with no legitimate role to play in the union or in political life generally.[17]

The existence of an anticommunist tendency within the Thomas-Addes-Leonard coalition had been apparent when the group coalesced at the UAW convention in March 1946. Some Thomas supporters had engaged in considerable anticommunist talk on the convention floor. Thomas had long been closer to the Reuther caucus than the Addes caucus and Leonard had been the number two figure within the Reuther group. The activists whom Thomas and Leonard brought with them into the merger with the Addes-left group had only recently left the Reuther group and some retained their hostility to the Communists. According to the *Detroit Times*, it was Leonard who pressed Addes on the idea of dropping the Communists from the caucus. As Doug Fraser, a close personal follower of Leonard's, and an advocate of dropping the Communists recalled it, the idea "just never worked out, it got blurred." Addes "came over" to the view of "those of us who began to resent . . . [the Communists'] politics within the caucus . . . [but] he never stayed there." The Addes-left alliance was a long-standing one and withstood the pressures resulting from the merger with the much smaller Thomas-Leonard group.[18]

Cochran argues that the Addes group held back from "throwing over their Communist supporters" because of "organizational calculation"—it would have cost them the margin of victory. On the contrary, it was "organizational calculation" that led to the consideration of such an action. The advocates of dropping the Communists like Fraser reasoned that the caucus would gain anticommunist votes whereas the Communists "had no place else to go. [They would] never go for Reuther." Addes, in particular, decided not to follow such a path because of an attachment to the caucus program, which included opposition to red-baiting, and because he had important personal ties to left-wing leaders, most notably to union attorney Maurice Sugar. Communists and allied left wingers remained active in the Thomas-Addes-Leonard coalition. As anticommunism increasingly permeated the national discussion of labor policy and foreign affairs, the gap between the Reuther and Addes groups widened, but no significant new fissures opened within the left-center coalition.[19]

When Michigan CIO delegates convened in June 1947 for their ninth annual convention, it was a critical moment for the labor movement: just one week earlier, Congress had sent the Taft-Hartley bill to the White House, and Truman was contemplating a veto. Although the political situation might have called for unity, the convention was marked by acrimony, disorder, and factionalism. The incumbents Scholle and Hopkins once again headed the Reutherite slate. As in 1946, the left-center caucus again selected middle-of-the-road candidates to lead its slate. Douglas Fraser was the opposition candidate for president, and John Skrocki, who had been elected a vice president on the Scholle slate in 1946 and had served as business manager of the *Michigan CIO News*, ran for secretary-treasurer. The right-wing slate once again emerged victorious, but the left-progressive bloc showed greater strength among UAW delegates than it had in 1946.[20]

Organized as the Committee for a Progressive Michigan CIO Council, the left-center coalition took the offensive at the convention. The progressives charged the incumbent administration with failing to mobilize the ranks of the CIO unions against several anti-labor and reactionary bills passed by the state legislature. They accused Michigan CIO President Scholle of supporting Republican Governor Kim Sigler, of encouraging division and secessionist movements in affiliated CIO unions, and of driving many CIO locals out of the state organization.[21]

The split between the two rival groups in the Michigan CIO was based on diametrically opposed approaches to the conservatives' antilabor drive in the state and nation. The left-progressive forces believed that the CIO should mobilize its membership, and indeed all progressives, to combat the attack on trade unionism. They advocated conferences, mass demonstrations in the state capital, and work stoppages as tactics to be used in fighting repressive legislation. The Reutherite CIO state administration opposed this approach, believing that the best way to deal with the overwhelmingly Republican legislature was to work behind-the-scenes with the governor and other state officials. Scholle saw mass demonstrations in the capital as counterproductive. Appointed by Governor Sigler to a commission studying unemployment compensation, Scholle told the CIO state board that attacks on him by R. J. Thomas were designed to force him to blast the governor and thereby bring about anti-labor legislation. Scholle, who had opposed a CIO endorsement of Sigler's

Democratic rival the previous fall, had come to regard the Republican governor as an opponent of antilabor legislation. He even joined Sigler in assailing as Communist the CIO United Public Workers (UPW), which was attempting to organize state workers.[22]

Scholle responded to UPW leader Yale Stuart's condemnation of his activity with the most vituperative red-baiting ever heard in the Michigan CIO. Scholle fairly frothed at the mouth as he decried the left-wing literature denouncing him. "They print every kind of scurrilous, stinking lie that is manufactured and originates from 900 'Liars Building'," he stated, "and then, like good stooges of the Party, they pass it out. I'll tell you the *CIO News* has never been used to do anything other than defend the actions of the members of this organization and expose the dirty, lying, stinking, slimy propaganda put out by 900 'Liars Building,' the Communist Party headquarters and carried out by stooges of that Party."[23]

Although the left-progressive group focused on the Scholle administration's qualified support of Sigler, it was also critical of the state CIO administration's backing of President Truman. "You can't mobilize the workers behind a machine politician like Harry Truman," Fraser declared.

> You don't mobilize by giving support, despite as some leaders of the CIO think, to Vandenberg on foreign or domestic policy. You don't get a dollar contribution to support the infamous Truman Doctrine. You can't get support or correct political action by having all the splinter groups like ADA and the rest . . . There is only one solution to this problem . . . a concrete program for political action that will shake us free from both the Democratic and Republican parties."[24]

The critical question of foreign policy referred to in Fraser's remarks was dealt with in a minor way in only one convention resolution. The convention paid far greater attention to the issue of political action. Strong support for independent political action and specifically for the formation of a labor party was a Michigan CIO tradition. After Scholle explained that the 1946 resolution authorizing immediate steps to form a third party had not been implemented because national CIO policy specifically forbade the establishment of a third party, the convention approved a resolution calling on the parent organization to alter its position because of the changed national situation and to move toward "the formation of a new political party of all liberal, nontotalitarian, American groups." Although approval of third-party action was not part of the Scholle administration's program, widespread support was evidenced for such a policy by right-wing, center, and left-wing delegates, which accounts for the decision taken by the convention.[25]

The political action resolution was weakened as a statement of support for third-party action by its call for uniting only "nontotalitarian groups," an implicit attack on the Communists in the labor and progressive movements. This exclusionary approach coincided with the thinking of the ADA, which was sharply opposed to third-party action. Whatever its shortcomings, the resolution went too far for Scholle and Hopkins. Before carrying out the final resolve to forward copies of the resolution to other CIO organizations, they asked CIO Secretary-Treasurer James Carey to rule on whether it was consistent with CIO policy and met the approval of national CIO officers![26]

The 1947 Michigan CIO convention paid greater attention to the problem of racial discrimination than any previous Michigan state convention had. Resolutions were passed opposing discrimination in restaurants, supporting fair employment practices legislation, and calling for the appointment of an additional full-time staff member to work with the state CIO's Fair Practices and Anti-Discrimination Committee. Coleman Young, then a representative of the United Public Workers in Detroit, provided evidence of the increasing prominence of Black workers by making a strong seconding speech in favor of Fraser's nomination as president. Young gained additional visibility when he declined a nomination for secretary-treasurer in favor of the candidate supported by the left-progressive caucus. Young turned down the nomination because Black delegates were not interested in making a "third force" bid against the two major caucuses. They hoped, instead, to gain agreement on the creation of a third full-time office in the state council and then to elect Young to the new position. Black delegates were not satisfied with increased visibility and greater attention to the issue of discrimination; they wanted more power within the state organization.[27]

A Black-led caucus met each day at noon to discuss the issue of increasing Black representation in the state CIO council. (Of those attending, 50 percent were white, mostly members of the left-center caucus.) The Black caucus developed a proposal for a third full-time elected office in the state council, an executive vice presidency. Although the office was not designated a Black office, the purpose of the proposal was to increase Black representation at the highest level of the state CIO. Black workers already served on the state CIO board, but none was a full-time elected officer.[28]

The Reuther caucus, which had opposed similar measures designed to achieve Black representation on the UAW International Executive Board, viewed such proposals as reverse discrimination. Because the Scholle administration once again refused to appoint opposition members to convention committees, the Black delegates were unable to persuade the constitution committee to present a minority report on the proposal. On the last day of the convention, Black delegates took over the platform. "We . . . just literally covered the stage," recalled Shelton Tappes, the caucus chairperson. "I can see Gus Scholle now ducking under the signs and standing there . . . with his gavel calling the meeting to order . . . just ignoring . . . it all, this mass of humanity and signs on the platform." Scholle proceeded with the convention bsiness for a while before recommending that Tappes be allowed to address the convention. Expressing the Black delegates' dissatisfaction with their failure to get a hearing for their proposal, Tappes asserted that Black workers refused to accept "excuses" that their proposal was either "political" or a form of "special privilege." "The truth of the matter is," Tappes proclaimed, "Negro workers are entitled to recognition . . . and they intend to get it if it takes from now until the end of time. We will get it."[29]

The Black workers' demonstration led to the formal consideration of their proposal by the convention. Their recommendation for an executive vice president was supported not only by Black delegates and white leftists but also by most centrist members of the progressive coalition, including Fraser. Effectively answering the argument advanced by Reutherite opponents of the measure that to accept a proposal of this sort was to establish Jim Crow in reverse, Fraser declared, "I am opposed to any setting up of the Negro in a corner because you have FEPC—automatically the Negro gets the job. That is Jim Crowism. But when you say you are setting up an executive vice-president you are not saying who gets the job . . . What do we do in local unions? We give Negroes representation in our local unions. And we run them on slates under that same understanding." As Hodges Mason, spokesperson for the caucus of Black delegates, saw it, the proposal was not a factional, left-wing idea, as some of its opponents claimed. The purpose of the amendment, Mason said, was "to right a wrong that has existed in this union for the last ten years . . . We want a Negro in a position that between conventions he can have some say about the policy of this union." Despite the greater support for the recommendation than similar proposals had received at UAW conventions, the convention delegates defeated the proposal.[30]

The prolonged discussion of Black representation in the state CIO convention prepared the way for a different result at the first constitutional convention of the Wayne County (Detroit area) CIO held just a few weeks later. The constitution committee, chaired by Fraser, recommended the creation of the office of director of organization as a third full-time office in the county council. After the convention adopted this provision, all three slates competing for office proposed a Black worker for the post. Left-winger Coleman Young then won election with the support of left and center delegates.[31]

When Young declined the nomination for secretary-treasurer at the state convention in favor of Skrocki, he declared that "unity is the only agent that will solve our grave problems." The left-center coalition maintained a united front throughout the convention. Leftists often encountered resistance within the Thomas-Addes-Leonard caucus to special measures to increase Black representation, but Fraser's vigorous support for the Black caucus proposal strengthened the unity of left and center forces. Fraser was among those who refused to vote for three leftist vice presidential candidates in 1946, but he voted for Young and other leftists on the 1947 ticket. Fraser was upset, however, when an angry confrontation broke out between a left-wing ally, UPW leader Yale Stuart, and Gus Scholle. "I could have killed Yale Stuart," Fraser recalled. "He got up on the stage . . . his general behavior, grabbing the mike . . . did who knows what damage."[32]

Although the right-wing slate again won all the offices at the 1947 state CIO convention and Scholle won reelection with 2,473 votes to Fraser's 1940, the left-center coalition improved its position among UAW delegates as compared to 1946. Fraser received about 47 percent of the auto unionists' votes compared to 42 percent garnered by Sigman in 1946. In the critically important local unions in the Big Three firms and among the independents, Fraser received 60 percent of the vote, an improvement over Sigman's 50 percent. Scholle increased his decisive share of the vote among the remainder of UAW locals, however, from 67 percent in 1946 to 70 percent in 1947. Scholle again won a majority among local unions with fewer than 5,000 members, but the variation in votes by the size of the local union was not as dramatic as it had been in 1946.[33]

Despite his vote total in the UAW delegation, Fraser did not come closer to victory than Sigman had in 1946 because he failed to retain Sigman's support among the non-UAW locals. Sigman has won nearly two-thirds of the non-UAW unions' votes, but Fraser received only about one-third of these ballots. At the end of 1946, most Steelworker local unions pulled out of the Michigan CIO because of their opposition to the conduct of the Scholle administration. This withdrawal, which was decided upon by the Steelworkers regional office, actually harmed the anti-Scholle group because it put an end to cooperation between the Steelworkers' representatives and the left-center coalition in the UAW.[34] Sigman had won the sizeable steel union delegation in 1946 by a margin of 149 to nine, but Fraser received only some seven of 36 votes from that group. In addition, there was a shift to the Scholle camp by the largest United Rubber Workers local and by all the locals of the Gas, Coke, and Chemical Workers union. The changed position of these unions alone provided Scholle with a net gain of about 300 votes, or more than one-half of his margin of victory.

The change in the alignment of the non-UAW unions may have been influenced by the altered policy of the national CIO; following its November 1946 convention, national CIO officials began supporting right-wing factions in local and state CIO councils. In a speech to the Michigan convention, Tony Smith, a representative of the CIO national office, praised the Scholle administration for carrying out CIO policy and asserted that the state council had done "an excellent job of holding its own and fighting back" on the legislative front. The national CIO's assistance to the right-wing was a serious blow to the left-center coalitions in the Michigan CIO and the UAW.[35]

Despite the shift of the national CIO leadership to the right, the events of the 1947 Michigan CIO convention showed that left-center forces were holding their own in the UAW factional conflict. The intensification of the cold war and the domestic anticommunist campaign, however, led to special challenges for the left and its allies. One of the most difficult situations occurred in the Milwaukee suburb of West Allis when the Allis-Chalmers Company attempted to weaken UAW Local 248 irreversibly and to destroy its left-wing leadership.

UAW Vice President Richard Frankensteen (left) and Secretary-Treasurer George Addes at an unidentified UAW convention.

Left to right: Coleman Young, UAW General Counsel Maurice Sugar, and unidentified individual, perhaps in Sugar's office at the time of his candidacy for Detroit City Council in 1941. Young was elected as director of organization of the Wayne County CIO in 1947.

George Crockett, executive director of UAW Fair Practices Committee, 1944.

Nat Ganley, business agent of UAW Local 155 and member of the National Committee of the Communist party.

Children picketing during the 1945-46 General Motors strike.

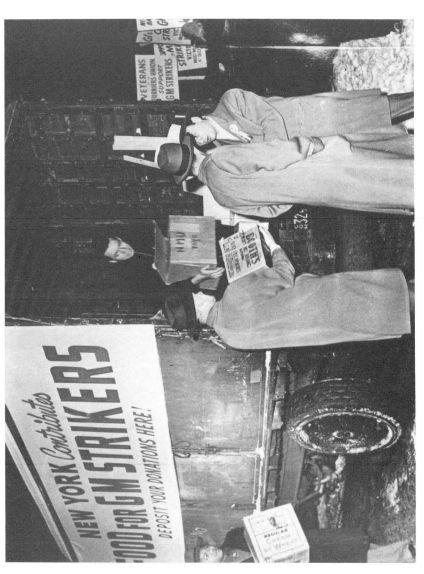

Food and toys collected by New York unions being loaded onto a truck to be sent to striking General Motors workers, 1945.

Walter Reuther being held aloft by his supporters after his election as UAW President at the 1946 UAW convention.

Officers elected at the 1946 UAW convention. Left to right: Vice President R.J. Thomas, Secretary-Treasurer George Addes, President Walter P. Reuther, and Vice President Richard T. Leonard.

Members of UAW Local 272 in a demonstration against anti-labor legislation, 1947.

A Detroit Labor Day parade float dramatizing opposition to the Taft-Hartley Act, 1947.

The Reuther slate candidates elected at the 1947 UAW convention. Left to right: Vice President Richard Gosser, Secretary-Treasurer Emil Mazey, President Walter Reuther, and Vice President John Livingston.

A Detroit Labor Day float from Local 600 supporting the presidential candidacy of Henry Wallace, 1948.

A large group of Ford workers outside the Ford Rouge plant during the 1949 Ford speed-up strike.

The "Walk to Freedom" in Detroit, June 23, 1963 prior to the March on Washington. UAW President Walter Reuther is third from left in the front row; Dr. Martin Luther King, Jr. is sixth from the left.

Chapter Ten

Defeat at Allis-Chalmers

The Reuther and Addes-Thomas groups differed sharply over the conduct of a difficult strike at the Allis-Chalmers plant in West Allis, Wisconsin, a suburb of Milwaukee. The company was a leading manufacturer of farm equipment. Local 248, which represented 11,500 workers at the plant and had 8,500 members, was a left-wing local that played a key role in the Milwaukee County and Wisconsin state industrial union councils of the CIO. The local was also an important force in UAW Region 4, the region with the largest UAW membership outside the Detroit area and one that was in the Thomas-Addes camp at the 1946 convention. Region 4 had swung back and forth between the two factions, however, and the director of the region, Joseph Mattson, had previously been a Reuther supporter. If the votes of the Allis-Chalmers local had been in the Reuther column at the 1946 convention, his supporters would have controlled Region 4. At the 1941 convention, in fact, the Reuther caucus had challenged the seating of delegates from the local, and the Reuther-aligned regional director had attempted to defeat the local's left-wing leadership.[1]

The Allis-Chalmers Workers Union, as Local 248 was known, prided itself on its autonomy, shop steward system, and militant processing of grievances. The local also was distinguished by its extensive educational classes, drama programs, town hall forums, films, and active women's auxiliary. A substantial force in local politics, Local 248 was active in the support of many progressive and left-wing causes. As one student by no means sympathetic to the left saw it, the local administration led by Harold Christoffel "fought relentlessly for improving the lot of the average worker . . . [and] brought tremendous strides in working conditions, job security and wages."[2]

On April 29, 1946, the Allis-Chalmers workers voted 8,091 to 251 to strike the plant, and they initiated the strike the next day. The Allis-Chalmers workers were seeking the pattern 18.5¢ wage increase, but, like the auto workers, they faced company demands designed to weaken the power of the union in the plant. The union wanted to retain the contract provisions established during the war as a result of War Labor Board rulings. Management, however, wanted to eliminate the maintenance-of-membership provision and to revise the grievance procedure so that the workers would first have to discuss a grievance with a foreman before securing a steward's aid.[3]

Although the workers began the strike with great enthusiasm, they were in a weaker position than the auto workers. Like the auto workers, they faced a corporation that was in large part insulated from the impact of a strike because it was to receive millions of dollars in legislatively mandated tax refunds for any losses suffered during reconversion. In addition, workers in the farm implement industry were weakened by the fact that the industry was only 70 percent organized, the union workers being represented by the Farm Equipment and Metal Workers Union (FE), the UAW, and several other unions. Jurisdictional conflicts between the UAW and the FE made cooperation between the two unions difficult; the UAW had even attempted to raid plants represented by the FE. Neither Allis-Chalmers nor the other major farm implement manufacturers had to contend with a single union representing all of its employees. Although, for example, the FE struck International Harvester in January 1946 after that company had rejected a federal fact-finding report, the corporation's plants represented by the UAW worked throughout the long strike.[4]

Despite division among several unions, Allis-Chalmers workers in seven plants were united at the start of the 1946 shutdown. Joining Local 248 in strike action against Allis-Chalmers were six smaller locals, including a CIO local industrial union and FE and UE locals. As the largest and strongest unit in the Allis-Chalmers chain, local 248 was the object of a special attack. Allis-Chalmers officials were long associated with the political right and were unyielding to their desire to restore traditional management prerogatives. The company's assault on the union became a national focal point in the conservative drive for antilabor legislation. Allis-Chalmers officials played a significant role in the development of the Taft-Hartley Act.[5]

Although management and the media charged that a Communist-run union was striking to delay reconversion, the reports of the government personnel involved in the dispute show that corporate intransigence was responsible for the prolonged impasse. Before the strike began, commissioners from the Labor Department's Conciliation Service observed that, in attempting to deal with an increased grievance load and the increased cost of writing agreements, the company had taken an "extreme" position, proposing not to pay stewards for the time consumed in writing up grievances. One week before the strike began, the Labor Department representatives noted that the company's negotiating team would not cooperate but that the union committee was "much more receptive" and could be "influenced and . . . guided by the advice and counsel of the Conciliators." Although the union agreed with the conciliatiors' proposal to submit unresolved issues to arbitration, the company refused. Like the conciliators, Assistant Secretary of Labor John Gibson, former president of the Michigan CIO and by no means sympathetic to Communists, also found the company uncooperative but "had no difficulty" in dealing with the local union officers, the union negotiating committee, or the international representatives.[6]

After failing in his attempt to secure a settlement, Secretary of Labor Lewis Schwellenbach recommended to the president that the federal government seize the corporation's plants. The UAW and the other unions on strike supported seizure because they wanted to maintain contractual gains won during the war through the War Labor Board. If the government were to operate the plants, they presumed, it would do so on the basis of the wartime contractual agreements. Secretary of Commerce Henry Wallace recorded in his diary that Schwellenbach's report on the Allis-Chalmers strike was a "hair-raising story in which justice was obviously on the side of labor." Wallace noted that Schwellenbach had suggested that Truman "go on the air . . . and make a speech as vigorous against Allis-Chalmers . . . as he had made" against the rail union leaders. Although Truman indicated interest in the idea and was certainly concerned about the heavy impact that the widespread farm implement industry shutdown was having on the nation's agriculture, he chose to go along with his more conservative advisers and refrained from using the power of seizure in this instance. He had used this power against oil, packinghouse, and railroad workers in response to strikes resulting from their demands.[7]

Truman's decision not to seize the struck plants in the agricultural implement industry greatly reduced the Labor Department's ability to pressure the company to settle the dispute. The key issue was the grievance procedure, and, although the federal conciliators were at first optimistic, they were in the end unsuccessful in persuading the company to compromise. Allis-Chalmers management was determined to eliminate any private discussion between the steward and the grievant in the first stage of the grievance procedure. Harold Story, Allis-Chalmers vice president, complained to Gibson: " . . . how are we going to meet our specifications of control unless we have somebody in the conference to know what they are talking about? It all [s]immers down to our lack of confidence in this particular group. The other people [in other local unions], we let them talk because they talk in good faith . . . . We have to continue to say 'no' on the first step . . . . " By the end of October 1946, all but one of the other Allis-Chalmers local unions had concluded that they had no choice but to return to work with unsatisfactory agreements that weakened their position on the shop floor. In any event, Story and company President Walter Geist turned aside Gibson's request to let the steward know the facts of the complaint and leave the union "enough expression to intelligently go about handling grievances."[8]

Following the collapse of negotiations in October 1946, the company initiated a major back-to-work movement. In response to this action, Local 248 called upon other unions in the area to aid the strike. UAW locals in Milwaukee formed a citywide strike strategy committee, and many non-Allis workers joined the picket lines. The company, on the other hand, enjoyed the support of the state's Republican governor and local authorities, and it benefited from a ruling by the Wisconsin Employment Relations Board (WERB) that mass picketing was illegal. Violent incidents occurred on the picket lines, and many Allis-Chalmers workers and their supporters were arrested. In mid-December more than 100 court cases were pending against union members and sympathizers on such charges as unlawful assembly and rioting. One union attorney recalled that the necessity for the union to direct its energies to these civil and criminal cases "delivered some pretty strong hammer blows at the union, . . . requiring us to spend a good deal of time . . . in areas that kept us away from the most important task of putting our minds to the resolution of the strike itself."9 Allis-Chalmers was using all the means at its disposal to break the strike.

The company resorted to red-baiting in an effort to discredit Local 248. It arranged with one of the two leading papers in Milwaukee, the *Sentinel*, for a series of articles on communism in the labor movement, with the focus on the leaders of Local 248. Between September 23 and November 21, 1946, the *Sentinel*, a Hearst paper, published daily articles against the union in what Communist leader Eugene Dennis called "a particularly vicious form of psychological warfare against the people of Milwaukee." The newspaper constructed a caricature of the Communist as "Red Fascist," opponent of "American prosperity," and agent of "Russia." The *Sentinel* characterized the leaders of Local 248 as Communists, fingering many local officials for their participation in various left and progressive organizations and causes. The newspaper concluded its series with a call to union members to vote out Communist leaders.10

In addition to supplying information to the *Sentinel* for its series, Allis-Chalmers officials publicly accused union representatives of being Communists. The company mailed to all Allis-Chalmers workers copies of Communist party gubernatorial nominating petitions that contained the signatures of many local union leaders. The anticommunist theme originated by the company was also taken up by the *Milwaukee Journal* and by national publications as well. Representatives of the House Un-American Activities Committee came to Milwaukee to investigate the strike and supplied information to the press. The anticommunist publicity, coinciding as it did with the development of the cold war, created a hostile climate that adversely affected the union's ability to conduct its strike.11

The UAW stepped up its assistance to Local 248 in an effort to alleviate the hardship of the workers as the result of the prolonged strike. "We gave it everything we had," Addes recalled. The UAW policy committee in November assigned Vice President Thomas to work fulltime in directing the drive to win the strike. Support also came from the CIO Executive Board, which ordered

CIO locals in Milwaukee to back the strike financially and on the picket line. "The whole strength of our organization," Reuther declared, "must be thrown behind the Allis-Chalmers workers." Reuther stressed, however, that unionists must not violate their contracts in rallying to Local 248's support, an admonition in line with Murray's views. Although the efforts of some strike supporters to have a work holiday proclaimed to back the Allis-Chalmers union were unavailing, some locals did stop work for short periods to join the picket lines.[12]

The Allis-Chalmers Workers Union faced a grave new difficulty when, as the *Sentinel* series reached its conclusion, a group within Local 248 began to attack the leadership of the union. The local leadership had not faced any serious opposition before the strike, all the officers having been elected without opposition in the local elections of February 1946. In the 1945 local elections, Robert Buse had been elected president by a four-to-one margin, and most other candidates had run unopposed. The new opposition group in Local 248 charged that the local union leaders were Communists. Failing to overturn the local leadership, the anticommunist group, comprised primarily of employees who had returned to work, organized an "independent" union in December 1946. The UAW characterized the new Independent Workers of Allis-Chalmers organization as a company union. The Wisconsin Employment Relations Board nevertheless scheduled a representation election for January 26, 1947, ignoring the UAW's protest that only the NLRB had jurisdiction. The "independent" group had collected about 180,000 signatures, far too few for an election sponsored by the NLRB, which, in any event, would have listened much more sympathetically to the UAW's complaint that the organization had no standing because it was a company union. A UAW plea for a federal injunction to block the WERB vote was turned aside by a judge who was the brother-in-law of Harold Story.[13]

The Independent Workers of Allis-Chalmers, which undoubtedly received material assistance from the company, was a significant threat to Local 248. The fact that some 4,000 workers had become demoralized and returned to work strengthened the hand of the new organization. The Independent Workers also hoped that it would receive the support of the Reuther caucus.[14]

Although Reuther had personally pledged support for the strike, the Reuther-aligned Wisconsin locals led by Walter Cappel withheld their support for the strike for more than seven months. Only after the CIO Executive Board called on CIO locals in Milwaukee to support the strike and after Reuther met with Cappel on the matter did the latter give his grudging support to the strikers. Cappel assured the press, however, that the right-wing's support for the strike in no way constituted support for Local 248 leaders. In fact, the right-wing caucus in the UAW concentrated its efforts on overturning the long-established left-wing leadership of both the Milwaukee County Industrial Union Council and the Wisconsin State Industrial Union Council. The right-wing drive for control of the councils was an hysterical, anticommunist campaign, no different in character from that of the Allis-Chalmers Company. The conservative press gave profuse coverage to the anticommunist effort, which succeeded first in the county council in October with the questionable seating of the newly affiliated Brewery Workers locals. At the state CIO convention in mid-December 1946, the right wingers, according to a reporter for the liberal *Madison Capital-Times*, were "yelling and screaming for order and refusing to permit the opposition to speak" and were "near rioting." Although the right-wing delegates were outnumbered at the convention, they were aided by the anticommunist turn that had taken place at the national CIO convention. National CIO officials intervened in the struggle, interpreting the rules in such a way as to give the right-wing control. Robert Buse, stepped down as president of the CIO council to make way for UAW Local 75 President Herman Steffes, a compromise candidate, but most other offices were won by right-wing caucus candidates.[15]

It is understandable that Independent Workers members took comfort from the right-wing UAW forces in the Wisconsin CIO because they were attacking the same enemy with the same anticommunist tactics. They publicly affirmed support for the right wing in the Milwaukee CIO and also for Reuther and Murray. Thomas charged that the right wingers were meeting with the Allis-Chalmers strikebreakers, but evidence to support this accusation is lacking. The UAW right wing had nevertheless strengthened the hand of the Independent Workers group by attacking the legitimacy of the Local 248 leadership. Cappel even attacked Regional Director Joseph Mattson, declaring, "We're giving no quarter to anyone who operates with Communist support, even if he is not a Communist." The moral authority of the union was thereby weakened, and strike breaking became acceptable to a large group of strikers.[16]

By mid-December Local 248 was the only one of the seven original striking Allis-Chalmers local unions still on strike. The union's strike newspaper asserted that the corporation had been able to force the members of the other locals to return on company terms because the locals were small. "These workers were literally starved out," the paper declared, "they could not find jobs elsewhere as most of our members have done with the help of Local 248." The success in finding work in other plants, however, meant many members had little time to devote to the strike. Also, some of the dispersed members of the Allis-Chalmers local were now at work in plants with right-wing local union officials who were politically opposed to the leaders of Local 248. Hearing their leaders attacked by fellow UAW members could only have had a demoralizing effect on these Local 248 members. The scattering of Local 248 members made it more difficult for the local union to get all its voters to the polls for the state-supervised representational election. The Independent Workers, on the other hand, had ready access to the compact group of some 4,000 workers who had returned to their jobs.[17]

Local 248 was still on strike as 1947 began, although it was weakened by the right-wing victories in the state and Milwaukee County CIO councils. In the new year, the Allis-Chalmers corporation was no longer able to receive excess profit tax refunds. The company could hope, however, that the Wisconsin labor board election at the end of January would result in a victory for the company union. As the union began to lose strength in December, Reuther told the UAW board that he thought the leadership of local 248 should resign because of the "attack being made by the corporation respecting the political character of the leadership." Reuther presented the idea of the resignation of local officials to the board as Addes's proposal. Addes acknowledged that he had advanced the suggestion, but he did not want Reuther to bring it before the board without first discussing it with Thomas. Both Thomas and Regional Director Mattson opposed the proposal. The local leadership had actually offered to resign in October provided that the company agreed to a satisfactory contract, but Allis-Chalmers management had rejected the offer. The majority of the executive board did not agree with Reuther's proposal, believing that an unconditional resignation of the local leadership in and of itself would not bring a resolution of the strike. In January, Reuther thought it was time to place the local union under an administrator, but the UAW policy committee overruled him.[18]

Reuther's attempt to eliminate the left-wing Local 248 leadership coincided with a new demand of the company. Allis-Chalmers representatives met with Reuther on January 11 and 14 and informed him that one of the conditions for a settlement was the elimination of the local leadership. Thomas reported to the UAW locals that "the company flatly refuses to sign a contract with the present officers and bargaining committee of the Local Union. The company insists that the officers and bargaining committee be ousted and it insists upon negotiating only with certain persons in the International Union." Thomas charged that this new company tactic was decided upon by the NAM at a meeting in December 1946 and that several auto companies were acting accordingly. Management, Thomas warned, had developed a "formula for destroying the secondary leadership of our Union . . . . Management in our industry is being encouraged to attempt to interfere in the affairs of local unions by playing international union politics. Management is trying to play off one group against the other with the hope of eventually destroying all groups."[19]

The company's principal aim by 1947 was to destroy Local 248 as an effective force by eliminating the local union leadership. It sought to use the threat of an electoral victory by the company union to get the international leadership to accomplish this task for it. On the eve of the election, the company proposed an agreement that involved the removal of local leaders, a weakened grievance procedure, and an inferior form of union security. Reuther thought that publicity about an impending settlement would aid the union in the election and that a January 23 declaration by Local 248 that there would be no further negotiations before the balloting damaged the union. John Brophy, the CIO representative, acted in concern with Reuther in approaching the company. In his autobiography, Brophy mistakenly credits Allis-Chalmers with a willingness "to make a reasonable settlement." Although the Milwaukee press reported that Reuther would have liked to settle the strike on the terms then under discussion, Reuther joined with the rest of the policy committee in voting down the company proposal. Reuther told the policy committee that the union "should work hard for a settlement in order to salvage the UAW as bargaining agent" if there were a danger of losing the election. Because Thomas reported that the UAW would win by a substantial margin, Reuther joined in rejecting the company's position. UAW leaders believed that a better settlement could be expected after an election victory.[20]

The UAW appeared at first to win a narrow victory over the company union in the Wisconsin labor board election, obtaining a plurality of slightly more than 100 votes out of 8,324 cast. With 117 votes going to no union and 50 ballots challenged, however, the UAW failed to gain a clear majority. Although on the night of the election the WERB was quoted in the press as stating that the vote outcome meant that the UAW retained its bargaining rights, it later reversed its position and refused to certify Local 248 as bargaining agent. The board first conducted a recount, which added a few votes for Local 248, and then instituted proceedings on the challenged ballots. The Independent Workers sought a runoff election, and the company claimed that there was no longer a legal bargaining agent in its West Allis plant. This was the turning point in the strike.[21]

Prior to the election, the Wisconsin CIO council had condemned the ordering of an election in a strikebound plant and characterized the danger to the union: "For nine months the workers have faced payless paydays, mounting bills—in some cases actual hunger," the Council declared. "To hold a representation election in such a period of induced hysteria* and weakening resolve is to invite the destruction of the union and the loss of the strike." Looking back, Christoffel saw exhaustion after nine months of striking as the principal reason for the union's failure to win a "good majority" of the vote. "The people were awful tired," Christoffel recalled, "and . . . they were hammered and hammered and hammered in the press day after day . . . it's bound to have an effect . . . ,maybe it's better to switch our allegiance . . . we had a good union but you can't have a good union under those circumstances and therefore we'll salvage what we can, ... Half finally had fatigue. They just were tired, they saw what they had was broken."[22]

---

*This is a reference to the impact of company and press propaganda against the union.

In the wake of the election results, the conflict between Reuther and Thomas over the strike escalated radically. Thomas charged that "Reuther swallowed the bait . . . in the form of . . . an opportunity to negotiate on a company proposal alone" and that Reuther's entrance "only served to confuse the workers." Reuther criticized Thomas for making a public attack on him and said he had not negotiated but had only "explored the company position," as the policy committee had authorized him to do. Reuther charged that Thomas's actions imperiled the strike. The charges and countercharges were publicized throughout the union. The open split in the international leadership only added to the Allis-Chalmers strikers' difficulties. The company persisted in its demand that the local leadership be ousted. Although Reuther and CIO President Murray were agreeable to this, the majority of the UAW leadership continued to reject the idea.[23]

Although Thomas asserted that Reuther jeopardized the strike's outcome, Reuther believed that the left-wing political character of the Local 248 leadership in and of itself endangered the union. " . . . what is happening in Local 248," he told the UAW board, "is just a small, a little dress rehearsal compared to what is going to happen in this country. I am not saying that we should run. I am prepared and will take my place to fight against the witch-hunt but I say it is nothing short of criminal negligence for a union not to recognize these basic facts and attempt to get its house in order and get in a position to resist the full impact of that attack." The gap between the Thomas and Reuther approaches could not have been wider.[24]

Already greatly weakened by the back-to-work movement, the WERB election, and the division in the international, Local 248 was subjected to new attacks in February and March. Both the House Education and Labor Committee and the House Un-American Activities Committee held hearings in these months in which the company's charges were warmly received and the union leaders were treated like criminals. The company charged that the union was prolonging the strike to further Thomas's ambition to regain the UAW presidency. Thomas called the accusation "stupid" and asserted, "I've never been in a strike I was more interested in settling." Although Thomas may have had hopes that a strike victory would enhance his position, by March 1947 little prospect of a favorable settlement existed.[25]

On March 23, 1947, Local 248 decided to call off the strike and return to work without a contract. "As we said many times before," union president Robert Buse declared, "we will go back without a contract before we will sign a sweatshop agreement." The company's refusal to bargain with the local, Buse said, "had created a deadlock which technically and legally could take months to break." Planning to go to court to protect its bargaining rights and faced with the prospect of another election, this time supervised by the NLRB, Buse asserted: "We must muster our forces to retain our bargaining rights and keep company unionism and sweatshop conditions out of Allis-Chalmers." The local officers hoped to rebuild the union's strength with the return to Allis-Chalmers of workers who had obtained jobs with other firms during the strike. Knowing the difficulties that faced them after a broken strike, about 1,800 workers failed to return to the company. The company responded to the local's shift in tactics, moreover, by firing 91 workers, including most union officers, committee persons, and stewards.[26]

The returning union workers had to work under open-shop conditions; they were told by management that there was no union in the plant. The local also had to contend with the efforts of the Independent Workers, which tried to benefit by the division in the international and distributed postcards in the plant calling for the UAW to place Local 248 under an administrator. The UAW local fought back against its opponents and, with the continuing assistance of the international, won a majority in the July 1947 NLRB election. The vote was once again close, and sufficient ballots were challenged to put the results in doubt once again. The NLRB refused to certify the election results because of the UAW's failure to file the non-Communist affidavits required by the recently passed Taft-Hartley Act even though the election itself had taken place before the act came into force. It was another year before the NLRB ruled that the UAW local had won the bargaining election. The Allis-Chalmers Workers Union had survived the biggest assault launched against any local union in the postwar period.[27]

Although the local survived the 11-month conflict, the strike itself was a terrible defeat for the union. The strike was not the only defeat suffered by the UAW in the postwar period. The UAW also lost a prolonged multi-plant strike against the J. I. Case Company. The company broke the strike at the plants in Rock Island and Rockford, Illinois. UAW Local 180, which represented workers at Case's Racine, Wisconsin plant, held out for 15 months and then, facing a threat by the corporation to close the plant, agreed to a less than satisfactory contract. Reuther's assertion that Local 180 had won a victory and Local 248 suffered a defeat because of the difference in the character of their leadership was wide of the mark. Reuther's appraisal ignored the strike defeats at the other Case plants and the poor contract that Local 180 had actually been forced to accept. Also, the international and the local labor movement were united behind the Case strikers whereas the international was divided and the UAW right wing gave less than full support to the Allis-Chalmers strike. The Allis-Chalmers workers were able to hold out as long as they did precisely because of the militant unionism they had learned under their left-wing leadership. The strike was defeated in spite of, not because of, the left-wing leadership of Local 248. Nevertheless, the strike had special significance because it was a defeat for a powerful left-wing local. The loss itself provided support for Reuther's argument that the UAW could no longer tolerate Communists in leadership.[28]

The left-wing leadership of Local 248 was not able to overcome the many obstacles it had faced. The defeated strike, the firing of its leading activists, and the indictment of union leader Harold Christoffel for perjury before a Congressional committee were heavy burdens for the local. The opposition, after the UAW convention, of the new Reuther-dominated leadership of the international was the final blow. The fired union leaders never returned to their jobs. They were among the first casualties in the cold war purge of left-wing activists.[29]

Chapter Eleven

Round Two in the Postwar Wage Negotiations

When the price control law expired on June 30, 1946, with Congress still debating the issue, an immediate 6 percent increase in the CPI occurred for all commodities and a 14 percent increase in food prices. Responding to the inflation, many auto workers demanded UAW action to increase wages and restore price control; Ford Local 600 called for a "cost-of-living bonus." The UAW's wage demands were directed primarily at the Chrysler Corporation because the union's contract with that company provided that negotiations on wages could be reopened on 60 days' notice. In addition to seeking a wage increase, Chrysler workers were angered by the corporation's "arbitrary reclassification" of many operations, the institution of a speed-up, and a general policy of "forcing the Chrysler workers to accept sweat shop conditions."[1]

A number of delegates present at the Chrysler conference of July 9–10, 1946, especially those who were Thomas-Addes-Leonard supporters, pressed for reopening negotiations with the company on the subject of wages. Norman Matthews, Chrysler Department Director and an independent in the union's factional politics, thought such action was premature and that it was necessary to coordinate the UAW's demands with the CIO as a whole. Although he had previously favored a one-company-at-a-time approach in the conduct of negotiations and UAW wage action independent of the CIO, Reuther, who attended the Chrysler conference, agreed with Matthews. Like Matthews, Reuther thought that an effort to secure wage increases was untimely and should be undertaken only if the price control fight failed. The Chrysler conference resolved to notify the Chrysler Corporation that, if Congress did not authorize OPA and restore prices to the June 30, 1946, level, the union would seek a wage increase equal to the rise in prices.[2]

The reluctance of Reuther and Matthews to seek immediate negotiations with Chrysler was in part a reaction to the increasingly antilabor climate in the country. The estrangement between the Truman administration and the labor movement was at its height following Truman's proposed actions against the railroad strikers. Reuther and Matthews were also concerned about the effect on the upcoming Congressional elections of pressing wage demands. Top leaders from the Thomas-Addes-Leonard camp also were concerned about these matters and were anxious to avoid the mistakes the UAW had made in the General Motors negotiations. Even though the Chrysler locals has supported Thomas and Leonard at the convention and it was Chrysler local union presidents aligned with the Addes-Thomas-Leonard group who were pressing for action, Thomas and Addes were even more cautious on the wage issue than Reuther. After several Chrysler local presidents appeared before the International Executive Board in August to demand action, Thomas told the board that he did not believe Chrysler workers could lead the fight for the second-round wage increase and that the UAW had to work with the CIO.[3]

Although he believed the time was not ripe for a wage action, Reuther proposed a policy statement to the board that promised future action. He told the board that Murray had approved the Statement and that he (Reuther) had promised Murray that the UAW would not go off "half-cocked" in the Chrysler negotiations. "The fight against inflation," the Reuther statement proclaimed, "has become the major front in our struggle to protect the living standards of our membership . . . . We must put chief reliance upon our power as consumers." The statement further called for combining consumer action and political action and for taking "preliminary steps in preparation for action on the wage front." In addition to providing that the union immediately give Chrysler the required 60 days' notice that it wished to reopen wage negotiations, the statement warned government and industry that the UAW would determine future action on the basis of the relations between prices and wages following the 60 day period. The suggested policy statement reaffirmed the Reuther concept that real wages would grow with the "wage increases . . . paid out of the higher profits of industry made possible by the economies of full production and improved technology and not passed on to the consumer in higher prices."[4]

Both Thomas and Addes expressed serious reservations about the Reuther statement. Thomas who, like Reuther, had just spoken with Murray at the CIO board meeting, argued that the CIO head did not want the UAW to pursue its wage demands at that time. In Thomas's view, the Chrysler Corporation was not big enough for a successful wage action directed against it to change the country's wage structure. Addes expressed his opposition to the UAW's once again pursuing a one-company-at-a-time policy. Although Thomas and Addes feared that the Reuther policy would lead to premature action by the UAW's members, Reuther insisted that he was simply offering a policy statement, not a particular strategy, and he believed that his approach was the best way to "control" the UAW membership. Thomas and Addes did not have an alternative program to offer. Reuther had once again assumed leadership in the collective bargaining arena, and the board adopted his proposal with only one negative vote.[5]

Shortly before the UAW adopted the Reuther statement, Congress enacted a new price control law. The measure, however, curtailed the OPA's authority, and prices continued to rise, although at a slower rate. Despite the price rise, the Truman administration continued to adhere to the wage stabilization order issued at the time of the steel strike and did not permit wage increases to match cost-of-living increases. George Addes protested that the administration was telling workers not to ask for wage increases but was merely requesting the big business forces responsible for the end of price control to reexamine their profit position. Addes charged that the "sole purpose" of the administration's wage-price policy was "to lend aid and comfort to the automobile manufacturers." In part because of the position of the Truman administration, the UAW delayed the launching of its wage drive.[6]

An additional factor that restrained the UAW was the spotty employment picture in the auto industry. Although the auto companies claimed that strikes at supplier plants were hampering production, the union blamed management provocation and a continued disinterest in high-volume production due to tax rebates for low production.[7]

Also affecting the UAW's readiness to engage in strike action was the Republican campaign against the CIO. Many in the union thought that union-supported candidates would be hurt in the November elections if the UAW took too aggressive a position in demanding a wage increase. The increasing difficulties experienced by the UAW in strikes at Allis-Chalmers and Case for first-round wage increases also slowed the drive to initiate a second round of wage hikes. Although Chrysler workers had demanded the reopening of negotiations in the summer, the unfavorable political and economic climate led to a decline in rank-and-file demands for action. UAW left wingers, nevertheless, called for a public relations campaign on the wage issue.[8]

The UAW formulated a new wage policy on October 20, 1946, as the basis for negotiations with Chrysler and the other auto firms. Because of what it characterized as the "complete destruction of effective controls of the cost of living," the UAW demanded a wage increase that would provide UAW members and their families with a "decent standard of living." The UAW did not name a specific wage figure, however. The UAW also called for the equalization of wage rates, a social security program covering health, hospital, disability, and death benefits, and a pension program. Although the policy statement embodying these demands was presented to the board by Addes, the new wage position followed the general lines of a Reuther proposal, and it was the UAW president who publicly announced the program. Reuther continued to maintain his leadership of the UAW's collective bargaining stance in the second round of wage negotiations.[9]

The UAW's social security demands, in Reuther's view, were noninflationary, sounder than a straight raise in pay, and had a better chance of success than a wage increase. Reuther's implication that an increase in hourly wage rates could be inflationary was a concession to the antilabor propaganda of business circles and contradicted the UAW board policy statement of the previous April. Addes's views on this question, however, were not very different from Reuther's. Addes told a UAW conference on health in September that there was a limit to what the union could expect to achieve in wage increases. The UAW had to look elsewhere than "the pay envelope," Addes maintained, for means to advance the social and economic welfare of its membership.[10]

UAW representatives met with Chrysler officials on October 30 to reopen wage negotiations. The company pressed the union to set a specific wage figure, alleging that this was required as part of the official notification to the company that the union wished to reopen wage negotiations. The UAW negotiators were, however, unable to take this step because the board had agreed to permit the Steelworkers to take the lead in the second-round wage struggle, and the steel negotiations were not scheduled to begin until mid-December.[11]

The union's focus on Chrysler in pursuing its wage demand enabled Reuther to develop a close working relationship with Chrysler Director Norman Matthews, who now moved into the Reuther camp. Reuther's ability to appear again as the union's chief economic spokesperson also strengthened his position with the rank and file.[12] Reuther's ability to lead in the collective bargaining arena was due in part to the strategic advantage that he derived from his position as UAW president. Reuther also retained his position as Director of the GM Department, whereas neither Addes nor Thomas headed a major collective bargaining department. Leonard was head of the Ford Department, but UAW negotiations with that company were not due to begin until the spring. The key factor in the failure of the leaders of the Addes group to contest Reuther successfully for leadership in the collective bargaining arena, however, was their tie to Philip Murray. The CIO president wanted to pursue a cautious policy in the second-round negotiations because of the prevailing antilabor climate. Although he arranged for the dissemination of the Nathan report, an effective study outlining the CIO's case for a substantial wage increase, Murray did not support the making of specific wage demands and wanted, if at all possible, to resolve the wage issue peacefully. "I don't think you have the slightest chance," Murray told the UAW board at its October meeting, to press Chrysler on wage or other demands. Murray foresaw no action in the steel industry "comprehending or anticipating or looking forward to [a] strike."[13] The Thomas-Addes-Leonard coalition found that its firm support for CIO policy and for Murray was a two-edged sword. As long as CIO policy was militant and progressive and enjoyed the support of UAW members, support for CIO policy aided the coalition. When CIO policy became cautious, confused, no longer consistently progressive, support for that policy began to hurt the coalition. The left-progressive forces had made a shibboleth of the phrase "CIO policy" and of Murray's leadership, and they now paid the price.

Despite Murray's opposition to specific wage demands the UAW board, on Reuther's advice, unanimously agreed on December 12, 1946, to seek a 23.5¢ wage increase. The wage demand supplemented the union's earlier request for fringe benefits. Although he eventually voted for the 23.5¢ wage demand, Thomas criticized the proposal, stating that it was more important to discuss how to win a wage demand than to fix the size of a wage increase. He pointed to the need for an educational campaign among the union's members because many believed that the cost-of-living increase was the result of the first-round wage increase. Thomas suggested that it would take a general strike in the auto industry to win the union's demands.[14]

In replying to Thomas, Reuther expressed the belief that the determination of the wage demand was simply a statistical question. The union executives could formulate a strategy for winning the demand, Reuther stated, once the demand was agreed upon. The board decided on this procedure and, after adopting the 23.5¢ demand, agreed to the holding of national and regional conferences to educate the union's secondary leadership on the wage question.[15]

The UAW stood alone among the big three CIO unions in announcing a specific wage increase figure. The Addes-Thomas supporters went along with Reuther on this matter, despite the opposition of Murray, because they did not want Reuther to appear more militant than they were. Nevertheless, Reuther's leadership allowed him to retain his image as a spokesperson for the economic needs of industrial workers.

Neither union faction thought that conditions were favorable for militant action. The UAW still planned to permit the Steelworkers to take the lead in the negotiations. Even the UAW's educational campaign for its wage demand developed slowly. The attention of union leadership and membership alike increasingly focused on the factional conflict within the union and the looming threat of restrictive labor legislation.[16]

Although the UAW had initiated its negotiations with Chrysler in October, GM was the first major company to make a wage offer. On April 12, 1947, ten days after the start of negotiations, GM offered the UAW a 10¢ wage increase subject to a reexamination in August. The UAW turned down the offer as inadequate. Two days later, however, GM reached an agreement with the UE on a 15¢ package increase for 30,000 electrical workers: a wage increase of 11.5¢ and the equivalent of 3.5¢ in the form of six paid holidays.[17]

As in the 1946 negotiations, Reuther criticized the UE agreement. He told the UAW board that the UE, the UAW, and the Steelworkers had agreed to report the maximum offer that each had received to a meeting in Pittsburgh before coming to terms with the affected company. Richard Leonard disagreed with Reuther's assertion that UE had violated a commitment to the UAW and the Steelworkers. Leonard contended that James Matles of the UE had mentioned the 15¢ figure during a meeting and that Murray had nodded in approval. UE's David Mates maintained that it was the UE that had pushed for consultations among the three CIO unions. He claimed that no one spoke against accepting the 15¢ package increase presented by UE leaders to a meeting of the three CIO unions. Although Leonard's recollection corresponded with that of Mates, he joined in a unanimous UAW board vote urging the UE leaders to withhold acceptance of the wage offer until they had discussed the matter with UAW officials. Reuther's telegram to UE president Fitzgerald went even further, stating incorrectly that the UAW board wanted UE officers to urge a rejection of the GM offer. At Murray's initiative, leaders of the big three CIO unions met to discuss the status of contract negotiations, but UE members ratified their contract with GM by April 21. Leaders of both UAW factions resented the fact that the UE, which represented only a small proportion of GM workers, had set the pattern for the largest auto firm. They did not believe, however, that a higher wage pattern could have been established than that set by the UE agreement.[18]

The UE had, in fact, succeeded in extracting a larger increase from GM than the UAW had yet been able to gain from GM or any other auto firm. The UE had filed a 30 day strike notice with GM on March 20 in accordance with the Smith-Connolly Act and was facing an April 22 strike deadline. The UAW did not file a strike notice with Chrysler until April 12, and it had not yet filed a notice with GM. Off the record, UE representatives explained they were under great pressure from the rank and file to settle before the contract expired. GM made an early offer because it wanted to avoid prolonged and possible acrimonious negotiations with the UAW.[19]

On April 16, GM presented the UAW with the same wage package that the UE had accepted, and two days later GM proposed to make the increase effective immediately instead of on May 31, the expiration date of the contract. On April 19 the UAW released a detailed economic brief prepared by Reuther's staff to back up its demands. Thomas criticized the brief, claiming it was poorly argued and underminded the union's wage case. Thomas apparently preferred to rely on the favorably received Nathan report prepared under the CIO's auspices with the UAW's assistance. Whatever the weaknesses of the Reuther-sponsored document, Reuther had once again demonstrated his leadership on the collective bargaining issue. In any event, the Reuther wage brief came too late to have any real impact on the negotiations. Within a week, the Steelworkers settled for 12.5¢ in the form of a direct wage increase and an additional 2.5¢ as compensation for wage inequities. UAW negotiators then agreed to the 15¢ increase but sought to have it distributed differently. They initially proposed that there be a wage increase of 12.5¢ and that 2.5¢ go to a social security fund. When GM turned down that proposal, the UAW suggested a straight 15¢ wage increase, but GM rejected this also. The UAW complained that since there was no difference in cost to the corporation, it was difficult for the GM workers to understand why General Motors insisted that workers "take something they did not ask for, while denying them something they did ask for." Reuther offered to arbitrate the differences with GM as he had in the previous negotiations, but GM once again rejected this proposal. Finally, with the corporation threatening to withdraw its proposal, the UAW agreed on April 24 to GM's offer of an 11.5¢ wage increase and six paid holidays. The UAW settled with Chrysler on the same terms two days later.[20]

When delegates from the GM locals met in conference to discuss the agreement, they booed a proposal to set a date for strike action. There were only three votes against acceptance of the agreement. Reuther told the conference that the union had achieved a major step forward in the vacation pay formula and that this made the UAW-GM agreement better than that accepted by the UE. The UAW had indeed improved its vacation pay plan by abandoning the calculation of vacation pay as a percentage of annual gross pay, as agreed on in 1946, and by accepting the pre-1946 formula of a specific number of hours of pay depending on seniority. Many veterans returning to their jobs at GM after the war had sharply criticized the 1946 percentage formula because it provided them with no benefits. The 1947 contract provided 40, 60, or 80 hours' pay for workers with one, three, or five years seniority, respectively. The provision of 60 hours' pay for those with three-to-five years' seniority was an improvement over the 1945 agreement because under that contract, workers with one-to-five years' seniority all received 40 hours' vacation pay. Although the new vacation pay formula was thus an improvement insofar as the UAW was concerned, Reuther's assertion that the UAW agreement was consequently superior to the UE contract was inaccurate. The UE vacation pay formula was identical to that of the UAW.[21]

The two major factions had each sought to ensure that it appeared no less militant than its rival in the negotiations. In the end, however, both sides followed Murray's lead while criticizing the UE for making essentially the same settlement. The fact that the UE accepted the GM proposal before the UAW did was of less significance than the fact that both UAW factions were following Murray's lead in seeking to avoid strikes if at all possible. Reuther's outspokenness in criticizing the UE settlement, however, made him appear to be the most militant of UAW and CIO leaders. The pro-industry *Detroit News* editorially credited Reuther's rivals in the UAW leadership for the settlement, and the GM-oriented *Flint Journal* praised UE leader James Matles's "statesmanship."[22]

The CIO had sought and achieved a compromise in consonance with its strategy of avoiding strikes in a hostile environment. Although political circumstances made it a poor time for the unions to strike, the corporations also preferred a compromise. John A. Stephens, vice president and chief negotiator for United States Steel, informed an American Management Association audience that his company saw a strike as the only alternative to a wage increase. A strike, Stephens asserted, would be costly to United States Steel and to the economy and would lead to the extension of government controls. The agreement proved that labor and managment could reach peaceful settlements, Stephens contended.[23]

The wage gain achieved by the CIO unions was a significant victory, but it did not compensate for the rise in prices since the first round of pay increases. Wages had been increased by 11-12 percent, but the CPI had jumped by 20.5 percent.[24] Although UAW members were greatly concerned about inflation, they did not develop an enthusiastic grass roots campaign to back up the union demands as they had in the first-round negotiations. Members and leaders alike were affected by the antilabor climate, the Truman administration's failure to secure enactment of progressive social legislation, and the CIO-PAC defeat in the 1946 elections. The rank and file were also burdened by the day-to-day problems of short work weeks, the rising prices of necessities, and shortages of housing and consumer goods.

Negotiations between the UAW and the Ford Motor Company began only after GM and Chrysler negotiations had been completed. When it met with Ford's representatives early in May, the UAW bargaining committee renewed the union's original demands for a 23.5¢ wage increase plus funding for social security and pension plans. The company made counterproposals that once again involved the company security theme. The union's negotiators, led by Ford Department Director Richard Leonard, refused to consider the company security demands because concessions by the UAW in this area would have violated the April 1946 board policy statement that Leonard had supported. Of greater importance, given the contest for power in the UAW, no leader seeking office could hope for support by making such obvious concessions to corporate demands. After the negotiations had been completed, Ford Vice President John Bugas complained that "the unions have come to regard the established pattern as a matter of right for which nothing need be traded." Failing to make progress in the negotiations, the union called for a strike vote. Immediately following this announcement, the company offered the UAW the pattern increase, but UAW negotiators rejected this because it failed to meet the union's pension and social security demands. "I have no desire," Leonard declared, "to see such social security benefits bypassed as they were by the General Motors Corporation and the Chrysler Corporation." The successful negotiation of social security or pension benefits would obviously have been an important victory for Leonard.[25]

Leonard's eagerness to exceed the pattern and make gains in an area where other UAW leaders had failed led him to announce prematurely that an agreement had been reached on a pension plan. He reported that the retirement plan would involve an expenditure of $200 million by the company for past service benefits alone. Without mentioning Leonard, Tommy Thompson, chairperson of the Ford National Negotiating Committee and a supporter of the Thomas-Addes-Leonard caucus, complained that a UAW press release of Leonard's report that a final agreement had been reached was erroneous because the Negotiating Committee had yet to act.[26]

The passage of the Taft-Hartley Act complicated the UAW-Ford negotiations. A provision of the new law permitted management to sue the union for damages resulting from a strike in breach of contract. The UAW demanded a contract clause protecting the union from the institution of such suits. To force action on this and other union demands, the UAW set an August 4 strike deadline. Henry Ford II telephoned Philip Murray asking him to prevent a strike over the Taft-Hartley issue. Following the conversation between Ford and Murray, Reuther, who was with the CIO head when he received Ford's call, put Murray in touch with Leonard; Leonard and Addes thereupon authorized a meeting between Ford and Murray.[27] Leonard told the board, however, that he "was rather shocked to receive a call from Philip Murray regarding Mr. Ford's little junket down in New York." Leonard was right in his assessment that the publicity surrounding the Ford and Murray interchange had hurt the UAW effort. Nevertheless, after a one-day postponement of strike action, the UAW was able to achieve an agrement providing for temporary protection from the institution of damage suits. The settlement of the issue came just moments before the new strike deadline. Although the wage and benefits provisions of the contract remained unresolved, the union delayed strike action.[28]

The Ford Negotiating Committee was divided regarding the merits of the pension plan proposed by the company. As a result, the UAW and Ford agreed that the union would present two packages to the membership. The first package, supported by Leonard, provided for a contributory pension plan and a 7¢ wage increase. The second package provided for a straight wage increase of 15¢.[29]

Although supplementing social security benefits with a union pension plan was an important UAW goal, Ford workers voted down the pension plan by a three-to-one margin. This vote reflected the desire of the workers for a large wage increase to meet the rising cost of living. Also, Ford workers found fault with the terms of the pension plan in several respects. Opponents believed that the workers were contributing more than the company; they also objected to the company's having sole control of the plan and to its right to cancel the plan unilaterally. Far from achieving a victory that would have enhanced his prestige and his political standing, Leonard had suffered an important setback. The Reutherites opposed the pension plan, as did the Communists and other left wingers, although the latter were allied with Leonard in the same caucus.

Unlike the Reutherites, however, the Communists praised Leonard's efforts to negotiate a pension plan and the presentation to the Ford workers of two wage-settlement options. The top leaders of the Thomas-Addes-Leonard caucus, on the other hand, pushed for the pension option. The defeat of the pension plan, therefore, weakened the entire caucus as well as Leonard personally on the eve of the convention.[30]

The Addes-Thomas-Leonard caucus had sharply criticized Reuther's approach to wages and prices in April 1946, but the caucus did not mount a major effort to secure higher wages or to roll back prices. Although caucus leaders occasionally disapproved of Reuther's actions in the second-round wage negotiations, they did not successfully distinguish their viewpoint from his. Reuther, generally speaking, appeared as the spokesperson for the auto workers economic demands.

In the one set of major negotiations in which a leader of the left-center coalition sought to set himself apart as a negotiator, Leonard was repudiated by the Ford workers. Although the UAW made important gains during the second round of postwar negotiations, Addes, Thomas, and Leonard failed to distinguish themselves as superior leaders in the collective bargaining field. Reuther continued to maintain his leadership in the economic arena.

Chapter Twelve

Shop Floor Issues and
Labor Relations Philosophy

The Reuther caucus had increased its strength during World War II by a greater responsiveness to rank-and-file restiveness with wartime restrictions than that displayed by the Addes caucus. Giving greater weight to the need for national unity in the war effort, the Addes group, and especially its Communist allies, lost some rank-and-file support because they showed too great a willingness to support incentive pay plans and depart from the UAW's traditional objection to piecework and the speed-up generally associated with it. The wartime shift in the balance of forces because of this issue was a modest one, however, not the decisive change depicted by Irving Howe and B. J. Widick.[1] Also, both before and after the war, it was the Reuther caucus that showed a greater willingness to favor plans for labor-management cooperation and to downplay the importance of the UAW's traditional goal of establishing and maintaining a militant shop steward system to fight on shop floor grievances. During the 1946–1947 battle for control of the union, the Thomas-Addes-Leonard coalition position on these issues was by no means consistent but it was somewhat more responsive to rank-and-file concerns than was the Reuther caucus and less influenced by pressure from the press and management circles for a more "statesmanlike" approach.

During the defense buildup prior to the United States's entry into the war, Reuther brought the umpire concept to auto labor relations and achieved a national reputation by publicizing a plan for production of "500 planes a day." The left, in particular, opposed the umpire system because it saw it as undermining the rank and file's ability to win concessions on shop floor grievances. The left also was critical of Reuther's "500 planes a day" plan because of its opposition to the defense program and because it saw the program as one which would lead to a speed-up. Both the left and Addes stressed the importance of the shop steward system as a factor in maintaining the union's strength.[2]

After the Soviet Union and the United States became involved in World War II, the positions of the Reuther and Addes caucus were reversed, with the

left-center group showing greater concern for responsibility to maintain uninterrupted production for the war and the Reuther caucus demonstrating more
responsiveness to rank-and-file militancy over difficult working conditions. The
Reuther group's greater support for shop floor militancy during World War II
ended with that conflict, however. Both caucuses thought an unauthorized strike
at Kelsey Hayes in the fall of 1945 undermined the union's attempt at a coherent
postwar strategy. Reuther designed his GM strike plan, partly, to "take the ball
out of the hands of the stewards and committeemen and put it back in the hands
of the national leadership."[3]

During the 1945–1946 negotiations, leaders of both caucuses took steps
to make themselves appear "statesmanlike." Reuther asserted that the UAW
would lower its wage demands if the facts showed that GM did not have the
ability to pay what the union was asking. Ford Director Richard Leonard led
the union into making the biggest concessions to management demands,
however, on the issue of company security against unauthorized strikes. Criticism
from the left led both union caucuses to reject the concept of company security
following the 1946 UAW convention.[4]

During the 1946–1947 factional conflict, it was Reuther as UAW president who showed the most concern about appearing as a "responsible" labor
leader. This became evident during the months following the first postwar wage
settlements when many auto workers experienced reduced take-home pay
because of shortened work weeks and temporary layoffs. Although auto
managements claimed that strikes in supplier plants had led to parts shortages
that disrupted production, the UAW charged that supplies were adequate and
that management was engaged in a conspiracy to wreck price controls and
further antilabor legislation. In line with his philosophy about the need for
a balanced economy, Reuther, with the support of the UAW policy committee,
proposed to the auto companies that there be a joint labor-
management conference to solve the production problem. In August 1946, three
small auto producers met with UAW officials in a conference boycotted by the
Big Three. At the conference, Reuther declared that "the greatest single obstacle
to automobile production is a shortage of basic materials." Although calling
for an investigation of the role of monopolistic practices in creating the shortage,
Reuther believed that factors such as the depletion of scrap iron during the
war were primarily responsible for the shortages and the consequent lag in
production.[5]

George Addes participated in the production conference, but Thomas and
Leonard were critical of the effort because they believed it created the impression
that the UAW was seeking "too intimate" a relationship with management.
Thomas said he was opposed to labor's interfering in management prerogatives
and vice versa. "I am convinced," he declared, "that industry's laying down
at this time. I object to any inference that labor is involved." Although Thomas

framed his criticism in ideological terms, his comments had strong factional overtones. Thomas deeply resented his defeat by Reuther and hoped to regain the presidency. After the UAW convention, Thomas initially refused to surrender the presidental office to Reuther, and he announced that he wanted Reuther's post as director of the GM Department. Although Thomas as president had appointed standing committees subject to the approval of the board, he unsuccessfully challenged Reuther's right to make such appointments on the grounds that the UAW constitution gave this power, except in certain circumstances, to the board. While criticizing Reuther's actions at the labor-management conference, Thomas said he was receptive to a presidential draft.[6]

Left wingers such as Hilliard Ellis, president of Local 453 in Chicago, also criticized Reuther's behavior. Ellis believed that "more production to management means 'more efficiency' in production, which in practice means speed-up . . . . It is not our job to solve the so-called problems of industry for the industrialists; such problems can only be solved at the expense of the workers and in direct opposition to their best interests." Agreeing with the charge that low auto production was part of a management conspiracy, Ellis told Reuther, "neither you nor I can do anything about it." Reuther defended his action on the grounds that it would contribute to "exposing the lies of industry with regard to the strike situation."[7]

Reuther received very favorable press coverage of his efforts, but the press highlighted the idea of labor-management cooperation rather than a possible management conspiracy against production. Reuther continued to emphasize the theme of labor-management cooperation as the solution to production problems. At a time when the UAW's left-wing Local 248 was receiving extremely hostile publicity because of the prolonged Allis-Chalmers strike in a Milwaukee suburb, Reuther received praise from that city's press for a Milwaukee speech supporting labor-management cooperation.[8]

The issue of labor-management cooperation became a subject of dispute within the UAW again in 1947. Toledo Regional Director Richard Gosser spoke to the Economic Club of Detroit, the leading organization of the city's business community, about the accomplishments of the Toledo Labor-Management-Citizens' Committee in achieving industrial peace and production. The UAW board decided to make an inquiry into the Toledo labor-management plan, but Thomas angrily denied Detroit newspaper reports that the UAW had approved any such plan. He assured delegates to a national UAW wage conference that any plan involving "any limitation on the right to strike or any kind of communitywide War Labor Board . . . will have my energetic opposition . . . we do not want collective bargaining to become a prize of City Hall politics." Although Reuther opposed any restriction on the right to strike, he supported the idea of voluntary labor-management cooperation and proposed a national labor-management conference. "In a democracy," Reuther declared, "there is no other way of solving the labor problem. Labor and management must sit down at the conference table and thrash it out themselves." Both Reuther and Addes agreed to sit on the Mayor's Labor-Management-Citizens' Committee in Detroit. The Committee's report called for "industrial peace," harmonious industrial relations based on free collective bargaining, technological improvements, management's right to direct the operation of its enterprises, and labor's right to organize and bargain collectively.[9]

At a time when the Taft-Hartley Act was being enacted into law, Reuther and Addes no doubt believed that it was important to demonstrate that labor leaders were reasonable in seeking industrial peace. Although labor leaders may have been perceived as conciliatory for joining the Detroit Mayor's committee, GM and other companies represented on the committee could claim the same for themselves. This apparent amity occurred as the UAW was accusing the corporations of a legislative conspiracy to destroy labor's rights; joint labor-management statements supporting labor peace may have undermined the effort to mobilize the rank and file to defeat the corporate drive.[10]

Although Reuther was the UAW leader most clearly identified with labor-management cooperation, Addes's participation in the Detroit committee indicated his philosophical agreement with the desirability of "industrial peace." The difference between the approach of Addes on the one hand and Thomas and UAW leftists on the other hand was an indication of the difficulties the Thomas-Addes-Leonard coalition faced in maintaining a united front and in implementing the UAW board program of April 1946. Although the board had rejected "any so-called partnership of industry and labor," it had also affirmed its "historic position that capital is entitled to a fair return on its investment." This pro-capitalist thinking led to Addes's acceptance of such concepts as labor-management cooperation.[11]

As the date of the eleventh UAW convention approached, the Addes-Thomas-Leonard coalition, hurt by the FE-UAW merger issue and the Taft-Hartley affidavits question, attempted an offensive against the Reuther caucus on the issue of speed-up.[12] The Addes group charged Reuther with supporting a speed-up because his name was attached to a statement issued in August 1947 by the National Planning Association (NPA) declaring that increases in real wages depended on increases in productivity. The NPA statement, which was also signed by other labor leaders, cited "improved personal efficiency of workers" as a factor contributing to increases in productivity. When the NPA declaration received widespread publicity, Addes supporters criticized Reuther, who thereupon repudiated the NPA statement. "My consistent position," Reuther declared, "has been that wages can be increased substantially without raising prices. What else can this mean but that real wages can rise now on the basis of present productivity?"[13]

Reuther's critics regarded his repudiation of the NPA statement as less than satisfactory because he failed to disavow an earlier NPA productivity statement to which his name was also attached and did not agree to resign from the organization. The majority of the UAW board also expressed concern about a statement in the wage brief issued earlier in the year by Reuther: "The familiar argument that labor should base its wage demands on higher productivity, when this is achieved at some time in the future, is a sound prescription for labor's wage demands in the years ahead."[14]

Reuther was criticized not only for these statements but also for advice he gave to Studebaker Local 5 that it must recognize that the "honeymoon" was over and that the industry was returning to a competitive situation. GM workers opposed to Reuther criticized speed-up conditions in General Motors plants. Reuther, of course, was codirector of the GM Department.[15]

The speed-up charges hurt Reuther. The reaction of local leaders to the NPA story was negative, and some of those who had supported Reuther in the past began to question their choice. In fighting this attack, the Reutherites revived the communist issue, claiming that "the same people who favored piecework during the war now pose as its militant opponents." Although the Communists and some of their allies had supported incentive pay schemes during the war, Reuther ignored the fact that some of the people opposing him on the speed-up issue had also resisted those proposals.[16]

Although the Addes caucus placed Reuther on the defensive on the speed-up issue, it was not able to disrupt the shift toward Reuther that was taking place in the last few months before the convention. Reuther somewhat deflected the effectiveness of the speed-up charge by raising the question of communism. More important, the charge looked like a last-minute election ploy by the Addes caucus. The Addes forces had implicitly criticized Reuther's economic concepts when they ratified the April 1946 policy statement, but they had ignored the issue since that time. Now, the Addes caucus on the board was citing old Reuther statements, including one in the wage brief that the board itself had authorized Reuther to publish, with Thomas casting the lone negative vote. Because opposition to speed-up was so important an issue to the UAW, it was possible to ask how Reuther could really have been so guilty and yet not have been called to account before.[17]

Shop floor issues and labor-management philosophy played only a minor part in the battle for control of the UAW. If there was more to criticize in the way grievances were processed in General Motors plants than in the plants of the other major companies, that had as much to do with GM's greater strength as it did with Reuther's policy. The idea that Reuther was the special champion of shop floor militancy is wide of the mark, however. Rather, it was Reuther who showed greater sensitivity to the value of appearing to be a responsible leader in the eyes of management groups and the press. Although his rivals also showed concern with this matter, they were more interested in maintaining the respect and good will of the "old timers," the 1930s activists in the local unions who had built the union.

Chapter Thirteen

Taft-Hartley and the Defeat of the Progressive Alternative in the UAW

The threat to the labor movement posed by the corporate drive to enact antilabor legislation became a factor of great importance in the auto union factional conflict. Although both sides opposed the industry campaign, the two caucuses disagreed on how to respond to the impending danger. Membership involvement and concern over this issue were greater than on any other because the union's ability to function effectively and obtain decent wages and working conditions appeared to be at stake. Although many members of the Reuther caucus wished to go all out in opposition to the proposed restrictive legislation, Reuther and some other key members of his caucus believed that a moderate, restrained opposition was needed; the union had to prepare to defend itself by getting its own "house in order."[1] With the insertion of the non-Communist affidavit requirement into the Taft-Hartley Bill, the Reuther caucus saw the opportunity to use this antilabor legislation against its factional opponents. In contrast, the left-progressive forces in the union, supported by the leaders of the Addes caucus, mounted a bold challenge to the antilabor legislation.

The peril of repressive legislation became immediate when the House of Representatives on April 7, 1947, approved the Hartley Bill by a wide margin, with a majority of Democrats voting for the measure. There were many demands within the UAW for the organization to pursue a united front strategy against the bill. A national CIO legislative conference responded to the critical legislative situation by designating April "Defend Labor Month." The UAW executive board, which supported the CIO call for action, assigned to Richard Leonard's Legislative and Political Action Department the responsibility of directing the UAW campaign. Leonard proposed UAW rallies in Detroit and other cities. At the request of a conference of 500 UAW local leaders in Detroit, the UAW board agreed to expand the Detroit demonstration into a work stoppage. The four Detroit regional directors, two from each faction, assumed the responsibility of organizing the demonstration.[2]

Two days before the demonstration Regional Director William Stevenson told the UAW board that some local unions were opposed to joining the walkout. Reuther reported to the board that GM had informed him that it was preparing to fire some people who participated in the demonstration and that, in reply, he had told company officials that UAW members had the right to assemble. The UAW president said that he doubted the corporation would actually take the disciplinary action it was threatening. Addes responded that the board had to back its decision to call the workers out by informing GM that the union would shut down GM's plants if the company disciplined any UAW members. The board minutes record Reuther's strong reaction to this suggestion: "President Reuther expressed the opinion that . . . no Board Member, no matter how righteous he may feel about the cause, has the right to shut down a General Motors Plant as a countermeasure to the company's discipline . . . . He did not for a moment doubt that the General Motors Corporation would hesitate to take the union on in the event the Union attempted to close its plants down . . . ." Reuther went on to assert that the union should protest any disciplinary action by GM through the grievance procedure. The talk of shutting down plants led Reuther to contend that the planned demonstration was a mistake but that it was now too late to abandon the action. Because Reuther, the GM Department director, opposed the idea, the board did not act on Addes's proposal to apprise GM that the union would shut down the plants in response to disciplinary action.[3]

On April 24, 1947, auto plants employing nearly 500,000 workers were shut down between 2:00 p.m. and 7:00 p.m. so that both day and afternoon shift workers could participate. A huge union crowd gathered in Cadillac Square, 200,000 by the UAW's estimate. UAW members were joined by the members of other CIO unions, the striking telephone workers, and some AFL and independent unions. The demonstration constituted a great "resurgence of militancy and fighting spirit," said Tony Czerwinski, president of Briggs Local 212 and a left-wing leader. In the view of UAW Vice President Leonard, the workers had been aroused for the first time in five years. The demonstration, Leonard believed, caused Truman to decide to veto the antilabor bills. The unity of the massive stoppage and rally was less than complete, however. The majority of General Motors workers in the Detroit area did not participate, and the plants in which they worked continued to operate.[4]

The fact that 24,000 of the 37,000 GM workers in the Detroit area did not join the stoppage gave the corporation the opportunity to discipline the leaders of the locals that had participated. GM discharged 15 local union officers, laid off 26 more for 30 to 60 days, and suspended about 400 workers for one day. A meeting of Detroit-area local union presidents observed with alarm that by disciplining local leaders who had carried out the order of the International Executive Board, GM had "seen fit to challenge the honor and prestige of the UAW-CIO." The local presidents resolved to support "actively, morally and financially any action necessary to overcome this '*Fear Psychology*' program . . . directed at the very foundation of our union movement . . . ."[5]

With the strong backing of the local union leaders, Addes and Stevenson initiated negotiations with GM to have these disciplinary measures immediately rescinded rather than processed through the grievance machinery, as Reuther had initially preferred. Reuther, who now also favored immediate top-level negotiations, joined the bargaining. The union was able to persuade the corporation to agree to reinstate all of those who had been fired, but the settlement provided that they were to be suspended for up to 90 days. Moreover, the Memorandum of Understanding on the punishments contained a UAW acknowledgement that the cessation of work had been in violation of the union's contract with the corporation. Although UAW officials believed that the contract's no-strike clause referred to disputes between the parties and not to political demonstrations, they thought it necessary to yield on this point. Reuther explained to the local presidents that conditions for a strike were poor: there were layoffs due to a steel shortage; GM workers had already lost income due to the 1945–1946 strike and, subsequently, to short hours; and Congress was "hell bent" on destruction. Under the circumstances, the local presidents did not object to the settlement.[6]

Although local leaders and activists from both factions had organized the demonstration, some leading figures in the Reuther group had weakened the effort by their actions. Art Johnstone, assistant director of the GM Department, had belittled the idea of the stoppage when talking with local unions. Reuther himself had failed to use his personal influence to persuade reluctant GM locals to participate. The failure of the majority of Detroit GM locals to join the demonstration and GM's success in imposing modified disciplinary penalties against demonstration leaders weakened the impact of the protest and took much of the steam out of the union's campaign against the proposed restrictive labor legislation.[7]

The difference between the Reuther and Addes caucus approaches to the antilabor drive was especially evident when the right-wing controlled Michigan state CIO met in convention in June 1947. The left-progressive forces advocated conferences, mass demonstrations in the state capital, and work stoppages as tactics to be used in fighting proposed repressive state and federal legislation, whereas the Reutherite CIO state administration contended that working behind-the-scenes with the governor and other state officials was the best way of dealing with an overhelmingly Republican legislature.[8]

On June 20, 1947, two days after the close of the Michigan CIO convention, President Truman vetoed the Taft-Hartley Bill. The veto came in response to a massive grass roots labor campaign. Both the AFL and CIO had fought the proposed legislation in Congress and, after its passage, had energetically urged a veto. The UAW effort included the huge Cadillac Square rally in April and similar demonstrations in other auto towns. In Muncie, Indiana, for example, more than 4,000 workers participated in a torch light parade; "Taft was hanged in effigy, and the audience responded with wild applause." UAW advocacy of a veto resulted in "Veto Day" proclamations by Detroit's Mayor Jeffries and by officials from several other Michigan cities. Truman was bombarded with several hundred thousand postcards, letters, and telegrams calling on him to exercise his veto power.[9] The unions hoped that groundswell of protest would not only secure a presidential veto but would prevent the Congress from overriding Truman's decision.

The varied protests against the Taft-Hartley Bill resulted from initiatives by the rank and file and by union officials. Ford Local 600, a conference of Cleveland-area UAW local unions, and other auto unionists called for a national work stoppage. CIO President Murray, however, turned aside appeals for work stoppages on the grounds that they usually violated collective bargaining agreements. At Murray's suggestion, the CIO's Executive Board adopted a motion advising its affiliates against participating in protest strikes in violation of their contracts.[10]

Whatever the shortcomings of labor's campaign against Taft-Hartley, Truman's veto message incorporated many of the union criticisms of the law. Truman's "liberal rhetoric," however, was "unsupported by thorough and vigorous action" to win support for his stand in Congress, with the result that the Taft-Hartley Act was enacted into law over his veto on June 23. Harold Ickes, former secretary of the interior under Roosevelt and Truman who had broken with the president, expressed the belief that "Truman wanted to have a chance to veto the Taft-Hartley Labor Bill, but he also wanted the bill passed over his veto." NLRB member James Reynolds, a supporter of Taft-Hartley, recalled a private meeting with Truman during which the president declared: "I'm convinced Taft-Hartley is a pretty good law . . . . I know that if I veto it my veto's going to be overridden . . . . And if I veto it, I'm going to hold labor support in the election next year." The unsuccessful veto, indeed, was sufficient for a number of union leaders to argue that labor once again had a friend in the White House and in the northern Democratic party.[11]

The Taft-Hartley Act was seen by union leaders as a major assault on the trade unions. Leonard Woodcock recalled that the measure "quite frightened" many secondary union leaders. The act outlawed the closed shop, political contributions by unions in national elections, secondary boycotts, and strikes by federal government workers. Union officials had to sign non-Communist affidavits annually if they wished their unions to be able to avail themselves of the machinery of the NLRB. A union shop agreement could be negotiated only after an NLRB vote of the workers. State laws forbidding union security provisions were given precedence over the federal law. Unions became subject to charges of unfair labor practices, and lawsuits against unions for damages were authorized. If the president declared that a dispute involved a national emergency, the federal government could delay a strike by 80 days through the injunctive process. Lobbyist for corporations such as Allis-Chalmers and Chrysler participated in drafting the legislation.[12]

Prior to the enactment of the Taft-Hartley Act, the two UAW caucuses were about equal in strength. Passage of the Taft-Hartley Act proved to be the turning point in the UAW's internal conflict. The requirement of the non-Communist affidavit gave the charge of "communism" a new potency within the labor movement. In the 11-month strike at Allis-Chalmers (April 30, 1946–March 23, 1947), Vice President Thomas had closely associated with local leaders branded by the press as Communists. Michigan's governor had called Thomas, Addes, and Leonard "captives of the Communist Party" when he appeared before the House Un-American Activities Committee.[13] Now, all unions with officials who refused to sign the non-Communist affidavits were deprived of their rights under the nation's labor laws. Increasing numbers of workers came to regard the Thomas-Addes-Leonard policy of toleration of Communists as harmful to the union.

The impact of the Taft-Hartley Act on internal union politics became apparent in a union referendum on a proposed merger between the UAW and the left-wing Farm Equipment Workers union (FE), which had 43,000 members and represented twice as many agricultural implement workers as did the UAW. Facing the likelihood that the Taft-Hartley Bill would become law, FE officials thought they needed a stronger organizational base, and so they sought a merger with the UAW. Representatives of the two unions concluded an agreement on June 3, 1947, that provided for retention of the FE staff, a UAW farm equipment division headed by a director selected by the FE, and full voting strength for the FE locals at the upcoming UAW convention. In the referendum that took place at local union meetings between June 5, 1947 and July 5, 1947, the Reuther group opposed the merger, arguing that the terms were so favorable to the FE that they constituted a grant of autonomy. For both caucuses, however, the struggle over whether the Addes forces would gain several hundred additional convention votes was the primary issue whereas the merits of the agreement were secondary.[14]

The conservative climate of the times made anticommunism an effective weapon against the merger. The Reutherites charged that the move was a coup attempt by the Addes group and that the FE was one of the strongest pro-communist unions in the CIO. Opponents of the merger reprinted a column by Joseph and Stewart Alsop attacking the agreement and claimed that the Taft-Hartley Act might not be able to stop a Communist party takeover of the UAW. Reuther himself used anticommunism to oppose the merger. He asserted that the farm equipment locals in the UAW were aware that FE officers had favored the incentive pay system and speed-up during World War II at a time when UAW locals had been fighting piecework. The introduction into the merger debate of this issue, which Reuther had successfully used against the Communists in the UAW, may have helped Reuther defeat the plan, but it did not contribute to the "sound and constructive" unity between the two unions that Reuther claimed he favored.[15]

Looking back on the merger referendum, George Addes agreed with Reutherites Leonard Woodcock, Ken Morris, and Jack Conway that the dispute was the turning point in the factional struggle in the UAW. With each local voting as a unit, the merger proposal was defeated by a two-to-one margin. Conway, who chaired the Reuther caucus at the 1947 convention, recalled that the merger issue "gave us a forum and we beat their ears off. And, in the process, converted a lot of the leadership to our point of view." Conway believed, however, that "the merger agreement would have stood on its own merits" if the board had completed the agreement without sending it to a referendum vote. The arguments in the debate over the merger "were really unimportant" in Conway's view.[16]

Decisive to the Reuther victory in the merger debate, as Martin Gerber recalled it, was the charge that the proposal was "an attempt . . . to upset the balance of power by an artificial means." Although there were unquestionably good trade union reasons for merging the two unions, the decision to conclude the agreement just a few months prior to the convention and to give the FE members equal representation there was motivated by political considerations. The Reuther caucus successfully linked the accusation that the merger was factionally motivated with the charge that the Addes group was tied to Communists. Leonard Woodcock recalled that the Reuther caucus was able to convince the UAW secondary leadership that the merger was "purely a manipulated, political factional deal simply to fasten a Communist grip on the UAW."[17]

A realignnment in the balance of forces in the UAW took place during the referendum, but the merger debate was the occasion rather than the cause of the realignment. With Communist-led unions in a questionable legal status as a result of Taft-Hartley, many UAW members believed it was the better part of wisdom to vote against association with a union labelled as Communist by the press and by many UAW leaders. The anticommunist issue had become so effective that union members advised Addes to get out of his own caucus because it was "branded." "It was unbelievable," Addes recalled, "that you could go out and wave the red flag, call names and convert membership" to the belief that there was a communist conspiracy to take over the union. A swing group shifted away from the Thomas-Addes-Leonard coalition, believing that its willingness to work with Communists was leading the union into dangerous waters. Some local leaders, Addes noted, failed to support his caucus because they were "afraid to go back to their local unions and be stigmatized [as

Communists] . . . . There would just be too much pressure on them and they'd be out of a position." The inclusion of an anticommunist provision into the nation's fundamental labor law had given anticommunism a new strength.[18]

Although the balance of forces in the union was shifting against the Addes group because of the Taft-Hartley Act's anticommunist provision, the law as a whole was extremely unpopular with union members and it was an open question whether the UAW would actually comply with the statute. The initial inclination of both the CIO and the UAW was against compliance with the law. In voting against taking cases to the new NLRB on July 9, 1947, the UAW board believed that this would not affect cases then in process. On July 17, however, Truman appointed as general counsel of the NLRB Robert N. Denham, a former board trial examiner and a Republican Wall Street lawyer opposed to the New Deal philosophy of the old NLRB. Denham ruled that existing cases were to be dismissed unless the union involved complied with the act. Denham further ruled that compliance required the filing of the non-Communist affidavits and financial statements by the officials of the local, the international, and the labor federation to which the union was affiliated. Denham's rulings put pressure on the UAW and CIO to change their positions.[19]

The left-progressive forces in the UAW continued to conduct anti-Taft-Hartley protest activities. Detroit's CIO Labor Day parade, organized by the left-center Wayne County CIO Council, was a massive demonstration with the emphasis on the "Destroy the Taft-Hartley Act" theme. Estimates of the numbers involved varied from 50,000 to 200,000. Board member Stevenson described the scene: "Float after float came down . . . local union after local union, with the only theme being drummed and drilled into everybody's head—get rid of the Taft-Hartley Act." At the head of the march was Henry Wallace, who told the assembled union members, "If we don't make the Democratic party into a party of peace and prosperity, we shall build a new party.[20]

Despite the rank-and-file sentiment exhibited in Detroit on Labor Day, right wingers on the UAW board sought to overturn its policy of noncompliance with the Taft-Hartley Act. Representatives of the Glenn Martin local in Baltimore appeared before the board on September 9 to urge compliance. The International Association of Machinists (IAM) had challenged the right of UAW Local 738 to represent the Glenn Martin workers in an NLRB election on August 2. Although UAW representatives believed that Local 738 would win a majority once the disputed ballots were counted, NLRB officials refused to complete the count because the UAW had not complied with the Taft-Hartley Act. "I am satisfied," the president of the Glenn Martin local said to the board, "we cannot hold our people there much longer unless there is something done. The people in the plant are not old militant union people; . . . they haven't gone through these things yet to get the feeling of unionism. They are young yet, and have read the papers, and they want to know the answers to certain questions that they have a right to ask."[21]

All the pro-Reuther regional directors supported compliance. "You just can't get workers to vote go out on strike," Martin Gerber argued, "knowing that they have the opportunity to vote for other unions that promise them the same things." Charles Kerrigan, who had supported the FE merger, now returned to the right-wing side. The Addes-aligned director from the West Coast, Cy O'Halloran, also favored compliance, asserting the UAW might thereby be able to double its membership in his region. Other Addes caucus members continued to oppose compliance. R. J. Thomas maintained that pioneer locals in Detroit and Flint would resent compliance, and William Stevenson asked, "Should we, the enlightened section of the labor movement, follow [the] IAM in this matter?"[22]

The resolution for compliance was defeated by a vote of thirteen to nine. Although he supported compliance, Reuther voted against the motion because he wanted first to effectuate a change in CIO policy. Indeed, the steadfastness of some Addes caucus members on this issue was to be shaken by a change in CIO policy.[23]

Although CIO President Murray thought it unfair to force labor representatives to sign loyalty oaths when management representatives were not required to do so, his opposition was essentially a personal one, and he did not oppose a campaign for compliance by CIO right wingers. When the NLRB overturned Denham's ruling that CIO and AFL officials would have to comply for their affiliates to have access to the NLRB, the CIO board and convention accepted Murray's view that CIO unions should now be "free to exercise their own judgement."[24]

As national UAW leaders disputed the Taft-Hartley issue, balloting for delegates to the eleventh union convention got underway. The election contests were close in many important locals, but it soon became clear to both sides that the Reuther caucus would have a majority of delegates at the convention. Although the local contests had not been fought on the issue of Taft-Hartley Act compliance, the passage of the law had made anticommunism, the Reuther caucus's principal concern, a winning issue.[25]

In the wake of both the CIO convention decision and local union balloting for convention delegates, Reuther directed that a poll be taken of the members of the UAW International Executive Board regarding the compliance question. Facing the dismissal of pending NLRB cases if the union did not comply by an October 3 deadline, a majority of the board members who voted now favored signing the Taft-Hartley affidavits. Of the 22 board members, 11 supported compliance, including all nine Reuther partisans and two Addes caucus members, O'Halloran, who had voted to comply in September, and Arnold Atwood. Only five Addes supporters voted against compliance—Addes,

Thomas, Stevenson, Percy Llewellyn, and Kenneth Forbes. Two other Addes supporters, Richard Reisinger and Joseph Mattson, did not vote but instead asked for a special board meeting. Leonard and regional directors Paul Miley and Jack Holt did not indicate their positions. George Burt of Canada refrained from voting on the grounds that this was a United States question. The absence of a united CIO response and the danger that pending UAW cases would be lost broke the already weakened solidarity of the Thomas-Addes-Leonard coalitions's top leadership on the Taft-Hartley issue.[26]

Denham's imposition of a preconvention deadline forced top leaders of the Addes group to choose between abandoning the caucus program of noncompliance and facing delegates from several locals angry that they as board members had permitted their NLRB cases to be dismissed. The Addes caucus members were, of course, aware that the Reuther group would have a majority at the convention. The only hope the caucus had was that Murray would make a stirring speech and help the Thomas-Addes-Leonard group win back some of the swing centrist elements. Although Murray was not opposed to Thomas, Addes, and Leonard as leaders of the UAW, his antileft animus was such that he was not likely to criticize the Reutherites nor make a strong pitch for united front action.[27] Cold war anticommunist attacks on the caucus by the media, corporate and government officials, and its union opponents had put the left-center group on the defensive. For a decisive swing group among the membership, the passage of the Taft-Hartley Act made the continuation in office of the Addes group undesirable. The eleventh UAW convention marked the end of the UAW's left-center coalition and the beginning of a new era in the history of the auto union.

Chapter Fourteen

A Victory for the Left: Coleman Young and the Wayne County CIO Council

Although the tide had begun to turn against the left-center forces in the UAW after the passage of the Taft-Hartley Act, they and their allies in other CIO unions achieved an important victory at the Wayne County CIO convention in late July 1947. After several unproductive efforts to elect a Black as a member of the UAW International Executive Board during the mid-1940s, Detroit Black trade unionists and their supporters succeeded in gaining Black representation in top union leadership with the election of Coleman Young as director of organization of the Greater Detroit and Wayne County CIO Industrial Union Council. Stressing the pervasive influence of racism on white workers, some historians have questioned whether either of the major auto union caucuses truly favored inclusion of Blacks in top union leadership.[1] Young's election and his tenure in office indicate, however, that racist influences in the Detroit labor movement were not the insurmountable barrier that many accounts imply; that many white union activists in Detroit were willing to accept Black leadership; and that the support given by most members of the left-center caucus for an affirmative action approach to including Blacks in leadership represented a true progressive commitment rather than mere political game playing.

According to Meier and Rudwick, UAW leaders of both factions had liberal leanings on the race question but were constrained in their behavior by racist tendencies among white rank-and-file workers. This formulation errs in several respects. Not all union leaders were liberal on the race question; the behavior of the two caucuses was not really the same; and the implication that racism of white workers was an elemental force that could not be opposed is exaggerated. Two important figures in the Reuther caucus, Richard Gosser and John Livingston, were quite illiberal on the race question. At the time of Reuther's election to the presidency in 1946, only one of the 13 Black staff members worked for a member of the Reuther caucus. During the war the Reuther-aligned board members defeated a recommendation by Fair Practices Committee director George Crockett that each board member should have at least one Black unionist on his staff. Although Meier and Rudwick cite the Packard local as an example of the Addes group's inability to influence its supporters in secondary leadership in an antiracist direction, the opposite was true. In fact, Addes succeeded in persuading local leaders who supported him to take positive action. It was Reuther caucus supporters in the Packard local who went along with the racist sentiment and profited from it politically. As Chris Alston, the leading Black figure in the local union recalled, the Reutherites took advantage of the situation and "our guys [the Addes partisans] got the hell beat out of them."[2]

As an organization of industrial unions, the CIO understood the need to overcome racial division if it were to succeed. It declared its opposition to discrimination, involved Black workers as organizers, and worked to establish a united front with the Black community. Important to the CIO's efforts at interracial unity was its decision to welcome into its ranks all partisans of industrial unionism regardless of their political affiliations. The Communist-led left was the most important trend to be included, both in terms of the number of its adherents and its influence on broader circles beyond the left. On the question of racial integration, the Communist-led left was in the forefront and influenced the CIO as a whole.[3]

The struggle for Black representation in the UAW leadership started early in the history of the union, but it was not until Black union membership reached substantial numbers after the organization of the Ford Motor Company in 1941 that proposals for Black representation in top leadership received serious attention.[4] The issue became especially important to Black union activists following the wartime "hate strikes" against Black upgrading and the 1943 Detroit race riot. The decisive battle on the Black representation question in the UAW took place at the October 1943 convention.[5]

The number of Blacks elected as delegates to the convention was about 150, twice as many as at any previous convention. Before the convention opened, Black leaders met with the leaders of the two major union caucuses, both of which went on record in favor of the idea of Black representation. The left-center caucus, led by Secretary-Treasurer George Addes and Vice President Richard Frankensteen, acted first, voting unanimously to support efforts to elect a Black to the International Executive Board. Vice President Reuther and Ford Department Director Richard Leonard, leaders of the rival caucus, reacted angrily to the Addes group's action, claiming that Addes had "made himself appear to a large segment of our Negro brothers as a savior of the Negro race" while his actions in the area were, in fact, blemished. For their part, Reuther and Leonard declared that "our record on the racial question is unblemished and . . . we are unalterably committed to Negro representation on the International Executive Board." Although they declared their support for "a Negro as an executive officer of this union," they noted "one reservation . . . we could not support or encourage the election of a Negro on a Jim Crow basis."[6]

Reuther and Leonard were attempting to tread a fine political line. If a "pure" ideological color blind approach had been their concern, they would simply have argued that Blacks should run on the same basis as anyone else and be given fair consideration by caucuses and delegates alike. Instead, they made a point of their commitment to the substance of the issue—Black representation on the executive board—disagreeing "only" on the form through which that representation might be achieved. After the convention opened, they retreated from their unalterable commitment, took no action on the substantive question, and opposed the only manner of achieving Black representation that was before the convention: electing the head of a new Minorities Department as a member of the union's Executive Board. The Reuther group's reservation thus became the sum total of its policy.

When Walter Reuther met privately with Black union leaders on various occasions, he told them that he agreed with them but that he was limited in what he could do by the views of his supporters. The Black unionists, for their part, urged Reuther to take an advanced position on the race question with his caucus, arguing that if he took such a position, his supporters would follow even though they were not responding to the same ideas when expressed by Black workers. Reuther chose not to follow this course.[7]

When the debate occurred on the convention floor, Reuther, apparently influenced by the idea of Black inferiority, asked, "Supposing you elect a man that is not competent to do the kind of job you want done on the minorities problem? Can you do anything about it?" This argument could be raised about any elective office so there is an implication that competence is a special problem when selecting a Black candidate. The most persuasive opponent of the Black representation proposal, however, was Victor Reuther, who asserted that the proposal constituted a "special privilege" for Blacks. "If there is a special post for Negroes," he said, "then in all justice there should be a post at large for the Catholics, the women, the Jews, the Poles, and all the rest."[8] The denial that Blacks faced special discrimination that called for special action was consistent with Reuther's Socialist background; the Socialist party historically had emphasized that the problem of the Black worker was essentially the same as that of workers in general. There was no "special" problem of racial discrimination to address.[9]

In supporting the Black representation proposal, Addes and Frankensteen were, to be sure, responding to the concerns of their suppporters, but they also showed an understanding of the principles of what today is called affirmative action. Whereas Walter Reuther claimed that "the problem [of racism] does not exist on the Executive Board," Frankensteen argued that "it would be most helpful if we could receive first hand the point of view of the colored people within this union . . . . It would acquaint the board members more with the problems than anything else we could do."[10]

Not surprisingly, most Blacks supported the Black representation proposal, but two prominent international representatives, Horace Sheffield and Walter Hardin, switched their positions and sided with the Reuther caucus at the last moment. Sheffield later wrote Walter Reuther that he had "snatched your and Dick Leonard's chestnuts out of the fire over the 'Negro Board Member at Large Issue'." Other Black union members and the Black press were quite critical of Sheffield and Hardin for their turnarounds.[11]

The immediate result of the divisive debate was that the proposal for the creation of a Minorities Department as such was defeated along with the recommendation for a Black board member. The long-range consequences were to solidify the Reuther caucus into a positon of hostility against the concept of special Black representation and to make more difficult future efforts at a united front of all Black union activists.

In the wake of the defeat of the proposal for a Minorities Department, the union's top leaders reached a compromise by agreeing to select a "top Black" to give leadership in the area of fighting discrimination. As a result, Thomas appointed George Crockett, an attorney with the federal FEPC, to the UAW staff as a consultant on minority and racial problems. The UAW board approved Crockett's recommendation for establishing a Fair Practices Committee to investigate complaints of discrimination by both management and the union and to educate the union's members in the principles of fair practices. Thomas named Crockett as the committee's executive director.[12]

Under Crockett's leadership, the Fair Practices Committee established the principle that "fair practices" were a basic union precept and priority.[13] Upon Crockett's recommendation, the number of Black staff members was increased. He brought together the Black staff for strategy sessions and organized a fair practices caucus. At the same time, Crockett assumed a highly visible role in the Black community through a column in the *Michigan Chronicle*. As Shelton Tappes, probably the most influential Black leader on the local union level, recalled it, Black union leaders "looked to Crockett as their representative among the hierarchy . . . [and] followed him."[14]

Recalling his experiences with the union's top officers, Crockett characterized Frankensteen as the best when it came to action on discrimination, followed by Addes, then by Thomas, and finally by Reuther. "Whenever there was an issue with respect to discrimination, we could generally count on Thomas to go along with the Addes faction," Crockett commented. "Sometimes, if it was politically expedient, you could count on Walter going along also." The political reality was that the Reuther caucus, while including many Socialists and liberals who were strongly opposed to racism, also included Richard Gosser, regional director from Toledo, who was openly antagonistic to Blacks, as well as the two southern regional directors, who asked, "How far are you going to let the Negroes go?" With its appeal to anticommunism, the Reuther caucus drew in the bulk of the union's conservative elements. Many Michigan members of the union had been strong supporters of Charles Coughlin or Homer Martin and some still accepted the anticommunist and generally conservative perspective of their former mentors. Not surprisingly, these union members and their white conservative Southern counterparts tended to be illiberal on the question of racial equality. Although they did not share Walter Reuther's social democratic philosophy, they did regard him as an ally in the fight against communism.[15]

The Addes caucus included the Communists who, according to Crockett, had been the "shock troops" in the UAW's battle against racial discrimination. Many other forces had since joined the battle against racism, and during World War II Communists opposed the slogan for a "Double Victory" over fascism abroad and racism at home put forward by A. Philip Randolph because they thought a single focus on the enemy abroad was necessary. Nevertheless, in the UAW and Michigan CIO, the Communists remained in the forefront of the struggle against bigotry. "I could always count on them to support whatever I came out for," Crockett said of white Communist leaders Nat Ganley and John Anderson of Local 155 and Bill McKie of Local 600. The Communists imparted a pro-Black outlook to the Addes caucus. The differences between the two groups were visible on the local as well as national level. "I would expect an Addes supporter to be in favor of and actively seeking to serve on the local union fair practices committee," Crockett commented. "I would expect the Reuther supporter to be opposed to even creating a fair practices committee in the local union." The perception that Addes supporters were more supportive of Black equality was shared by Black leaders active in the local unions.[16]

The passage at the 1946 UAW convention of a constitutional amendment to create a securely funded Fair Practices and Anti-Discrimination Department was an indication of the success of Crockett's work in improving the race relations climate in the union. Black workers had survived the reconversion period and retained 10 percent of the jobs in the industry;[17] they had become a permanent part of the union's political system. Given this reality and the context of an all-out fight for control of the union that followed the 1946 convention, the Reuther caucus moved to correct its historic weakness among Black workers. Although the Reuther group paid more attention at this time to issues of discrimination and appointed more Blacks to the union's staff than it had in the past, it remained hostile to proposals to provide for Black representation in top elective office. With Thomas's and Leonard's record of opposition to this concept, it is not surprising that the official program of the new Thomas-Addes-Leonard group did not include endorsement of the idea. Most members of the Thomas-Addes-Leonard caucus did support such proposals, but the task of organizing a campaign to achieve the objective of Black representation fell to the Black caucus and the left wing.[18]

Blacks interested in achieving representation on the union's executive became more active during 1946–1947, a period of intensive factional fighting and caucusing in the UAW. They formed a caucus with that specific goal in mind and sought support from Black trade union leaders from all over the country. The caucus was broadened to include non-UAW members in preparation for the 1947 state CIO convention. Coleman Young, then a representative with the United Public Workers, joined in these efforts. Although the state CIO leadership consisted of Reuther supporters who oppposed the caucus's efforts, the state CIO convention provided a good opportunity for a "dry run" on the Black representation issue in preparation for the county convention. Black delegates raised the representation issue in a dramatic manner and gained the vocal support of Douglas Fraser, the left-center caucus's presidential candidate. Young, in the process, emerged as an important new figure in the Michigan CIO. In the end, however, the Black representation proposal was defeated because the right-wing caucus retained a convention majority.[19]

The balance of forces in the Wayne county CIO council was much more favorable for the advocates of the Black representation proposal than was the balance in the state CIO. During the war, the left-center group had gained control of the Wayne council. Refusing to accept defeat, the Reuther forces had succeeded in establishing a new organization, the Wayne County Political Action Committee, as a regional CIO organization with responsibility in the electoral arena. The two leaders of the Wayne County PAC, however, were William Stevenson and Tracy Doll, both close supporters of Richard Leonard. The coalescing of the Thomas-Leonard group with the Addes-left caucus created the basis for a merger of the Wayne County CIO Council and the Wayne County PAC, which was consummated at a September 1946 conference. Several Reuther locals refused to participate in the merged organization.[20]

Hodges Mason had been elected vice president of the Wayne Council when the left-center forces gained control in 1943. Under the terms of the 1946 merger, he and other officers retained their positions. Although Mason did not have a full-time paid position, he played an important role in the leadership of the council and helped prepare the way for greater representation of Blacks in union leadership.[21]

Following the 1947 state CIO convention, the left and the Black caucus intensified their efforts to secure Black representation in the leadership of the Wayne County CIO. The Communist party made it a "control task" for its members in the trade union movement. "Everybody had to define themselves in relation to the task of getting [a] Black in [the] Wayne CIO leadership," Communist leader James Jackson recalled. The Communists cultivated support at the local union level. Black caucus and left-wing leaders approached council leaders Tracy Doll and Sam Sage, who "weren't necessarily in favor of it" but agreed not to oppose it.[22]

Although most representatives to the council from UAW locals were Addes caucus partisans and favorably disposed to the Black representation proposal, the campaign met some opposition from within the UAW left-center coalition. The newspaper *FDR*, which leaders of the Thomas-Addes-Leonard caucus had established to assist them in their fight against the Reuther caucus for control of the UAW, viewed proposals for special Black representation as divisive and predicted that there would be a split in the left-center coalition over the issue at the Wayne County CIO convention. *FDR's* stance reflected the position long-espoused by Thomas and Leonard, but the newspaper's stance did not dissuade any significant section of the Addes caucus members in the council from supporting the proposal. Doug Fraser, a close friend and follower of Dick Leonard, worked to convince other delegates about the need for the special measure.[23]

Aside from the bulk of the Addes caucus delegates, another important source of support for the Black representation proposal came from the coalition of non-UAW unions in the council. The council had been formed to gain a greater voice for the non-UAW unions in both the state and county councils. The coalition included both left-wing unions like the Fur and Leather Workers, the Public Workers, and the Office and Professional Workers and non-left unions such as the Steelworkers, Rubber Workers, and Packinghouse Workers. According to Fur and Leather Workers leader and coalition chair, Harold Shapiro, the group "set as one of our objectives the inclusion of Black leadership, full-time paid leadership, in the Wayne County Council." On the floor of the convention, Shapiro was an outspoken advocate of Black leadership.[24]

As the convention opened, leaders of the left-wing and centrist blocs discussed the need to elect a Black as one of the full-time officers of the council. Fraser chaired the constitution committee, which had formal responsibility for recommending what offices should exist in the council. Centrist forces suggested the creation of a director of special projects to be filled by a Black representative. The left wingers, for their part, proposed that the vice presidential position, then held by Hodges Mason, be made a full-time post. The two groups compromised on the idea of a director of organization, which the convention affirmed with the understanding that the position would be filled by a Black. Once the victory on the main question was achieved, attention shifted to which individual would be elected to the new office.[25]

At first, the Black caucus selected Hodges Mason as its candidate for the new position. President of the Bohn Aluminum local as well as vice president of the county council, Mason was a leading Black spokesperson in the UAW. He was associated with the UAW left but was not a Marxist. "A 33rd degree mason" opposed to communism ideologically, Mason felt "forced into the left" by the hostility of the Reutherites. The leftists in the council preferred a more ideologically reliable left winger, Coleman Young, and, in the end, their view prevailed.[26]

Born in Tuscaloosa, Alabama in 1918, Coleman Young moved to Detroit with his family in the 1920s. While still a student, Young was initiated into politics at the neighborhood barbershop of a Black Marxist named Williams. It was a scene of lively discussion and a place for political education. Landing a job at Ford's in the mid-1930s, Young began as an electrical apprentice, but discrimination prevented him from advancing to electrician. He joined the UAW in the underground days but was fired when, as Young recalled it, he "picked up a steel pipe and laid it across" the head of a company man who was baiting him. As a leader of the National Negro Congress, Young assisted the Ford drive and participated in the Sojourner Truth housing struggle. In 1942, Young entered the army and became an officer. He participated in struggles against segregation and was put in the stockade. Returning from the war, he obtained a job with the U. S. Post Office but soon came to the attention of the leaders of the Public Workers union and was placed on the staff as an international representative.[27]

One of the reasons Young became the choice of the convention to serve as director of organization was the fact that he came from a non-UAW union. Shelton Tappes recalled that the Steelworkers led the fight against another UAW choice and sought the post for Alex Fuller, a member of Steelworkers Local 1299 who functioned as a full-time coordinator for the county council. At a meeting of the Black caucus attended by a large complement of white delegates, several names were placed in nomination. Yale Stuart, a leader of the Public Workers, proposed a recess during which a committee could review the names being suggested and bring a recommendation back to the caucus. Stuart stated that he would like to appear before the committee. This proposal was accepted and Tappes, as chair, appointed the committee. Stuart, who was the only person to appear before the committee, "put up a real good plea" for the miscellaneous unions. The committee then chose Young over Fuller by a four-to-one vote.[28]

The personal factor was another important reason for Young's selection. For one thing, as a relatively new figure on the trade union leadership scene, Young, unlike Mason and Tappes, did not have a record of significant participation in the factional politics of the union movement.[29] Even more important assets for Young were his personal ability and style. State Senator Stanley Nowak, a member of the council executive board, recalled Young in that period as a "very promising young man" and a "brilliant young fellow." Harold Shapiro characterized Young as a "tremendous personality, a good guy with a lot of drive, extraordinarily articulate, a guy who made friends easily and with the very force of his personality he was in the opinion of many, head and shoulders above any possible [other] candidate." James Jackson saw Young as a "a marvelous popularizer" of left-wing policies who was "nimble and facile in debate [and] leaflet writing."[30]

Three slates contested for office in the elections at the convention. The left-center coalition slate consisted of Tracy Doll for president. Sam Sage for secretary-treasurer, and Coleman Young for director of organization. C. Pat Quinn, who had served as president of the council prior to the merger with the Wayne County PAC and continued to hold that post under the terms of the merger, ran against Doll with the unethusiastic backing of the pro-Reuther forces. On Quinn's slate were Joseph Hoffman of Local 600 and Alex Fuller. Also backing Fuller was a middle-of-the-road slate organized by Glen Sigman, assistant regional director of the Steelworkers and, as we have seen, the 1946 candidate of the left-center caucus for state CIO president. Of the three candidates for top office, Sage had the largest margin of victory, 1,531 to 764 votes, or 66.7 percent of the total. Young won by the smallest margin, with 1,280 votes to Fuller's 873, or 59.4 percent of the total. In addition to Young, three of the 17 vice presidents elected to serve on the board were Black.[31]

The development of a third slate that took some votes away from Young was due not only to the Steelworker officials' desire to achieve representation in CIO leadership but to Young's leftism as well. Left-center coalition slates tended to be dominated by centrists, with leftists usually receiving seondary posts that were not full-time positions. With the increasing cold war pressures, some within the coalition sought to reduce further left wing representation in leadership positions.[32] Insofar as a Black representative was concerned, however, it was difficult to deny a left-wing choice because most Detroit area Black union activists were on the left.[33]

One of the most notable aspects of the election was the right-wing caucus's acceptance of the restructuring of offices to achieve Black representation in leadership. The Reuther caucus had oppposed this idea in the past as reverse discrimination and CIO rightists had raised the same argument at the previous month's state CIO convention. Now, however, with a majority clearly in the hands of the left-center coalition—and in the hands of supporters of the Black representation principle—they chose not to fight the proposal. They supported a Black candidate for the newly created office rather than adhering to the reverse discrimination stand. Although unwilling to pioneer in the fight for increased Black representation, the right-wing caucus accepted this development when it came; it did not fight a rear-guard campaign by appealing to anti-Black feelings. Nat Ganley, who presented the unsuccessful 1943 Black representation proposal to the UAW convention, concluded that the running of Black candidates on all three slates demonstrated that "the majority of white unionists will eradicate the 'second-class citizenship status' of their Negro brothers if they are given the chance to do so."[34]

The different outcomes at the state and county conventions on the issue of Black representation stemmed in part from the fact that they represented different sections of the CIO membership. Although both organizations represented CIO unions in Wayne County, the state council also included many small locals from more conservative areas of Michigan. The CIO membership represented by the Wayne Council was politically more sophisticated and included a larger proportion of Black workers than was true for the state council. Equally important was the contrasting factional situations in the two organizations. The left-center caucus controlling the Wayne county council was sympathetic to the demand for Black representation while the right-wing caucus controlling the state council was hostile to it. Apart from the accidental twists and turns of factional politics, however, other differences existed between the two councils. The delegates elected to the county council convention continued to serve throughout the year as delegates to the county council, which met biweekly. Delegates to the state convention by contrast, did not participate in that council's decisionmaking between conventions unless they were elected as members of the state executive board. As Douglas Fraser recalled, the county council was a scene of lively debate and political discussion in which the left wing was an influential force. Despite irregular delegate attendance, the county council delegates had a much greater opportunity to adopt new positions as a result of political discussion and personal interaction with fellow delegates. Given the commitment to after-hours meetings throughout the year that election as a county convention delegate implied, these delegates were probably more politically involved than were state council delegates, just as the latter tended to be more aware and interested in politics than UAW convention delegates were.[35]

Other actions taken by the county convention also illustrated its left-center character. Most notable was the convention's unanimous vote to support the nomination of Henry Wallace for president on the 1948 Democratic ticket. The delegates also voted to help launch campaigns to repeal Michigan's anticommunist Callahan Act by referendum vote and to prevent evictions and improve the housing situation in Detroit.[36]

At the first council executive board meeting following the convention, Doll commented that Young "should be a great help on racial problems, and on other minority group matters, but will be assigned to other organizational work of any nature as the need arises." One of Young's first tasks was the organization of council participation in the effort to collect 150,000 signatures to place repeal of the Callahan Act on the ballot. Young's talents as a speaker and organizer immediately became evident. He successfully argued that the petition campaign could be used as a tool to build the local union political action committees and make them ready to "swing into full action in the November election." Young oversaw the distribution of leaflets and petitions, organized shop gate meetings. and mobilized a large contingent of canvassers for the Labor Day parade. There was a "life and death necessity" to build the union's political machinery, Young reported to the council, thereby making "the indignation, unity and power of labor's political strength felt in November." In two month's time, 110,000 signatures were collected and filed, but the Secretary of State refused to certify them.[37]

The repeal campaign showed Young would be a major force in the council's leadership. In some people's view, Young became the predominant leader. Young "has an instinctive bent that makes it very easy for him to become a prevailing influence with a group of people," according to Shelton Tappes. "His depth of perception and his ability to trust himself . . . had a lot to do with influencing Sage and Doll," and he "had the energy and aggressiveness" to be a forceful leader, Tappes recalled. Apparently, Doll and Sage harbored no resentment over the prominent role Young so quickly assumed. The three shared the same programmatic objectives and remained united even when the council was subjected to a full scale onslaught by the Reuther forces in 1948.[38]

Young assumed a new prominence in the community as well as in the labor movement and was equally self-confident in that arena. On the Sunday following his election, Young joined Benjamin Davis, Black Communist council member from New York City in a Greater Macedonia Baptist Church event. When, five years later, the House Un-American Activities Committee questioned Young about introducing Davis at this meeting, he asserted: "I think that any meeting in which the first Negro councilman ever elected to office in the State of New York were to attend would be of interest to a great number of Negroes. It would be to the credit of any party if that Negro were elected under the label of that party."[39]

The importance of Young's election was such that the Public Workers sponsored a testimonial banquet for him about two months after his victory. "Hundreds pay tribute to Coleman Young," read the headline in the *Michigan Chronicle*. Artists and civic and labor leaders appeared, including Mayor Edward Jeffries, R. J. Thomas, Reverend Charles Hill, and Doll and Sage. Serving as master of ceremonies was Hodges Mason.[40]

As a full-time officer, Young was the most important Black leader in the county council, but other Blacks provided leadership as well. The three other Black council executive board members served on an 11-person council committee that organized a massive 1947 Labor Day parade. It was "the largest and most spectacular Labor Day demonstration ever held in Detroit," reported the *Michigan Chronicle*, and "Negro unionists were represented fully" in the parades of both the AFL and CIO. Young, one of three speakers at the CIO rally, told the crowd that "Michigan must lead the way" to repeal of the Taft-Hartley Act by moving to rescind the Callahan Act.[41]

Another major focus of council activity in which Young was involved was the 1947 Detroit city elections. Reverend Charles Hill, who was running for the city council for a second time, received the endorsement of the county council, as did council president Doll and board member and state senator Stanley Nowak, among others. Young played a prominent role in Hill's campaign. With anticommunism on the upswing, none of the three candidates the Wayne council was most interested in getting elected was successful.[42]

Under Young's leadership, the council became more actively involved in the community in a variety of struggles. Young assisted union members faced with the threat of evictions, he involved the council in a community coalition against police brutality when a Black youth was shot, and, when Blacks moving into a new area were threatened by racist attacks, he mobilized a group of trade unionists to ensure their safety.[43]

Despite Young's innovative leadership and the broad support among left and center unionist for the Wayne County Council, national events were moving the UAW as a whole toward the Reuther caucus. The left-center leadership of the council would not long survive the victory by its caucus opponents in the dominant international union in the area. Nevertheless, the victory on the Black representation issue did outlast the demise of the left-center caucus. When it obtained the council's leadership, the Reuther group included Alex Fuller among the council's full-time officers. Black trade unionists had attained a permanent role in the Wayne County council's top leadership.

Chapter Fifteen

The Reuther Caucus Wins Control

As the campaign for delegates to the November 1947 UAW convention got underway, both sides made numerous charges and countercharges. The Thomas-Addes-Leonard group made intense personal attacks on Reuther, attempting to portray him as an ally of reactionaries. It gave extensive publicity to a false report, probably originated by opponents of Reuther, of efforts to develop a 1948 Taft-Reuther presidential ticket. The Addes partisans claimed that Reuther supported Taft-Hartley. The *FDR*, a factional sheet of the Addes group, reproduced a purported letter from the fascist Gerald L. K. Smith to his supporters urging quiet support for Reuther. Actually, Smith's publication attacked Reuther as a Marxist. The Addes group used the undeniable fact that the media was giving Reuther favorable coverage to claim that he was the "bosses' boy."[1]

Reuther secretly placed a "Report to the Membership" in the September issue of the *United Automobile Worker* in which he assailed the board majority for factionalism, blocking the enforcement of the union constitution's anti-communist clause, and "scandalous waste of union funds" in an organizing drive. Although the Reuther report had overstated the amount, the union had, indeed, expended considerable funds on the Thompson Products drive without achieving success. The company was one of the most antiunion employers in the automobile parts industry. The UAW again failed to organize the company after the Reuther caucus gained complete control of the union. Although Reuther's general attack on the Thompson Products organizing effort was disingenuous, he pointed to specific abuses of correct financial procedures that the Addes caucus did not refute. Until the Reuther report was issued, Addes had always enjoyed a reputation for meticulousness in the performance of his financial duties.[2]

In reply to Reuther's charges the board majority passed a resolution censuring the UAW president and issued its own "Report on the State of Your Union." By picturing the union as "corrupt, . . . as a squanderer of dues, as dominated by 'reds,' as unpatriotic and unAmerican," the Addes-Thomas-

Leonard report charged, Reuther had aided the campaign of the NAM and the Congressional supporters of Taft-Hartley. The Addes report asserted that the Reuther report had overstressed factionalism and that the union's finances were in order. Devoting considerable attention to the "totalitarian issue," the Addes group maintained that the real issue was a fair trial; Reuther, the report stated, "seeks absolute power to drive from the ranks of the Union any person or group of persons who blocks his plans to achieve one-man control of the UAW-CIO." The Addes report also accused Reuther of aiding the speed-up drive and failing to mobilize the union politically.[3]

The Reuther and Addes reports contained the two caucuses' election platforms, which included such common points as support for labor unity and social security and opposition to speed-up, inflation, and Taft-Hartley. On the issue of political action, the Reuther report continued to favor "the eventual formation" of a new party and sharply criticized the reactionary Congress. The Reuther report contained no criticism of the Truman administration, but the Addes report declared: "The common people of America no longer may count on the present Administration for any effective opposition to a reactionary Congress dominated by the National Association of Manufacturers." Foreign policy was not a major point in either report. Whereas the Addes report contained no mention of the question, the Reuther document stated: "America's productive power is the most important economic asset that free men have in the world. What we do with the American economy will in large measure determine whether we have a world at peace or at war." Two important points included in the Addes program but not mentioned by Reuther were oppositon to company security clauses and support for measures to strengthen the power of stewards and union committeemembers and weaken management's disciplinary authority. The Addes report also affirmed support for the IEB policy of bypassing the "antilabor NLRB," but four weeks after the report was issued, the coalition lost its board majority on this issue.[4]

Convention platforms at the local level were more limited in scope than those published by the national leaders. Reuther partisans at the local level emphasized their support for Reuther and their opposition to financial squandering, a dues increase, communism, speed-up, factionalism, and Taft-Hartley. In line with some Reuther proposals, his supporters recommended constitutional amendments calling for the keeping of verbatim minutes of the executive board and establishing a board of trustees to review the union's books. The main themes of the right-wing campaign were unity behind President Reuther, an end to disruptive factionalism, and elimination of any association with communism. Since the Allis-Chalmers dispute, Reuther had successfully adopted the garb of the unity candidate, the leader who was trying to do an effective job but whose activities were disrupted by factional opponents. Also, he stood apart as the one union officer who was trying to put the UAW's "house in order" on the question of communism so that the union could deal more effectively with its opponents. The media as well as his supporters portrayed Reuther in these terms.[5]

Whereas the Reuther supporters at the local level emphasized their support for their presidential candidate, Reuther's opponents were far less united. In some locals, two slates of candidates ran against the Reuther slate, and the Reuther opponents did not always identify themselves as Addes-Thomas-Leonard supporters. Some Addes supporters even ran on Reuther slates in order to have an opportunity to attend the convention. In their preconvention statements, the forces associated with the left-center coalition emphasized the fight against the speed-up, Taft-Hartley, and company security and advocated a progressive political program. The top leaders of the coalition, however, had not successfully projected an image of themselves as fighters for these policies. The Addes caucus was also weakened by Murray's support for Reuther and anticommunism. At the national CIO convention in October, Reuther was reelected as vice president but Thomas was not. Both Murray and Reuther spoke at that convention in favor of the Marshall Plan, and Marshall himself addressed the delegates. On the issue of Taft-Hartley, the CIO convention left it up to each affiliate to decide whether to comply with the act. The national CIO provided no reinforcement for the program advanced by Addes, Thomas, and Leonard.[6]

Addes, Thomas, and Leonard also found their strength undermined by the success Reuther achieved in characterizing them as disruptive factionalists. Thomas had indeed been attacking Reuther since his accession to the presidency. Thomas was weakened by the accurate charge that he had brought the union into disrepute by attacking Reuther publicly over the handling of the Allis-Chalmers strike and by the defeat of the strike itself. Leonard was harmed by the defeat of the inadequate pension plan at Ford and by a concentrated attack on him by the *Detroit Free Press* for his strong stand against Taft-Hartley. Addes was damaged by the allegation that he and the board majority were guilty of financial mismanagement. Although many long-time Reuther opponents were still respected leaders and activists with a base of support in their local unions, they were weakened by their association with the Addes-Thomas-Leonard coalition and their opposition to Reuther. Formerly neutral elements within the secondary leadership now tended to align with Reuther. Formerly neutral elements among the rank and file also began to shift to the Reuther camp. In additon, some defections were seen from the ranks of Addes supporters into the opposing camp. Although the shift at the local level was not overwhelming, it was enough to enable Reuther supporters to win many hotly contested local elections by small margins. The balance had tipped to Reuther's side before the convention opened; he had a majority of delegates going into the convention, and the neutral bloc had been considerably weakened. The

Reuther group had presented its issues effectively, organized well, maintained its traditional areas of strength, and improved its position in areas where it had previously been weak.[7]

Although he did not alter his ideological position, Reuther took steps to develop a base among Black members. He gained the support of a majority of the board in April 1946 to appoint himself director of the new Fair Practices and Anti-Discrimination Department, with William Oliver, a Black worker who had been on Leonard's staff, being named as codirector. Control over the Fair Practices and Anti-Discrimination Department put Reuther in a position to speak out regularly in opposition to racial discrimination and to express concern about the issue. Reuther had voiced opposition to intolerance and discrimination in the past, but his new role gave him the opportunity to identify himself more closely with the concerns of Black workers.[8]

Reuther not only spoke out against discriminaton, he met with Black workers to develop a strategy for increasing his support among the union's Black membership, and he and his supporters on the board placed additonal Black members on the union's staff. The Thomas-Addes-Leonard caucus, however, retained the support of a strong cadre of Black members.[9]

UAW activists from both factions participated actively in two anti-discrimination struggles in 1946 and 1947. The union campaigned to secure a referendum vote on a Michigan fair employment practices bill and challenged discrimination in the American Bowling Congress (ABC). The referendum campaign was intitiated at an October 1946 conference organized by the left-wing Civil Rights Congress (CRC). In a rare departure from his usual policy of refusing to associate with leftists, Reuther joined in cosponsoring the conference, which resulted in the formation of a Committee for a State FEPC. Instead of joining the committee, however, Reuther and other right-wing UAW members worked with a rival organization, the Michigan Council for Fair Employment Practices Legislation. Bishop Francis Haas acted as honorary chair of the council. A broad array of organizations and individuals, including the NAACP, the National Negro Congress, the Jewish Community Council, and the American Veterans Committee, joined CIO unions in the referendum campaign. More than 180,000 signatures were gathered on the petition, but the effort to get the legislature to act favorably on the proposal was weakened by the division between the left and anticommunist groups. Both sides claimed to have done the most to collect signatures, and each accused the other of sabotaging the campaign. The right-wing coalition, which refused to associate with Communists, did not challenge Governor Sigler's statement that he would not assist the endeavor because legislators believed it was Communst-inspired. Although sufficient signatures were submitted, the state Supreme Court ruled the fair practices initiative off the ballot due to a technicality. Nevertheless, the active participation in the campaign by the Reuther caucus enhanced the group's reputation as a fighter against racial discrimination.[10]

Members of both factions also participated in the UAW's campaign against racially discriminatory practices of the ABC. The Reuther-led Fair Practices Department recommended in December 1946 that the UAW pull out of the ABC at the end of the 1947–1948 season if the group did not abandon its segregationist policy. In the board discussion on the issue, Addes was the most determined to shift from verbal criticism to action. The board decided that the withdrawal should occur at the end of the 1946–1947 season and that the UAW should set up its own bowling league. Although Reuther staff members helped to carry out the policy, they did not attempt to implement it in Toledo because of the opposition of Richard Gosser, the regional director. Nevertheless, the leadership role in the campaign of Reuther supporters such as Olga Madar, head of the union's Recreation Department, won Reuther new support.[11]

Outside support for Reuther as a nationally prominent advocate of liberalism also helped the right-wing group to overcome its weakness among Black workers. Among those praising Reuther's liberalism on racial matters were Eleanor Roosevelt, Walter White of the NAACP, and Lester Granger of the Urban League. The *Michigan Chronicle*, Detroit's leading Black newspaper, which in the past had been sympathetic to the UAW's left wing, now endorsed Reuther. Philip Murray, despite the fact that he had serious personal reservations about Reuther, presented the UAW president the CIO's special anti-discrimination award in September 1947.[12]

The Reuther caucus's attempt to garner support among Black workers was aided by a retreat on the issue of discrimination by the Addes forces. As the convention neared, the newspaper of the Addes faction, *FDR*, attacked proposals to ensure the election of a Black to the executive board. Also, leaders of the Addes caucus began making deals with local union groups characterized as racist by the left wingers who supported the caucus.[13]

As the factional controversy moved toward a climax, some union members attempted to form a new caucus. Disaffected members of the Reuther caucus took the lead in these efforts. Matt Hammond, chair of the National Third Caucus of the UAW-CIO, had been an initiator of the "draft Reuther" effort in 1946. Making opposition to factionalism its cause, the new group opposed the UAW-FE merger as unconstitutional and factional and characterized Reuther's Report to the Membership as the "most vicious attack made against our Union since the days of Homer Martin, 1938." The caucus also charged that Reuther's release of his report indicated "complete coordination between the National Manufacturers Association [sic] and the internal forces within our union." Despite this harsh condemnation, leading members of the caucus elected as delegates to the November convention voted for Reuther in the end. Another supporter of Reuther involved in a breakaway effort was Lloyd T. Jones, president of Local 2 and a former Socialist. Speaking to the Committee for Unity in the UAW-CIO, Jones, although saying he liked both Reuther and Addes, sharply criticized factionalism. "Let's fight for a program instead of losing our heads by fighting one another over personalities and job seeking power politicians who fear a few Communists and the loss of their jobs more than they fear our next Congress," Jones declared. Jones, who had led his local in a successful strike to win contractual protection against the initiation of Taft-Hartley suits, voted for Reuther, Addes, and the Reuther vice presidential nominees at the convention. As in previous third-force attempts, the strength of the two principal coalitions was too great for the new group to make significant headway. The abortive movement indicated the existence of some discontent and questioning in the ranks of the Reuther supporters as well as the decline of the Addes group as an attractive alternative to Reutherism.[14]

The eleventh UAW convention opened on November 9, 1947, once again in Atlantic City, New Jersey. The nearly 2,000 delegates represented 750,000 union members. In the opening address of their first-term president, the delegates heard a mixture of radical and anticommunist statements. Reuther declared that the UAW was "building the kind of labor movement that will remake the world where working people will get the benefits of their labor." Industry was making the "most scandalous profits ever known," Reuther declared, and important segments of industry were "controlled by powerful monopolies which officially control the level of production and the price level." Interspersed among these progressive comments, however, was a heavy dose of anticommunism. "The answer," Reuther asserted, "will not be found in any of the so-called magic totalitarian formulas where you trade freedom for bread." He reaffirmed the CIO's policy to "resent and reject . . . interference" by the Communist party or any other political party. Declaring that the UAW membership would oppose injustice, he pledged, "we will fight with equal determination anyone in this Union or anyone in this country who attempts to sell the membership, the Union, or our country down the river to any foreign power in the world." Reuther had in the past expressed antagonism to communism and equated communism with fascism and with loyalty to a foreign power. He now gave greater emphasis to these concepts and implicitly expressed his support for the idea of driving supporters of the Soviet Union out of political life in the United States.[15]

As president, Reuther opened and chaired the convention, but the board majority controlled the convention's committees. It quickly became apparent, however, that the Reutherites had a working majority at the convention. They won a test vote on the question of electing officers earlier rather than later in the proceedings by a better than two-to-one margin. The outcome of the elections was foreshadowed in this vote, but the delegates still had some important issues to discuss.[16]

The key debate at the 1947 UAW convention was whether to comply with the Taft-Hartley Act. Both sides condemned the act as a part of management's antilabor conspiracy, but the Addes caucus majority on the convention's resolutions committee opposed compliance while the Reutherite minority favored it. Although it is unlikely that many votes were changed in the debate, it was of sufficient length for both points of view to be heard and to indicate the radically different approaches of the two caucuses.[17]

The Addes caucus argued its case against compliance by recalling the heroic early days of the UAW, a period of united front action. The Reuther caucus framed its argument in terms of pragmatism and assisting the weaker locals in the union. Although these arguments were important, the caucuses' contrasting positions on compliance stemmed largely from their differing attitudes toward communism. The Addes caucus regarded the requirement for the filing of the non-Communist affidavits as an illegitimate interference in the internal affairs of the union which threatened both the caucus's united front policy and its political strength because some of its leading activists in the local unions were Communists. Although opposed to the Taft-Hartley Act, the Reuther caucus saw that the non-Communist affidavits could be used to put the Addes group on the spot. Moreover, the Reuther caucus, which had attempted to strengthen enforcement of the UAW's anticommunist constitutional clause, agreed with the view that Communists should be excluded from holding union office.[18]

The opponents of compliance were unable to muster the support of the 500 delegates needed for a roll call vote on the issue. The position taken by Herman Steffes, president of Local 75 representing Seaman Body workers in Milwaukee, illustrated the thinking of those centrist local leaders who had shifted from support for Thomas and Addes to support for Reuther. Steffes pointed out that Addes and Thomas has asked his local to aid the Allis-Chalmers workers. "We have gone out, the Local Union, three different times," Steffes told the convention. "A lot of us boys have been put in jail. I have been picked up myself. I want to know what the hell we went out there for, if we did not try to see there was supposed to be a union in that plant . . . . If we can't get those people to come up here and state . . . that they want to be on that ballot . . . perhaps we wasted a lot of time, and our wives got sick by having their boys being in prison over night."[19]

Murray's speech at the UAW convention reinforced the shift to the right by the center forces. Although he spoke at length on the evils of the Taft-Hartley Act, Murray, whose address was delivered before the vote on the compliance question, did not even mention that the policy of his Steelworkers was one of noncompliance. Instead, he stressed the right of each union to make its own decision. Murray assured the delegates that the position of the CIO Executive Board was that any affiliate that "for good, sound and substantial reasons

believed that their interests would best be protected through filing and quali-
fying should feel free to do so." Such action could be taken, Murray emphasized,
"without violating any National CIO policy." Addes, understandably, thought
Murray had made "a lousy speech."[20]

Whereas the delegates had the opportunity to discuss Taft-Hartley
thoroughly, the issue of foreign policy as such did not come before the convention. There were, however, occasional references to the question. In his
presidential report submitted to the convention, Reuther strongly endorsed
the Marshall Plan. "You and I," Reuther declared on the convention floor, "can
appreciate how important a job we are doing in America in terms of the whole
fight to win peace in the world." John DeVito, who ran an independent campaign for president against Reuther, asserted: "I say the kind of fear psychology
that Walter Reuther is preaching today can drive you into World War III through
his hatreds." Although the cold war was a background factor shaping the conflict within the UAW, leaders of both sides were primarily concerned about
union matters.[21]

Although Reuther, in his opening address, stressed that political action
should be put at the top of the union's agenda, the eleventh UAW convention
also failed to consider the question of political action in any formal way.[22] The
delegates may not have been fully aware of the direction in which Reuther
intended to lead the union on the issues of foreign policy and political action,
but it is apparent that Truman's veto of the Taft-Hartley Act, although overridden, allowed Reuther and others supporting the president's policies to
forestall a wholesale abandonment of the administration. For all its shortcomings, many unionists believed that the union's alliance with the Truman
administration should be preserved at a time when so many other forces in
society were arrayed against the labor movement.

Although the delegates supported the recommendations of committees
led by the Addes forces on a number of issues, they did not look favorably upon
opposition to anticommuism. The most vigorous speech against anticommunism was made by John DeVito, a progressive from the Cleveland Fisher
Body local who had been nominated for president without the support of the
Thomas-Addes-Leonard caucus. DeVito characterized Reuther's activity as

> the best job of Red-baiting and fear psychology that I ever saw in my life . . . .
> It goes down in the Local Unions . . . . And today the state of the Union is
> the left fighting the right and the right fighting the left and wasting all our
> energies and having nothing left to fight the companies . . . . Reuther has got
> so many progressives and liberals scared, if they get up to talk against him they
> are afraid they might be labelled a Communist.

Many delegates booed DeVito's allegation of red-baiting.[23]

Although the Reuther leadership did not win convention approval for initiating sharp policy changes, its convention majority was decisive. This fact was especially evident in the contest for the presidency. The Thomas-Addes-Leonard coalition could not agree on a candidate for the top office. Although Thomas had seemed the most likely caucus candidate earlier in the year, caucus members just before the convention discussed the possibility of running Addes for president, thinking he was the strongest caucus candidate. Reuther's strength was so great, however, that the Thomas-Addes-Leonard coalition decided not to run any candidate against him. Two left-wing candidates, DeVito and John Murphy, contested for the presidency, and were soundly defeated: Reuther received 5,593 votes to 304 votes for DeVito and 36 votes for Murphy; there were 1,219 abstentions and 344 votes were held by absent delegates. Reuther received nearly three-quarters of the total convention vote, and he failed to receive a majority in only three regions—the two Cleveland-based regions and the West Coast region. Reuther won majority support among the delegates from each of the Big Three companies, from the independent manufacturers, and from aircraft, agricultural implement, and miscellaneous firms. He also received a majority of the Black delegates' votes.[24]

The closest vote in the balloting for the four top offices was in the contest for secretary-treasurer, in which Emil Mazey received 4,833 votes to 2,599 for George Addes. The incumbent achieved a majority in only four regions, the three that Reuther had failed to win and the Canadian region. The directors of all four regions were members of the Thomas-Addes-Leonard caucus. Addes received between 33 and 46 percent of the votes in the other regions with directors allied with his caucus. The pro-Addes directors were still able to bring substantial votes to Addes but, with the exception of the West Coast region, not the decisive majorities most had been able to muster in the past.

Addes received fewer votes than Mazey in each of the Big Three companies, in aircraft, independent automobile manufacturers, the agricultural implement plants, and the remaining miscellaneous plants. Addes came closest to Mazey's vote in the farm equipment industry, receiving 47 percent of that vote. Because of Addes's solid record as an opponent of racial discrimination, a 56 percent majority of Black delegates overlooked the Addes caucus leaders' pre-convention maneuvering on the race issue and voted for him.

In the first vice presidential race, Toledo regional director Richard Gosser defeated incumbent R. J. Thomas by a vote of 5,084 votes to 2,019 votes. Gosser won a majority in the same 12 regions in which Mazey had prevailed. Gosser also won a majority in each industrial section of the union. Thomas did less well than Addes in each industry and in every region except one. Despite Gosser's opposition to racial equality, he received 55 percent of the ballots of Black delegates who were, for the most part, voting a straight Reuther ticket.

In the contest for second vice president, Richard Leonard was again opposed by John Livingston, the Reutherite director of Region 5 who served as codirector of the GM Department. Leonard was also opposed by Shelton Tappes, a Black leader from Local 600. Livingston won by a wide margin, receiving 5,025 votes to 1,627 for Leonard and 560 for Tappes. Livingston won a majority in all but two regions, in each of the Big Three companies and in the other industrial sections of the union. He also received a slight majority of the Black delegates' votes. The combined total of 440 votes of Leonard and Tappes among Ford delegates was higher than the vote among those delegates for any other Thomas-Addes-Leonard coalition candidate, but it still fell far short of Livingston's total of 681 votes. The strength of Leonard's Ford Department directorship had been eroded by the factional battle. In fact, Leonard's total of 176 votes among Ford delegates was considerably less than the 264 Ford votes that Tappes received. Tappes drew 40 percent of his strength from his home local, which had a strong left wing. Tappes's candidacy represented an assertion of independence by Black delegates and the left wing of the Thomas-Addes-Leonard coalition, which had long advocated electing a Black worker to a top union office. Tappes received 41 percent of the votes cast by the convention's Black delegates, but only 21 votes from Black delegates who voted for two or three Reuther candidates on the first three ballots.

The Thomas-Addes-Leonard caucus won only four regional directorships, the two Cleveland-based districts and the West Coast and Canadian regions. The victory margins for the four successful center-left candidates were reduced in all but the West Coast region as compared with the vote totals for Thomas and Leonard at the 1946 convention. O'Halloran, the West Coast director, had supported Reuther on the issues of Taft-Hartley and the automatic disqualification of Communists from union office. In the Canadian region, George Burt, the Addes candidate, received 139.7 votes to 131.1 for his opponent, but in 1946 Thomas had led Reuther in Canada by more than 50 votes. An anticommunist drive similar to that in the United States was underway in Canada at that time. The convention of the Canadian Congress of Labor in October adopted resolutions condemning "Communist imperialism" and denouncing Communist party activity in the labor movement. David Lewis, a leader of the social democratic Canadian Commonwealth Federation, wrote Reuther after the convention, "I am . . . sorry that our people were unable to deliver a victory in the Canadian region . . . . It is only a matter of time now and . . . continuing work will ensure a victory at the next convention."[25]

The candidates of the Thomas-Addes-Leonard caucus were defeated by small margins in two regions. In Wisconsin-based Region 4, site of the Allis-Chalmers strike, Joseph Mattson lost to Patrick Greathouse by 30 votes out of more than 600 votes cast. In the Flint-Lansing region, the Addes candidate, an assistant to retiring regional director Jack Holt, lost by 12 votes out of 391 votes cast. In Regions 1A, 1D, and 3, however, the incumbent Thomas-Addes caucus regional directors lost by large margins, receiving only 30 to 40 percent of the votes. All the right-wing regions remained in the hands of the Reuther caucus. None of the contests in these regions was close, and in three regions, the Reuther candidate ran unopposed.

The vote totals indicated that the power of the Thomas-Addes-Leonard caucus as a vote-getting machine based on officeholding had been undermined. More sharply divided than at any time since Homer Martin's tenure, the UAW's leadership in the rival caucuses had devoted themselves to preconvention organizing to a much greater extent than in the past. Each side had organized in territories where members of the rival caucus held office. Control of the international was at issue and office-seeking ambition was a factor in developing a challenge to the incumbents in the various regions, but ideology and program were also of consequence. Although Reuther later claimed to have waged his fight against "Communists" with a positive program, the issues at the forefront of his campaign were negative ones such as charging that his opponents were factionalists and tolerant of communism. Aided by strident anti-communism in the media and the union's need to deal with the threat of Taft-Hartley, Reuther won over most of the previously nonaligned elements to his side. Many center elements in the union agreed with Reuther on the issue of communism and saw him as a more pragmatic leader who could manage a retreat from an exposed position.[26]

The shift of the neutral elements to the right can be seen in the ballots cast by those who attended both the tenth and eleventh UAW conventions. Of 49 delegates who had supported the Thomas-Addes candidates on two of the three 1946 roll calls, almost two-thirds now supported three or four of the four Reuther candidates for the top offices. One such delegate was Victor Scott, a leader of Continental Motors Local 113 in Muskegon, Michigan. Scott recalled that he had supported Thomas at the 1946 convention to avoid a split in his local. After the convention, he became involved in the "anti-left-wing" group in the international. Scott supported Reuther and the entire Reuther slate in 1947 because he saw Reuther as a leader with a better program. He thought the "commies were trying to control the UAW," whereas the Reutherites were not "using the union as a stepping-stone for themselves or some other philosophy."[27]

The Addes caucus position also deteriorated among those who voted solidly for the group at the 1946 UAW convention. Only 45 percent of the 196 delegates voting a straight Thomas-Addes-Leonard slate in 1946 voted against the Reuther slate on all four ballots in 1947, with another 22 percent voting against the Reuther candidates on three ballots.[28] Anticommunism was one factor weakening the solidarity of the Addes group. The split that occured in the Addes group at the 1946 Michigan CIO convention over the nomination of three left wingers to the caucus slate was evident once again. Only 65 percent of those who had refused to support the 1946 left-wing candidates voted against three or four Reuther-backed candidates at the 1947 UAW convention, compared to 88 percent of those delegates who had cast ballots for the left wingers in 1946.

The deterioration of the position of the Addes caucus between the two UAW conventions was indicative of the pull of patronage as well as the weakening in the group's political base. With defeat for the Addes forces becoming increasingly clear, its less committed supporters dropped away and established relationships with the soon-to-be dominant Reuther group. For example, Charles Kerrigan, a regional director who had left the Reuther camp to join the Addes group in 1946, now rejoined Reuther.[29]

The Addes group retained more of its strength among Black delegates than among union delegates in general. From an estimated 90 percent backing in 1946, the left-center group was able to retain 56 percent of the Black delegates' votes in 1947 in the contest for secretary-treasurer. Black delegates were a swing group in the eleventh convention. Although 63 percent of Black delegates' votes went to Reuther for president, Blacks demonstrated their independence by their large vote for Shelton Tappes in the second vice presidential race. The Reuther caucus responded to this growth of Black indepedence by nominating and electing a Black candidate for one on the positions on the newly created Board of Trustees. Although the position was one without real power or influence, The *Michigan Chronicle* praised the Reuther caucus for the action and compared it favorably with the Addes group's failure ever to nominate a Black for top union office.[30] The *Chronicle*, to be sure, had chosen to support the Reuther group before the convention opened but its criticism of the Addes group's failure was well-founded. The Addes group was able to make some headway on the Black representation issue in the Wayne County CIO council, where the left was particularly influential. In the national UAW set-up, however, where centrist office holders were much more influential than the left, the Addes group took no forward steps on the Black representation issue after the 1943 convention. After the Addes group merged its forces with the Thomas-Leonard forces, the new center-left coalition took some steps backward on the issues of electing a Black to the UAW executive board.

The decisive reason for Reuther's victory in the factional fight was that the rank and file viewed him as a more pragmatic leader for the difficult times the union was facing. Reuther's willingness to use the facilities of the NLRB despite the Taft-Hartley Act won the support of workers concerned with the loss of cases pending before the labor board and with the threat to UAW representation posed by rival unions. Reuther's well-known anticommunism, which was shared by most union members, meant fewer attacks on the union because of alleged links with Communists. The triumph of one faction after the chaotic warfare of the past 18 months meant that the leadership would now be able to devote more attention to servicing the membership. The passage of the Taft-Hartley Act, a decisive event in the United States labor history, helped to create the conditions for the overwhelming triumph of the Reuther caucus. An era had come to an end in the history of the UAW and of the United States labor movement as a whole.

Chapter Sixteen

The Consequences of the Reuther Victory

The Reuther caucus's winning of overwhelming control of the UAW International Executive Board led to many changes in the structure of the union, its role in United States social and political life, and the character of its internal political life. One immediate effect was the firing of 77 staff members who had been part of the Addes-Thomas-Leonard caucus. Among those dismissed were Maurice Sugar, the union's general counsel, George Crockett, director of the union's first Fair Practices Committee, and Irving Richter, legislative representative. Many other Addes supporters were retained, however, including Douglas Fraser, who had been on the staff of West Side Regional Director Percy Llewellyn but now joined the Chrysler Department under Norman Matthews.[1]

The new administration's retention of a number of staff members who had been aligned with the Addes caucus was a sign not of the continued vitality of the anti-Reuther coalition but of its disintegration. The Addes-Thomas-Leonard coalition disappeared from the scene as a major vote-getting union machine. The central fact of the coalition's existence had been its role as an instrument of the majority of top union officials who had control over a large part of the union's staff. The removal of most of these top officials from office eliminated the principal point of cohesion of the coalition. The caucus could no longer provide jobs for its supporters, an avenue of advancement to potential allies, or services to local union leaders. The top leaders of the caucus, for the most part, were insufficiently committed to the caucus's program to persevere in union activity in a minority role. Top UAW leaders with a variety of past caucus affiliations had formed the Thomas-Addes-Leonard coalition to oppose Reuther. In cooperation with UAW Communists, they had adopted an alternative program to the one projected by Reuther. The top leaders had generally ignored the program, however, and focused instead on factional maneuvering. It was not surprising, therefore, that many regarded the caucus defeat primarily from a personal standpoint and made decisions about their futures on that basis.

R. J. Thomas, who had been pro-Reuther, then independent, and then anti-Reuther in the union's factional politics, immediately took a position on the CIO staff and joined the growing campaign against the Communists. George Addes, long-time leader of the center-left caucus, was disheartened by the defeat and left the labor movement. "You put in fifteen years doing the best job you know how to do," Addes recalled, "then they come along and they say, 'Hey out' . . . they decided you're no longer needed. I was tired. I was tired of the fight. I was tired of constantly pulling knives out of my back and the bickering that had taken place . . . . I just gave it up." Richard Leonard, who, like Thomas, had shifted from a pro-Reuther to an anti-Reuther stance, went back to work in an auto plant. He was elected president of DeSoto Local 227 and engaged in anti-Reuther caucusing, but he left the UAW within a year. Leonard recalled that he decided to take a CIO job in the West because his wife had fallen ill.[2]

The opposition forces not only lost their three national leaders but a number of regional officials as well. Regional directors Joseph Mattson and William Stevenson took staff jobs with the new Reuther administration. None of the four Addes-aligned regional directors who were reelected challenged Reuther: Cy O'Halloran and George Burt came to terms with the UAW president and received his support for the retention of their positions in 1949; Paul Miley and Richard Reisinger did not seek reelection in 1949 but instead accepted UAW staff positions. Some former board members continued to oppose Reuther, notably Percy Llewellyn, who returned to his job in the Ford River Rouge plant and became a leader of the anti-Reuther, pro-left-wing Local 600 "progressive" caucus. Llewellyn recalled rejecting Vice President John Livingston's offer of a staff position because the UAW vice president would not tell him what the job entailed. "I'm not going to . . . take a job," Llewellyn told him, "where I go out and hit my friends over the head." Another board member, Kenneth Forbes, returned to his job in a Saginaw foundry and remained actively opposed to Reuther for a few years before eventually taking a UAW staff position.[3]

The limited opposition to Reuther among former top union leaders reflected the fact that the Reuther administration's decisive control of the UAW after the 1947 convention far surpassed that of any previous UAW administration. The Reuther group controlled 18 of 22 seats on the executive board, the entire staff, and all departments of the international. It had won a large majority of the convention delegates from the largest local unions and from the Big Three companies. The Reuther group used its considerable resources to consolidate its position. In a departure from past practice, Reuther insisted on the dismissal of several of Canadian regional director Burt's staff members on the grounds that the convention was a mandate to remove "Party guys" and those close to the Communists from the UAW payroll.[4] To safeguard their power, the Reutherites sought to gain as complete control of the union at the bottom as they had at the top. Although concerned with all oppositional elements, the Reuther caucus concentrated its attack on left-led locals that had supported the now defunct Thomas-Addes-Leonard caucus.

The Reuther administration used the Taft-Hartley non-Communist affidavits requirement to isolate Communists and those close to Communists in local leadership. The 1947 auto union convention had directed UAW international officers and board members to sign the affidavits but had not called for compliance by local officials. Interpreting the convention decision as a mandate for compliance by those locals wishing to use the NLRB, the UAW board directed such locals to sign the affidavits. Most of the leaders of the left-wing Allis-Chalmers Local 248, which still awaited an NLRB ruling on the results of a new representation election, resigned rather than sign the affidavits. The international appointed an administrator to take over the affairs of the weakened local, once the largest UAW local in the UAW's Region 4. Buick Local 599 in Flint, the biggest General Motors unit and an Addes local, reversed its position and voted in favor of compliance.[5]

In Ford Local 600, the UAW's largest local, the General Council overturned the executive board's preconvention opposition to compliance and directed local officers to sign the affidavits. Five union officials, including the financial secretary and the recording secretary, refused to comply. As a result, the local held a referendum vote of the membership. Local 600 president Tommy Thompson, a past supporter of the Thomas-Addes-Leonard caucus, advocated compliance and related the debate to the international question of "democracy versus communism." Thompson asserted that the vote would demonstrate Local 600's "Americanism to all the world and throw the lie into the teeth of all those who have presumed otherwise." With the international leadership also calling for a "yes" vote, the rank and file supported compliance by a margin of 7,539 to 4,650, but 80 percent of the members did not vote. Following the Local 600 referendum vote for compliance, the five dissenting local officials offered to sign the affidavits when and if the local needed to use the NLRB. When the General Council refused to accept this proposal, two of the five officers resigned and three signed the affidavits.[6]

In some local unions, anticommunists sought to have workers who held positions of any kind in the local sign the affidavits, not just those who were officers of the union. Anticommunists in Local 216, which represented workers at a California GM plant, won the support of a local membership meeting for requiring all executive board members and committeemembers to sign the oaths. Six leaders of this traditionally pro-Addes local who refused to sign the affidavits were tried but were acquitted. Cy O'Halloran, director of the West Coast UAW region, the only region to vote strongly in favor of the Thomas-Addes-Leonard caucus at the 1947 convention, supported the campaign against those refusing to sign the affidavits. O'Halloran had earlier supported Reuther's unsuccessful proposal to the UAW board to have known Communist party members automatically removed from union office.[7]

The Taft-Hartley affidavits were an effective tool for eliminating Communists and their supporters from local union leadership. Local union officers were required to affirm that they were not members of or affiliated with the Communist party and that they did not "believe in" or "support" any organization that favored the overthrow of the United States government by force or by illegal or unconstitutional means. Any union officers making a false statement could be imprisoned for ten years and fined $10,000. Supporters of compliance at Ford's asked, "Are some people afraid to sign" the affidavits because of the threatened penalities? Members of the Communist party had good reason to be afraid of the penalties and so did non-Communist leftists who were supporters of popular front alliances. After Harold Christoffel, honorary president of UAW Local 248, told a congressional committee he was not a member of the Communist party, he was indicted for perjury based on the testimony of former Communist Louis Budenz. Some potential signers of the non-Communist affidavits no doubt believed that the same fate might await them.[8]

Compliance with the Taft-Hartley affidavits was only one of the problems confronting supporters of the old Addes group. The Reuther caucus used its administrative powers to weaken centers of opposition at the local level. The UAW board appointed newly elected Region 4 Director Pat Greathouse as administrator of Allis-Chalmers Local 248. Greathouse's goals were to rebuild the membership of the local, regain legal recognition, win a new contract, and eliminate the old left-wing leadership. Although the UAW constitution limited the period of an administratorship to 60 days, the UAW board revoked and then reissued the local's charter in order to continue the administratorship for a second 60 days. Greathouse found evidence of mishandling of union funds and organized a trial of the former top leaders of the local, all of whom had already been fired by the company. Ex-president Robert Buse testified that, with the knowledge and support of Secretary-Treasurer George Addes, money given the local by the international for relief and welfare had actually been used for organizing activities. Buse explained that Addes had instructed him to submit expenditure statements in this manner because President Reuther insisted that the funds contributed by the international be used for welfare purposes only. The local trial committee, which included members who had returned to work while the local was still on strike, expelled the nine former officers of the local from membership in the union. The action of the local was upheld by the 1949 UAW convention. Local 248 no longer served as a strong center of left-wing opposition to Reuther. [9]

A number of local union elections in the spring of 1948 were tests of the ability of forces aligned with the old Addes caucus to retain office and a power base. John Anderson, president of Local 155 since its founding and an avowed Communist, had won reelection in 1947 by only 59 votes out of nearly 4,000 cast. With the international participating in the 1948 campaign against Anderson, he lost by nearly 700 votes out of 7,500 cast. Reutherites also defeated three incumbent Addes-aligned officers in Local 212, gaining about 55 percent of the votes. Reuther supporters also won in Local 157, the large tool and die local on Detroit's east side. Opposition forces retained power, however, in such large units as Packard Local 190, Plymouth Local 51, and Buick Local 599, as well as in the 2,500 member DeSoto Local 227, in which former international Vice President Leonard was elected president.[10]

Ford Local 600, with its 65,000 members, was a traditional source of strength for Addes and the Communist party. The debate regarding compliance with Taft-Hartley, however, had brought about a split in the old left-center caucus that had won the local union elections in 1946 and 1947. This division carried over into the 1948 local union elections. Tommy Thompson, no longer opposed to Reuther, was reelected president, defeating both a right-wing candidate and Percy Llewllyn, who had the support of the local's left-wing. Candidates on the right-wing slate defeated the incumbent recording and financial secretaries, who initially had refused to sign the Taft-Hartley affidavits and sought reelection on Llewellyn's slate.[11]

Some of the old Addes forces attempted to regroup on a broader basis than the local union. Tracy Doll, president of the Wayne County CIO Council, chaired the UAW Progressive Union Group; and a Michigan Progressive Statewide Steering Committee met in Flint to plan for the June 1948 state CIO convention. When the anti-Reuther forces caucused at the latter convention, Richard Leonard argued that they were too weak to run candidates against the incumbent Reutherite administration of Gus Scholle. The caucus, amid "cat-calls," rejected Leonard's position and ran a full slate of candidates.[12] Although the opposition group remained very dissatisfied with the activities of the Scholle administration, the results of the balloting indicated the change in the balance of forces in the Michigan UAW and CIO since the Reuther victory. In the two previous conventions, Scholle had received 55 percent of the votes. Now he was reelected with 76 percent of the ballots; such large oppositional locals as Buick Local 599, Plymouth Local 51, and the UE locals boycotted the meeting. Nearly three-quarters of the UAW delegates voted for Scholle, as did 89 percent of delegates from other unions.[13]

In addition to winning an easy reelection, the Scholle administration took command of the convention's discussion of policy questions. Whereas the opposition at the 1947 convention had kept the administration on the defensive regarding its conciliatory approach to Republican Governor Kim Sigler, Scholle now spoke out sharply against state antilabor legislation and called for a petition drive to require reapportionment of the Michigan legislature. The administration won endorsement for its positions on most issues. Two out of five delegates, however, voted against the credentials committee report, which denied seating to a local union that had changed from a CIO local industrial union to an affiliate of the left-wing UPW against the wishes of the national CIO. As was true in 1947, the majority of delegates defeated an administration proposal to hold state conventions biennially rather than annually. Although they gave a decisive majority to the candidates of one faction, the delegates still valued their independence and their participation in state CIO conventions.[14]

A few weeks after the 1948 Michigan state CIO convention Richard Leonard launched his own opposition group, the Committee for Democratic and Militant Action. Among those joining the new group were Tracy Doll; Melvin Bishop, a former regional director and Reuther staffer; Lloyd Jones, president of Local 2 and an independent; Ralph Urban, the Addes-aligned president of Local 190; and Paul Silver, former aide to R. J. Thomas. The new group criticized Reuther as a "self-styled labor statesman" who permitted a speed-up in GM plants. Reuther responded that the new caucus was "the same old gang up to the same old factional tricks." At a meeting of 350 persons, however, the new group sharply departed from the approach of the Addes-Thomas-Leonard caucus and voted by a two-to-one margin to condemn Communist policies in the labor movement. Leonard favored the exclusion of Communists from the caucus. The anti-Reuther opposition thus had become divided between a group that favored the traditional popular front, progressive approach and a group with an anticommunist tendency.[15]

The new tack of the Leonard-led group led to the rupture of some longstanding friendships. Tracy Doll attended the meeting of the new organization but did not advocate moving in an anticommunist direction. Long a close friend and follower of Leonard's, Doll could not accept Leonard's move away from the popular front approach. "Tears were running down his face," Betty Yochim recalled, as "Tracy took his [Leonard's] picture off the wall, smashed it . . . [and] threw it in the wastepaper basket."[16]

The growth of anticommunism in the anti-Reuther camp was caused by increasing anticommunism in the country's political life and by the development of an open split on major issues between CIO President Philip Murray and the Communist-led wing of the CIO. Whatever differences Reuther and Murray had over compliance with the Taft-Hartley Act, the two union leaders were in complete agreement on support for the Marshall Plan and opposition to the third-party presidential aspirations of Henry Wallace, who had announced his candidacy in December 1947. Murray brought these two issues to a head at the CIO Executive Board meeting in January 1948 and secured approval of his position by a majority vote of 33 to 11. The CIO board majority, which rejected the argument that a Wallace bid would increase voter turnout and thereby improve the electoral chances of pro-labor congressional candidates, declared that the Wallace candidacy was divisive and would lead to the election of reactionary Republicans.[17]

Communists in the national CIO had attempted to maintain an alliance with Murray despite the adoption, at his insistence, of a resolution at the 1946 CIO convention to "resent and reject" Communist interference and his strong support for the Marshall Plan at the 1947 CIO convention. The leaders of the Communist-led left wing now had to recognize that their alliance with Murray was dead. Ignoring the CIO tradition of union autonomy, the new center-"right" alliance regarded refusal to oppose Wallace or to support the Marshall Plan as defiance. Murray aligned the CIO organizationally with the ADA in February, thus making clear his support for the anticommunist side of the liberal split.[18]

In endorsing the CIO's rejection of the Wallace candidacy in March, the UAW executive board denounced the third-party effort as a "Communist party maneuver designed to advance the foreign policy interests of the Soviet Union at the expense of democracy and freedom throughout the world." The UAW board set its sights, however, on the formation of an anticommunist liberal party after the 1948 elections.[19]

Whereas the anti-Wallace stance of the national CIO and UAW gave implied support to the Democratic party, the Michigan CIO was more explicit. With the support of the UAW and the national CIO, the Michigan CIO-PAC decided in March to inaugurate a policy of working through the Democratic party from the level of precinct delegates on up. The June state CIO convention adopted a resolution that endorsed this policy and attacked the Wallace party for "splitting the progressive vote . . . playing into the hands of the Communist party . . . and strengthening the isolationists and communists who with equal vigor oppose the CIO-endorsed Marshall Plan to aid the war sufferers of Europe." There was some resistance to the policy of working within the Democratic party, a policy that had been initiated by Michigan CIO President Gus Scholle. The *Detroit Free Press* observed that delegates "listened coolly as . . . Scholle laid down the law on political action." The new policy was, indeed, a sharp departure from the position taken in previous state CIO conventions when delegates had called for the formation of a labor party. Scholle had long been opposed to a labor party, and the Reuther caucus was now strong enough to enable Scholle to secure acquiescence for the policy he favored. The delegates were aware that Scholle had secured the expulsion from the PAC of those who had voted against the new policy when it was proposed. The convention resolution did contain the caveat, however, that action would be taken to form a new progressive party if the new policy proved unsuccessful. Pro-Reuther delegates who did not agree with the policy of working inside the Democratic party did not see the Wallace candidacy as an alternative because of its association with the CIO leftwing and the Communists.[20]

The UAW had participated in the Democratic party in the past. In the 1936 elections the infant union had endorsed Roosevelt without involving itself deeply in his campaign. The UAW supported Democrats regularly in elections thereafter, but it had worked primarily through an independent labor electoral arm, first Labor's Non-Partisan League and then the CIO-PAC. Even in 1944, when several UAW members were elected state representatives in Michigan, union leaders negotiated with Democratic party leaders to achieve party recognition for UAW aspirants without sending union activists into the party *en masse*. Although union leaders like Richard Frankensteen had been prominent Democrats or, like George Addes, had attended Democratic party conventions, the UAW and Michigan CIO in 1948, for the first time, urged all key union activists to involve themselves directly in the Democratic party. Some UAW local leaders were cool to the idea because they had strongly supported the building of a labor party, but union activists now became a key component of the Democratic party in Michigan. In becoming active Democratic party workers, UAW members added a new element to the UAW's internal life. UAW Democratic activists developed a dual loyalty to the union and the party. Opponents of the UAW often remarked on the UAW's important influence in the Democratic party in Michigan. Less often noted is the fact that the Democratic party has had a strong influence on the UAW as a result of the qualitatively new level of party involvement that began in 1948.[21] In deciding some union policies, UAW local and international officers gave greater weight to the interests of the Democratic party than was previously true. This characteristic of the new union-Democratic party relationship can be glimpsed in a memorandum from Labor Secretary W. Willard Wirtz to President Lyndon Johnson during the 1964 negotiations between the UAW and GM:

> Walter Reuther is being pressed very strongly by some of his *local* union leaders on some 'rules' issues . . . on which GM has historically been tighter than the other companies . . . he knows (and I have emphasized with him) that a strike now would make him look very bad—and would hurt us . . . . He will probably suggest [to you] that the situation leaves him no choice but to strike. *I recommend that you tell him that this would be a serious mistake* from every standpoint. My information is that Walter can control this situation (with his local people) if he tries hard enough . . . . We should not at this point lift any of the pressure he is under to get a settlement without a strike.[22]

Despite the UAW and CIO rejection of the Progressive party in 1948, many local leaders of the old Addes caucus supported the Wallace candidacy. When Wallace campaigned in Detroit in May, he joined the picket line of UAW members engaged in a national strike against the Chrysler Corporation. The *New York Times* reported that a crowd of striking workers applauded a call to put Wallace in the White House. During his Detroit visit, Wallace met with 900 local officers, stewards, and committee members. About 13,000 people paid to hear Wallace speak at Detroit's Olympia Stadium. Presidents of local unions and units representing about 50,000 Detroit area auto workers formed an Auto Workers National Committee for Wallace and Taylor in 1948. Bob Travis, a leader of the 1937 Flint sit-down strike, acted as executive secretary; other leaders included Percy Llewellyn; Dave Miller of Cadillac Local 22; Francis Danowski of Plymouth Local 51; Ralph Urban of Packard Local 190; and Shelton Tappes, William Johnson, and James Couser of Ford Local 600. Pro-Wallace committees were formed in a number of local unions.[23]

The top leadership of the UAW strenuously opposed the pro-Wallace activity. International representatives supported the filing of charges against members of one Wallace committee for conduct unbecoming union members in putting their local union number on their leaflets. International officers wrote letters to members of local unions whose officers backed Wallace, attacking them for this stance. The UAW leadership opposed not only unionists who actively supported Wallace but those who refused to express opposition to his candidacy. The Reutherites did not accept neutrality on Wallace or the Marshall plan from those who had been their factional opponents.[24]

At the urging of the Reuther forces in Michigan, the national CIO intervened to eliminate the left-center leadership in the Greater Detroit and Wayne County CIO Council of Tracy Doll, Sam Sage, and Coleman Young. At first the Reutherites charged that the council was backing Wallace, but centrist forces in the council leadership had opposed a pro-Wallace stance and the council had refrained from any such action. John Brophy, director of Industrial Union Councils for the national CIO, demanded that the Detroit council follow CIO policy by directly opposing the third-party effort and supporting the Marshall plan. When the council voted to receive and file the Brophy letter, the Reutherites petitioned the national CIO to appoint an administrator over the council. Although the national CIO refrained from appointing an administrator, Murray's representatives pressured the council's officers to allow pro-Reuther locals that had been boycotting the council to participate equally in the organization's convention by making one-month per capita payments to the council and three-month payments into an escrow fund instead of the 12-month payments required by the council constitution.[25]

Although the council leadership eventually sent out a convention call to all locals, when the convention opened September 2, the convention's credentials committee delayed seating the locals that had been disaffiliated. Reuther delegates and UAW staff members prevented conducting orderly business while negotiations proceeded. Before a vote could be taken on the credentials committee report, national CIO representative Adolph Germer announced that he was taking control of the council in the name of the CIO and led a walkout from the convention. The seceding CIO-sanctioned group held its own convention and elected a pro-Reuther leadership. Subordinate to the national CIO, the center-left Detroit CIO group had no choice but to accept its defeat; it no longer constituted a rival center of leadership in the Michigan labor movement.[26]

In addition to its actions against those who supported or might be sympathetic to the Wallace candidacy, the Reuther leadership also attacked the candidate himself. Although the UAW had historically supported Wallace, the union now delved into Wallace's record to find points of disagreement. The UAW and CIO leadership charged that the Wallace campaign was controlled by the Communist party. The ADA also attacked the Progressive party in a similar manner. Press characterization of the movement as Communist-inspired and a tool of the Soviet Union coincided with an intensification of the cold war. The U. S. media condemned the Soviet Union and Eastern European Communists for the blockade of West Berlin, the seizure of power in Czechoslovakia, and other events. Given the national consensus on the cold war, Wallace and the Progressive party's advocacy of a restoration of the policy of cooperation with the Soviet Union fell on hostile ears. Wallace had spoken before a series of large mass rallies in the spring of 1947 and again in the spring of 1948. In the last few months of his presidential campaign, however, the turnouts for his rallies declined in most places, with New York a notable exception. On Wallace's second campaign appearance in Detroit in August, the Progressive party was able to organize a meeting of only 450 people. The Wallace campaign had become isolated.[27]

Although strongly opposed to Henry Wallace's presidential race, the Reuther administration did not look favorably on Truman as a candidate. Leonard Woodcock recalled that only Richard Gosser and he were consistent Truman supporters in the Reuther group. Reuther, CIO President Murray, and ADA leaders engaged in a search for an alternative candidate. Reuther thought Truman was "not adequate for the job he inherited" and feared that "a lot of decent guys" would vote for Wallace if Truman were nominated. Reuther, the CIO, and the ADA were critical of Truman's qualities as a candidate, not his policies. Like most political observers, they thought Truman's unpopularity was such that he had no chance of being elected president in his own right.[28]

The CIO's choice of alternative candidates for president made evident the limited nature of its criticism of Truman. The CIO and ADA jointly selected General Dwight Eisenhower as their first preference and Supreme Court Justice William O. Douglas as their second choice. Eisenhower's views and even his political affiliation were not well known. The CIO-ADA forces were unsuccessful in blocking Truman's nomination, but they did succeed in gaining the adoption by the Democratic convention, against Truman's wishes, of a strong civil rights plank.[29]

After the Democratic party nominated Truman, the CIO-PAC on September 1, 1948 called for an all-out effort on his behalf. A few days later, Truman opened his campaign in Detroit at a Labor Day celebration. A crowd of 125,000 heard the president speak in Cadillac Square at a rally sponsored jointly by the AFL and CIO. Wallace had been the featured speaker the previous Labor Day, but the national CIO takeover of the left-center Detroit-Wayne County CIO eliminated any challenge to a pro-Truman position. Truman spoke forthrightly against the Taft-Hartley Act and warned of worse to come if the Republicans won the election. In mobilizing a massive get-out-the-vote effort and propaganda campaign, the CIO gave priority to electing liberal Democrats to Congress. Truman, however, waged a more effective campaign than many had expected. He concentrated on domestic economic issues and supported the civil rights plank adopted by his party's convention. He successfully projected himself to many voters as a liberal alternative to Thomas Dewey, the Republican presidential nominee.[30]

Persuaded by the vigor of the campaigns of Truman and the CIO-PAC, most UAW rank and filers, union activists, and secondary leaders decided that a vote for Wallace was a wasted vote. They thought Harry Truman would attempt to preserve most of the gains of the New Deal, whereas they believed that Dewey represented conservative forces that would turn the clock back. Most UAW members agreed with the view expressed by the Reuther administration that the Wallace bid, however well intentioned, was divisive. Although Henry Wallace had been personally popular among auto workers, only a small number of them actually voted for him for president in 1948. Wallace received 2.2 percent of the vote in Michigan, 3.5 percent in Detroit's Wayne County, and 2.3 percent in Flint's Genesee County. The Wallace campaign and Wallace's poor showing further isolated the Communists and other popular front supporters in the labor movement.[31]

The UAW leadership made use of the weakened position of the left in the labor movement to undermine not only the strongholds of its factional opponents in the auto union and the Michigan CIO but of left-wing CIO unions as well. The UAW embarked on a raiding campaign against the UE, the FE, the Mine, Mill and Smelter Workers, and other unions. Although denying any raiding intentions, the UAW International Executive Board declared in March 1948 that it would issue charters to CIO members who were "in open revolt against their international leaders because these leaders are in defiance of national CIO policy." The UAW, in fact, initiated raiding campaigns and responded to secession movements by groups within left-wing unions. In some instances, the UAW intervened where a left-wing union was on strike. A number of UAW locals protested this raiding but to no avail. The UAW leadership was "hungry for the carrion," recalled Father Charles Owen Rice, a leader of the fight against communism in the CIO who called on the UAW to take over dissident UE locals but later questioned the wisdom of the anticommunist drive.[32]

The UAW raiding campaign gained strength because many left-wing unions were refusing to sign the non-Communist affidavits and could not participate in NLRB elections. Although UAW raiding attempts were frequently rebuffed, the UAW gained nearly 30,000 members at the expense of other CIO unions in the 14-month period ending on October 31, 1948. The UAW continued its raiding activities even after other CIO unions signed the Taft-Hartley affidavits.[33]

Violent incidents occurred during the course of the UAW raids against left-wing CIO unions. Violent attacks also occurred against Walter and Victor Reuther. On April 20, 1948, Walter Reuther was seriously wounded at home by a shotgun blast that struck him in the arm and chest. Another shotgun blast 13 months later cost Victor Reuther an eye. Detroit newspapers asserted that the attempted assassination of Walter Reuther was a "Communist plot," and police called in many of Reuther's union opponents for questioning. Reuther and his supporters themselves made statements that employers, Communists, or fascists might have been involved, but the UAW board advised union members not to take action against innocent persons. A union investigation found evidence pointing to organized crime elements as the culprits. A jury, however, acquitted the only person ever indicted for either crime, a former leader of the Reuther caucus who had gambling connections and had been dropped from the Reuther slate.[34]

One result of the assassination attempts was that the Reuthers became very security conscious and changed their living style considerably. Walter and his family, for example, moved from a Detroit neighborhood to a secluded and well-protected rural area. Another consequence of the shootings, in the view of Carl Haessler, was to make a "living martyr" out of Reuther and win him sympathy with "large circles of public opinion."[35]

The events of 1948—the Reuther shootings, the Truman victory, the intensification of the cold war and of domestic anticommunism—strengthened the Reuther administration. Following the election, the UAW leadership increased the pressure on local union leaders who had backed Wallace. Ralph Urban, the president of Packard Local 190, complained that the international had twice threatened to replace him with an administrator. The International Executive Board investigated Plymouth Local 51 and charged in January 1949 that the union's newspaper "slavishly adhered to the Communist party line." The board censured Local 51 President Francis Danowski and the officers associated with him and ordered them to comply with UAW and CIO policies. Because all groups in the local opposed the appointment of an administrator, the international refrained from this action. A local membership meeting objected to "dictatorial methods and interference" in the affairs of the local and charged that the attack on individual officers "smells to high heaven with preelection politics." Danowski was subsequently defeated by a Reuther candidate, but most other anti-Reuther officers retained their positions, and the local continued to be an opposition force.[36]

Despite some continuing opposition, the new Reuther administration was in a position to consolidate its power if it could successfully advance the economic interests of the auto workers. In the first two post-war wage negotiations, competition between the two union caucuses had been a factor in leading to the UAW's submission of demands for substantial wage increases of 30 percent (33.5¢ in General Motors) in 1945–1946 and 23.5¢ in 1947. Officials affiliated with the two union caucuses had worked together to win wage gains of 18.5¢ in the first round and 15¢ in the second round of negotiations. Neither of the first two wage increases, however, had compensated workers for the rising cost of living, which increased an additional 7 percent in the seven months following the 1947 GM and Chrysler settlements. Untroubled by the rivalry of the Addes group, the new Reuther-led executive board took no immediate action on the collective bargaining front. Reuther declared that no third round of wage demands would be presented if Congress and the employers rolled back prices.[37]

Although the Reuther administration was proceeding cautiously on the wage issue, five local union presidents in Flint initiated a movement in December 1947 for a 25¢ wage increase plus a cost-of-living bonus in contract renewals. Detroit GM locals, Ford Local 600, Plymouth Local 51, and Briggs Local 212 immediately endorsed the program of the Flint presidents, whose locals represented 50,000 workers. The Reuther leadership responded quickly to the rank-and-file movement for wage increases. The union's executive board adopted a demand for a 25¢ wage increase, 5¢ per hour for a health insurance plan, a guaranteed weekly wage, increased vacation pay, and pension plan demands at the discretion of local unions and corporation councils. The executive board's endorsement of the 25¢ per hour wage demand was weakened, however, by the decision of the GM conference to use 10¢ of the 25¢ for a pension plan. The UAW board, moreover, failed to support the Flint presidents' proposal for a cost-of-living clause in the new contract. Reuther, indeed, went to Flint to argue against the escalator concept.[38]

Disagreement within the union's ranks on the amount and form of the wage demand was only a minor problem compared with the stiff resistance the UAW anticipated from the companies. Taking advantage of the Taft–Hartley Act and the split in the CIO, United States Steel, General Electric, and Chrysler asserted that they would grant no wage increases, and Ford called for a wage cut. The Packinghouse Workers struck the five leading meat packers for ten violence–wracked weeks but received little support from the CIO and were unable to improve on the companies' initial offer of 9¢ per hour. In the face of a strike threat, Chrysler offered the union a 6¢ increase. After the UAW rejected the proposal, Chrysler withdrew the 6¢, and it had no offer on the bargaining table when the UAW commenced strike action on May 12 under the leadership of Acting President Emil Mazey. (The assassination attempt had sidelined Reuther.) Chrysler locals set up mass picket lines, Ford Local 600 donated $125,000, and many other locals voted special assessments to aid the 75,000 Chrysler strikers.[39]

While the Chrysler workers combated the company's antistrike tactics, the UAW conducted a strike vote among its General Motors members. In contrast to the one-company-at-a-time strategy the union had employed in 1945–1946, the UAW now pursued a two-pronged strategy. Most GM locals voted to authorize strike action, but 16 plants employing 38,000 workers, including the old Addes-aligned Buick Local 599, turned down the proposed action. Workers voting no complained that Reuther had promised that it would not be GM's turn again this time, but anti-Reuther factionalism no doubt played a role in their decision. Despite the division, the UAW achieved a third-round negotiations breakthrough at GM when the company proposed an 11¢ wage increase that the UAW accepted on May 25, 1948. In addition to the wage gains, the UAW won noneconomic concessions, including a reduction of the probationary period from six months to 90 days and the right of committeemembers to represent workers in discipline cases. In view of the gap between the UAW wage demands and the negotiated increase, however, UAW Vice President John Livingston and GM Department Assistant Director T. A. Johnstone called the wage settlement "a victory only in the context of today's economic and political reaction."[40]

The new UAW-GM agreement not only marked a break with general managment resistance to a new round of wage increases; it also incorporated several innovative concepts, proposed by GM, that proved to be of lasting significance. GM declared that it recognized that auto workers' purchasing power should be protected from increases in the cost of living. Therefore, of the wage increase, 8¢ was a cost-of-living adjustment designed to restore the workers' buying power to the 1940 level, as measured by the increase in the CPI. Under an up-and-down escalator provision, wages were to increase or decrease quarterly by 1¢ for each 1.14-point change in the CPI. In a concession to UAW negotiators, GM agreed that 3¢ of the 8¢ would not be subject to a reduction should the CPI decrease. To bring the total wage increase to 11¢, GM offered 3¢ (2 percent) in the form of an annual improvement factor (AIF) or productivity increase. Under the terms of the two-year agreement, UAW members were to receive an additional 3¢ productivity increase in 1949.[41]

The agreement on a two-year contract, with no wage reopener, was a concession by the UAW; GM had proposed a three- or five-year contract. Fully aware of the favorable prospects for long-term expansion of its business and the change in the UAW leadership, GM offered its innovative proposals in the hope of stabilizing its labor relations. By building small automatic improvements and cost-of-living protection into the wage structure, GM officials thought they would reduce the likelihood of strikes. GM was especially concerned with increasing the length of contracts, regarding annual contracts as a cause of labor-management tension. Subsequent events proved that GM achieved its objective of securing more peaceful labor relations. The UAW waged no corporate-wide strike against GM until 1970.[42]

Although GM secured its goals in the 1948 negotiations, UAW leaders regarded the settlement as a result of the "seeds planted" during the long 1945–1946 negotiations and strike. Reuther asserted that the UAW had educated GM to an understanding that workers had a legitimate interest in the relationship between wages, price, and profits, something the corporation had refused to concede in 1945–1946. UAW officials also credited GM with recognizing the principle, advanced by the UAW, that workers were "entitled to a share in the growing output of an expanding economy." Despite the union's claim to having educated GM, corporation officials had actually been seeking an opportunity to present the program it brought forward in 1948 since 1941. GM had made what it characterized as a cost-of-living offer during the 1945–1946 negotiations, the company had stated in 1945–1946 that higher wages had to be based on increased production and productivity, and the 1948 contract made no mention of GM's prices and profits. GM's position in 1948 was really consistent with its earlier stance.[43]

Both GM and the Reuther leadership sought a stable balance between wages and prices and production and consumption. The two sides still disagreed, however, on the level of wages and the point at which wages and prices, production and consumption, would truly balance. However committed to their belief that a balanced economy would produce automatic progress for workers and peaceful labor relations, Reuther and his colleagues in the UAW leadership remained attuned to the demands of rank-and-file auto workers for a greater share of the income produced by their industry. In their victory statements, therefore, Livingston and Johnstone were frank about the shortcomings of the new GM contract. They criticized the selection of 1940 as the base year for the cost-of-living calculation as unjust given the reality of "an army of eight million unemployed" in that prewar year. They also asserted that GM had failed fully to apply the principle it espoused that workers should share in economic expansion and characterized "the assumption that workers can expect no more than to remain on an economic treadmill, inching up 3¢ an hour per year" as "the trickle down theory of prosperity, slightly modified." Reuther, for his part, stated that the UAW's goal "from now on" would be to "increase and accelerate" the extent of the workers' participation in the benefits of increasing production and productivity. UAW leaders viewed the agreement as a "foot in the door" for important principles.[44]

The new concepts embodied in the GM contract became an auto industry pattern only in later years. Three days after the GM settlement, the UAW and Chrysler concluded a strike settlement providing for a straight 13¢ per hour wage increase and the right to reopen wage negotiations after one year. The

Ford and United States Steel agreements followed the Chrysler pattern. Only the UE accepted the pattern set by the UAW-GM contract when they came to terms with GM.[45]

One reason the GM-UAW agreement did not set the pattern for the auto and other industries was that workers in many industries would have been unable to secure a cost-of-living wage increase on the basis of the 1940 standard because their wages had advanced more rapidly than the CPI since that time. Some criticized the use of the CPI because of the labor movement's long-standing argument that the index was a very inadequate measure of both retail prices and living costs. Given widespread predications of a recession and deflation, the prospect that inadequate wage rates might be cut, as was possible under the GM agreement, disturbed many. Like the UAW negotiators themselves, many others in the labor movement criticized the 2 percent productivity increase for falling short of the actual increase in productivity. They also thought that larger increases were justified in view of the record profit rates of industrial concerns.[46]

During the life of the 1948 agreement, GM workers received some cost-of-living increases and a second 3¢ productivity increase, but they also saw their wages cut when the CPI fell. The wage cuts sanctioned by the recessionary drop in the CPI caused serious dissatisfaction among GM workers. The corporation, in a minor concession, agreed in August 1949 to a 0.8 upward adjustment in the index because of its inadequate reflection of rents. The union was so disillusioned with the cost-of-living clause that it announced on July 9, 1949, that the formula would be dropped in the next contract negotiations.[47]

The hourly increase in wages of GM workers during their two-year contract averaged 13.25¢, the equivalent of 12.75¢ the first year and an additional 0.75¢ the second year.[48] Chrysler and Ford workers had won 13¢ in their 1948 agreements and had the right to reopen negotiations in 1949 on all issues at Ford and on wages at Chrysler. Because the GM contract could not be reopened, however, the other auto companies were in a position to resist UAW demands that would raise wage rates and labor costs above those at GM. Although the 1948 victory of President Truman and Democratic liberals strengthened labor's hand in the 1949 negotiations, the recession that began at the end of 1948 and the division in the ranks of the CIO that culminated in the expulsion of the left-wing unions weakened the union's position. Increased attention on international problems connected with the cold war also had a negative impact on labor's effort to win support for its economic and social demands. As Emil Mazey later avowed about the Korean War, labor's "enemies [were given] the excuse and opportunity of stymying . . . necessary progressive social legislation."[49]

A cost-of-living increase—eventually specified as 11¢—was only the third highest UAW priority in the 1949 negotiations. The top union priority was a $100 per month employer-financed pension at age 60 after 25 years of service.

The UAW's second demand was a health, hospital, and security plan financed by employer payments of 5 percent of its payroll. The UAW proposed joint union-management administration of the two separate trust funds that its demands were intended to create. To back up the union's demands, both Ford and Chrysler workers voted heavily in favor of strike action in August 1949. The union returned to a one-company-at-a-time strategy and targeted the Ford Motor Company, whose work force was considerably older than Chrysler's or GM's. Three thousand Ford UAW members 60 years and older attended a rally at which Reuther pledged that the union would not sign a contract without a pension program.[50]

On September 29, 1949, the UAW achieved its historic pension agreement with the Ford Motor Company. Under terms of the agreement, the company guaranteed that it would supplement social security payments (then averaging $30 per month for Ford retirees) so that retiring Ford workers 65 years and older would receive a total of $100 per month beginning April 1, 1952. Union and management were to be equally represented on a Board of Administration that was to govern the pension fund, and the two parties were to select a neutral chairperson. The union claimed that the company had agreed to a specific contribution of 8.75¢ per hour to the pension fund and that the addition of a hospitalization benefit to the company paid group insurance plan brought the value of the package to 10¢ per hour. President Truman's steel fact-finding board had recommended the latter figure in the dispute in that industry over pension and health plans.[51]

Recognizing the pension plan as an impotant breakthrough in the field of social security, Ford workers ratified the new agreement by a four-to-one margin. Many secondary union leaders, however, sharply criticized the terms of the pact during and after ratification. Delegates to the Ford Council approved the agreement by only a 659 to 381 margin, and Flint leaders and UAW left wingers pointed out shortcomings in the agreement. The critics were dissatisfied with the fact that an increase in social security benefits would reduce the company-paid benefits. The plan was not truly noncontributory, the critics noted, because workers and the company would equally share the cost of an increase in social security benefits. Also, the fact that Ford could deduct the full amount of contributions to the pension fund from its taxable income meant that the general public shared the cost of the plan.[52]

The critics generally failed to realize that the cost of the plan to the company was unknown. Although the contract mentioned the 8.75¢ cited by the union in its explanation of the agreement, it did not require the company to contribute this amount into the fund. Ford negotiators agreed to insert mention of the 8.75¢, at Reuther's request, "to increase the salability of the plan by enabling the employees to attach some value to it." The 8.75¢ "had no real meaning," UAW Ford Department Director Ken Bannon later recalled.[53]

The union won the right to participate in the administration of benefits under the pension plan, but unmentioned by the union was the fact that the company maintained sole control of the financial operation of the trust fund. The critics believed that few workers would actually receive any substantial benefits because of the strictly defined eligibility rules. Workers received full credit toward the needed 30 years only for those years in which they had worked 1,800 hours. Able workers working fewer than 30 years had no vested rights under the plan. To receive maximum pension benefits, workers had to wait until they attained 65 years of age. Social security experts expressed concern that few younger workers would remain with one company long enough to receive benefits under a Ford-type plan. There was also criticism of provisions for mandatory retirement, with some exceptions, for 68-year-old workers and the right of the company to retire at 65 any worker unable to perform his or her assignment "efficiently." Critics also complained about the fact that the contract ran for two and one-half years and that there was a two-year waiting period before the contract could be reopened on wages.[54]

Despite the shortcomings of the Ford plan, it established an important new benefit for Ford workers. Under the leadership of the Reuther administration, the union had laid a foundation on which it could and did build. It is noteworthy that the UAW won a pension plan at Ford without resort to strike action whereas the steel workers were obliged to strike for more than four weeks to establish a similar plan in their industry.[55] Achievement of the Ford pension plan was a factor in the consolidation of the Reuther leadership. The critics of the plan, while numerous, were not in a position to show that they could have secured greater benefits than those won by the Reuther administration. The Ford rank and file rejected calls to defeat the plan. It should be noted, however, that workers at the Ford River Rouge and Lincoln plants (three-fifths of all Ford workers) had recently struck the company for 25 days against speed-up and were not eager for another long strike.[56]

Following the Ford negotiations, the UAW set out to win similar pension plans at other automobile corporations, achieving success at Nash, Kaiser-Frazer, and Budd Manufacturing. Negotiations with Chrysler dragged on, however, as the union extended its strike deadline. As criticism of the Ford agreement mounted, the union's Chrysler Department set its sights on improving the terms of the Ford pact, and considerable rank-and-file sentiment for wage increases developed. On the eve of strike action at Chrysler, the UAW board offered to settle for 10¢ per hour in the form of pension and health benefits or as a straight wage increase and expressed a willingness to arbitrate the details of the pension plan. Chrysler offered to pay pensions but refused to establish a trust fund. Believing that the Chrysler offer was worth less than 3¢, the UAW began strike action on January 25, 1950, thereby automatically terminating the contract.[57]

During a difficult 100-day strike most Chrysler locals followed the UAW leadership's advice and organized only token picket lines. Occasional rallies allowed for some rank-and-file participation in the strike. As had been true of GM workers in their long strike, Chrysler workers strongly supported their leadership and resented attacks on it, whether from the press or UAW oppositionists. The victory of the United Mine Workers on March 5, 1950, in its strike for higher pay and improvements in the union's health and welfare plan strengthened the UAW's position. The UAW and Chrysler finally came to terms on May 4, 1950, agreeing on a Ford-type pension plan and improvements in the group health-insurance plan that the union valued at 7¢ and 3¢ per hour, respectively. The union also won wage increases for workers in 45 classifications and in certain geographical areas. For the first time, Chrysler agreed to a dues check-off. Although the basic features of the Chrysler pension plan were similar to Ford's, the Chrysler plan was superior because it required 25 instead of 30 years of service and 1,700 instead of 1,800 hours of work to establish one year's pension credit. In a concession to the corporation, the UAW ageed to a three-year contract but retained the right to open the pact twice on wages and insurance. The rank and file ratified the agreement by an overwhelming margin.[58]

Following the long, drawn-out battle at Chrysler, General Motors took the initiative in the 1950 negotiations and arrived at an agreement with the UAW before it took a strike vote. GM agreed to a Ford-type pension plan and significant improvements in the hospital and medical insurance plan. The pension plan provided for an increase in monthly benefits from $100 to $117.50 if Congress approved a 22 percent increase in social security benefits then under discussion. Other gains included an increase in the annual improvement factor to 4¢, an improvement in the vacation pay plan, and an extra 5¢ wage increase for skilled workers. In the noneconomic area, the UAW won a modified union shop provision for the first time. The UAW appraised the value of the GM pension and health plan improvements at 12¢ and the total economic worth of the package at 19¢. Although the union initially planned to discard the escalator clause, it agreed to its continuation. In a significant concession to GM, the union agreed to a five-year contract that specifically excluded reopening of negotiations on any matter. Although many Reuther opponents were once again critical of the agreement, rank-and-file members ratified the contract by a large margin.[59]

GM workers had won greater immediate wage increases than had other automobile workers, but the new agreement tied them to real wage increases of less than 3 percent per year and to no further improvements in fringe benefits over the next five years.[60] Reuther hailed the agreement, however, as "the most significant development in labor relations since the mass production industries were organized in 1936–1937." The GM-UAW contract was a good example of labor and management making democracy work, Reuther told the press, and thereby reducing the need for nationalization.[61]

The new GM agreement influenced other auto workers to seek higher wages from their companies. Shortly after signing the GM agreement, the United States became involved in the Korean War, and the rising prices and falling unemployment that accompanied the beginning of the war gave impetus to the wage movement. Workers took advantage of a growing shortage of experienced workers to launch a series of unauthorized strikes. Responding to the pressure, Chrysler and Ford agreed to new concessions to the UAW even though their contracts were not open for negotiation. In the Ford talks, the UAW won significant improvements in wages and fringe benefits, but it also agreed to rewrite the contract to make it conform to the GM pact, which meant a five-year contract that included a wage escalator and an annual improvement factor. Although opposition among Ford workers was substantial, the contract was ratified.[62]

The agreements of 1948, 1949, and 1950 set the pattern for the UAW's future collective bargaining efforts. The escalator clause provided partial protection from the inflation that became an endemic feature of the United States economy. The annual improvement factor provided modest, automatic increases in base wage rates. In return for these gains and improvements in fringe benefits, the UAW accepted longer contracts than it had in the past. Three-year contracts became the norm beginning with the 1955 contracts.

With the successful negotiation of health and retirement plans, the UAW began to stress the increase in worker compensation in the form of fringe benefits, which had been very limited prior to 1948. Health and retirement plans had been a union goal for a number of years, and both sides in the 1946–1947 factional fight had favored them. It was under the Reuther administration's leadership, however, that these benefits were won. In subsequent years, the union was able to secure an increase in the level of benefits under these plans, and it also won new fringe benefits, notably the establishment of Supplemental Unemployment Benefits in 1955.[63]

Union success in winning fringe-benefit improvements was accompanied by a partial retreat on the political front. At the end of World War II, the union had hoped that union political action would help secure an expanded New Deal, with legislation for improved old age security, a national health plan, and full and fair employment. The union's commitment to these goals was no less than in the past, but its "sense of urgency" about the reforms was lessened, Leonard Woodcock recalled, because of the protection won for union members in UAW contracts. The cold war and the strength of conservative forces in Congress, despite Truman's 1948 victory, made progress toward an expanded New Deal difficult. The negotiation, however, of company-paid pension plans that were integrated with social security lessened corporate opposition to a reform of social security in 1950 that involved expansion in the number of beneficiaries and the level of benefits. Still, in contrast to the UAW's initial decade, in the 1950's, the UAW and its fellow CIO unions were generally unable to win gains for the greater community through the political process while it won new benefits for its members. This failure led to a weakening of the industrial union alliance with nonlabor groups, even though the unions retained their collective bargaining strength.[64]

The increased wages and security won by auto workers were not accompanied by corresponding improvements in working conditions. Management continued its efforts, as it saw the matter, to redress the balance of power within the factory. Ford and Chrysler had achieved some success in winning strengthened company security clauses in the 1946 negotiations and such clauses remained a permanent feature of most UAW-auto industry contracts. Although both sides in the UAW's factional battle had declared their opposition to company security clauses and the tying of wage increases to productivity, the Reuther group accepted both after it gained complete control of the union.

The AIF or productivity wage increase provided for modest, annual wage increases based on the concept of giving workers a share in the advancing productivity of the national economy. The terms of the AIF clause made clear that a "cooperative attitude" by the union and workers was a necessary ingredient for increased productivity. Although the stated objective was "to produce more with the same amount of human effort," the company's use of time study to measure "scientifically" the amount of work that could be done caused great strife. Worker protests and strikes against speed-up were widespread, but the company security clauses gave the Big Three and other auto companies the right to discharge workers who failed to meet production standards or engaged in work slowdowns or stoppages in violation of the contract. GM President Charles E. Wilson praised union leaders for supporting the philosophy of the productivity wage clause and rejecting the "make work" and "feather bedding" that would undermine the new approach.[65]

The greatest protest against the speed-up was a 25-day strike of 65,000 workers at the Ford River Rouge and Lincoln plants in May 1949. Workers at Ford and other companies had been complaining for some time that production standards were too high. Ford workers, moreover, were dissatisfied with a company policy inaugurated in March 1948 to run production lines as much as 25 percent above the standards to make up for production delays. Most of the workers' complaints about production standards were not processed as grievances because union committeemen lacked the technical skills to challenge time studies, which were accepted in principle by the international. [66]

Auto workers expressed their dissatisfaction with their working conditions in spontaneous work stoppages in various buildings at the River Rouge complex and in numerous other auto plants of other companies as well. In the fall of

1948 the Communists, who were still a strong force in Local 600, began a campaign for general action to halt the Ford speed-up drive. The *Michigan Worker,* a Communist paper, published articles about speed-up conditions in various River Rouge buildings, and left wingers in Local 600 wrote leaflets, circulated petitions, and called for strike action. Although the Local 600 leadership condemned outside intervention and the international denounced Communist agitation concerning the speed-up, most rank-and-file workers supported the campaign. During the course of the local's election contest, consequently, the Local 600 administration of Tommy Thompson began protesting the speed-up. Thompson was reelected, but his left-wing opponent received 38 percent of the vote, and left wingers were elected presidents of several buildings. Thompson criticized the use of time study, and the local voted to strike against the speed-up by a margin of 34,000 to 4,000.[67]

Although the immediate cause of the strike was the union's contention that speed-up conditions at the Lincoln and Dearborn Assembly plants violated the health and safety clause of the contract, the union also raised general policy issues. The union demanded that lines be maintained at a constant speed and at 100 percent of production standards, with equal spacing of work; that a sufficient number of workers be allocated to the lines to prevent a speed-up and to meet problems of absenteeism or unusual mixes of body types; that an adequate number of relief workers be employed to provide all employees with their rightful 24 minutes of relief time; and that no one involved in the strike be penalized. Although it raised some policy questions, the union did not contend that there was a general speed-up involving high production standards at the River Rouge plant, nor did it question the company's prerogative to determine production standards on is own nor its use of time study. Ford, which charged that the strike was caused by intraunion politics, offered to arbitrate the dispute. Recalling that workers at the River Rouge plant had lost their traditional 20-minute paid lunch period by an arbitraton decision in 1948 and aware that the contract gave the company the sole power to determine production standards, the union at first rejected arbitration.[68]

UAW President Reuther, who immediately took over leadership of the strike, told a cheering rally of 14,000 strikers, "there is nothing to arbitrate." The enthusiasm of the rank and file was great; a management representative who toured the picket lines counted 3,000, 4,800, and 2,100 workers picketing on three occasions. The union had strong public support as well. Dearborn Mayor Orville Hubbard announced that his sympathies were with the union, and a company-commissioned public opinion poll showed that 43 percent of the general public supported the union in the strike as compared to 27 percent who supported the company.[69]

Despite the strength of the strike, the UAW leadership was anxious to see it ended because Ford was refusing to open negotiations on the new contract.

The UAW leadership's primary 1949 goal was to establish a pension plan, and it feared that prolongation of the speed-up strike might make the production standards and company security clauses of the contract prime issues for renegotiation. The Reuther leadership arrived at a settlement with the company on six of the strike issues and agreed to the arbitration of the principal issue in dispute: whether the company could require employees to perform a work assignment "on any unit" in less time than specified in the company's time study, provided that the total work assigned did not exceed 480 minutes in an eight-hour shift. The agreement was ratified at a meeting of 7,000 workers over the Memorial Day weekend.[70]

The company agreed under the terms of the settlement to maintain each line at a constant speed and to space units to provide a uniform flow of work. The company further agreed that normal work loads would not increase because of absenteeism or because of an unexpected mix of body types on the line. The union did not gain any increase in the number of relief workers, but it received a pledge that "necessary" relief would be provided. The parties agreed that penalty discharges and layoffs against 27 workers would be reduced to reprimands. The arbitration panel ruled on the issue submitted to arbitration that the company could operate its lines at a speed in excess of the production schedule but that it had to "seek to make the individual employee's work assignment as measured by standard work minutes equal to or within the actual production cycle time available to him." The arbitration panel credited the company with having achieved this distribution of work on most assignments. Although Reuther considered the settlement a victory, his left-wing opponents at Ford termed it a "betrayal." The real loss from the workers' viewpoint was that the union did not challenge the company's establishment of production standards that were too high, the company's sole right to set production standards, or the company's use of time study. The speed-up remained a continuing problem for auto workers.[71]

The 1949 Ford speed-up strike was an indication that Communists retained an important influence in Local 600. Because Local 600 was so large, it carried substantial weight in the international union. Although no danger existed that an opposition to the Reuther administration based in Local 600 could successfully challenge the administration, the international leadership remained committed to the old Reuther caucus policy of denying Communists any legitimate role in the union's affairs. The Communists and their partners in the Local 600 Progressive Unity caucus won new strength in the 1950 local elections by allying with workers associated with other caucuses who agreed with them on issues. Candidates endorsed by the Progressive Unity group won three of the four top local union offices and the majority of local building presidencies. Reuther supporter Carl Stellato won the local presidency with 600 votes more than Tommy Thompson, who had abandoned his alliance with

Reuther after the 1949 speed-up strike and pension negotiations. Stellato ran on a militant program, condemning the Ford decentralization program and the settlement of the speed-up strike, but he was also openly anticommunist.[72]

With Reuther's support, Stellato launched an anticommunist campaign in Local 600. By a 75-to-63 margin, the local's General Council supported Stellato's call for endorsement of Truman's Korea policy and the requirement that all 550 local union representatives and appointees sign an anticommunist loyalty oath. Stellato then charged five officers with being Communists and thus not eligible to hold union office under the UAW's constitution. Although the trial committee found the accused guilty, opposition to the purge was strong in the local. Left and center opponents of the anticommunist campaign gained new strength in the elections for the council later in 1950 and for local union office in 1951. Stellato, who retained his presidency by defeating a left-wing candidate by 429 votes, decided to drop the anticommunist campaign. The local's general council eventually dismissed the charges against the accused local officers. During and after the 1951 UAW convention, Stellato emerged as an outspoken opponent of Reuther.[73]

An anti-Reuther opposition was present at the 1949 and later UAW conventions, but it did not represent a significant challenge to the administration. The eleventh UAW convention in July 1949 was the first after the Reuther caucus had won complete control of the union's executive board and showed that the Reuther group now enjoyed ideological hegemony in the union. The convention endorsed the CIO policy of expelling affiliates accused of following the Communist party line. At the two previous UAW conventions, no general foreign policy resolution had been adopted, but the delegates now went on record in favor of the Marshall Plan, Point Four, and the establishment of the North Atlantic Treaty Organization. In keeping with Reuther's past advocacy of a middle-of-the-road position, the resolution supported "constant vigilance" against "possible Soviet aggression" but also "constant readiness to cooperate with the USSR" as long as principles were not sacrificed.[74]

The anti-Reuther forces, now without any base in international office or staff positions, consisted mostly of left wingers and their closest allies. Reuther was reelected president over W. G. Grant of Local 600 by a margin of 8,021 to 639 votes. William Johnson, a Black leader from Local 600, received 875 votes, the highest opposition total, in his race for vice president. The opposition's strength was concentrated in a few locals that had traditionally been left wing. Ford Local 600 provided Grant with nearly 30 percent of his total vote, and other substantial blocs of opposition votes came from Plymouth Local 51, Packard Local 190, Fisher Body Local 45, and amalgamated Local 453 in Illinois.[75]

Although only about 10 percent of the delegates voted against one or another of the top union leaders, the contests for some of the regional directorships were closer. An oposition candidate received 545 votes to 1,113 for one of the incumbents, Norman Matthews, in Region 1. Administration candidates won office in the Flint region, in one Cleveland region, and in the Wisconsin-based region by margins of only 19, 30, and 44 votes. Much of this opposition reflected dissatisfaction with the performance of individual directors rather than a serious questioning of the Reuther administration. These contests evidenced the existence of a bloc of independent delegates that was larger than the predominantly left-wing opposition bloc.[76]

Because of the continuing existence of independent sentiments, the convention rejected some administration proposals and only narrowly approved others. The delegates defeated the administration-sponsored constitutional amendment for biennial conventions but agreed to a proposal for a 20-month interval between conventions. The convention refused to agree to a dues increase or to the appointment of international administrations over local unions without hearings. By a narrow margin, the convention approved the division of Region 4, which critics accurately charged was designed to prevent the defeat of the region's director. There was also dissent over the decision to expel Tracy Doll and Sam Sage, leaders of the Progressive Unity caucus, from the union because of their distribution of a brochure alleging toleration of gangsterism by the UAW leadership that the FE had used in their fight against UAW raiding. Although the constitution provided that union members were to be tried by their local unions, the executive board convinced the convention to try and convict the opposition leaders, whom Reuther charged with "treason." The convention then agreed to amend the constitution to provide for international trials of union members.[77]

Although the Reuther leadership had dominated the 1949 convention, it was self-critical about its failure to win the dues increase and the two-year conventions. The Reutherites had not engaged in the kind of year-round organizing and caucus activity for which they had been known in the past but instead relied on their administrative control. They resolved to return to the old methods in the future.[78]

The Reuther administration maintained firm control of subsequent UAW conventions. The left wing still remained the core of the anti-Reuther opposition, and the Reutherites still used the Communist charge against all their opponents. The United States's involvement in the Korean War caused cold war anticommunism to reach a fever pitch and made it more difficult than ever for opposition elements to function in the union.

Extremist actions against alleged Communists in the UAW had begun in 1948. In March of that year, threats of violence by a mob of fellow workers forced three union members accused of distributing Communist and Wallace literature from their jobs in the Briggs Vernor plant in Detroit. Production was interrupted for three days because of the incident. Although the leaders of Local 212 and the international affirmed that Communists had the right to work until they were "outlawed by legislation," they also suggested to those opposing the alleged Communist presence in their plant that a charge could be filed against the three workers for "conduct unbecoming a union member."Anticommunists in other local unions also filed charges against union members who had distributed Communist literature.[79]

There were numerous physical attacks on alleged Communists in the auto industry in 1950. Attacks on left-wing auto workers took place in Detroit, Flint, Milwaukee, Linden, New Jersey, and Los Angeles. Some of the victims suffered serious injuries, loss of their jobs, or arrest.[80]

Hearings by the House Un-American Activities Committee in Detroit in 1952 resulted in public identification of numerous auto workers as Communists. The press gave banner headlines to the hearings and publicized the names, work places, and addresses of those identified. In some plants, workers forced "unfriendly witnesses" out of the plant. Black unionists who were victimized were subjected to racial harassment as well. Some employers suspended and fired individuals who did not cooperate with the committee. The union processed grievances successfully for some of the fired workers, but international representatives also cooperated with the committee's investigation of alleged Communist domination of Local 600. Although Communists were far from dominating the local, they and their allies remained an important element in the life of the local union. Following the hearings, the international itself charged Communist domination of Local 600 and established an administratorship. The administrator removed 20 local staff and lesser officials from office, including the five building leaders who had previously been tried by the local. The international then barred the five building leaders from office for several years. Although Carl Stellato, the anti-Reuther president of the local, was reelected after the administratorship was ended, the pressure exerted by HUAC and the international succeeded in reducing the left-wing role in the local.[81]

The HUAC returned to Michigan in 1954, concentrating on an investigation of communism in Flint. Once again, individuals were named and violent attacks occurred both inside and outside the plants against many of them. Although hourly paid auto workers conducted the in-plant attacks, indirect evidence of GM management's involvement was found in the assaults in Flint. Whatever the degree of management complicity in the violence, employers suspended and fired individuals who were the objects of physical attack as well as many of those who were named in the hearings but not attacked. On the other hand, GM did fire four of the mob leaders a few weeks after the hearings.[82]

The UAW at first hesitated to attempt to combat the hysteria, but it eventually decided that the constitutional rights of union members had to be protected. The UAW board stated that the union would henceforth process the grievances of those who lost pay or who were discharged due to mob violence. If the victims affirmed that they were no longer Communists, they sometimes received strong support from their local union. Charles Shinn, a leading activist in Fisher Body Local 598, received the unanimous backing of a local membership meeting the day after he was thrown out of the plant. As Shinn recalled it, although he enjoyed the solid support of the union activists, the large majority of the rank and file was hostile to him. The *Flint Weekly Review*, the paper of the city's UAW locals, noted with concern that many rank and filers did not support the UAW's policy of protecting the rights of the accused Communists and asserted that this was weakening the union's solidarity.[83]

Many of those named in the Flint hearings were "colonizers" for the Communist party who had come to the city only recently to get jobs in auto plants. Most of the colonizers lacked roots in Flint and were unable to survive in the hostile environment created by the hearings. Most left the city, further weakening the already weak Communist and left-wing groups in Flint.[84]

By the mid-1950s the Reuther group had effectively consolidated its leadership of the UAW. Its solid control of the union's administrative staff put it in position to provide numerous services to the union's membership, and it used the union's publicity, educational, and political machinery to win the membership to its ideological viewpoint. The Reutherites retained the tactical flexibility to respond to rank-and-file movements and, at the same time, it put into place more and more restrictions on its opponents in the local unions. Most importantly, the Reuther leadership won measured advances for the UAW membership in wages and economic security. The left-center coalition that had been a leading power in the UAW for the first ten years of its existence had been weakened by factionalism, anticommunism, and a weakening of the ties between top leadership and the rank and file. Losing its base in the union apparatus after the defeat of its top leaders, the coalition fell apart. The coalition's center forces were dispersed, and the left-wing groups were isolated. The Communist-led left wing had been able to build new coalitions after previous setbacks in 1938 and 1940–1941, but it was now unable to reestablish an alliance that could link it with the mainstream of the union. The fact that the Soviet Union and the United States were now the principal contenders on the world stage made anticommunism a much more potent force than ever before. Left-wing UAW members faced hostility from the media, the major political parties, and public opinion as well as the leadership of the UAW and CIO. They experienced repression at the hands of congressional committees, their employers, and their own union leaders. The UAW leftists became a relatively isolated minority active mainly in a few big cities. As a result, no force emerged to challenge the Reuther trade union philosophy. It became the norm accepted by the vast majority of automobile union members in the years to come.

Chapter Seventeen

The Cold War and
the End of the Popular Front

Although foreign policy issues were not debated in depth or at length during the factional fight for control of the UAW, the cold war was the underlying reality shaping the conflict. The breakdown of the alliance between the United States and the Soviet Union and the initiation of a "get-tough-with-Russia" policy by Truman had immediate and, for the UAW's left-center coalition, detrimental domestic consequences. Conservative forces such as the Hearst newspaper chain whose attacks on communism had not abated even during the wartime alliance stepped up their offensive. "Straight" reporting by other newspapers of the growing conflict between the United States and the Soviet Union helped in the building of a wave of anticommunist sentiment. Charges of Communist spying in Canada on behalf of the Soviet Union added to the hysteria. Republican politicians and conservative organizations picked up the theme, especially during the 1946 election campaign. In 1947, anticommunism became firmly rooted in foreign policy as a result of the Truman Doctrine and the Marshall Plan and in domestic policy as a consequence of Truman's Loyalty Order and the Taft-Hartley Act. The hysteria of McCarthyism soon followed.

Domestic anticommunism was nothing new nor was the connection of antiradicalism with a foreign danger new. The anticommunism of the cold war period was more intense and far-reaching than previous bursts of antiradicalism, however, because of the fact that the United States and the Soviet Union had become the two major contenders on the world stage. Leaders of government and the press charged that Communist support for the Soviet Union amounted to potential or actual disloyalty to the United States. When the Soviet Union acquired nuclear weapons, the fear that the Soviet Union represented a threat to the United States became even greater. The United States's goals as a world power were more ambitious, the radical foe more powerful, and the danger stemming from nuclear weapons development was more frightening than ever before. The leaders of the Thomas-Addes-Leonard coalition began their battle with Walter Reuther and his supporters just as this new wave of anticommunist hysteria was beginning to build. They had no idea that the wave would not only force them from leadership but continue to mount until many of their radical supporters at the local level had been silenced, isolated or forced out of union activity.

The defeat and disintegration of the UAW left-center coaliton contributed to the ending of the popular front presence in United States political life. It was the conclusion of a period in United States political history as well: The division between the 1935–1946 period and the subsequent period in United States history is immense. Communists were not accepted as equal participants in the political process during the popular front period, to be sure. There was an openness to Communists and Communist ideas in both working-class and professional communities, however, that came to an end with the cold war. The cold war ushered in a period in which the fear of communism dominated our political culture until the broad outpouring of opposition to the Vietnam War in the late 1960s and early 1970s. Cold war anticommunism resulted in the creation of an intellectual and psychological wall between the Communist party and the rest of the body politic. As a result, many radical ideas were closed off from consideration and the nation's overall political dialogue shifted substantially to the right. Although events since the 1960s have led to the weakening of this invisible structure of fear, it continues to affect public thinking and psychology. Many are still influenced by the idea of Communists as Soviet agents. Perhaps more important for the story of the UAW, many liberals and radicals feel a need to distinguish themseleves from the Communists because they do not want to be outside the bounds of normal society or subject to public rebuke or job loss.

To understand what was lost with the defeat of the left-center coalition in the UAW and its equivalents in other areas of our political life requires the comprehension of a time when the Communist party was different from other political organizations but not "other," not viewed as a pariah with whom association had to be avoided at all costs. The period of the popular front (1935–1946) was an era of relative openness of broad sections of the population to Communist individuals and ideas. Communist party officials met regularly with UAW leaders to discuss policy and areas of mutual cooperation. Even at a time when he led a powerful anticommunist coalition in the UAW, Walter Reuther met with Communist officials John Williamson and Pat Toohey to urge that the party not oppose him for UAW vice president. This meeting occurred at the 1944 UAW convention and, as Leo Fenster, who was present, recalled it, Reuther told Williamston and Toohey: "You and I have our differences, but at least we're both Marxists."[1]

More important than meetings with opponents, of course, were the Communists' meetings with friends and allies, the cooperation between Communists and non-Communists in developing trade union programs, in conducting organizational campaigns and strikes, in fielding slates of candidates, and in solving daily problems on the shop floor and in the neighborhood. Even though they lost representation at the highest level of the UAW when Wyndham Mortimer was not returned to the UAW executive board in 1939, Communists continued to have input into UAW board policy. They were regularly consulted by UAW officials and they had a leading role in such key developments as the UAW's 1939 constitution and the April 1946 board program. There were similar arrangements in many local unions. Many UAW activists knew individual Communists or Communist supporters who had played important pioneering roles in their local unions. The Communists and their supporters were known for their facility at developing a program of action, their advocacy of Black equality, their interest in broader political and social questions of the day, and their commitment to the cause of unionism. They influenced how non-Communist activists thought about the union and politics and the latter, in turn, influenced the Communists' thinking. Through their cooperation with centrist allies on the local, international union, and national CIO levels, Communists influenced the thinking of rank-and-file members with whom they may not have been in immediate contact. As John Earl Haynes has argued, through the medium of these popular front alliances, Communists were a factor influencing mainstream politics in the United States.[2]

The special significance of the defeat of the left-center alliance in the UAW and in other unions and the subsequent near destruction of left-wing influence in the trade unions lies in the fact that these organizations had millions of members and had a powerful role in the nation's political life. If the popular front forces had continued to be a significant factor in the leadership and activist ranks of the UAW and other CIO unions, they could have served as voices of opposition to the cold war. The development of the stultifying "cold war consensus" would thereby have been averted and alternative policies would have been up for discussion. Whether the issue was war in Korea or Vietnam, ghetto rebellions, busing for racial integration, the challenge of advancing technology, the crisis of the cities or the crisis of manufacturing, the unions proceeded, by and large, without the benefit of the left's thinking and activism.

Although the popular front alliance was demolished and left-wing influence reduced to a meager level, many of the popular front's accomplishments remained. Industrial unionism, interracial unity, the active involvement of unions in the political arena, and concern for the needs of the oppressed all continued as features of the trade union movement. The popular front groups were not alone in endorsing these concepts, but the left had pioneered in bringing these ideas foward and the popular front coalitions had been the means by which they were consolidated. Although there was less progress in some areas—such as advancing Black workers into leadership positions—than might have been the case if the left-center forces had remained in leadership,

these had become the values of the industrial wing of the trade union movement and they persist to this day.

With the left wing's isolation from the mainstream of the nation's politics,
the Reuther-led UAW was about as far to the left of the political spectrum of
"respectable" politics of any major organization. The core of the Reuther leadership's liberalism remained, necessarily, its responsiveness to the economic needs
of its membership. It secured regular wage increases, health and retirement
plans (1949–1950), supplemental unemployment benefits (1955), and the right
to retire after 30 years of service (1970). In the political arena, it was the chief
support for the liberal administration of G. Mennen Williams in Michigan and
a major sponsor of Lyndon Johnson's Great Society. The UAW did not limit
itself to supporting liberal Democratic administrations. It joined in the sponsorship of a major civil rights demonstration in Detroit which served as a prelude
to the 1963 March on Washington. It has been a principal source of financial
and political support for the United Farm Workers.[3] The UAW has also been
one of the leading forces working for national health insurance, a reform that
has yet to be won.

On foreign policy questions, the UAW, while continuing to accept the
cold war consensus, began to advocate a more flexible approach after the end
of the Korean war. The 1953 UAW convention called for summit negotiations
between the United States and the Soviet Union.[4] In the mid-1950s, Walter
Reuther argued that nonalignment was a fact of international life against
Secretary of State John Foster Dulles's attempt to stigmatize nations choosing
such a course as Communist.[5] Reuther and the UAW board also tolerated the
far more critical approach to foreign policy questions being taken by Secretary-
Treasurer Emil Mazey.

With the close ties to President Lyndon B. Johnson, Reuther supported
administration policy in the Vietnam War. The severe domestic consequences
of the war and the massive opposition movement led Reuther and the
UAW into the antiwar camp after Richard Nixon assumed office. The
union supported the Vietnam Moratorium demonstrations in the fall of
1969.[6] Just before his death in 1970, Reuther issued a statement highly
critical of the United States's invasion of Cambodia. At its 1972 convention,
the UAW called for an immediate end to United States involvement in
Indochina and supported the new policy of East-West detente.[7] The cold
war consensus had come asunder, never to be put together again. Since
the Vietnam War crisis, the "doves" have been a significant and accepted part
of the body politic. Although the UAW leadership does not usually go as far
as the organized peace movement would like, it generally takes a dovish position on major foreign policy questions. Thus it opposes aid to the contras in
Nicaragua, supports divestment from South Africa, and advocates a nuclear
arms freeze.

The UAW has undeniably been a significant factor in the achievement of the progressive reforms of the past 40 years: Medicare, Medicaid, civil rights legislation, the expansion of higher education, and the establishment of affirmative action programs for minorities and women. When viewed from the standpoint of the popular front coalition, however, the UAW's liberal politics have had several shortcomings. The remarkable feature of the popular front period was the degree of rank and file involvement in committees, caucuses, political campaigns, and social causes in the community. There were picket lines, demonstrations, caravans, and protests of all sorts. This popular front style of protest activity declined precipitously with the elimination of left-progressive catalysts at the local level. The UAW's approach has generally been a top-level one: Walter Reuther might speak at a civil rights rally, but there would usually be little effort to mobilize the UAW membership. Often there would be an antagonism to doing so, as when the UAW opposed the efforts of the left-led Detroit Negro Labor Council to place a Fair Employment Practices ordinance on the Detroit ballot in 1951.[8] More importantly, there has been a reluctance to take on the more difficult issues, most notably busing in the early 1970s. The failure to provide leadership on this issue allowed racist sentiment to expand rapidly among white members and made racial division a major internal problem for the union.[9]

For many years, the UAW stood firm against the nationalist and protectionist positions adopted by so many other unions, but when the crisis of the auto industry reached a new depth in the late 1970s, the UAW took the road of advocating the "Buy American" approach. At the same time, it accepted major concessions on wages and benefits. There is, to be sure, no easy solution to the situation that the UAW has faced in the last dozen years. When faced with substantial layoffs due to a major economic crisis in 1937–1938, the left-center forces opposed Homer Martin's capitulationist approach and instead sought both to preserve the union's bargaining position and to organize its unemployed members.

There have been some moves in recent years to establish a left-progressive movement within the UAW. The most notable example at the rank-and-file and secondary leadership level was a movement for shorter hours that gained considerable support in the Detroit area in the 1970s. UAW leaders have even taken steps to provide an opening for a left-progressive approach. In 1977, UAW President Douglas Fraser initiated the formation of a national organization and movement called the Progressive Alliance. It included nearly 100 labor, civil rights, consumer, women's, environmental, and citizen action organizations and advocated an advanced progressive agenda.[10] The limitation of the formation, however, was that it did not provide for grass roots local organizing. It remained principally a letterhead organization and failed to become a substantial force in the nation's politics. Another leadership initiative was an abortive attempt to have the anticommunist clause removed from the UAW constitution at the union's 1980 convention.[11] These initiatives suffered from the fact that the left has remained too weak to serve as a reliable and powerful partner for centrist leaders.

The major achievement of the movement against the Vietnam war in the 1960s and early 1970s was the defeat of the cold war consensus that anticommunism had to guide all aspects of United States foreign policy. Critical studies by historians and other scholars of the origins of the cold war and of the history of Vietnam played an important part in the development of the antiwar movement and the ending of the cold war foreign policy consensus. The new scholarly studies on the legacy of the popular front may contribute to the erosion of the other central feature of the cold war consensus, the idea that Communists were illegitimate and had to be walled off from the rest of the body politic. Before the wall was constructed, the alliance of left and center in the UAW played the decisive role in the organization of the automobile industry and in the building of a large, powerful, democratic, and politically active union. The left-center alliance's advocacy of a foreign policy based on peaceful relations with the Soviet Union and a domestic policy that recognized the right of Communists to participate in the country's political and trade union life may be examined anew today.

Abbreviations

ACTU	Association of Catholic Trade Unionists
BLS	Bureau of Labor Statistics
DFP	*Detroit Free Press*
DN	*Detroit News*
DT	*Detroit Times*
DW	*Daily Worker*
FEPC	*President's Committee on Fair Employment Practices*
FMC	*Ford Motor Company Archives*
FP	*Federated Press*
FPCB	*Federated Press*, Central Bureau
FPEB	*Federated Press*, Eastern Bureau
IEB	UAW International Executive Board
JFK	John F. Kennedy Library
LFB	*Labor Fact Book*
MLR	*Monthly Labor Review*
NA	National Archives
NYT	*New York Times*
SW	*Sunday Worker*
UAW	*United Automobile Worker*
WPR	Walter P. Reuther
WSU	Archieves of Labor History and Urban Affairs, Wayne State University

Notes

Chapter One

1. Sidney Fine, *The Automobile Under the Blue Eagle* (Ann Arbor, Mich., 1963), p. 1; General Motors Corporation, *Annual Report, 1943* (n.p., n.d.), p. 60; Automobile Manufacturers Association, *Automobile Facts and Figures, 1946-1947* (n.p., n.d.), pp. 34, 70; Donald M. Nelson, *Arsenal of Democracy* (New York, 1946), pp. 217-42, 276-77.

2. Fine, *Automobile Under the Blue Eagle,* p. 3; Charles E. Edwards, *Dynamics of the United States Automobile Industry* (Columbia, S.C., 1965), pp. 13-16.

3. U. S. Congress, Senate, Committee on the Judiciary, *Concentration in American Industry: Report of the Subcommittee on Antitrust and Monopoly* 85th Cong., 1st sess. (Washington, D.C., 1957), pp. 216, 400-10.

4. Lawrence J. White, *The Automobile Industry since 1945* (Cambridge, Mass., 1971), pp. 79-90.

5. Peter F. Drucker, *Concept of the Corporation* (2nd Edition, New York, 1972), pp. 98-114.

6. White, *Automobile Industry,* pp. 110-13; Robert F. Lanzillotti, "The Automobile Industry," in Walter Adams, ed. *The Structure of American Industry* (3rd Edition, New York, 1961), pp. 339-42; David L. Lewis, *The Public Image of Henry Ford* (Detroit, 1976), pp. 437-46.

7. White, *Automobile Industry,* pp, 124-25.

8. General Motors Corporation, *Annual Report, 1950* (n.p., n.d.), p. 49; White, *Automobile Industry,* p. 251.

9. White, *Automobile Industry,* p. 152; Kathy Groehn ElMessidi, *The Bargain: The Story Behind the 30-Year Honeymoon of GM and the UAW* (New York, 1980), p. 32; GM, *Annual Report, 1950,* pp. 45, 48; J. Mel Hickerson, *Ernie Breech* (New York, 1968), pp. 145-57.

10. David L. Lewis, *Public Image of Henry Ford,* pp. 425-26; Allan Nevins and Frank Ernest Hill, *Ford: Decline and Rebirth, 1933-1962* (New York, 1962), pp. 313-45; Hickerson, *Ernie Breech,* pp. 129-44.

11. U.S. Department of Commerce, Bureau of the Census, *Census of Manufacturers, 1954* (Washington D.C., 1957), II: 37A3; *Annual Survey of Manufacturers, 1949 and 1950* (Washington D.C., 1952, pp. 38-39; BLS, *Handbook of Labor Statistics, 1950,* Bulletin No. 1016 (Washington, D.C. 1951), p. 100.

12. *Handbook of Labor Statistics, 1950,* pp. 73, 100; *Census of Manufacturers, 1954,* II: 37A3.

13. Alfred P. Sloan, Jr., *My Years with General Motors* (New York, 1963). p. 388; UAW, Quarterly Report on Economic Conditions [1947], WPR Coll., WSU; *FP*CB, Jan. 5, 1952, *FP* Coll., Columbia University, Butler Library.

14. Sloan, *My Years with General Motors,* pp. 375–88; Alfred Sloan to James Forrestal, April 17, 1946, Papers of Harry S. Truman, Official File 1010, Harry S. Truman Library, Independence, Mo.

Chapter Two

1. Sidney Fine, *Sit-Down: The General Motors Strike of 1936–1937* (Ann Arbor, Mich., 1969), p. 54; Robert Dunn, *Labor and Automobiles* (New York, 1929), pp. 63–74 "Place of Birth and Citizenship of Persons at Present Employed" [circa 1925], Henry Ford Archives, Acc. 572, Box 28, 12.7.3 Policies, Dearborn, Mich.; Bureau of the Census, *Fifteenth Census of the United States: 1930, Population Bulletin 2d Series, Michigan, Composition and Characteristics of the Population* (Washington, D.C. 1931). pp. 45–71; *Population,* 5 (Washington, D.C., 1932): 468–70; 3, Part 1:721, 744; 3, Part 2: 502–7, 536.

2. Dunn, *Labor and Automobiles,* pp. 59–66, 101–33; Sidney Fine, *The Automobile Under the Blue Eagle* (Ann Arbor, Mich., 1963), pp. 13–16; Joyce Shaw Peterson, "A Social History of Automobile Workers Before Unionization" (Ph.D. thesis, University of Wisconsin-Madison, 1976), pp. 31–32, 81.

3. Fine, *Sit-Down,* pp 55–59; Dunn, *Labor and Automobiles,* pp. 78–91; Keith Sward, *The Legend of Henry Ford* (New York, 1948), pp. 342–61; Peterson, "Automobile Workers Before Unionization," pp. 105–6.

4. George Douglas Blackwood, "The United Automobile Workers of America, 1935–51" (Ph.D. thesis, University of Chicago), p. 9; Fine, *Sit-Down,* pp. 37–42, 59–63, 102; Dunn, *Labor and Automobiles,* pp. 164–75; Jerold S. Auerbach, *Labor and Liberty* (Indianapolis, 1966), pp. 97–114; Fine, *Automobile Under Blue Eagle,* pp. 152–54; Peterson, "Automobile Workers Before Unionization," pp. 115–16.

5. Jack W. Skeels, "Early Carriage and Auto Unions: The Impact of Industrialization and Rival Unionism," *Industrial and Labor Relations Review* 17 (July 1964):566–83; Peterson, "Automobile Workers Before Unionization," pp. 197–99; Roger R. Keeran, "Communist Influence in the Automobile Industry, 1920–1933: Paving the Way for an Industrial Union," *Labor History* 20 (Spring 1979): 193–96; Blackwood, "United Automobile Workers," pp. 15–17.

6. James R. Prickett, "Communists and the Automobile Industry in Detroit before 1935," *Michigan History* 57 (Fall 1973): 188–93; Roger Roy Keeran, *The Communist Party and the Auto Workers Unions* (Bloomington, Ind., 1980), pp. 47–59; Keeran, "Communist Influence," pp. 213–24.

7. Keeran, "Communist Influence," pp. 199, 206-7, 225; Keeran, *Communist Party and Auto Workers,* pp. 38-39, 58-59. For evidence of radical trends among Detroit immigrants, see Lois Rankin, "Detroit Nationality Groups," *Michigan History* 23 (Spring 1939):135-36, 151, 168, 175-76, 180-81, 193. See also "Report to C. M. Culver from J. Spolansky 'Communism—Detroit'," 1928, Frank Ernest Hill Papers, Acc. 940, Box 17, Ford Motor Co. Archives.

8. Fine, *Automobile Under Blue Eagle,* p. 17. The real income figure was computed from employment, payroll, and cost-of-living data in *Monthly Labor Review* 38 (1934):402, 479.

9. Irving Bernstein, *The Lean Years* (Baltimore, 1966), pp. 300-1, 335-45; Alex Baskin, "The Ford Hunger March-1932," *Labor History* 13 (Summer 1973):331-360; Prickett, "Communists and the Automobile Industry," pp. 194-98; Sward, *Henry Ford,* pp. 231-42; Wyndham Mortimer, *Organize!* (Boston, 1971), pp. 51-53; Walter Galenson, *The CIO Challenge to the AFL* (Cambridge, Mass., 1960), p. 132; Sidney Fine, *Frank Murphy: The Detroit Years* (Ann Arbor, Mich., 1975), pp. 403-6; Maurice Sugar, *The Ford Hunger March* (Berkeley, Calif., 1980), pp. 30-38, 64-71.

10. Fine, *Automobile Under the Blue Eagle,* pp. 25-43, 85-95, 163-71, 180-82, 259-60, 284-88, 299; Keeran, *Communist Party and Auto Workers,* pp. 84-95, 101-7, 118-19, 128; Prickett, "Communists and the Automobile Industry," pp. 197-208.

11. Bernstein, *Lean Years,* pp. 345-57; Fine, *Automobile Under Blue Eagle,* pp. 142-50, 218-30; Jack Skeels, "The Background of UAW Factionalism," *Labor History* 2 (Spring 1961): 158-59.

12. Fine, *Automobile Under Blue Eagle,* pp. 150-58, 193-94, 284-88, 291-92; Henry Kraus, *The Many and the Few* (Los Angeles, 1947), pp. 9-12.

13. Michael S. Clinansmith, "The Black Legion: Hooded Americanism in Michigan," *Michigan History* 55 (Fall 1971): 243-62; George Morris, *The Black Legion Rides* (New York, 1936); A. B. Magil and Henry Stevens, *The Perils of Fascism* (New York, 1938), pp. 98, 114, 175-77, 183, 193. 209-14; *NYT,* June 4, 1936; A. B. Magil, *The Truth About Father Coughlin* (New York, 1935); Kraus, *Many and the Few,* pp. 13-14, 32-38; Neil Betten, *Catholic Activism and the Industrial Worker* (Gainesville, Fla., 1976), pp. 90-107; Oral History Interview of Mort Furay, Apr. 6, 1960, p. 14, Michigan Historical Collections, Ann Arbor, Mich. Coughlin's influence before 1936 was such that New Deal Democrat Frank Murphy characterized the National Union for Social Justice program as "splendid" and said that he was "a close friend and admirer" of the radio priest. Sidney Fine, *Frank Murphy: The New Deal Years* (Chicago, 1979), pp. 219-22. See also William E. Leuchtenburg, *Franklin D. Roosevelt and the New Deal* (New York, 1963), pp. 100-3, 180-83.

14. Fine, *Automobile Under Blue Eagle,* pp. 223-24, 291-93, 386. See also Oral History Interview of Ted LaDuke, Aug. 5, 1960, pp. 10-13, Michigan Historical Collections; and Keeran, *Communist Party and Auto Workers,* pp. 108-10.

15. Fine, *Automobile Under Blue Eagle,* pp. 150, 260-11, 238-42, 263-66, 274-83, 407-8; Keeran, *Communist Party and Auto Workers,* pp. 101-2, 110-18.

16. Fine, *Automobile Under Blue Eagle*, pp. 293–306, 381–409; Keeran, *Communist Party and Auto Workers*, pp. 121–34; Blackwood, "United Automobile Workers," pp. 41–42; Skeels, "UAW Factionalism," pp. 161–65.

17. Fine, *Automobile Under Blue Eagle*, pp. 406–8, 416–21; Fine, *Sit-Down*, p. 82; *Proceedings of the First Constitutional Convention of the International Union, United Automobile Workers of America, Detroit, August 26-31, 1935* (n.p., n.d., pp. 11–19, 29, 40–46, 68–79.

18. Galenson, *CIO Challenge to AFL*, pp. 3–10; Fine, *Sit-Down*, pp. 84–88; Edward Levinson, *Labor on the March* (New York, 1938), pp. 108–21; Mortimer, *Organize!*, pp. 90–100.

19. Harry Dalheimer, *A History of the Mechanics Educational Society of America in Detroit from Its Inception in 1933 through 1937* (Detroit, 1951), pp. 3–13, 25–28, 36–37; Fine, *Automobile Under Blue Eagle*, 163–75, 427; Fine, *Sit-Down*, p. 90.

20. Fine, *Automobile Under Blue Eagle*, pp. 299–300, 337–44; Irving Bernstein, *Turbulent Years* (Boston, 1970), pp. 503–4; Mortimer, *Organize!*, p. 80; Margaret Collingwood Nowak, "The Making of an American: The Story of Stanley Nowak," undated ms., pp. 175–76, Stanley Nowak Coll, WSU; Morris, *Black Legion*, pp. 16–17; Peter Friedlander, *The Emergence of a UAW Local, 1936-1939* (Pittsburgh, 1975), pp. 115–16, 127–28, 145–46; Kraus, *Many and Few*, pp. 13–14; Betten, *Catholic Activism*, pp. 96–98; The Reminiscences of R. J. Thomas, 1956, pp. 24–38, Oral History Collection, Butler Library, Columbia University, New York; Oral History Interview of Joe Hattley, Aug. 4, 8, 1961, pp. 9–10, Michigan Historical Collections; Oral History Interview of John A. Zaremba, Aug. 11, Sept. 29, Oct. 6, 1961, pp. 14–16, *ibid.*; Galenson, *CIO Challenge to AFL*, p. 132; Skeels, "UAW Factionalism," p. 174. The weight of the evidence indicates that Coughlin had a strong influence on the AIWA. For a contrary view, see Ray Boryczka, "Seasons of Discontent: Auto Union Factionalism and the Motor Products Strike of 1935–36," *Michigan History* 61 (Spring 1977):20n.

21. Fine, *Sit-Down*. pp. 87–94; Keeran, "Communists and Auto Workers," pp. 216–19; James Robert Prickett, "Communists and the Communist Issue in the American Labor Movement, 1920–1950" (Ph.D. thesis, University of California at Los Angeles, 1975), pp. 171–74; Galenson, *CIO Challenge to AFL*, pp. 130–33; Blackwood, "United Automobile Workers," pp. 52–56; Oral History Interview of Frank Manfred, June 26, 1960, pp. 17–20, Michigan Historical Collections.

22. Fine, *Sit-Down*, pp. 95–98, 128–33; Fine, *Automobile Under Blue Eagle*, p. 149; August Meier and Elliot Rudwick, *Black Detroit and the Rise of the UAW* (New York, 1979), pp. 35–38; Oral History Interview of Wyndham Mortimer, June 20, 1960, pp. 31–32, Michigan Historical Collections; Mortimer, *Organize!*, pp. 110–11; Nowak, "Making of an American," pp. 169–70, 183–94, 200–5; "McKie Book sugg. by Nat Ganley," May 1952, Ganley Coll., WSU.

23. Fine, *Sit-Down*; Sward, *Henry Ford*, pp. 375–86; William Weinstone, *The Great Sit-Down Strike* (New York, 1937).

24. Fine, *Sit-Down*; Weinstone, *Great Sit-Down*. Kraus reported that: "The sound car particularly attained nightmarish proporations to the authorities and company agents everywhere where repeated attack upon it almost partook of a religious fervor—as though this instrument were a new god or idol that must be destroyed," *Many and Few*, p. 181.

25. Fine, *Sit-Down*; Kraus, *Many and Few*, pp. 141, 219–24, 267–69, 275; Mortimer, *Organize!*, pp. 124–32. Murphy did approve the police eviction of 120 mostly women sit-downers in the Yale and Towne strike and was prepared to enforce an injunction against the UAW in the Chrysler strike because of the shift in public opinion against the sit-down. On balance, however, Murphy's "refusal to shoot strikers out of the plants they occupied, even though it was at the expense of prompt enforcement of the law, helped to attract workers to their government rather than to alienate them from it." Fine, *Murphy: New Deal*, pp. 331–52. See also Weinstone, *Great Sit-Down*, pp. 15–17.

26. Fine, *Sit-Down*, pp. 323–27; Nat Ganley, "UAW-Pact Discussion," 1954, Ganley Coll.

27. Ganley, "UAW-Pact Discussion"; George B. Heliker, "Grievance Arbitration in the Automobile Industry" (Ph.D. thesis, University of Michigan, 1954), pp. 109–17.

28. Fine, *Sit-Down*, pp. 327–28.

29. Fine, *Sit-Down*, p. 281; Kraus, *Many and Few*, p. 166.

30. Fine, *Sit-Down*, pp. 78–80, 88–90, 320–28; Irving Howe and B. J. Widick, *The UAW and Walter Reuther* (New York, 1949), p. 68; Skeels, "UAW Factionalism," pp. 164–79; Victor Reuther, *The Brothers Reuther and the Story of the UAW* (Boston, 1976), pp. 178–82, 185; Claude Hoffman, *Sit-Down in Anderson* (Detroit, 1968), pp. 68–73; Friedlander, *Emergence of a UAW Local*, pp. 56–62; Roger R. Keeran, "The Communists and UAW Factionalism, 1937–1939," *Michigan History* 60 (Summer 1976):121. Unionism was new to the majority of auto workers, too, but the UAW moved quickly to educate its members in the philosophy of unionism and to train the many new leaders thrown up by the struggle. Harvey Klehr argues that Martin's charge that Communists were "behind" a series of "wildcat" strikes was accurate and that the Communists were therefore responsible for the UAW factional conflict. Klehr shows that there were disagreements among Communist leaders over how to respond to the unauthorized strikes, deal with non-Communist union leaders, and, more generally, over how to implement the popular front policy in the UAW. He offers no evidence, however, that Communists were responsible for the unauthorized strikes or initiated the factional conflict. Harvey Klehr, "American Communism and the United Auto Workers: New Evidence on an Old Controversy," *Labor History* 24 (Summer 1983): 403–11.

31. Galenson, *CIO Challenge to AFL*, pp. 152–62; Mortimer, *Organize!*, pp. 100–2, 151–62; Reuther, *Brothers Reuther*, pp. 183–91; Len DeCaux, *Labor Radical* (Boston, 1970), pp. 251–53, 300, 305; Skeels, "UAW Factionalism," pp. 166–76; Melvyn Dubofsky and Warren Van Tine, *John L. Lewis* (New York, 1977), pp. 317–18; *NYT*, Aug. 10,

1938; Keeran, "Communists and UAW Factionalism, pp. 117–27. An indication of Martin's early conservatism is contained in letters he wrote Father Coughlin in 1935: "I listen at every opportunity to your broadcasts and have done so since you started . . . . I have been urging the people of my own union to join the National Union for Social Justice [Coughlin's organization]." Cited by Betten, *Catholic Action*, p. 103. Martin began secret meetings in 1936 with former Dillon supporters on the executive board and "pursued a perplexing policy with regard to the CIO. Publicly he sought CIO aid in the form of money and organizers, but privately he attempted on occasion to exclude the CIO representative in Detroit from GEB [General Executive Board] deliberations." Fine, *Sit-Down*, pp. 78, 93–94.

32. Keeran, "Communists and UAW Factionalism," pp. 123–27; "Union Program of the Martin-Frankensteen Caucus," Unity Caucus, For a United Democratic Union," (1937). Carl Haessler Coll., WSU; Reuther, *Brothers Reuther*, p. 186; Jack William Skeels, "The Development of Political Stability within the United Auto Workers Union" (Ph.D. thesis, University of Wisconsin, 1957), pp. 42–51; Galenson, *CIO Challenge to AFL*, pp. 150–56; Oral History Interview of Wyndham Mortimer, June 20, 1960, p. 53. The "Greer outfit" referred to by Mortimer was the AAWA.

33. Skeels, "Political Stability within the Auto Workers Union," pp. 55–59; Keeran, "Communists and UAW Factionalism," pp. 125–26.

34. Keeran, "Communists and UAW Factionalism," pp. 123–32; Sward, *Henry Ford*, pp. 382–83; Galenson, *CIO Challenge to AFL*, pp. 7–65; Skeels, "Political Stability within the Auto Workers Union," pp. 61–93; Dubofsky and Van Tine, *Lewis*, pp. 318–19; Bernstein, *Turbulent Years*, pp. 566–67. Germer suspected Martin involvement with Ford and the AFL as early as January, 1938. Lorin Lee Cary, "Institutionalized Conservatism in the Early CIO," *Labor History* 13 (Fall 1972):502–3. See also Louis Columbo to C. B. Sorenson, Sept. 19, 1938, and Sorenson to Columbo, Sept. 20, 1938, Acc. 940, Henry Ford Archives; and Oral History Interview of Martin Jensen, Nov. 1, 1960, pp. 27–29, Michigan Historical Collections.

35. Skeels, "Political Stability within the Auto Workers Union," pp. 89–98; Galenson, *CIO Challenge to AFl*, pp. 165–77; *Labor Fact Book* 5 (New York, 1941):129.

36. Len DeCaux, *Labor Radical*, pp. 102–3; Frank Emspak, "The Break-Up of the Congress of Industrial Organizations (CIO), 1945–50" (Ph.D. thesis, University of Wisconsin, 1972), pp. 2–6.

37. The withdrawal of Communist support for Victor Reuther's election as secretary-treasurer of the Michigan CIO at that organization's 1938 convention is sometimes cited as the reason for the break between Communists and Socialists. Keeran cites Socialist and Communist statements from the period to show that substantive policy differences were the cause of the split and the incident at the Michigan CIO convention was just "the final break." Keeran, "Communists and UAW Factionalism," pp. 128–29; Prickett, "Communists in the American Labor Movement," pp. 217–29; Persky, "Reuther and Third Party Politics," pp. 81–87; Cary, "Institutionalized Conservatism in CIO," p. 502; Bert Cochran, *Labor and Communism* (Princeton, 1977), pp. 98–99, 124–25, 363, 368;

Socialist Call, Jan. 22, Feb. 5, 12, Apr. 2, 1938; "Confidential Report of the Socialist Party on the Inner Situation in the Auto Industry," June 7, 1938; Arthur G. McDowell to Socialist Trade Unionists [circa May 1938], Richard T. Frankensteen Coll., WSU. Aside from the Lovestonites, others who worked closely with Martin included Charles Millard, the executive board member from Canada, and various Trotskyites. Irving Martin Abella, *Nationalism, Communism, and Canadian Labour* (Toronto, 1973), pp. 30–33; *Proceedings of the Special Convention of the International Union United Automobile Workers of America, Detroit, Michigan, March 4 to 8, 1939* [Martin group] (n.p., n.d.), p. 177.

38. Reuther moved away from the Socialist party when he supported the reelection of Governor Murphy in 1938. Frank Warren notes that Reuther "was persuaded to withdraw" his resignation, but it is evident that he stopped participating in the party. Frank A. Warren, An *Alternative Vision* (Bloominton, Ind., 1974). pp. 224–25; Keeran, *Communist Party and Auto Workers*, pp. 203–6; Persky, "Reuther and Third Party Politics," pp. 85–91, 100–4; Galenson, *CIO Challenge to AFL*, p. 172; *Socialist Call*, Apr. 8, 1939.

39. Keeran, "Communists and UAW Factionalism," pp. 129–30; Persky, "Reuther and Third Party Politics," pp. 88–94; Fine, *Murphy: New Deal*, pp. 492–93, 502–7; Oral History Interview of Arthur Case, Aug. 4, 1960, p. 25, Michigan Historical Collections; *Proceedings of the Third Convention*, pp. 164, 174–75; *First Annual Constitutional Convention, Michigan State IUC CIO, Grand Rapids, June 29–July 1, 1939*, pp. 135–36, 169–71.

40. Earl Browder, *Second Imperialist War* (New York, 1940), pp. 111–17, 170, 245–46; Bruce Minton and John Stuart, *The Fat Years and the Lean* (New York, 1940), pp. 415–24; DeCaux, *Labor Radical*, pp. 335–63; *Michigan CIO News*, May 31, 1940; Keeran, *Communist Party and Auto Workers*, pp. 207–12. The resolution on national defense passed at the May 1940 Michigan CIO convention concerned the need for maintaining labor standards, but the UAW fully endorsed the national defense program at its midsummer convention. The UAW convention, however, enacted a strong antiwar resolution similar to that endorsed at the Michigan CIO convention. *Michigan CIO News*, May 31, June 3, 10, 1940; *Proceedings of the Third Convention*, pp. 221–22, 281–84.

41. David A. Shannon, The *Socialist Party of America* (Chicago, 1955), pp. 254–56; Skeels, "Political Stability within the Auto Workers Union," pp. 150–53; Persky, "Reuther and Third Party Politics," pp. 105, 122; DeCaux, *Labor Radical*, pp. 326–27, 355–63; Reminiscences of R. J. Thomas, 6:18.

42. Betten, *Catholic Activism and the Industrial Worker*, pp. 124–45; Harold Wattel, "The Association of Catholic Trade Unionists" (M.A. thesis, Columbia University, 1974), pp. 35, 54, 73–78; Richard (Joseph) Ward, "The Role of the Association of Catholic Trade Unionists in the American Labor Movement" (Ph.D. thesis, University of Michigan, 1958), pp. 56, 61, 68–69, 223; "Confidential ACTU Newsletter," No. 2, Nov. 1, 1943, Haessler Coll. The statement of purpose is from the constitution of the ACTU Detroit chapter, as amended Jan. 19, 1948. Association of Catholic Trade Unionists Coll., Detroit Chapter, WSU. The reference to local conferences is from Father Hubbell's Report to Cardinal Mooney (1956), ACTU Coll., Box 4.

43. *Proceedings Fifth Convention*, pp. 292–302, 425–40, 498–506; Keeran, *Communist Party and Auto Workers*, pp. 210–11; *DN*, Aug. 4, 5, 6, 1940; Persky, "Reuther and Third Party Politics," p. 123; Transcript of Interview with Leonard Woodcock by Frank Cormier and William J. Eaton, June 20, 1968, Cormier and Eaton Papers, JFK Library, Boston, Mass.

44. *Proceedings Fifth Convention*, pp. 161, 221–22, 281–84, 405–40; *DW*, July 31, Aug. 3, 8, 1940.

45. Sward *Ford*, pp. 324-27, 408-16; Lloyd H. Bailer, "Negro Labor in the Automobile Industry" (Ph.D. thesis, University of Michigan, [1943]), pp. 136–179; Meier and Rudwick, *Black Detroit and the UAW*, pp. 6–22; Martin Halpern, "The 1941 Strike at the Ford Motor Company" (ms., 1973), pp. 16–23.

46. Sward, *Henry Ford*, pp. 399–422; Meier and Rudwick, *Black Detroit and the UAW*, pp. 82–107; Bailer, "Negro Labor," pp. 136–79; Halpern, "The 1941 Strike," pp. 26–43.

47. Mortimer, *Organize!*, pp. 174–85; Prickett, "Communists in the American Labor Movement," pp. 247–62; Galenson, *CIO Challenge to AFL*, pp. 184–87, 508–9. Cochran, like Galenson, takes the traditional view that the North American Aviation strike was a Communist "political strike," that is, a strike against the defense program rather than for trade union demands. His argument seems to be that Frankensteen's opposition to the strike and the international's support of Frankensteen's position meant that the "Communists" must have had some nontrade union motive. The simpler explanation is that there was a difference over trade union policy and tactics. Most North American workers were making 50¢ per hour and their enthusiasm for strike action was high. The picket lines at the huge plant were the largest in California history. Mortimer supported this militancy and hoped it would lead to the organization of the industry. Frankensteen opposed the strike, believing that the path to progress for the UAW in the industry lay in close cooperation with government agencies such as the National Defense Mediation Board. *Labor and Communism*, pp. 176–84. Roger Keeran argues that it was the "moderate labor leaders who were "changing their line" on strikes while the Communists continued to support aggressive struggles for economic demands. *Communist Party and Auto Workers*, pp. 214–17. See also James Prickett, Communist Conspiracy or Wage Dispute?: The 1941 Strike at North American Aviation," *Pacific Historical Review* L (May 1981):215–33.

48. *Proceedings of the Sixth Convention UAW-CIO, Aug. 4-16, 1941, Buffalo, N.Y.* (n.p., n.d.), pp. 683–702; R. J. Thomas, *Automobile Unionism (1942)* (n.p., n.d.), p. 5.

49. *Proceedings Fifth Convention*, pp. 292–302; *Proceedings Sixth Convention*, p. 700; DeCaux, *Labor Radical*, pp. 395–402; Cochran, *Labor and Communism*, pp. 153–55.

50. Roger R. Keeran, " 'Everything for Victory': Communist Influence in the Auto Industry during World War II," *Science and Society* XLIII (Spring 1979):28; Martin Glaberman, *Wartime Strikes: The Struggle Against the No-Strike Pledge in the UAW*

During World War II (Detroit, 1980), pp. 1–2; Alan Clive, *State of War: Michigan in World War II* (Ann Arbor, Mich. 1979), pp. 59–61; Joshua Freeman, "Delivering the Goods: Industrial Unionism During World War II," *Labor History* 19 (Fall 1978):590–93.

51. *Labor Fact Book* 6 (New York, 1943). pp. 77–79, 86–90; Clive, *State of War*, pp. 60–70; Glaberman, *Wartime Strikes*, pp. 5–8; Skeels, "Political Stability within the Auto Workers Union," p. 159.

52. *Labor Fact Book* 6, pp. 90–100; Clive, *State of War*, pp. 65–68; Hoffman, *Sit-Down in Anderson*, pp. 91–92.

53. Clive, *State of War*, p. 60; Joel Seidman, *American Labor from Defense to Reconversion* (Chicago, 1953), pp. 80–84.

54. Seidman, *American Labor*, pp. 94–123; "Smash the Little Steel Formula," UAW Local 51 Coll., Box 14, WSU; Clive, *State of War*, p. 70; Daniel B. Crowder, "Profile in Progress: A History of Local 287, UAW-CIO" (Ph.D. thesis, Ball State University, 1969), pp. 144–52; R.J. Thomas, *Automobile Unionism (1942)*, p. 5; typescript of UAW membership by month, Ganley Coll., Box 8.

55. Clive, *State of War*, pp. 64–76, 103–12, 193–98; Keeran, " 'Everything for Victory'," pp. 12–21; Glaberman, *Wartime Strikes*, pp. 35–50; B. Y. Mikhailov *et al.*, *Recent History of the Labor Movement in the United States, 1939–1965* (Moscow, 1979), pp. 93–104; Ed Jennings, "Wildcat! The Wartime Strike Wave in Auto," *Radical America* 9 (July–August 1975): 77–113.

56. Keeran " 'Everything for Victory'," pp. 13–25; Skeels, "Development of Political Stability", pp. 163–200; Elizabeth Hawes, *Hurry Up Please Its [sic] Time* (New York, 1946), pp. 43–45, 107–22; Cochran, *Labor and Communism*, p. 218.

57. Keeran, " 'Everything for Victory'," pp. 14–18; *DW*, Apr. 6, 1943; Skeels, "Political Stability within the Auto Workers Union," pp. 166–68; Nelson Lichtenstein, "Industrial Unionism Under the No-Strike Pledge: A Study of the CIO During the Second World War" (Ph.D. thesis, University of California, Berkeley, 1974), pp. 393–442.

58. Michael Devereaux Whitty, "Emil Mazey: Radical as Liberal" (Ph.D. thesis, Syracuse University, 1969), pp. 104, 145–47; Keeran, " 'Everything for Victory'," pp. 18–24; Clive, *State of War*, pp. 72–81; Glaberman, *Wartime Strikes*, pp. 73–81; *Proceedings Sixth Annual Convention Michigan CIO Council, June 28–July 1, 1943, Detroit* (n.p., n.d.), pp. 136–51; Ford Industrial Relations Dept. report "Re: Renegotiations Proceedings for 1944–1945," Dec. 2, 1946 cited in George Heliker, "Report on Labor, 1933–1957," p. 301, Acc. 958, Box 2, Henry Ford Archives, Dearborn, Mich. See also an untitled typescript of an unidentified observer's conversation with Addes in Earl Browder Papers, Series 2–155, Syracuse University, Syracuse, N. Y.

59. Skeels, "Development of Political Stability," pp. 190–201; Keeran, " 'Everything for Victory'," pp. 22–24; typescript, "Votes for No-Strike Super Minority Resolution," WPR Coll.; Glaberman, *Wartime Strikes*, pp. 98–120.

60. Oral History Interview of Leonard Woodcock, Apr. 30, 1963, pp. 36–37, Michigan Historical Collections.

61. Local 155 to Edward Levinson, May 14, 1943, Ganley Coll., Box 8; Persky, "Reuther and Third Party Politics," pp. 122–23; 129–31; *Proceedings Sixth Annual Convention Michigan CIO*, pp. 164–76, 27–28; Theron F. Schlabach, *Edwin E. Witte, Cautious Reformer* (Madison, 1969), pp. 209–10; Lichtenstein, "Industrial Unionism Under the No-Strike Pledge," pp. 554–59.

62. Oral History Interview with Nat Ganley, UM-WSU ILIR, April 16, 1960, p. 37; Victor G. Reuther, "Labor in the War—and After, *Antioch Review* III (Fall 1943): 311–27; Lichtenstein, "Industrial Unionism Under the No-Strike Pledge," pp. 537–39. Members of the Socialist party remained an important part of the Reuther caucus. The Detroit Socialist party paper, *Labor Comment*, observed: "We can only make this war result in a better world, and in a world free of war, if we work now for a better postwar settlement than is foreshadowed by the Soviet land-grab." March 1944. Copy in Socialist party of America Coll., Duke University.

63. Keeran, " 'Everything for Victory'," pp. 14–25; Oral History Interview of Leonard Woodcock, p. 20.

64. Herbert R. Northrup, "The Negro in the Automobile Industry," in Northrup *et al., Negro Employment in Basic Industry* (Philadelphia, 1970), pp. 65–66; Robert Weaver, *Negro Labor* (New York, 1946), p. 289; Meier and Rudwick, *Black Detroit and UAW*, pp. 108–206; Sheila Tobias and Lisa Anderson, "What Really Happened to Rosie the Riveter? Demobilization and the Female Labor Force, 1944–47," MSS Modular Publications, Inc. New York, Module 9 (1974), pp. 20–25; "Seniority in the Automobile Industry," mimeo, UAW War Policy Div. Coll., Box 22, WSU.

65. Weaver *Negro Labor*, pp. 69–74, 289; Northrup, "The Negro in the Automobile Industry," pp. 65–66; Meier and Rudwick, *Black Detroit and UAW*, pp. 123–74; Tobias and Anderson, "What Really Happened to Rosie the Riveter?," pp. 20–25; Paddy Quick, "Rosie the Riveter: Myths and Realities," *Radical America* 9 (July–Aug. 1975):115–31; Lyn Goldfard *et al., Separated and Unequal: Discrimination against Women Workers after World War II (the U.A.W. 1944-54)* (Washington, n.d.).

66. Hawes, *Hurry Up Please*, pp. 97–100, 136–38; James Caldwell Foster, *The Union Politic: The CIO Political Action Committee* (Columbia, Mo., 1975). pp. 3–40; Joseph Gaer, *The First Round: The Story of the CIO Political Action Committee* (New York, 1944).

Chapter Three

1. *DFP*, Aug. 15, 1945. The Soviet forces rejected as improper the United States directive to terminate hostilities. Fighting between the Japanese Army and the Red Army continued until Sept. 2, 1945, when representatives of the Allies and Japan signed the instrument of unconditional surrender. G. Deborin, *Secrets of the Second World War* (Moscow, 1971), p. 262–64.

2. *UAW*, June 1, 1945; Automobile Manufacturers Association, *Automobile Facts and Figures*, 27th ed. (Detroit, 1946 and 1947), p. 35.

3. *DFP*, Aug. 15, 1945; John Lewis Gaddis, *The United States and the Origins of the Cold War* (New York, 1972), pp. 230, 289; Montgomery quoted in *UAW*, Sept. 1, 1945.

4. BLS, *A Brief History of the Labor Movement*, Bull. No. 1000 (Washington, 1970), p. 65; *UAW*, May 5, 1945; *LFB*, 7 (New York, 1945): 22, 97–103; Thomas E. Linton, "An Historical Examination of the Purposes and Practices of the Education Program of the United Automobile Workers of America" (Ed.D. thesis, University of Michigan, 1961), pp. 109–37.

5. *LFB* 8 (New York, 1947): 14; Alfred P. Sloan, Jr., *My Years with General Motors* (New York, 1965), p. 377; Barton J. Bernstein, "The Automobile Industry and the Coming of the Second World War," *Southwestern Social Science Quarterly* 47 (June 1966): 25–33; Richard Polenberg, *War and Society* (Philadelphia, 1972), pp. 73–98; David Brody, "The New Deal and World War II," in John Braeman *et al.*, eds., *The New Deal: The National Level* (Columbus, Ohio, 1975) pp. 287–99; N. Sivachyov and E. Yazkov, *History of the U.S.A. since World War I* (Moscow, 1976), pp. 168–80, 196–205; N. V. Siovachev, *Government and Labor in the U.S.A. during World War II* (Moscow, 1974), in Russian, summary in English, pp. 367–77. Sloan declared in 1944 that the philosophy of "something for nothing that prevailed in the Thirties is finished . . . . I believe it died in the war." [*NYT*, Oct. 6, 1944], UAW Washington Office—Donald Montgomery Coll., Box 73, WSU, Detroit.

6. The War Labor Disputes (Smith-Conally) Act, enacted over President Roosevelt's veto in 1943, contained provisions requiring unions to give notice of a strike and the NLRB to supervise strike votes in war plants. The act also outlawed political contributions by unions in federal elections. Among provisions of some state laws were the banning of certain types of strikes and secondary boycotts and restrictions on picketing and union political contributions. Joel Seidman, *American Labor from Defense to Reconversion* (Chicago, 1953), pp. 188–93. Some states adopted "right to work" constitutional amendments. Bureau of Labor Standards, *Growth of Labor Law in the United States* (Washington, 1967), pp. 215–17.

7. *NYT*, May 3, 1945; *UAW*, May 1, 1945; George Romney, *Automotive Council Statement to the Senate War Investigating Committee on Manpower Problems and Their Effect on War Production* (Detroit, March 9, 1945), pp. 24–38. Romney, then head of the Automotive Council, wrote: "I am completely and utterly convinced that the Government must redistribute the power of the unions on a local basis if we are to continue to have a free country." Romney to Folks, Nov. 13, 1945, George Romney Papers, Michigan Historical Collections, Ann Arbor, Mich., Truman's letter is cited by R. Alton Lee, *Truman and Taft-Hartley* (Lexington, Ken., 1966), p. 15.

8. Seidman, *American Labor*, pp. 254–69; Carl Haessler, "Press Magnifies Detroit Labor Situation," *FBCB*, Sept. 18, 1945, FP Coll., Butler Library, Columbia University, New York; James Caldwell Foster, *The Union Politic: The CIO Political Action Committee* (Columbia, Mo., 1975), pp. 49–75. See also Lee, *Truman and Taft-Hartley*, pp. 10–44.

9. Seidman, *American Labor*, pp. 238–40; Barton J. Bernstein, "The Truman Administration and the Steel Strike of 1946," *Journal of American History* 52 (March 1966): 771–803; *LFB* 8: 38–41; BLS, *Handbook of Labor Statistics*, Bull. No. 916 (Washington, 1947), p. 107; Barton J. Bernstein and Allen J. Matusow, eds., *The Truman Administration: A Documentary History* (New York, 1966), pp. 80–85.

10. Raymond E. Paul, *Taxation in the United States* (Boston, 1954), pp. 321–22, 420–21; *Business Week*, Dec. 1, 1945, pp. 15–16, 100.

11. *LFB* 7: 97–103, 171; 8: 109.

12. Samuel Lubell described the change in Detroit's Chrysler Local 7, which he visited in 1940 and 1948: "In 1940 the flavor of the local was one of street barricades and sit-down strikes; eight years later it was almost like a lodge hall." *The Future of American Politics*, 3rd ed., rev. (New York, 1965), pp. 174–79. See also Len DeCaux, *Labor Radical* (Boston, 1970), pp. 430–45; James J. Matles and James Higgins, *Them and Us: Struggles of a Rank-and-File Union* (Englewood Cliffs, N. J., 1974), pp. 164–65; Sivachyov, *History of the U.S.A.*, pp. 181–87; Brody, "The New Deal," p. 298; Interview with Jack White, June 1976.

13. For statistics on Black and women auto workers, see below. Tensions between white and Black workers were the most serious. The principal factor motivating "hate strikes" was the entry of Black workers into areas and jobs from which they had previously been excluded. A secondary factor was a racist "concern" by some white men for white women in plants where Black men were also workers. Robert C. Weaver, *Negro Labor* (New York, 1946), p. 65–74; "Summary of Strike at Wright Aeronautical Co., Lockland, Ohio," Tension Files, Records of the President's Committee on Fair Employment Practice, Record Group 228, National Archives and Record Service, Washington. Tensions between white Southerners and Blacks was an additional problem, because many new white migrants from the South no doubt brought racist attitudes with them. By 1950, about 9 percent of Michigan's population consisted of people born in the South; these were almost equally divided between Blacks and whites. U.S. *Census of Population, 1950*, IV, Part 4, Ch. A (Washington, 1953), 22. See Alan Clive, *State of War* (Ann Arbor, Mich., 1979) and August Meier and Elliot Rudwick, *Black Detroit and the Rise of the UAW* (New York, 1979). Harriet Arnow's novel *The Dollmaker* (New York, 1954) shows the tensions in a war workers' neighborhood in Detroit, particularly between white Southern migrants and Catholics. The difficulties of urban adjustment are brilliantly depicted in the novel. Ben Field's novel *Piper Tompkins* (Garden City, N. Y., 1946) is the story of the transformation from antiunionism to unionism of an individualistic New England farm boy who goes to work in a war plant. Although Piper becomes a good trade unionist, he retains much of his individualism and does not become radical. Piper quotes the technocratic ideas of William Knudsen and praises Henry Ford to the left-wing shop steward (pp. 146–49). Field had worked in an electrical plant during the war and later reported on the 1946 strike wave for the *Daily Worker*.

14. Alonzo L. Hamby, *Beyond the New Deal* (New York, 1973), pp. 60–113; *LFB* 8: 162–63; Harvard Sitkoff "Years of the Locust: Interpretations of the Truman Presidency since 1965," in Richard S. Kirkendell, ed., *The Truman Period as a Research Field: A*

Reappraisal, 1972 (Columbia, Mo., 1974), pp. 75–112; Donald R. McCoy, *Quest and Response: Minority Rights and the Truman Administration* (Lawrence, Kan., 1973), pp. 27–28. Thomas quoted in *UAW*, Aug. 15, 1945.

15. Foster, *Union Politic*, pp. 39–43, 58–70. In many UAW locals fewer than 25 percent of the members were registered to vote in 1946. "Report of UAW Pol. Action and Legislative Dept. to the IEB," Richard T. Leonard, Director, Dec. 1946, WPR Coll., WSU.

16. Strong CIO support for international labor cooperation and peace is indicated in several sources. See Mary Sperling McAuliffe, *Crisis on the Left: Cold War Politics and American Liberals, 1947–1954* (Amherst, Mass., 1978), p. 12; Proceedings of the CIO Executive Board, Nov. 1–2, 1945, pp. 8–10, WSU; *Proceedings of the Third Constitutional Convention of the United Steelworkers of America, May 14–18, 1946* (n.p., n.d.), pp. 48–49, 56–57, 183, 199–200; *CIO News*, Sept. 3, 10, 1945; and James Carey, *Report of the CIO Delegation to the Soviet Union* (Washington, n.d.). Foster believes that CIO leaders were not circumspect enough and should have moved in an anti-communist direction sooner than they did. *Union Politic*, pp. 68–69. The idea that CIO leaders were essentially cautious on foreign policy is developed by DeCaux, a leftist on the CIO national staff, in *Labor Radical*, pp. 460–62, 470–77. A reading of the *United Automobile Worker* in the period shows that foreign policy was not given much emphasis. See also Hamby, *New Deal*, pp. 91–113, 154–56.

17. Foster, *Union Politic*, pp. 58–60; Carl O. Smith and Stephen B. Sarasohn, "Hate Propaganda in Detroit," *Public Opinion Quarterly* 10 (Spring 1946): 24–52; Henry Lee Moon, "Danger in Detroit," *Crisis* 52 (Jan. 1946): 12–13, 28–29.

18. *UAW*, October 1945; *DFP*, Nov. 1, 1945; *DN*, Oct. 24, 1945; R. T. Frankensteen, "Jeffries linked with Plot against Labor," transcript of radio speech, Oct. 19, 1945, UAW Local 212 Coll., Box 15, WSU; Gloster B. Current, "The Detroit Elections: Problem in Reconversion," *Crisis* 52 (Nov. 1945): 319–325; Arthur Clifford, "Was Detroit a Defeat?" *New Masses* 25 (Nov. 23, 1937): 13. CIO membership estimates given in Jack Skeels, "The Background of UAW Factionalism," *Labor History* 2 (Spring 1961): 178–79; Foster, *Union Politic*, pp. 58–60; Smith and Sarasohn, "Hate Propaganda," pp. 24–27. The estimate of the number of Blacks voting for Frankensteen was derived from data presented in several sources. Smith and Sarasohn stated that 90 percent of Blacks in their sample precincts voted for Frankensteen. "Hate Propaganda," pp. 50–51. Moon reported a total vote of 60,321 to 12,110 in Frankensteen's favor in 172 predominantly Black precincts and noted that the turnout was 60 percent of the registered voters in those precincts. "Danger in Detroit," p. 13. Current stated that the total eligible Black electorate was 120,025, with 15 percent of these votes residing in areas other than the 172 predominantly Black precincts. Current, "Detroit Elections," p. 321.

19. *DN*, Aug. 5, 1945; Current, "Detroit Elections," pp. 319–25; Moon, "Danger in Detroit," pp. 12–13, 28–29; Smith and Sarasohn, "Hate Propaganda," pp. 24–52. The quotation is from *New Republic* 113 (Nov. 26, 1945): 703–4.

20. Moon, "Danger in Detroit," p. 28; Current, "Detroit Elections," pp. 319–20. The quotation about housing is from Robert C. Weaver, *The Negro Ghetto* (New York,

1948; reissued, 1967), pp. 86, 115–121, 228, 247. See also Dominic J. Capeci, Jr., *Race Relations in Wartime Detroit: The Sojouner Truth Housing Controversy of 1942* (Philadelphia, 1984).

21. Smith and Sarasohn, "Hate Propaganda," pp. 24–52; *FPCB*, Nov. 5, 1945, *FP* Coll.; *Michigan CIO News*, Oct. 26, 1945.

22. *Michigan CIO News*, Aug. 10, 1945; Smith and Sarasohn, "Hate Propaganda," pp. 48–51. James D. Friel, a Democrat and Wayne County auditor, received 12 percent of the primary vote and endorsed Frankensteen in the final election. *DN*, Aug. 6, 8, 1945. Foster, *Union Pacific*, pp. 58–60, is inaccurate in saying that Polish and white southern workers turned to Jeffries in overwhelming numbers; Jeffries's main base of support was the wealthier WASP districts. Jeffries, however, did gain important support in working-class areas, as Smith and Sarasohn's statistical analysis shows. For an analysis of the general impact of the nonpartisan electoral system, see Edward C. Banfield and James Q. Wilson, *City Politics* (Cambridge, Mass., 1963), pp. 157–60.

23. Joseph Goulden, *Meany* (New York, 1972), p. 140. For the goal of 200,000 cars, see *NYT*, May 17, 1945, and *FPCB*, July 4, 1945, *FP* Coll. The actual car sales total is given in *Historical Statistics of the United States: Colonial Times to 1970*, Part 2 (Washington, 1975): 716. Detroit-area unemployment data are based on a UAW survey of auto plants. "Layoffs in Representative UAW-CIO Plants," Aug. 24, 1945; UAW press release, Aug. 26, 1945, Region V, *FEPC* Records. The figure on the overall decline in auto employment is derived from *Labor Statistics*, p. 18.

24. Michigan Unemployment Compensation Commission, *Unemployment Compensation, 1942-1946* (Detroit, 1947); *Public and Local Acts of the Legislature of the State of Michigan* ([Lansing, Mich.,] 1945), pp. 603–8; "UAW Intensifies Campaign Against Wage Cuts," UAW press release, Aug. 16, 1945, UAW Ford Dept. Coll., WSU; *Labor Statistics*, p. 62; *LFB* 8: 60.

25. *UAW*, Sept. 1, 1945; *Automotive and Aviation Industries*, Sept. 15, 1945, p. 42; Minutes of the IEB, Sept. 10–18, 1945, pp. 45–6, George Addes Coll., WSU; Haessler, "Press Magnifies Detroit Labor Situation," *FPCB*, Sept. 18, 1945, *FP* Coll.

26. *Labor Statistics*, p. 62, 107; *MLR* 54 (Feb. 1942): 292; Proceedings of GM Dispute Panel, Dec. 20, 1945, pp. 48–51, Records of the Federal Mediation and Conciliation Service (FMCS), RG 280; Goulden, *Meany*, pp. 98–115.

27. Crockett column clipping and draft, Nov. 17, 1945, Feb. 23, 1946, George Crockett Coll., WSU; Crockett to Edward L. Cushman, Nov. 29, 1945, CIO Sec'y-Treas. Coll., Box 172, WSU; Dept. of Labor, Div. of Labor Standards, *President's National Labor-Management Conference*, Bulletin No. 77 ([Washington,] 1946), pp. 13, 22, 84; Robert Weaver, *Negro Labor* (New York, 1946), pp. 289–92; Seymour L. Wolfbein, "Postwar Trends in Negro Employment," *MLR* 65 (Dec. 1947): 665. The Leininger quotation is in (UAW) *Research Report* Vol. 5, No. 5 (July 1945), and in Crockett column, "Labor Looks Ahead," *Michigan Chronicle*, June 30, 1945, Crockett Coll.

28. Philip Foner, *Organized Labor and the Black Worker: 1619-1973* (New York, 1974), pp. 269-70. Houston is quoted in McCoy, *Quest and Response*, pp. 26-33 and in Herbert Hill, *Black Labor and the American Legal System* (Washington, 1977), pp. 326-29. The FEPC report is quoted in Seidman, *American Labor*, p. 250.

29. Weaver, *Negro Labor*, pp. 69-74; UAW press release, Apr. 7, 1946, Region V, FEPC, affidavit by Edward Swan, Admin. Files, FEPC Coll.; Crockett column, May 11, 1946, Crockett Coll.; Minutes of the IEB, Nov. 26-28, 1945, pp. 27-31, Addes Coll.

30. Weaver, *Negro Labor*, p. 289; (UAW) *Research Report*, Vol. 4, No. 7 (August 1944); J.H. Wishart memorandum to WPR, May 20, 1947, with attached employment surveys, WPR Coll.; Herbert R. Northrup, "The Negro in the Automobile Industry," in Northrup et al., *Negro Employment in Basic Industry*," (Philadelphia, 1970), pp. 65-66; Wolfbein, "Negro Employment," p. 665; War Manpower Commission, *Labor Market*, Dec. 1944, p. 25; Mar. 1945, p. 41; Nov. 1945, p. 40; Jan 1946, p. 55; Mar. 1946, p. 62; Apr. 1946, p. 40; and May 1946, p. 40.

31. *Labor Statistics*, p. 18; "No. of Negro Women Employed," Sept. 21, 1943, folder, Negro Question—General UAW Research Dept. Coll., WSU; (UAW) *Research Report*, Vol. 4, No. 7 (August 1944); Women's Bureau, *Negro Women War Workers*, Bull. No. 205 (Washington, 1945), p. 7; Weaver, *Negro Labor*, p. 289; U. S. Dept. of Commerce, Bureau of the Census, *United States Census of Population: 1950*, vol. 2, *Characteristics of the Population*, pt. I, *United States Summary*, pp. 400-11; Women's Bureau, *Women Workers in Ten War Production Areas and Their Postwar Employment Plans* (Washington, 1946), pp. 40-47; *Research Report*, Vol. 5, No. 2 (March 1944); Sheila Tobias and Lisa Anderson, "What Really Happened to Rosie the Riveter? Demobilization and the Female Labor Force, 1944-47," MSS Modular Publications, Inc., New York, Module 9 (1974), pp. 20-25. See also Paddy Quick, "Rosie the Riveter: Myths and Realities," *Radical America* 9 (July-Aug. 1975): 115-31; Lyn Goldfarb *et al., Separated and Unequal: Discrimination against Women Workers after World War II (the U.A.W. 1944-54)* (Washington, n.d.); and Nancy Gabin, "Women Workers and the UAW in the Post-World War II Period: 1945-1954," *Labor History* 21 (Winter 1979-80): 5-30. The proportion of women placed in auto industry jobs through the United States Employment Services (USES) declined from about 26 percent in the summer of 1944 to 8 percent in the last quarter of 1946. The comparable figure for all nonagricultural employment was a stable 30 percent. See *Labor Market* issues cited in note 30 herein.

32. R. J. Thomas memorandum to Regional Directors, "Seniority of Women Workers during the Reconversion Period," Nov. 13, 1944, Emil Mazey Coll., Box 13, WSU; *DW*, Oct. 14, 1945; BLS, "Seniority in the Automobile Industry," mimeo, UAW War Policy Div. Coll., Box 22, WSU; Leonard to M. N. Cummins, July 31, 1946, Ford Dept. Coll.; Larry Yost to WPR, Aug. 14, 1946, Ford Dept. Coll., Box 6; Report of Fair Practices and Anti-Discrimination Department to IEB, Dec. 10, 1946, WPR Coll.; UAW, *Proceedings of Ninth Constitutional Convention, Sept. 11-17, 1944* (n.p., n.d.), pp. 119-121; *Proceedings of Tenth Constitutional Convention, Mar. 23-31, 1946* (n.p., n.d.), pp. 51-54, 328-330; copy of 1946 convention resolution with notation of unanimous action by women delegates in Neal Edwards Coll., Box 9, WSU. For dominance of conservative attitudes toward women working, see public opinion survey in *Fortune* 34

(August 1946): 510. The idea that keeping women as a low-wage labor pool hurts all workers was discussed by Ruth Young, "Full Employment and Women," transcript of remarks to CIO-PAC conference, Jan. 15, 1944, Mary Heaton Vorse Coll., Box 128, WSU, and in *Women's Auxiliary News*, Oct. 1945, Mazey Coll., Box 3.

33. R. J. Thomas, Report of UAW Women's Conference (Dec. 8–9, 1944), Jan. 22, 1945, UAW War Policy Coll., Box 27; clippings [*NYT*, Dec. 10, 1944; *DW*, Dec. 17, 1944], UAW Research Dept. Coll., Box 3; Anna Long, "Women Workers After the War," *Political Affairs* 24 (March 1945): 258–67. On the contradiction between attempts to involve women in union activity and the failure to deal with discrimination see Elizabeth Hawes, *Hurry Up Please Its [sic] Time* (New York, 1946), pp. 31–36, 97.

34. Philip S. Foner, *Women and the American Labor Movement: From World War I to the Present* (New York, 1980), pp. 316, 364–67; *Proceedings of the Tenth Convention*; Donald T. Critchlow, "Communist Unions and Racism," *Labor History* 17 (Spring 1976): 233.

35. Davis R. B. Ross, *Preparing for Ulysses: Politics and Veterans During World War II* (New York, 1969), pp. 89–124; Keith W. Olson, *The G. I. Bill, The Veterans, and the Colleges* (Lexington, Ken., 1974), pp. 23–24.

36. Ross, *Politics and Veterans*, pp. 160–89; *UAW*, June 1, 1945; *Labor Market*, Dec. 1946, pp. 38, 40; Jan. 1947, pp. 38, 40; Feb. 1947, pp. 38, 40; Crockett columns, Nov. 17, 1945, Feb. 23, 1946, Crockett Coll.

37. *FP*, Nov. 29, 1945, Dec. 8, 1945, *FP* Coll.

38. Ross, *Politics and Veterans*, pp. 148–59; *FPEB*, Nov. 26, 1945, *FP* Coll.; *NYT*, Jan. 13, 1946. *Fortune* surveys indicated that veterans were more pro-labor than people in general: 34 (Dec. 1946): 5–6.

39. A very moderate Labor-Management Charter in April 1945 agreed to by heads of the CIO, AFL, and the U. S. Chamber of Commerce promised support for labor peace and private enterprise, but it was opposed by auto industrialists and other conservative employers. *NYT*, Apr. 10, 1945, *UAW*, May 1, 1945. The November 1945 Labor-Management Conference sponsored by the Truman administration found management—and the AFL—opposed to dealing with the wage issue. Barton Bernstein, "The Truman Administration and Its Reconversion Wage Policy," *Labor History* 6 (Fall 1965): 229. Bernstein notes that steel companies like Bethlehem refused a compromise on the wage issue because "it was not for 4.5¢ but against the union they were fighting." Bernstein, "Steel Strike," p. 794. The quotation in the text is from *Automotive and Aviation Industries*, Sept. 15, 1945, p. 42.

Chapter Four

1. Barton Bernstein, "Walter Reuther and the General Motors Strike of 1945–1946," *Michigan History* 49 (September 1965): 260–65; Proceedings, Dec. 20, 1945, pp. 48–51,

GM Dispute Panel Hearings and Exhibits, Records of the Federal Mediation and Conciliation Service (FMCS), RG 280, NA.

2. U. S. Bureau of the Census, *Historical Statistics of the United States: Colonial Times to 1970*, Part 1 (Washington, 1975): 179.

3. Chronology of the GM-UAW Case," Appendix A, File Strikes-GM, Lewis B. Schwellenbach, General Subject File, 1945–1947, Conciliation Service, Records of the Office of the Secretary, Dept. of Labor, RG 174, NA. The quotation is from *DN*, Aug. 18, 1945. See also Bernstein, "General Motors Stike," pp. 261–62. Reuther's letter to Wilson is in *UAW: GM Facts Edition*, Oct. 10, 1945.

4. Bernstein, "General Motors Strike," pp. 260–65; *FP*EB, Oct. 22, 1945, *FP* Coll. Butler Library, Columbia University, New York, New York.

5. UAW, *Purchasing Power for Prosperity* (Detroit, 1945), pp. 22–45; Art Hughes's notes on UAW-Chrysler negotiations, 1945–46, Art Hughes Coll., WSU; *NYT*, Mar. 25, 1946; Max Hall, "What Reuther Said and What He Didn't Say: A Newspaper Reporter Examines His Notes on the UAW Convention," Hall to J. B. S. Hardman, Apr. 20, 1946, J. B. S. Hardman Coll., Tamiment Library, New York University, New York; Proceedings of GM Dispute Panel, Dec. 20, 1945, pp. 55–67. According to Howell John Harris, GM "had made its point, on behalf of the entire business community that basic managment rights were not negotiable." *The Right to Manage: Industrial Relations Policies of American Business in the 1940's* (Madison, Wisc., 1982), pp. 140–46. Public opinion polls showed GM had a greater degree of support for its position than did steel, meat packing, electrical, and coal companies. Hadley Cantril and Mildred Strunk, eds., *Public Opinion, 1935–1946* (Princeton, N. J., 1951), pp. 825–27. Citing one public opinion poll which showed more than twice as many persons blamed the union for the dispute as GM, Harris overstates the weakness of the union's attempt to influence public thinking. Two of the three polls reproduced in *Public Opinion* showed the union with a slight plurality of support, and one gave a slight plurality to the company. See below, p. 64, for evidence of active public support of the union's position.

6. Thomas to all UAW Local Officers in Detroit Area, Nov. 1, 1945, Ford Dept. Coll., WSU. Reuther even conceded that the union was willing to scale down its demands if it were wrong on the arithmetic: "If they can show we are wrong—that they cannot give a 30 percent increase without increasing prices—we will scale down our demand down to whatever they can pay without a price increase. We don't want to rob Peter to pay Paul." *UAW*, Nov. 1945.

7. WPR, "Our Fear of Abundance," *NYT Magazine* , Sept. 16, 1945, reprinted in *Walter P. Reuther: Selected Papers,* Henry M. Christman, ed. (New York, 1961); WPR, "The Challenge of Peace," *International Postwar Problems* 2 (Apr. 1945): 143–64; WPR, "GM Versus the Rest of Us," *New Republic* 114 (Jan. 14, 1946): 41–42. The first WPR quote is from Transcript of the Negotiations, Oct. 23, 1945, GM Dept.—Negot. & Strike, WPR Coll., WSU. See also Reuther's comments in Transcript of the Negotiations, Dec. 13, 1945, GM Dept.—Negot. & Strike, WPR Coll. The second WPR quote is from his testimony before the GM Dispute Panel, Proceedings, Dec. 20, 1945, p. 20 and the

quote from the GM executive is in "Transcript of GM Press Conference," Nov. 29, 1945, also included in GM Dispute Panel Hearings and Exhibits.

8. Minutes of the IEB, Sept. 10–18, 1945, pp. 46–48, George F. Addes Coll., WSU; *DFP*, Sept. 12, 13, 16, 18, 1945; Max Hall, "What Reuther Said . . . .", Hardman Coll. Matt Hammond, a key figure in the antileadership demonstration, was also a prime mover in Reuther's presidential bid. Hammond, leader of a group of Detroit area local union presidents, threatened that he and other local presidents would not recognize board decisions if a convention were not held in 1945. The UAW constitution at the time required annual conventions. The convention call was initially delayed due to the federal government's wartime restrictions on transportation. Although the four officers of the UAW proposed a December convention, the majority of the board (including both pro-Reuther and anti-Reuther members) voted to delay the convention until March so as not to interfere with the Frankensteen mayoralty campaign. The drive for an immediate convention petered out before its objective was obtained. Hammond soon lost his office as president of UAW Local 157. See Minutes of the IEB, Sept. 10–18, 1945, pp. 7–8.

9. Minutes of the IEB, Sept. 10–18, 1945, pp. 48–54; *UAW,*Oct. 1, 1945.

10. Minutes of the IEB, Sept. 10–18, 1945, pp. 48–54; *DFP*, Sept. 14–18, 1945; *NYT*, Sept. 15–16, 1945; *DN*, Sept. 14–18, 1945. The Reuther prediction was reported in the *Detroit Free Press*, Sept. 17, 1945. The union's executive board authorized a strike at GM, Ford, or Chrysler on November 10 and left the final decision to a strategy committee. Minutes of the IEB, Nov. 7–12, 1945, pp. 62–65.

11. *DFP*, Sept. 15, 1945; Carl Winter, "Background of the Auto Strike," *Political Affairs* 25 (Dec. 1945): 1075–76; Bernstein, "General Motors Strike," pp. 260–67. The Reuther quotation is in [UAW,] "Chronological History of the Negotiations between the UAW and General Motors," *Congressional Record*, 79 Cong., 1 Sess., Oct. 26, 1945, pp. A5117–19.

12. Barton J. Bernstein, "The Truman Administration and the Steel Strike of 1946," *Journal of American History* 52 (March 1966): 792; Raymond E. Paul, *Taxation in the United States* (Boston, 1954), pp. 321–22, 403–21; *Business Week*, Dec. 1, 1945; *NYT*, Nov. 11, 1945; Detroit to Washington Offices of Conciliation Service, Dec. 11, 1945, GM Corp. (System Wide), FMCS Case #453–3486, FMCS Records, RG 280, NA, General Archives Div., Suitland.

13. Proceedings of the Executive Board, Congress of Industrial Organizations, Nov. 1–2, 1945, pp. 73–77, WSU. The view that "there was no CIO strategy" is expressed by Bert Cochran, *Labor and Communism* (Princeton, N. J., 1977), p. 254. Cochran bases his conclusion on the fact that Murray hoped to avoid strikes. The desire to avoid a strike does not, of course, exclude the possibility of having a bargaining strategy that includes the making of necessary strike preparations. Cochran incorrectly states that Murray waited "to work his way through Truman's fact–finding board" before calling a strike when, in fact, Murray dealt directly with the president and ignored the steel fact–finding board.

14. Proceedings of the Executive Board, Congress of Industrial Organizations, Nov. 1–2, 1945, pp. 17–121.

15. *Ibid.*

16. *NYT*, Dec. 16, 1945; *DFP*, Dec. 7, 1945; *DW*, Feb. 16, 1945, *SW*, Mar. 17, 1946. See also Elizabeth Hawes, *Hurry Up Please, Its* (sic) *Time* (New York, 1946), pp. 123–32.

17. *Moody, Manual of Investments American and Foreign, Industrial Securities*, 1946 (New York, 1946), pp. 2299–3000. Proceedings of the CIO Executive Board, Nov. 1–2, 1945, pp. 117–18. Strikes in steel, for example, were reported by the *NYT*, Sept. 6, 8, 12, 15, 1945.

18. *DN*, Sept. 10, 1945; *Wage Earner*, Sept. 28, 1945, Victor Reuther to William Becker, Sept. 25, 1945, Socialist Party Papers, Duke University, Durham, N. C.. For discussions of strike pressure, including long lists of locals requesting strike authorizations, see Minutes of the IEB, Sept. 10–18, 1945, pp. 13–14, 45–6, 99–104; Minutes, Nov. 7–12, 1945, pp. 71–76, 107–81. For the WPR quote, see Minutes of the IEB, Nov. 26–28, 1945; Interview with Leo Fenster October 23, 1982; Interview with George Addes, January 23, 1982. The strategy committee consisted of the UAW offficers—Thomas, George Addes, Reuther, and Frankensteen— and Ford Department director, Richard Leonard and Chrysler Department director, Norman Matthews. After the strike, Thomas, in reviewing the decisions that led up to the strike, stated that he had told the UAW executive board that it would be better to wait until after the first of the year "but Walter had his idea so sold by that time there was no use in a fellow breaking his skull" trying to change the plan. Reuther's September announcement that GM was the target was "on his own hook." The board approved the plan and the strategy committee the date "because after Reuther had already announced the plan, the others didn't want to hurt the cause of the strikers." Had Reuther "been willing to work together and call the strike when it ought to be made we could have brought the wildcat strikes under control." Max Hall, "What Reuther Said . . . ." The *New York Times* on March 25, 1946 quoted Thomas as saying that Reuther's action of selecting GM as the target could not be disavowed "because we would have been undercutting General Motors workers. So we had to go along."

19. Lillian Stone, "Labor and the Community," *New Masses* 57 (Oct. 23, 1945): 1–4; Frank Emspak, "The Break-Up of the Congress of Industrial Organizations (CIO), 1945–1950" (Ph.D. thesis, University of Wisconsin, 1972), pp. 59–64.

20. Haessler, "Is Ford Playing Lone Wolf Again?", *FPCB*, July 4, 1945, *FP* Coll.; *DFP*, Sept. 5, 1945; Winter, "Auto Strike," 1075–76; Keith Sward, *The Legend of Henry Ford* (New York, 1948), pp. 464–81; *NYT*, Nov. 16, 1945.

21. *NYT*, Nov. 16, 1945; "Progress Report," Dec. 18, 1945, Chrysler Corp. (System Wide), FMCS Case #453-3508, FMCS Records, RG 280, NA, General Archives Div.

22. *NYT*, Nov. 16, 1945.

23. *NYT*, Nov. 16, 24, Dec. 11, 1945; *Time* 46 (Dec. 3, 1945): 19–22; Minutes of the IEB, Nov. 26–28, 1945, p. 11; FPCB, Mar. 14, 1946, FP Coll.; Detroit to Washington, Dec. 1, 1945, Chrysler, FMCS Case #453-3508.

24. The CIO's expectation of support was based on the decade–long alliance with the Democratic administration. The CIO had played a key role in the 1944 Roosevelt reelection campaign. R. J. Thomas noted a "rightward deviation" by Truman as early as August 1945 and said the new president was "on trial." *UAW*, Aug. 15, 1945. On October 17, 1945, Henry Wallace noted in his *Diary* that Murray had stated that he "had lost faith in the administration because they had not grappled courageously with the wage and price problem." John Morton Blum, ed., *The Price of Vision, The Diary of Henry A. Wallace, 1942–1946* (Boston, 1973), p. 493. Murray's detailed description of the problems he was having with the administration is recorded in the Proceedings of the CIO Executive Board, Nov. 1–2, 1945, pp. 15–33. The open break between the CIO and Truman came in December. See below, pp. 65–66.

25. *Public Papers of the Presidents: Harry S. Truman, 1945* (Washington, 1961), pp. 220–22; Barton Bernstein, "The Truman Administration and Its Reconversion Wage Policy," *Labor History* 6 (Fall 1965): 220–25; Joseph C. Goulden, *The Best Years* (New York, 1976), pp. 114–15; Chester Bowles, *Promises to Keep: My Years in Public Life, 1941–1969* (New York, 1971), pp. 130–31. Goulden and Bowles contend that Reuther was involved in the discussions concerning the extension of the no–strike pledge and a 10 percent wage increase, but this is probably an error. Reuther was not yet a top CIO leader. For Truman's belief that Murray and others made a no–strike commitment, which was contradicted by Eric Johnston of the Chamber of Commerce, see *Wallace Diary*, pp. 529, 555–56, 575, and Truman to J. Percy Priest, Jan. 14, 1946, Harry S. Truman Papers, PSF Box 137, Harry S. Truman Library, Independence, Mo. Wallace proposed an immediate increase in wages of at least 10 percent without a general increase in prices. Wallace proposal, Cabinet Meeting, Aug. 17, 1945, Papers of Matthew J. Connelly, Truman Library. The close personal ties between CIO leaders and Roosevelt apparently did not continue under Truman. Alonzo Hamby, *Beyond the New Deal* (New York, 1973), pp.65–66. An Atlanta publisher with ties to Murray and presidential secretary Matt Connelly wrote the latter that "Mr. Murray feels very keenly that the president is attempting to do the whole job of reconverting without so much as asking labor to kiss his royal ass . . . . Mr. Murray is as sore as hell at labor being ignored and is going to do something about it that is going to hurt somebody . . . . These men who carry millions of votes around in their pockets have been ignored and neglected. They were Roosevelt's intimates; his chief reliance in many tough spots [.] Now they are on the outside without even a look in; and they resent it like hell . . . ." Ed O'Connell to Matt [Connelly], Aug. 23, 1945, Truman Papers, OF 170.

26. Goulden, *The Best Years,* pp. 114–15; Bernstein, "Reconversion Wage Policy," pp. 224–25; *Truman Papers, 1945*, pp. 264–65. Truman declared in this address: "Hold wages in line where their increase would cause inflationary price rise." See Nat Ganley analysis in "Memorandum on Aspects of Reconversion Problem and Auto Union Situation," Sept. 29, 1945, Nat Ganley Coll., Box 9, WSU.

27. *NYT*, Apr. 28, Oct. 2, 3, 1945, Jan. 13, 1945; Winter, "Auto Strike," p. 1075.

28. Note 10 above; *Wallace Diary*, p. 540; *Congressional Record*, 79th Cong., 1 sess., Oct. 26, 1945, pp. 10092–93. When the steel companies in January brushed aside his attempt at a compromise, Truman still did not support efforts by Congressional

liberals to revise the tax refund law. *Truman Papers, 1946*, pp. 91–93. See also Bernstein "Reconversion Wage Policy," pp. 226–8.

29. The Murray quotation is from the Proceedings of the CIO Executive Board, Nov. 1–2, 1945, pp. 25–31, 54–61. See also "Facts Relating to Wage–Price Policy," [Oct. 24, 1945], Records of the Office of War Mobilization and Reconversion (OWMR), RG 250, Box 392, NA; Minutes of the OWMR Advisory Board, Oct. 24, 1945, p. 4; Oct. 29–30, 1945, pp. 2–4, 37–56, *ibid*, Boxes 392–93; and Bruce R. Morris, Industrial Relations in the Automobile Industry," in Colston E. Warner, *et al.*, eds., *Labor in Postwar America* (Brooklyn, 1949), pp, 406–7.

30. *NYT*, Nov. 2, 1945; *DN*, Nov. 19, 1945; Bureau of Foreign and Domestic Commerce, "Domestic Economic Developments" (Confidential), Oct. 25, 1945, Auto Industry Reports, Papers of Alfred Schindler, Truman Library. The Commerce report was accompanied by considerable controversy. See "Chronology of the Study on Wage, Prices and Profits in the Automobile Industry," *ibid*.

31. *Truman Papers, 1945*, pp. 439–49.

32. Proceedings of the CIO Executive Board, Nov. 1–2, 1945, pp. 17–111; *NYT*, Oct. 31, Nov. 1, 1945; Bernstein, "Reconversion Wage Policy," pp. 226–28.

33. U. S. Dept. of Labor, *The National Wage Stabilization Board, Jan. 1, 1946–Feb. 24, 1947* (Washington, n.d.), pp. 28–30, 107–8. Murray fought hard against the draft of Executive Order 9651 that administration officials presented to the OWMR Advisory Board. The only provision in the draft not included in the final text of the order was the declaration that an 8–1/3 percent wage increase was appropriate when hours were cut from 48 to 40 (corresponding to the saving to employers on the cost of overtime rates). OWMR Advisory Board Minutes, Oct. 24, 1945, pp. 24, 12, Records of the OWMR, Box 392; OWMR Advisory Board Minutes, Oct. 29–30, 1945, pp. 51–56, *ibid*, Box 393.

34. Bernstein, "Reconversion Wage Policy," pp. 226–28; Benjamin J. Fairless to J. Snyder, Nov. 13, 1945, Records of the OWMR, Box 153. The Romney quotation is in *DW*, Nov. 1, 1945. GM's demand and UAW reply is in [UAW], "Chronological History of Negotiations."

35. Connelly notes on Cabinet Meeting, Oct. 19, 1945, Connelly Papers; Schwellenbach memorandum to Truman, Oct. 19, 1945, Bowles to Truman, Oct. 19, 1945, Wallace to Truman, Oct. 19, 1945, Truman Papers, OF 98.

36. *NYT*, Nov. 2, 6, 9, Dec. 1, 1945; Div. of Labor Standards, *President's National Labor-Management Conference*, Bull. No. 77 ([Washington,] 1946), pp. 11–15, 42–47, 51–6; N. Sivachyov and E. Yazkov, *History of the U.S.A. since World War I* (Moscow, 1976), pp. 220–221.

37. [UAW,] "Chronological History of Negotiations."

38. Bernstein, "General Motors Strike," pp. 260–67; *DFP*, Nov. 29, 1945. In answering a reporter's question, Truman said on November 20 that his office would not be taking a hand in the Detroit strike trouble. Truman's November 29 remark that

GM should sit down and talk with the strikers represented a slight tilt toward the union because GM was refusing to negotiate at the time. *Truman Papers, 1945*, pp. 493–94, 509. Schwellenbach's shift was noted by Wallace in his *Diary* on November 23, 1945, p. 518. See also Connelly notes on Cabinet Meeting, Nov. 23, 1945, Connelly Papers.

39. George Morris, "The New Stage in the Wage Struggle," *Political Affairs* 25 (Jan. 1946): 21; *DW*, Nov. 23, 1945; Interview with Leo Fenster, Oct. 23, 1982; Claude E. Hoffman, *Sit-Down in Anderson: UAW Local 663, Anderson, Indiana* (Detroit,1968), p. 96.

40. FPCB, Nov. 29, 1945, *FP* Coll.; Minutes of the IEB, Nov. 26–28, 1945, p. 33.

41. UAW Supplementary Charge before the NLRB, Nov. 27, 1945, in *Congressional Record*, 79 Cong., 1 Sess., Jan. 14, 1946, p. A6–7; Minutes of the IEB, Nov. 26–28, 1945, p. 33; *NYT*, Dec. 15, 1945; *DFP* Dec. 18, 1945; Strike Strategy Committee to all Local Unions and Plants Re Corporation's Injunctions, Dec. 19, 1945, R. J. Thomas Coll., Box 9 WSU. *DFP* clipping, Jan. 8, 1946, Records of the Labor Mediation Board, Box 5, Acc. 63-38-A, State of Michigan Archives, Lansing.

42. *UAW*, Jan. 1946; *NYT*, Dec. 12, 15, 1945; *DW*, Dec. 18, 1945; FPCB, Nov. 29, FPEB, Dec. 13, 21, 1945, *FP* Coll.; Abner Berry, "What Will Win the Auto Strike?", *New Masses* 57 (Dec. 18, 1945): 13–14; "Report of the National Citizens Committee on GM–UAW–CIO Dispute," Dec. 6, 1945, WPR Coll.

43. Thomas to Wilson (copy), Dec. 1, 1945, Thomas Coll. Box 9; *Business Week*, Dec. 8, 1945; *DFP*, Dec. 2, 1945; *NYT*, Dec. 5, 1945; FPEB, Dec. 3, 1945; telegrams to Thomas from Greater Flint I.U.C.; Chairman, Local 581 Strike Committee; and President and Chairman, Local 651 Strike Comittee, Dec. 1, 1945, Thomas Coll., Box 9.

44. FPEB, Dec. 3, 4, 1945, *FP* Coll. On December 4, a telegram was sent by Thomas's assistant, David Connery, to editors of local union papers telling them not to publicize the letter "supposedly sent by Thomas." Connery to editors, UAW Local 212 Coll., Box 8, WSU. According to the *New York Times*, Dec. 5, 1945, Connery was the assistant who drafted the letter. For Reuther's role in reviewing the letter, see [*NYT*, Dec. 4, 1945,] Blair Moody Papers, Michigan Historical Collections, Ann Arbor, Mich. and *NYT*, Dec. 5, 1945.

45. *NYT*, Dec. 4, 1945; Bernstein, "Reconversion Wage Policy," p. 230; *Labor-Management Conference*, pp. 11–15, 24–28. "In the past half dozen years," former UAW Vice President Wyndham Mortimer noted, "labor had obtained action from the White House without extraordinary pressure." This was no longer true, Mortimer said. *SW*, Dec.9, 1945.

46. *NYT*, Dec. 4–6, 1945. AFL President Green disagreed with Truman's plan but also opposed Murray's harsh criticism of the proposal. Green thought Truman was sincerely trying to ward off vicious antilabor legislation. Regarding some Congressional antilabor proposals, Green said: "We are no different from the laboring men of Great Britain. When driven to desperation we too will turn to the left." *NYT*, Dec. 5, 1945.

47. *NYT*, Dec. 4, 5, 1945; FPEB, Dec. 4, 5, 1945, *FP* Coll.

48. *NYT,* Dec. 4, 5, 1945.

49. *NYT,* Dec. 6, 1945; Marjorie Thines Stanley, "The Interrelationships of Economic Forces and Labor Relations in the Automobile Industry" (Ph.D. thesis, Indiana University, 1953), p. 318; GM mimeo, Dec. 13, 1945, "General Motors' Wage Proposal . . . " GM Dispute Panel Hearings and Exhibits. GM's offer actually exceeded the amount that would qualify under the new regulations. The official history of the Wage Stabilization Board noted that the cost of living increase appropriate under the formula would have been 9.9¢. *Wage Stabilization Board,* pp. 111–13.

50. *FPCB,* Dec. 8, 1945, *FP* Coll.

51. *NYT,* Dec. 11, 1945. The *Federated Press* reported that Thomas and Reuther exempted Ford from what seemed like an industry conspiracy. *FP* (Washington), Nov. 29, 1945, *FPCB,* Dec. 8, 1945, *FP* Coll.

52. *NYT,* Nov. 16, Dec. 10, 11, 21, 1945.

53. *NYT,* Dec. 21, 1945. The first quotation is from a "Resolution Opposing the 'Company Security' Proposal," Bendix Local 9, (c. Dec. 21, 1945). WPR Coll. The Detroit strike committee's protest against the Leonard proposal is contained in John W. Anderson to Thomas, Thomas Coll., Box 9. The Flint strike committee was quoted in *DFP,* Dec. 16, 1945. For other protests, see *DW,* Dec. 12, 1945; Minutes Ford Sub-Council 8, Jan. 13–14, 1946, Ford Dept. Coll., Box 17; Ford Rouge foundry petition, "Our Union is Not for Sale for 18 cents . . . ", *ibid.,* Box 8; and Tony A. Nicol, Secretary, (L.A.) District Auto and Aircraft Council #5 to WPR, Feb. 19, 1946, WPR Coll.

54. *NYT,* Dec. 11, 21, 1945.

55. Neil Brant, Int'l. Rep. UE to WPR, Jan. 16, 1946, WPR Coll.; Emspak, "CIO Break-Up," p. 65; Albert Fitzgerald to Thomas, Feb. 22, 1946, CIO Secretary Treasurer Coll., Box 62, WSU. The UE publicly disassociated itself from the UAW arbitration offer in November, saying that the CIO would have to be consulted before arbitration could be considered as a means of resolving the electrical industry dispute. The UAW had not consulted CIO president Murray before proposing arbitration to GM. However, in January 1946, UE President Albert Fitzgerald told the Senate Education and Labor Committee that the UE did favor arbitration. *NYT,* Jan. 18, 1946; *DFP, Dec. 7, 1945.*

56. *NYT,* Dec. 12, 1945.

57. Bernstein, "General Motors Strike," p. 269; Bernstein, "Steel Strike," p. 793; "Chronology of the GM-UAW Case;" *DW,* Dec. 21, 1945; *Truman Papers, 1945,* pp. 535–36, 568.

58. Proceedings of the GM Dispute Panel, Dec. 20, 1945, pp. 79–104, 150–1.

59. *Ibid.,* Dec. 21, 1945, pp. 174–75.

60. *NYT,* Dec. 22, 23, 1945; *Commercial and Financial Chronicle,* Dec. 27, 1945; *Business Week,* Dec. 29 1945. The *New York Times,* Dec. 23, 1945, editorially criticized the administration for treating statutory authority lightly on the wage–price issue; under the Price Control Act, wages were supposed to be kept at the September 15, 1942, level.

61. Proceedings of the GM Dispute Panel, Dec. 28, 1945, pp, 196–203, appendix B–1; "Corporation Statement of . . . Withdrawal . . . ," "Comment by the Fact-Finding Board on General Motors' Statement . . . ," Dec. 28, 1945, Schwellenbach, General Subject File, 1945–47, Conciliation Service, Records of the Office of the Secretary, Department of Labor, RG 174, NA.

62. C. E. Wilson testimony, U. S. Congress, Senate, Committee on Education and Labor, *Hearings on S1661: Labor Fact-Finding Boards Act*, 79 Cong., 2 Sess., (Washington, 1946), pp. 234–45.

Chapter Five

1. *Detroit Times*, Jan. 8, 1946. Thomas was quoted in *FPEB*, Jan. 9, 1946. See the testimony of Reuther and DuBrul, U. S. Congress, Senate, Committee on Education and Labor, *Hearings on S1661: Labor Fact-Finding Boards Act*, 79 Cong., 2 Sess., (Washington, 1946), pp. 348, 359–60.

2. The quotation is from "Excerpts from the Official Proceedings Before the NLRB," Case No. 7 C–1496, Feb. 14, 1946, pp. 310–329, 428–29, UAW Washington Office— Donald Montgomery Coll. Box 72, WSU. See also *NYT*, Feb. 15, 1946; *DW*, Feb. 14, 15, 1946.

3. *NYT*, Jan 4, 11, 12, 1946; Chester Bowles, *Promises to Keep: My Years in Public Life, 1941–1969* (New York, 1971), pp. 47; Barton J. Bernstein, "The Truman Administration and the Steel Strike of 1946," *Journal of American History* 52 (March 1966); *Public Papers of the Presidents: Harry S. Truman, 1946* (Washington, 1961), pp. 4, 16.

4. *NYT*, Jan. 11, 12, 1946.

5. *NYT*, Jan. 12, 1946.

6. *NYT*, Jan. 13, 17, 19, 1946; Murray testimony, *Hearings on Fact-Finding*, pp. 684–5; John Morton Blum, ed., *The Price of Vision, The Diary of Henry A. Wallace, 1942–1946* (Boston, 1973), p. 540.

7. *NYT*, Jan. 14, 1946. UAW leaders informed Truman that they were withdrawing their acceptance of the fact–finding board's proposal and reinstating the original union demands because the president had not secured GM's agreement. Thomas *et al.* to Truman, Jan. 22, 1946, Truman Papers, OF 407B. Despite this formal withdrawal of acceptance, the union still sought to win GM's adherence to the fact–finding board's proposal.

8. *NYT*, Jan. 14, 1946.

9. *FP* (Washington), Feb. 28, 1946, *FP* Coll., Butler Library, Columbia University, New York, N. Y.

10. *NYT,* Mar. 1, 1946. In announcing its decision to authorize a complaint in January, the board stated: "At this point . . . the national interest requires action . . . ." NLRB press release, Jan. 13, 1946, Harry S. Truman Papers, OF 145, Harry S. Truman Library, Independence, Mo.

11. Telephone transcripts, Herzog and Paul Sifton, Nov. 25, 1945; Herzog and WPR, Nov. 27, 1945; Herzog and John Gibson, Jan. 10, 1946, Paul Herzog Papers, Truman Library. Herzog told Schwellenbach that "the Board would take no action . . . without notifying him first." Herzog memorandum to file, Nov. 28, 1945, Herzog Papers. Herzog sent a note to a top Truman aide advising that the board was seriously considering issuing the complaint against GM around Jan. 1, 1946 "in case you wish to discuss problem with President." Herzog to John R. Steelman, Dec. 29, 1945, Truman Papers, OF 145. When sending Steelman a copy of the board statement of Jan. 13, 1946, Herzog cited the explanation for the delay and concluded, "Perhaps you will want to show it to the Boss." Memo, Herzog to Steelman, Jan. 14, 1946, *ibid.*

12. *Truman Papers, 1946,* p. 22.

13. *NYT,* Jan. 14, 16, 17, 1946; Fitzgerald testimony, Jan. 16, 1946, *Hearings on Fact-Finding,* pp. 190–91.

14. Bernstein, "Steel Strike," pp. 794–96; *NYT,* Jan. 17, 18, 1946.

15. Bernstein, "Steel Strike," pp. 794–96; *NYT,* Jan. 17, 18, 1946. Although the unions protested that extortion and robbery were crimes already, the Hobbs, "antiracketeering" Act was signed into law on July 3, 1946. *LFB* 8: 137.

16. *NYT,* Jan. 18, 1946. A preliminary draft of Truman's statement contained language placing "full responsibility for the present failure of production of automobiles in the General Motors plants" on GM and declaring that United States Steel "will have to bear the responsibility for the situation" if it failed to adopt the President's recommendation. "Statement by the President," [Jan. 18, 1946,] Truman Papers, PSF Box 137.

17. *NYT,* Jan. 14, 19, 1946. Truman privately expressed a view similar to Murray's on the seriousness of the situation. "I fear very much," Truman wrote, that the steel industry aim is " . . . to eliminate all the accomplishments the Roosevelt Administration made for the improvement of the lot of the people who work." Truman to Bernard M. Baruch, Jan. 24, 1946, Truman Papers, PSF Box 137.

18. *NYT,* Jan. 24, 26, 27, 1946; Leslie F. Orear and Stephen H. Diamond, *Out of the Jungle* (n.p., 1968).

19. *NYT,* Jan. 27, 1946; James J. Matles and James Higgins, *Them and Us* (Englewood Cliffs, N. J., 1974) pp. 144–45. The importance of Truman's intervention in the steel dispute to the resolution of the Ford, Chrysler, and RCA disputes is indicated by the remarks made by K. T. Keller, president of Chrysler, to Prentiss Brown of Detroit Edison: "When the President told us 18 1/2 cents was necessary and fair, I felt it was the thing to do and I did it. The President was speaking for the Country and we want

to get on with our work." Prentiss M. Brown to Truman, Jan. 30, 1946, Truman Papers, PSF Box 137.

20. *NYT,* Jan. 27, 29, 1946; *UAW,* Feb. 1946; *Detroit Labor Trends,* Feb. 2, 9, 1946; *Dodge Main News,* Feb. 23, 1946.

21. *UAW-Ford Agreement,* Feb. 26, 1946; *Detroit Labor Trends,* Mar. 2, 1946. The UAW had only a limited form of union security at Chrysler, lacking the union shop and checkoff provisions in effect at Ford.

22. *UAW-Ford Agreement*; Progress Report, Mar. 1, 1946, Ford Motor Co. Plants, FMCS Case #453-3644, Records of the Federal Mediation and Conciliation Service (FMCS), RG 280, NA, General Archives Div., Suitland, Md.; *DW,* Mar. 2, 1946; *Business Week,* Mar. 16, 1946; *Detroit Labor Trends,* May 4, June 1, 1946;*DFP,* Apr. 23, 1946.

23. *New Masses* 58 (Jan. 15, 1946): 18; *DW,* Jan. 22, 1946; *NYT,* Jan. 27, Feb. 8, 1946; *Congressional Record,* 79 Cong., 2 Sess., p. A390.

24. *FP,* Jan. 28, Feb. 4, 1946; *GM Picket,* Feb. 6, 1946, UAW Veterans' Department Coll., WSU; Carl L. Hunter to Thomas, Jan. 15, 1946, UAW Ford Dept. Coll., WSU; *DW,* Feb. 6, 11, 1946; Minutes of City–Wide Strike Committee (Pontiac), Dec. 17, 1945, Jan. 14, 1946, Thomas to N. J. Raymond, Jan. 31, 1946, WPR Coll., WSU.

25. *DW,* Mar. 3, 1946.

26. Interview with Jack White, June 1976; Claude E. Hoffman, *Sit-Down in Anderson: UAW Local 663, Anderson, Indiana* (Detroit, 1968) pp. 95–96. Community general strikes took place in 1946 in Stamford and Hartford, Connecticut; Lancaster, Pennsylvania; Houston, Texas; Rochester, New York; Camden, New Jersey; and Oakland, California. *LFB* 8: 159–61. In New York and Massachusetts general CIO shutdowns to protest police violence were cancelled at Murray's request. *DW,* Feb. 8, 1946.

27. *Hearings on Fact-Finding,* pp. 306, 696–98; David L. Lewis, *The Public Image of Henry Ford* (Detroit, 1976), pp. 431–32.

28. Matles and Higgins, *Them and Us,* pp. 142–49; Frank Emspak, "The Break–Up of the Congress or Industrial Organizations (CIO), 1945–50" (Ph.D. thesis, University of Wisconsin, 1972), pp. 59–64; Herbert R. Northrup, *Boulwarism* (Ann Arbor, Mich., 1964), pp. 20–22; C. E. Wilson's testimony, *Hearings on Fact-Finding,* pp. 640–50.

29. Bernstein, "Steel Strike," p. 800.

30. Bernstein, "Steel Strike," pp. 791–803; Bowles, *Promises to Keep,* pp. 138–47; *Truman Papers,* 1946, pp. 117–23; Harvey C. Mansfield and associates, *A Short History of OPA* (Washington, 1947), pp. 96–98.

31. *NYT,* Feb, 23, 1946; *Detroit Times,* Mar. 10, 1946, WPR notes, "GM Conference," GM Dept.—Negot. & Strike, WPR Coll.; Victor Reuther, *The Brothers Reuther and the Story of the UAW* (Boston, 1976), p. 253.

32. *Hearings on Fact-Finding,* pp. 682–98. Mass demonstrations and consumer boycotts were organized in the spring and summer of 1946. See, for example, leaflets

for July 16 "Protest Against Inflation," Nat Ganley Coll., Box 2, WSU. See also the "Report of the Officers," *Proceedings of the Third Constitutional Convention of the United Steelworkers of America, May 14-18, 1946* (n.p., n.d.), pp. 20-24.

33. *NYT,* Feb. 3, 1946. For an indication of the Reuther staff's concern over the prospective CIO strikes, see typescript, "Material to Get Together to WPR," Jan. 11, 1946, GM Dept.—Negot. & Strike, WPR Coll. The GM Department's 1945-46 "Yearly Report," written during the strike, contended that the steel strike removed competitive and public pressure from GM. WPR Coll.

34. W. V. Henson to R. T. Leonard, Jan, 22, 1946, Ford Dept. Coll., Box 7; *DW,* Dec. 31, 1945, Jan. 17, 18, 23, Feb. 17, Mar. 2, 1946; Thomas to Murray [, Feb. 20, 1946], WPR Coll.; Murray to Thomas, Feb. 20, 1946, Philip Murray Coll., Catholic University, Washington; typescript of report to WPR on "Board Meeting —CIO," Mar. 15, 1946, WPR Coll.; *NYT,* Mar. 17, 1946. Murray denied a series of rumors directed against him in his speech to the 1946 UAW convention. He cited a telegram from members of the GM Fact-Finding Board to refute the rumor that he had intervened in its decision-making in an effort to lower the wage recommendations. UAW, *Proceedings of the Tenth Convention,* pp. 91-101.

35. *NYT,* Feb. 11, 12, Mar. 22, 1946; Minutes of the IEB, Feb. 22-24, 1946, p. 4, WSU; Neil Brant to WPR, Jan. 16, 1946, WPR Coll.; James Robert Prickett, "Communists and the Communist Issue in the American Labor Movement, 1920-1950" (Ph.D. thesis, University of California at Los Angeles, 1975), p. 279; A. Fitzgerald to Thomas, Feb. 22, 1946, CIO Sec'y-Treas. Coll., Box 62, WSU. Although a UE spokesperson initially claimed that the union kept its national contract with GM intact, the UE in fact accepted a modification of its maintenance-of-membership clause. The UE agreement did ensure vacation pay benefits for veterans, a weak point in the UAW-GM agreement (see below, p. 90). UE's right-wing was critical of the GE and Westinghouse settlements but not of the GM agreement. *DW,* Feb. 18, 1946; *Proceedings of the Eleventh Convention, United Electrical Workers, Sept. 9-13, 1946* (n.p., n.d.), pp. 39, 99, 104, 274.

36. *NYT,* Feb. 13, 1946.

37. *NYT,* Feb. 17, 18, 1946.

38. *NYT,* Feb. 21, 22, 23, Mar. 1, 3, 4, 1946; *DFP,* Mar. 2, 1946; Local 602 Bargaining Committee Report, Mar. 9, 1946, UAW Local 602 Coll., WSU.

39. *NYT,* Mar. 4-6, 1946.

40. *NYT,* Mar. 4, 7, 1946; *Detroit Labor Trends,* Mar. 9, 1946.

41. The *New York Times* reported on February 2 that there had been no weakening in striker morale. "The strikers, to the last man," the newspaper declared, "seem to be in a mood to carry on as long as necessary to win their fight." Most plants had not completed local negotiations, and many still faced tough bargaining on local issues. After the national agreement was signed, mass picketing was renewed at many plants

to bring pressure on management to settle local issues. *NYT*, Mar. 19, 20, 1946; *Lansing State Journal*, Mar. 20, 21, 1946.

42. *NYT*, Mar. 1, 7, 8, 1946; telegrams from officials in Pontiac, Flint, Saginaw, Cleveland, and other cities, GM (System–Wide), FMCS Case #453–3486, FMCS Records; *Washington Post*, Mar. 5, 1946.

43. *Truman Papers, 1946*, pp. 144–45; Alonzo Hamby, *Beyond the New Deal* (New York, 1973), p. 76; *NYT*, Feb. 15, Mar. 1, 7, 8, 15, 1946. Union negotiators complained to Truman that "since January 30 we have met with a government conciliator who not once to our knowledge has expressed any interest in the settlement which you recommended." They appealed to the president not to allow GM and other large corporations "to destroy your stabilization program . . . . The GM workers have a right to expect you, Mr. President, to fight as hard for your own policies and recommendations as they are fighting . . . ." Top GM Negotiating Committee to Truman, Mar. 9, 1946, Truman Papers, OF 407B. See also Walter Millis, ed., *The Forrestal Diaries* (New York, 1951), p. 143 and Cabinet Meeting, Feb. 15, 1946, Matthew J. Connelly Papers, Truman Library, for two different versions of a cabinet discussion on the GM strike. The union eventually withdrew the charges filed with the NLRB because Thomas's statements that Reuther was responsible for the delay in the settlement of the strike undermined the UAW's case. (See below pp. 85–86.) WPR to GM locals, May 17, 1946, UAW Washington Office—Montgomery Coll., Box 74.

44. *DN*, Mar. 10, 1946; *DT*, Mar. 10, 1946; *DFP*, Mar. 10, 1946; Bert Cochran, *Labor and Communism* (Princeton, N. J., 1977), p. 219.

45. Interview with George Addes, Jan. 23, 1982; *NYT*, Mar. 22, 1946; *DW*, Mar. 23, 1946.

46. *DN*, Mar. 11 1946; *Milwaukee Journal*, Mar. 16, 1946; *DW*, Mar. 12, 1946.

47. Addes to Barney Hopkins, Mar. 9, 1946, Leo Goodman to WPR, Mar. 2, 1946, memorandum to Walter, Mar. 2, 1946, Paul Sifton memorandum to Goodman, Feb. 28, 1946, Goodman memorandum to WPR, Mar. 18, 1946, WPR Coll.; *NYT*, Mar. 7, 1946.

48. *UAW*, Mar. 1, 1946; *NYT*, Jan. 27, Feb. 8, Mar. 13, 1946; Goodman to WPR, Mar. 2, 1946, Dubinsky to WPR, WPR Coll.; *DW*, Mar. 13, 1946.

49. Typescript of "CIO Board Meeting," Mar. 15–16, 1946, WPR Coll.; *DW*, Feb. 27, Mar. 1, 13, 1946; *NYT*, Mar. 24, 1946; *New Leader*, Feb. 23, 1946; Max D. Danish, *The World of David Dubinsky* (Cleveland, 1957), pp. 168–69; David Dubinsky and A. H. Raskin, *David Dubinsky: A Life with Labor* (New York, 1977), p. 243; Interview with David Dubinsky by C. Eaton, Feb. 25, 1968, pp. 1–2, Charles Eaton and Frank Cormier Papers, JFK Library, Boston.

50. *DN*, Mar. 14, 1946; *NYT*, Mar. 14, 1946; Interview with Louis B. Seaton by Cormier and Eaton, 1968, pp. 1–3, Eaton and Cormier Papers; "Reminiscences of R. J. Thomas," 1956, p. 223, Oral History Collection, Butler Library, Columbia University.

51. *NYT,* Mar. 14, 1946. The quotation on local demands is from UAW mimeo, "Strike Settlement Agreement," pp. 14–15, UAW Local 602 Coll. (emphasis in original).

52. WPR notes, "GM Conference," GM Dept.—Negot. & Strike, WPR Coll.

53. *NYT,* Mar. 16, 1946.

54. *DFP, Mar. 21, 1946; Lansing State Journal,* Mar. 21, 1946; *DN,* Mar. 22, 1946; *NYT,* Mar. 19, 20, 22, 1946.

55. *NYT,* Mar. 26, 1946.

56. Listing of plants demanding "Changes from Incentive Payment to Straight Hourly . . . ," GM Dept.—Negot. & Strike, WPR Coll.; *UAW-GM Agreement,* Mar. 19, 1946; *Fisher Eye Opener,* Sept. 12, Oct. 17, 1947. Local 45 leader Leo Fenster voiced the same criticism, in more moderate terms, on the floor of the UAW convention in March 1946, while the local was still out on strike. *Proceedings of the Tenth Convention,* pp. 38–43.

57. In early negotiations, the union proposed that the 30 percent demand include 1 percent for intraplant inequities, 3 percent for interplant inequities, and 3 percent for hospitalization, death benefits, and social security. *DFP,* Sept. 15, 1945. A top UAW GM Department official criticized UAW local unionists who believed that GM was required to spend at least 1/2¢ to correct inequities. Art [Johnstone] memorandum to WPR, Aug. 16, 1946, GM Top Negotiating Committee, WPR Coll. For an acknowledgement that the UAW did not win the extra penny, see Interview with Leonard Woodcock by Cormier and Eaton, May 5, 1968, p. 4, Cormier and Eaton Papers.

58. *UAW-GM Agreements,* Oct. 19, 1942, Apr. 16, 1945, Mar. 19, 1946; *Umpire Decisions: 1946 Agreement, GMC and UAW,* E 44—E 49; *NYT,* Mar. 3, 1946.

59. *UAW-GM Agreements,* Apr. 16, 1945, Mar. 19, 1946; WPR notes, "GM Conference," GM Dept.—Negot. & Strike, WPR Coll.; Minutes of the IEB, Feb. 22–24, 1946, p. 5, WSU.

60. *NYT,* Mar. 14, Aug. 15, 1946; WPR to H. Anderson, May 2, 1946, A. G. Schultz to WPR, July 26, 1946, and Minutes, Top GM Negotiating Committee, July 30, 1946, WPR Coll.

61. Robert M. McDonald, *Collective Bargaining in the Automobile Industry* (New Haven, Conn., 1963), pp. 32–33; *UAW-GM Agreement,* Mar. 19, 1946, paragraphs 8, 47, 117.

62. Bernstein, "GM Strike," pp. 276–77; BLS, *Handbook of Labor Statistics,* Bull. No. 916 (Washington, 1947), p. 107.

63. McDonald, *Collective Bargaining,* pp. 230–36; *UAW-Chrysler Agreement,* Jan. 26, 1946; *Detroit Labor Trends,* Feb. 9, 1946.

64. *MLR,* May, 1947, pp. 765–69.

65. Minutes of the IEB, Nov. 26–28, 1945, p. 27, WSU; *Michigan Chronicle,* May 4, 11, 1946, WPR to Crockett, Aug. 29, 1945, Feb. 8, 1946, George Crockett Coll., WSU;

UAW press release Feb. 16, 1946, Ford Dept. Coll.; *DW*, Feb. 3, 1946. Under the occupational group seniority system, workers accumulated seniority rights in a limited job category and had no right to transfer to another job area even though they were capable of doing the job. Black workers were concentrated in low–skilled job classifications and were unable to transfer to other jobs. Inequitable layoffs were also a consequence of this system. The transfer clause sought by the UAW in 1946 concerned transfers within the existing occupational groups. Crockett, Report to Local 25, Oct. 25, 1945, p. 5, WPR Coll.

66. Victor Reuther defined the aims of the strike as the winning of two principles— the right to share in the fruits of advancing technology and the right not to be victimized by inflation—and concluded that "the UAW did not win that strike." Reuther, *The Brothers Reuther*, pp. 304–6. The conclusion that the strike was a victory is based on defining the aims of the strike as the winning of a substantial increase in wages and maintenance of the strength and position of the union.

67. H. M. Douty, "Review of Basic American Labor Conditions," Colston E. Warne, *et al.*, eds., *Labor in Postwar America* (Brooklyn, 1949), pp. 128–31.

68. Curtis D. MacDougall, *Gideon's Army* 3 vols. (New York, 1965), 1: 41–47; *FP*CB, Dec. 8, 1945, *FP* Coll.

69. Oral History Interview of James Cleveland, Oct. 3, 1961, pp. 20–21, 26–27, Michigan Historical Collections, Ann Arbor, Mich.; Interview with George Addes, Jan. 23, 1982.

70. *Time*, 46 (Dec. 3, 1945): 1922; Victor Reisel column, *New York Post*, Mar. 7, 1945; Else Maxwell column, *New York Post*, Apr. 22, 1946; Jack William Skeels, "The Development of Political Stability within the Auto Workers Union" (Ph.D thesis, University of Wisconsin, 1957), pp. 219–21.

Chapter Six

1. *DFP*, Mar. 22, 1946; *NYT*, Mar. 22, 1946.

2. UAW, *Proceedings of Tenth Constitutional Convention*, pp. 6–10, *DFP*, Mar. 24, 25, 27, 1946; *Washington Post*, Mar. 30, 1946.

3. Reuther for President Committee, "The Issue is Wages—Real Wages—and Prices," ACTU Coll., Box 35, WSU; Oral History Interview of Carl Haessler, Nov. 27, 1959–Oct. 24, 1960, p. 174, Michigan Historical Collections, Ann Arbor, Mich.

4. *DFP*, Mar. 26, 1946, *NYT*, Mar. 26, 1946, *DW* Mar. 25, 26, 1946; UAW, *Proceedings of Tenth Constitutional Convention*, pp. 91–101.

5. Typescript from Tom [Doherty], Monday [Mar. 25, 1946], ACTU Coll. Box 35; WPR, "I Challenge R. J. Thomas to Debate," *ibid.*; UAW, *Proceedings of Tenth Constitutional Convention*, pp. 138–43; *DFP*, Mar. 26, 1946.

6. Edwin A. Lahey, "Reuther Takes Over," *New Republic* 114 (Apr. 8, 1946): 468–69; Len DeCaux, *Labor Radical* (Boston, 1970), p. 413; Elizabeth Hawes, *Hurry Up Please, Its* [sic] *Time* (New York, 1946), pp. 112–205.

7. Hawes, *Hurry Up Please*, p. 110.

8. *Ibid*, pp. 110–11; DeCaux, *Labor Radical*, pp. 317, 412; Roger Keeran, *The Communist Party and the Auto Workers Unions* (Bloomington, Ind., 1980), pp. 199–200, 255, Haessler interview, p. 172; *Wage Earner*, Mar. 29, 1946; Therton F. Schlabach, *Edwin E. Witte, Cautious Reformer* (Madison, Wisc. 1969), pp. 209–10; August Meier and Elliot Rudwick, *Black Detroit and the Rise of the UAW* (New York, 1979), pp. 11–34, 167–72, 193–97; Interview with George Addes, Jan. 23, 1982. See Chapter Three for Thomas's remarks during the GM strike.

9. Oral History Interview of George Addes, June 25, 1960, pp. 35–37, Michigan Historical Collections; Addes interview, Jan. 23, 1982. Most delegates voted a straight ticket in the three contested ballots. Reuther received 223 votes from delegates who cast Thomas–Addes caucus ballots in the two vice presidential races, 80 percent higher than the comparable figure for Thomas. *Proceedings of the Tenth Convention*, pp. 336–463.

10. *Proceedings of the Tenth Convention*, pp. 30–32, 35–36, 51–54, 68–69, 328–30; *UAW-CIO Leader*, Mar. 24, 1946, "Spike the Lies," Ernest J. Moran Coll., Box 6, WSU. Women union members objected that a resolution on "Government Responsibility to Women Workers" ignored the union's responsibility to protect women union members from discrimination. The Council of Women Delegates drafted a strong resolution on "Protection of Women's Rights in the Auto Industry" that sharply criticized union leaders at all levels for tolerating and even approving discrimination against women. Both resolutions were adopted by the convention. Neal Edwards Coll., Box 9. See Chapter Three herein for a discussion of management's postwar drive to exclude women from the auto plants and the union's response to this campaign.

11. *UAW-CIO Leader*, Mar. 24, 1946, "Spike the Lies," Moran Coll.; "The Issue is Wages–Real Wages—and Prices," ACTU Coll., Box 35.

12. *Nation*, 162 (Mar. 23, Apr. 6, 1946): 333, 385.

13. *Michigan Chronicle*, Apr. 6, 1946; *Proceedings of the Tenth Convention*, pp. 103–17, 336–463. The alignment of the committee members is based on the Roll Call included in the *Proceedings*.

14. *Proceedings of the Eighth Convention*, pp. 370–88; *Proceedings of the Tenth Convention*, pp. 103–17.

15. *Michigan Chronicle*, Mar. 30, 1946. See Chapter Three for description of the role of the Fair Practices Committee.

16. *Proceedings of the Tenth Convention*, pp. 6–10.

17. "Foreign Policy—Majority Report," ACTU Coll., Box 35; *Proceedings of the Tenth Convention*, pp. 15, 336–463.

18. "Minority Report (Peace)," Paul Silver Coll., WSU.

19. Reuther and Ganley drafts on "Political Action, " Silver Coll.

20. *DFP*, Mar. 28, 1946; *Proceedings of the Tenth Convention*, p. 8; *NYT*, Mar. 23, 1946.

21. *DFP*, Mar. 31, 1946; Marvin Persky, "Walter Reuther and Third Party Politics" (Ph.D. thesis, Michigan State University, 1974), pp. 130–31, 143–49; Michael Deveraux Whitty, "Emil Mazey: Radical as Liberal" (Ph.D. thesis, Syracuse University, 1969), pp. 145–47.

22. According to one Reuther staff member, the Reuther approach on foreign policy was "to steer a middle course between the sterile 'get tough' approach of the conservatives and the pious fawning of the fellow travelers." "Proposal: A Major Speech on Foreign Policy by Walter Reuther, (CIO Conv. [1946]), WPR Coll.

23. Resolutions on "Wages and Prices," Minutes of the Resolutions Committee, Tenth Annual Convention, Mar. 23, 1946, Silver Coll.

24. "So-Called Company Security," Silver Coll.

25. Mary Sperling McAuliffe, *Crisis on the Left* (Amherst, Mass., 1978), pp. 12–13; Keeran, *Communist Party and Auto Workers*, p. 256. For an indication of the CIO's strong support of U.S.-U.S.S.R. cooperation in early 1946, see *Report of the CIO Delegation to the Soviet Union* (Washington, n.d.).

26. McAuliffe, *Crisis on the Left*, pp. 10–13. For the formation of the Reuther coalition, See Chapter Two herein.

27. "In Support of Philip Murray's Message," Minutes of the Resolutions Committee, Tenth Annual Convention, Mar. 21, 1946, Silver Coll.; *Proceedings of the Tenth Convention*, pp. 91–101, 330–31.

28. Keeran, *Communist Party and Auto Workers*, pp. 199–200; Interview with Carl Winter, June 6, 1974. The quotation is from Wyndham Mortimer, *Organize!* (Boston, 1971), pp. 362–73.

29. *Proceedings of the Tenth Convention*, p. 213; *DW*, Apr. 7, 1946.

30. Jack William Skeels, "The Development of Political Stability within the United Auto Workers Union" (Ph.D. thesis, University of Wisconsin, 1957), pp. 225–28. *NYT*, Mar. 10, 23, 1946; Oral History Interview of Carl Haessler, p. 173. Addes recalled that the merger between his group and Thomas's occurred before the convention. Addes, Thomas, and other top leaders no doubt caucused before the convention, but the formation of a single joint organization took place at the convention. Interview with George Addes, Jan. 23, 1982; *DW*, Mar. 23, Apr. 7, 1946; *DFP*, Mar. 23, 1946; Typescript from Tom [Doherty], Monday [Mar. 25, 1946], Doherty notes, ACTU Coll., Box 35.

31. Bruce Minton, "The Auto Workers Meet," *New Masses* XL (Sept. 2, 1941): 16–18. See Chapter Two herein for Thomas's prior position.

32. Oral History Interview of Nat Ganley, Apr. 16, 1960, pp. 40–42, Michigan Historical Collections; Skeels, "Development of Political Stability," pp. 140–201.

33. Skeels, "Development of Political Stability," pp. 190–203, 226, 233–34, 240; Oral History Interview of Leonard Woodcock, Apr. 30, 1963, pp. 36–38, Michigan Historical Collections; Interview with Leonard Woodcock, Feb. 10, 1982.

34. *Proceedings of the Tenth Convention; Proceedings of the Ninth Convention.* In this and the following paragraphs tabulations are based on votes recorded in the *Proceedings*.

35. Hawes, *Hurry Up Please*, pp. 111–12; Keeran, *Communist Party and Auto Workers*, p. 256; Oral History Interview of Richard Frankensteen, Oct. 10, 1959–Dec. 7, 1961, pp. 49–50, Michigan Historical Collections; *DW*, Apr. 7, 1946.

36. Cochran, *Labor and Communism*, p. 256; *Report of George Addes*, Jan. 1, 1944–May 31, 1945 (n.p., n.d.), pp. 10–25; *Report of George Addes*, Jan. 1, 1945 to May 31, 1946 (n.p., n.d.), pp. 10-23. Most notable among delegations from closed plants was that from UAW Local 50 at Willow Run, which cast 132 votes for the Reuther candidates. The *Daily Worker* saw this as one of "several glaringly phony Reuther delegations" that should have been challenged. Given the decline of the aircraft industry, this phenomenon could not have been restricted to Reuther caucus delegations. *DW*, Apr. 7, 1946.

37. *NYT*, Mar. 28, 29, 30, 1946; Tom Doherty to *Wage Earner*, Mar. 28, 1946, ACTU Coll., Box 35; Oral History Interview of Kenneth Bannon, Feb. 28, 1963, pp. 18–19, Michigan Historical Collections; *DFP*, Mar. 29, 1946; Oral History Interview of Carl Haessler, pp. 178–79. Leonard drew 116 votes from delegates who had voted for Reuther for president and 83 votes from those who had supported Thomas.

38. Interview with George Addes, Jan. 23, 1982; Oral History Interview of Carl Haessler, pp. 178–79; C. Kosmalsku to Ernest Mazey, July 31, 1945, WPR Coll.; Local 212 Investigating Committee, "Press Statement on Dollinger Beatings," WPR Coll.; UAW Press Release, Jan. 24, 1946, ACTU Coll., Box 9; Memo on Daily Labor Situation, Mar. 11, 1946, Records of the State Police, Intelligence and Security Bureau, RG 65–31, Michigan State Archives, Lansing, Mich.

39. Gary M. Fink, *Biographical Dictionary of American Labor Leaders* (Westport, Conn.), pp. 199–200.

40. *Ibid.*, pp. 206–7; *DW*, Mar. 30, 1946; *NYT*, Mar. 28, 1946. With the approval of the convention, Thomas appointed a committee to investigate those and other charges of gangster influence. *Proceedings of the Tenth Convention*, pp. 259–60, 270. See Convention Investigating Committee, "Report to UAW International Executive Board," Mar. 21, 1947, James Couser Coll., Box 1, WSU.

41. Votes cast for Leonard in the first vice presidential race were counted as independent rather than Addes–Thomas caucus votes. Totals for delegates casting two of three ballots for a particular caucus include the votes of split ticket voters and the votes of those absent or abstaining on one of the ballots.

42. Skeels, "Development of Political Stability," pp, 248–57.

43. Skeels, "Development of Political Stability," pp. 248–57, 263; *Proceedings of the Eighth Convention*.

44. Interview with George Addes, Jan. 23, 1982, *New Leader*, Apr. 6, 1946; Joseph Mattson to WPR, Jan. 26, WPR Coll., Box 7; *Call*, Aug. 30, 1941.

45. *Proceedings of the Tenth Convention*, pp. 218–19; Oral History Interview of Carl Haessler, pp. 181–82.

46. *Proceedings of the Tenth Convention*, p. 224.

47. *Ibid*; *NYT*, Apr. 17, 1946; Oral History Interview of George Addes, June 25, 1960, Michigan Historical Collections; *DW*, Apr. 7, 1946; Oral History Interview of Carl Haessler, p. 173; Interview of George Addes, Jan. 23, 1982.

48. *NYT*, Mar. 31, 1946; *DFP*, Mar. 31, 1946; *DW*, Apr. 2, 1946.

49. *DFP*, Mar. 29, 1946; *Detroit Labor Trends*, Mar. 30, 1946.

50. Minutes of the IEB, Apr. 16–26, 1946, pp. 35–43, WSU; "Report by Nat Ganley," May 5, 1946, Communist Auto Conference, Nat Ganley Coll., Box 9, WSU.

51. Minutes of the IEB, Apr. 16–26, 1946, pp. 35–43, 60; Walter Reuther, "A Program and Statement of Policy for the UAW–CIO Membership," Apr. 25, 1946, ACTU Coll., Box 33, WSU; Nat Ganley, Report to 1948 Communist party Convention, (Copy in author's possession); *NYT*, Apr. 19, 1946. The board program is printed in *UAW*, May, 1946.

52. *DN*, Apr. 11, 1946; *NYT*, Apr. 12, 1946.

53. *Wage Earner*, Apr. 26, 1946; *Militant*, July 13, 1946.

54. *UAW Constitution*, adopted Mar. 23–31, 1946, Atlantic City, N. J.

55. "Report by Nat Ganley," May 5, 1946. The Supreme Court decision in *Schneiderman v. United States* actually turned on the question of "force and violence," not allegiance to a foreign power. Because significant evidence was found both for and against the idea that Communists advocated "force and violence," the Court ruled that the Government could not revoke Schneiderman's citizenship. The Government had not proved, the Court said, that Schneiderman lacked "attachment" to the U. S. Constitution. 320 U. S. 118 (1943).

56. *UAW Constitution*, 1946, Article 13 Section 5, Art. 14, Section 4.

57. Minutes of the IEB, Apr. 16–26, 1946, pp. 7–14, 109–30; [Maurice Sugar,] "Memorandum on Existing Situation in the International Union," May 23, 1946, Maurice Sugar Coll., Box 1, WSU; Harold L. Wilensky, *Intellectuals in Labor Unions* (Glencoe, Ill., 1956), pp. 99–100.

58. Minutes of the IEB, Apr. 16–26, 1946, pp. 1, 109–21.

59. Minutes of the IEB, Apr. 16–26, 1946, pp. 1, 7–14, 109–25; *Wage Earner,* May 3, 1946. There was no immediate appointment of a woman codirector.

60. *Ibid.* Victor Reuther attests to the importance of the Education Department in allowing the Reutherites "to break out from under the hard-core group that dominated the Executive Board." The board minutes do not sustain Reuther's statement that Thomas supported his appointment to head the Education Department. Victor G. Reuther, *The Brothers Reuther and the Story of the UAW* (Boston, 1976), pp. 259–60.

61. Keeran, *Communist Party and Auto Workers,* pp. 261–65; *NYT,* June 5, 1946. Minutes of the IEB, Aug. 5–18, 1946, pp. 213–20; *Wage Earner,* Aug. 23, Sept. 13, 1946.

62. [Maurice Sugar,] "Memorandum on Existing Situation in the International Union," May 23, 1946, Maurice Sugar Coll., Box 1; Christopher H. Johnson, "Maurice Sugar: Law, Labor and the Left in Detroit, 1912–1950," manuscript, pp. 533–35, to be published by Wayne State University Press; Minutes of the IEB, Apr. 16–26, 1946, pp. 109–24; Mar. 17–26, 1947, pp. 159–74; *Wage Earner,* June 7, 1946.

Chapter Seven

1. John Barnard, *Walter Reuther and the Rise of the Auto Workers* (Boston, 1983), p. 131.

2. Interview with Leonard Woodcock, Feb. 10, 1982.

3. Interview with Leonard Woodcock, Feb. 10, 1982.

4. Victor Reuther, *The Brothers Reuther and the Story of the UAW* (Boston, 1976), pp. 20–21, 36–37; Barnard, *Walter Reuther,* pp. 2–5.

5. Barnard, *Walter Reuther,* pp. 2–5.

6. *Ibid.,* pp. 4–17, 36–40; Reuther, *The Brothers Reuther,* pp. 50–59; Frank Marquardt, *An Auto Worker's Journal* (University Park, 1975), pp. 81–82.

7. Reuther, *Brothers Reuther,* pp. 188–90; Lorin Lee Cary, "Institutionalized Conservatism in the Early CIO," *Labor History* 13 (Fall 1972): 502; Christopher H. Johnson, "Maurice Sugar: Law, Labor and the Left in Detroit, 1912–1950," manuscript to be published by Wayne State University Press, pp. 413–20, 482–85. See Chapter Two, note 37.

8. Sidney Fine, *Frank Murphy: The New Deal Years* (Chicago, 1979), pp. 490–93; Barnard, *Walter Reuther,* p. 59; Walter Reuther, "Our Fear of Abundance," *New York Times Magazine,* Sept. 16, 1945, reprinted in Henry M. Christman, *Walter P. Reuther: Selected Papers* (New York, 1961), p. 13.

9. Interview with Stanley Nowak, Apr. 4, 1984.

10. Jack William Skeels, "The Developmet of Political Stability within the United Auto Workers Union" (Ph.D. thesis, University of Wisconsin), pp. 248–52; Francis Carlton, "The GM Strike: A New Stage in Collective Bargaining" *Antioch Review* VI (Sept. 1946): 426–41; Bert Cochran, *Labor and Communism* (Princeton, N. J., 1977), pp. 257–58; Victor G. Reuther, *The Brothers Reuther*, pp. 246–59; *Labor Comment*, March 1944, Socialist Party of America Coll., Duke University (Microfilm Edition); Interview with Leonard Woodcock, Frank Cormier and William J. Eaton Papers, JFK Library, Boston; Interview with Leonard Woodcock, Feb. 10, 1982.

11. Douglas Paul Seaton, "The Catholic Church and the Congress of Industrial Organizations: The Case of the Association of Catholic Trade Unionists, 1937–1950," (Ph.D. dissertation, Rutgers University, 1975); Confidential ACTU Newsletter, No. 2 (copy), Nov. 1, 1943, Carl Haessler Coll., Box 8, WSU.

12. Seaton, "The Catholic Church and the Congress of Industrial Organizations," p. 24; Statements of Policy Recommended by the Policy Committee to the Third Annual Convention, Detroit ACTU, Dec. 13, 1947, and Minutes, Third Annual Convention, Detroit ACTU, Dec. 1947, ACTU Coll. Box 2.

13. Seaton, "The Catholic Church and the Congress of Industrial Organizations, pp. 160–61, 211, 285, 294; Minutes of Detroit ACTU Convention, Oct. 28, 1945, ACTU Coll., Box 2; Confidential ACTU Newsletter, No. 2 (copy), Nov. 1, 1943, Carl Haessler Coll., Box 8, WSU.

14. Minutes of Detroit ACTU Conference, Oct. 28, 1945, ACTU Basic Training Course [1946], "Errors of Collectivism," ACTU Coll., WSU; The quotation is from "Statement of Policy in United Automobile Workers," ACTU Coll., Box 3. See Chapter Two herein.

15. Seaton, "The Catholic Church and the Congress of Industrial Organizations," pp. 77, 205; Detroit ACTU Constitution as amended by third annual convention, Jan. 19, 1948. ACTU Coll., Box 1.

16. Roger Keeran, *The Communist Party and the Auto Workers Unions* (Bloomington, 1980), p. 254; "Statement of Policy in United Automobile Workers," ACTU Coll., Box 3. Both ACTU critic Haessler and leader Thomas Doherty saw the organization as having the leading role in the right–wing caucus, at least in Detroit. The weight of the evidence indicates, however, that Reuther–social democratic elements had the leading role. Oral History Interview of Carl Haessler, Nov. 29, 1959–Oct. 24, 1960, p. 264, Michigan Historical Collections, Ann Arbor, Mich.; Thomas Doherty to Joseph Lime, Apr. 9, 1946, ACTU Coll., Box 1. See Cochran, *Labor and Communism*, p. 287. ACTU's social conservatism led it strongly to support the idea that women's proper place was in the home. During the war, ACTU had opposed the "promotion of nursery schools designed to lure mothers of small children into war plants." Copy of "Confidential ACTU Newsletter," Nov. 1, 1943, Carl Haessler Coll., Box 8, WSU.

17. Art Preis, *Labor's Giant Step* (New York, 1964), pp. 280–82, 324–35; Art Preis, "The Atlantic City Auto Union Convention," *Fourth International* 7 (May 1946): 149–52;

"The Strike Wave," *New International* XII (January 1946): 3–5; *Labor Action*, Mar. 18, 25, Apr. 1, 8, 15, 1946.

18. Keeran, *Communist Party and Auto Workers*, pp. 240, 259–60; Earl Browder, "The Strike Wave Conspiracy," *The Communist* 22 (June 1943): 490–94; Nat Ganley, "Michigan's Decisive Battle for Victory, Peace and Security," Report to State Conference of the Communist Political Association (CPA), Apr. 22, 1945, Ganley Coll., WSU; Report by Pat Toohey to State Committee, CPA, June 10, 1945; *DW*, Mar. 26, 1946; Americus [Earl Browder], *Labor and Socialism in America* (n.p., Sept. 1, 1948), pp. 12–18.

19. George Crockett to WPR, Oct. 23, 1945, Crockett Coll.; *DW*, Sept. 12, 1945, Apr. 13, 1946; Shelton Tappes to Reuther, Apr. 14, 1945, WPR to Tappes, Apr. 23, 1945, WPR Coll. The *Michigan Chronicle* estimated that 90 percent of the Black delegates voted for Thomas for president and vice president, Apr. 6, 1946. The quotation is from *ibid*, Jan. 19, 1946.

20. August Meier and Elliot Rudwick, *Black Detroit and the Rise of the UAW* (New York, 1979), pp. 108–211.

21. *Ibid.*, pp. 209–211; clipping of Crockett column, *Michigan Chronicle*, May 11, 1946, Crockett Coll., Box 1, WSU. The quotation is from *Michigan Chronicle*, Apr. 20, 1946.

22. *Michigan Chronicle*, Feb. 2, Apr. 20, May 4, 1946.

23. Report by Nat Ganley to Auto Conference, May 5, 1946, Ganley Coll.

24. Irving Howe and B. J. Widick, *The UAW and Walter Reuther* (New York, 1949); *NYT*, Sept. 16, 1945; Interview with George Addes, Jan. 23, 1982.

25. Steve Babson, "Living in Two Worlds: The Immigrant Experience in Detroit," *Michigan Quarterly Review* XXV (Spring 1986): 369–85. See Robert H. Zeiger, "Toward the History of the CIO: A Bibliographic Report," *Labor History* 26 (Fall 1985) 500–3, for a listing of several recent works in this area.

26. Peter Friedlander, *The Emergence of a UAW Local, 1936–1939* (Pittsburgh, 1975), pp. 97–100, 121–26; Interview with Harold Christoffel, Dec. 2, 1983; Interview with Jack White, June 1976.

27. Interview with Arthur McPhaul, October 7, 1984. The quotation is from Friedlander, *Emergence of a UAW Local*, p. 123.

28. Interview with Leo Fenster, Oct. 23, 1982.

29. A stratified random sample of 1,215 delegates was drawn so that there would be equal numbers from each of three voting tendencies (left-center, right, and other) and from each of three types of UAW regions (right-aligned, the two Detroit regions, and all other regions). A total of 989 names were identified according to their national origin (or in a handful of cases, where the author had independent documentation of a delegate's actual ethnicity). There was some variation in the pattern by region, but the numbers were too small to draw definite conclusions. Names, of course, are only

a very rough guide to actual ethnic affiliation. The source for the identification of names was Elsdon C. Smith, *New Dictionary of American Family Names* (New York, 1973).

30. Interview with William Allan and Jack White, June 1976.

31. K. B. Gilden, *Between the Hills and the Sea* (New York, 1971), p. 244.

Chapter Eight

1. *NYT*, July 17, 1946; *UAW*, Aug. 1946.

2. Curtis D. MacDougall, *Gideon's Army*, 3 vols. (New York, 1965) I:104–10; Alonzo Hamby, *Beyond the New Deal*, (New York, 1973), pp. 102–4, 154–56; Norman D. Markowitz, *The Rise and Fall of the People's Century: Henry A. Wallace and American Liberalism, 1941–1948* (New York, 1973), pp. 201–4,

3. MacDougall, *Gideon's Army*, I:109–10.

4. *Ibid*, pp. 50, 111; *LBF* 8:104, 107, 186.

5. Mary Sperling McAuliffe, *Crisis on the Left* (Amherst, Mass., 1978), pp. 10–13.

6. *DW*, Jan. 14, 29. 1947; Douglas P. Seaton, *Catholics and Radicals* (London, 1981), pp. 195–96; Len DeCaux, *Labor Radical* (Boston, 1970), pp. 471–76; MacDougall, *Gideon's Army*, I:106.

7. Richard Leonard, "Report of UAW Political Action and Legislative Department to the Board," December 1946, WPR Coll.; *UAW*, Nov. 1946; *Michigan Manual*, 1947, pp. 309–10, 555–59; *LFB* 8 (New York, 1947): 167–72; MacDougall, *Gideon's Army*, I:99–101; Alonzo Hamby, *Beyond the New Deal* (New York, 1973) pp. 134–36.

8. Leonard, "Report . . . Political Action", MacDougall, *Gideon's Army*, I:100.

9. Marvin Persky, "Reuther and Third Party Politics" (Ph.D. thesis, Michigan State University, 1974), p. 169; Leonard, "Report . . . Political Action;" MacDougall, *Gideon's Army*, I:99–100. The quotation is in *UAW*, Nov. 1946.

10. MacDougall, *Gideon's Army*, I:99–100; *DN*, Sept. 10, 1946; Persky, "Reuther and Third Party Politics," p. 169; *Wage Earner*, July 26, 1946. "Warning to the Voters of the 4th Congressional District," Wisconsin Industrial Union Council Coll., Box 3, Wisconsin State Historical Society, Madison, Wisc.; Fred Blair to William T. Evjue, Oct. 28, 1946, Fred Blair Coll., Box 1, Wisconsin State Historical Society, *Milwaukee Journal*, Nov. 6, 1946.

11. DeCaux, *Labor Radical*, pp. 474–76; James R. Prickett, "Some Aspects of the Communist Controversy in the CIO," *Science and Society* XXXIII (Summer–Fall 1969): 302–5; *DW*, Nov. 18, 19, 26, 1946; *Michigan Chronicle*, Dec. 14, 1946, *Michigan CIO News*, Dec. 13, 1946.

12. MacDougall, *Gideon's Army*, I:118–20.

13. *Ibid.*, pp. 121–24; Hamby, *Beyond the New Deal*, pp. 33–38, 153; Mary Sperling McAuliffe, *Crisis on the Left* (Amherst, Mass., 1978) pp. 5–8; Clifton Brock, *Americans for Democratic Action* (Washington, 1962), pp. 44–58.

14. *Proceedings of the Eighth CIO Convention*, pp. 277–81. Expressing his disappointment with the CIO resolution, UDA leader James Loeb told Walter Reuther that he hoped "the so-called 'compromise' is not too disastrous from your point of view." Loeb to WPR, Nov. 28, 1946, Papers of the Americans for Democratic Action (Microfilm Edition), Series III, No. 59, State Historical Society of Wisconsin, Madison, Wisc.

15. McAuliffe, *Crisis on the Left*, pp. 6–8, 17–18; MacDougall, *Gideon's Army*, I:121–24; Prickett, "Communist Controversy in the CIO," 308; James Loeb to Eleanor Roosevelt, Oct. 30, 1946, ADA Papers, Series I, No. 30; *NYT*, Feb. 28, 1947.

16. Brock, *ADA*, p. 60.

17. McAuliffe, *Crisis on the Left*, pp. 23–24.

18. MacDougall, *Gideon's Army*, I:114–17. Although his caucus was the "right-wing" in the UAW, Reuther's position on the U. S. political spectrum was left of center.

19. MacDougall, *Gideon's Army*; Markowitz, *Rise and Fall of the People's Century*; Richard J. Walton, *Henry Wallace, Harry Truman, and the Cold War* (New York, 1976).

20. Local 659 Education Committee, "Build a Labor Party," June 8, 1947, Charles Chiakulas Coll., WSU; Local 659, "Labor Party Resolution for UAW Convention," n.d., Lansing CIO Council Resolution, May 7, 1947, UAW Local 51 Coll., WSU. Emil Mazey continued to oppose both the Democratic and Republican parties in 1947. Mazey to Local presidents, Region I and IA, Apr. 30, 1947, UAW Local 212 Co., WSU.

21. MacDougall, *Gideon's Army*, I:174–75; Brock, *ADA*, pp. 44–52.

22. Barton J. Bernstein and Allen J. Matusow, eds., *The Truman Administration* (New York, 1966), pp. 251–56, 356–63; McAuliffe; *Crisis on the Left*, pp. 23–29; Walton, *Henry Wallace*, pp. 142–51; Hamby, *Beyond the New Deal*, pp. 170–78. Labor Secretary Schwellenbach proposed the outlawing of the Communist party and the barring of Communists from holding office in local unions. *NYT*, Mar. 12, 1947.

23. Minutes of the IEB, Mar. 17–26, 1947, pp, 38–39, WSU; Interview of Percy Llewellyn, Jan. 1, 1982; "A Program for Unity in the UAW–CIO," Louisville, Mar. 20, 1947, WPR Coll., WSU.

24. *NYT*, Aug. 4, 6, 1946, Mar. 17, 1947; Interview of Percy Llewellyn, Jan. 1, 1982; Interview of George Addes, Jan. 23, 1982. See Chapter Ten for details of the Allis-Chalmers strike and the dispute between Thomas and Reuther.

25. *NYT*, Mar. 23, 1947; Minutes of the IEB, pp. 159–61, 174–86.

26. *NYT*, Mar. 29, 1947; *UAW*, Apr. 1947; Roger Keeran, *The Communist Party and the Auto Workers Union* (Bloomington , Ind., 1980), p. 263. The ACTU quotation

is from Irving Howe and B. J. Widick, *The UAW and Walter Reuther* (New York, 1949), p. 151n.

27. *UAW*, April 1947.

28. Minutes of the IEB, Apr. 22–28, 1947, pp. 201–25. On the Schneiderman case, see Chapter Six, note 55.

29. *Ibid.* After the 1940 UAW convention adopted a constitutional amendment barring office–holding by members of illegal organizations, the international terminated some Commmunist and Socialist staff members. Oral History Interview of Leonard Woodcock, Apr. 30, 1963, Michigan Historical Collections, Ann Arbor, Mich.

30. *Ibid.* Keeran states incorrectly that Addes and Thomas supported the right to hold office regardless of political affiliation in Apr. 1946, and then criticizes their retreat from this position. *Communist Party and Auto Workers*, p. 265.

31. Keeran, *Communist Party and Auto Workers, pp. 223-24.*

Chapter Nine

1. Irving Howe and B. J. Widick, *The UAW and Walter Reuther* (New York, 1949). Bert Cochran, *Labor and Communism* (Princeton, N. J., 1977), pp. 214–20, 255–65, 272–79; Harvey A. Levenstein, *Communism, Anticommunism, and the CIO*, (Westport, Conn., 1981), pp. 196–206.

2. *Wage Earner*, May 31, 1946; *DN*, June 11, 1946.

3. *Wage Earner*, June 14, 1946.

4. "Here We Go Again . . . ," "The CIO is Behind Them (Sigman and Grant)," Detroit Association of Catholic Trade Unionists Coll., Box 27, WSU; *Proceedings of the Eighth Annual Convention of the Michigan CIO Council, June 19-22, 1946, Detroit, Michigan* (n.p., n.d.), pp. 7, 85. For Reuther's attempts to remove left–wing staff members, see *Wage Earner*, May 24, May 31, June 7, 1946.

5. August Scholle and Barney Hopkins, *Supplement to Eighth Annual Report, Michigan CIO Eighth Annual Convention, June 10-12, 1946* (n.p., n.d.), p. 4; *Proceedings Eighth Convention Michigan CIO*, pp. 45–46, 70–76, 139–40. See pp. 171–72 above.

6. *Proceedings Eighth Convention Michigan CIO*, pp. 116–21; *Detroit Free Press*, June 15, 1946.

7. "Program Adopted by Michigan State Conference (Sigman and Grant)," Mar. 24, 1946, UAW Local 51 Coll., Box 6, WSU; "The CIO is Behind Them (Sigman and Grant)," ACTU Coll., Box 27.

8. Scholle and Hopkins, *Report*, p. 24; "Program (Sigman and Grant)"; *Proceedings Eighth Convention Michigan CIO*, pp. 127–28; *Proceedings Ninth Annual*

Convention Michigan CIO Council, June 16–18, 1947, Detroit, Michigan (n.p., n.d.), p. 30.

9. Program (Sigman and Grant); *Michigan Chronicle*, June 1, 1946; Minutes Michigan CIO Executive Board, Jan. 19–20, 1946, Paul Brooks *et al.*, "Open Letter to the Delegates of the Eighth Convention of the Michigan CIO Council," ACTU Coll., Box 27.

10. *Proceedings Eighth Convention Michigan CIO*, pp. 16–17. Both caucuses were "in-groups" in the UAW but only the Reuther caucus was truly an "in-group" in the Michigan CIO apparatus. Prior to the convention, the right-wing had a substantial majority on the state CIO executive board, but one staff member, the editor of the *Michigan CIO News*, had not been a Scholle supporter. After the convention, Scholle fired the editor on the grounds that he had "politicked" against him. *Wage Earner*, June 21, 1946.

11. Len DeCaux, *Labor Radical* (Boston, 1970), pp. 316–18; Interview with Percy Llewellyn, Jan. 1, 1982; "Reminiscences of R. J. Thomas," 1956, pp. 205, 233, Oral History Coll., Butler Library, Columbia University; *DT*, June 9, 1946.

12. Interview with Alex Wasilew, June 11, 1984; Interview with Douglas Fraser, August 8, 1984; Interview with Harold Shapiro, August 16, 1985. Previous accounts of this dispute, based principally on the *Wage Earner*, do not mention pressure from the Reuther caucus as a factor. *Wage Earner*, June 14, 1946; Cochran, *Labor and Communism*, pp. 264–65; Jack William Skeels, "The Development of Political Stability within the United Auto Workers Union" (Ph.D. thesis, University of Wisconsin, 1957), p. 279.

13. *Michigan CIO News*, June 21, 1946; *Proceedings Eighth Convention Michigan CIO*, pp. 151–202.

14. *Michigan CIO News*, June 14, 1946; Cochran, *Labor and Communism*, p. 265.

15. The Michigan CIO voting figures in this and subsequent paragraphs are based on the roll call in the *Proceedings Eighth Convention Michigan CIO*, pp. 151–202, and the record of the number of votes carried by the delegates listed in "Michigan CIO Council Convention, 1946," ACTU Coll., Box 27. The UAW convention voting figures are from the roll call in UAW, *Proceedings Tenth Constitutional Convention, Mar. 23–31, 1946, Atlantic City, N. J.* (n.p., n.d.), pp. 336–463.

16. *Proceedings Eighth Convention Michigan CIO*, pp. 22–36, 58–63, 151–202; UAW, *Proceedings Tenth Constitutional Convention*, pp. 290–92.

17. Interview with Douglas Fraser, August 8, 1984; *DN*, June 27, 29, 30, 1946; *Detroit Times*, June 28, 30, 1946; UAW press release, June 30, 1946, UAW Secretary-Treasurer Emil Mazey Coll., Box 2, WSU; *UAW*, July 1945; Walter Reuther, "A Program and Statement of Policy for the UAW–CIO Membership," Apr. 25, 1946, ACTU Coll., Box 33. In his account of the Michigan CIO convention, Cochran states that Addes told reporters "buzzing around convention lobbies" he opposed interference by all outside groups and that Leonard advocated throwing Communists out of the caucus. I could

not confirm in the sources cited by Cochran that these convention incidents occurred. The description of Addes's view is an accurate paraphrase of his postconvention *United Automobile Worker* column, cited by Cochran, and the *Detroit Times* did give Leonard the principal credit for the postconvention proposal to drop the Communists. More importantly, Cochran's presentation is flawed because he ignores the prompt repudiation of the purge idea by both Addes and Leonard and the fact that the Addes–Thomas–Leonard group generally continued to challenge the anticommunist drive. Cochran, *Labor and Communism*, pp. 264, 377.

18. UAW, *Proceedings Tenth Convention* pp. 103–17; June 28, 1946; Interview with Douglas Fraser, August 8, 1984.

19. Cochran, *Labor and Communism*, p. 264; Interview with Douglas Fraser, August 8, 1984; Interview with Leonard Woodcock, February 10, 1982.

20. *Proceedings Ninth Convention Michigan CIO; Michigan CIO News,* June 21 1946; *Wage Earner,* June 13, 1947.

21. "The Speech Scholle Didn't Want You to Hear," 'Sad But True," ACTU Coll., Box 27; "The Issues are Clear," Michigan AFL–CIO Coll., Box 90, WSU; *Proceedings Ninth Convention Michigan CIO,* pp. 55–58.

22. "Scholle Wins CIO Election," *DN* clipping, Michigan CIO Legislative Conference Minutes, Mar. 6, 1947, Michigan CIO Executive Board Minutes, Apr. 1, June 10–11, 1947, ACTU Coll., Box 27; *Ford Facts* reprint, Nov. 9, 1946, Local 51 Coll., Box 6; *Proceedings Ninth Convention Michigan CIO,* p. 55. Shortly after the state CIO convention, Sigler signed several pieces of legislation strongly opposed by the labor movement; mass picketing was outlawed, as were strikes by state employees. *Public and Local Acts of the Legislature of the State of Michigan passed at the Regular Session of 1947* (Lansing, Mich., 1947), pp. 418–19, 467, 524–28, 633–34.

23. *Proceedings Ninth Convention Michigan CIO,* p. 56. The address of the Communist party's Michigan office was 900 Lawyers Building.

24. *Proceedings Ninth Convention Michigan CIO,* p. 41.

25. *Ibid.*, pp. 30, 76–78, 103–4.

26. Barney Hopkins to James Carey, June 27, 1947, CIO Secretary–Treasurer Coll., Box 106, WSU. Carey's reply was not located.

27. *Proceedings Ninth Convention Michigan CIO,* pp. 86–90, 99–102, 110, 119; "It is Fair Practice!! . . . We Negro Delegates Demand!!," Michigan AFL–CIO Coll., Box 90; Interview with Arthur McPhaul, Oct. 7, 1984.

28. Interview with Shelton Tappes, June 3, 1984.

29. *Ibid.; Proceedings Ninth Convention Michigan CIO,* pp. 107–10; *Wage Earner,* June 20, 1947.

30. *Proceedings Ninth Convention Michigan CIO,* pp. 119–25; Interview with Douglas Fraser, Aug. 8, 1984; Interview with Shelton Tappes, June 8, 1984.

31. *Michigan Herald*, July 27, Aug. 3, 1947. Young defeated Alex Fuller of the Steelworkers by a 3-to-2 margin. Some middle-of-the-roaders supported Fuller, including both Glen Sigman and Douglas Fraser. *Wage Earner*, Aug. 1, 1947; Interview with Douglas Fraser, Aug. 8, 1984. For Young's recollection, see Studs Terkel, *American Dreams Lost and Found* (New York, 1980), p. 398. See Chapter Fourteen below for a detailed account of Young's election.

32. *Proceedings Ninth Convention Michigan CIO*, p. 90; *Michigan Herald*, Sept. 7, 1947; Interview with Douglas Fraser, Aug. 8, 1984.

33. Official Report of Election Committee, Michigan CIO Convention, June 18, 1947, Michigan AFL–CIO Coll., Box 7. The analysis of voting patterns is based on the roll calls included in the *Convention Proceedings* and the record of the number of votes carried by the delegates listed in "Michigan CIO Council Convention, 1946," ACTU Coll., Box 27. The latter document has the 1947 vote figures in pencil for locals with 78 percent of the vote. The votes for the remaining locals were estimated, based on the number of delegates and the votes cast at the 1947 UAW convention and the 1946 Michigan CIO convention.

34. *NYT*, Dec. 27, 1946; Homer Watson to Barney Hopkins, Dec. 11, 1946, CIO Secretary–Treasurer Coll., Box 106.

35. *Proceedings Ninth Convention Michigan CIO*, pp. 45–52; Scholle to Alan Haywod, January 16, 1947, Haywood to Scholle, January 27, 1947, Michigan AFL–CIO Coll., Box 7. Antilabor laws were enacted in Michigan shortly after the convention. See note 22 herein.

Chapter Ten

1. Oral History Interview of George Addes, June 25, 1960, pp. 31–32, WSU; Bert Cochran, *Labor and Communism* (Princeton, N. J., 1977), pp. 166–70 , 184–89. In the presidential contest at the 1946 Convention, Thomas led Reuther in Region 4 by 360 votes to 256; Local 248 cast 82 votes for Thomas. *Proceedings of the Tenth Convention*, pp. 337–463.

2. Interview with Harold Christoffel, in Harry Dannenberg *et al.*, "Strike at Allis–Chalmers, 1946–47," Milwaukee Independent School, 1970–1971, copy in author's possession. The quotation is from Robert Ozanne, "The Effect of Communist Leadership in American Trade Unions" (Ph.D. thesis, University of Wisconsin, 1954), pp. 278–81, 287–88, 313.

3. *UAW*, May 1946; Roger Keeran, *The Communist Party and the Auto Workers Unions* (Bloomington, Ind., 1980), pp. 268–69.

4. Robert Ozanne, *A Century of Labor-Management Relations at McCormick and International Harvester* (Madison, Wisconsin, 1967), pp. 208–19; UAW, *Horses, Tractors, and Monopolies* ([Detroit, 1947]), pp. 17–18.

5. *UAW*, May 1946; Keeran, *Communist Party and Auto Workers*, pp. 266–71; Final Report, Oct. 30, 1946, FMCS Case #466–146, FMCS Records, RG 280, National Archives, General Archives Div., Suitland, Md.

6. "Progress Report," Mar. 14, 1946, "Progress Report," Apr. 22, 1946, Conciliation Service Press Release, Apr. 23, 1946, FMCS Case #4466–75, FMCS Records; John Gibson to John R. Steelman, July 10, 1946, Gibson Papers, Harry S. Truman Library, Independence, Mo.

7. Lewis Schwellenbach to Harold Smith, June 4, 1946, General Subject File, Conciliation Service, Records of the Office of the Secretary, Department of Labor, RG 174, NA, Washington; *Racine Labor*, Aug. 16, 1946; Resolution of UAW Local 530, July 15, 1946, UAW press release, June 21, 1946, Gibson Papers; John Morton Blum, ed., *The Price of Vision: The Diary of Henry A. Wallace* (Boston, 1973), p. 576; Resolutions on Government Seizure, UE Local 765, [circa Apr. 1, 1946], FE Local 119, [circa Mar. 20. 1946], FMCS Case #466–75, FMCS Records.

8. Telephone conversation transcript, Gibson, Walter Geist, and Buck Story, Oct. 25, 1946, Gibson Papers; Mr. J. O'Connell to Gibson and Edgar Warren, Oct. 7, 1946, Asst. Secretary John W. Gibson, General Subject File, Records of the Office of the Secretary of Labor. On the situation of the other Allis–Chalmers locals, see Minutes, Allis–Chalmers Workers Council, Sept. 23, 1946, Neil Brant to WPR, Oct. 21, 1946, Local 248 Coll., WSU; Joseph Smith to Fred McStroul, Dec. 8, 1946, Local 248 Coll., Box 5.; R. W. Davis to employees, Sept. 29, 1946, Esther Tice to Brother, May 8, 1947, *UE, Local 765 News*, Feb. 19, 1947, UAW Local 248 Coll.

9. *NYT*, Oct. 30, 31, Nov. 25, 26, Dec. 1, 28, 30, 31, 1946; Keeran, *Communist Party and Auto Workers*, pp. 269–72; Max Raskin to Maurice Sugar and Joseph Mattson, Dec. 17, 1946, Sugar Coll., Box 71, WSU; Interview with Attorney Daniel Sobel in Dannenberg, "Strike at Allis–Chalmers, 1946–1947"; Addes and Mattson to local executive boards and members, Nov. 4, 1946, UAW Local 51 Coll., WSU; Thomas W. Gavett, *Development of the Labor Movement in Milwaukee* (Madison, Wisc., 1965), p. 191.

10. Eugene Dennis, *The Un-Americanism of Hearst's John Sentinel* ([Milwalukee, 1946]), p. 4; Keeran, *Communist Party and Auto Workers*, pp. 269–71; *Milwaukee Sentinel*, Sept. 23, 25, Nov. 21, 1946 in "Strike at Allis–Chalmers, 1946–1947."

11. Keeran, *Communist Party and Auto Workers*, pp. 269–71, Cochran, *Labor and Communism*, p. 273.

12. *DW*, Nov. 25, 26, 28, 1946; *Madison Capital-Times,* Nov. 23, 25, 26, 1946; *UAW*, Dec. 1945; *Milwaukee Journal*, Dec. 12, 1946; Interview with George Addes, Jan. 23, 1982.

13. *NYT*, Nov. 21, 25, Dec. 1, 29, 1946; *Milwaukee Journal*, Dec. 3, 4, 6, 1946; *UAW*, Jan. 1947; Election Committee Reports, Feb. 26, 1945, Feb. 20–21, 1946, UAW Local 248 Coll., WSU; "Duffy Formula," *Federated Press* release, Jan. 24, 1947, UAW Local 248 Coll., Box 3, WSU.

14. Minutes of the IEB, Dec. 9–18, 1946, pp. 10–11, 54, WSU. Estimates of the number returning to work varied. In December the sheriff reported that about 7,400 employees entered the plant, of whom about 2,500 were production workers. Reuther reported to the UAW board in mid–March that 5,000 to 6,000 had returned to work. Based on these figures, I have estimated that 4,000 members of the Local 248 bargaining unit were back to work by January 1947. *Milwaukee Journal*, Dec. 11, 1946; Minutes of the IEB, Mar. 17–26, 1947, p. 19.

15. *Milwaukee Journal*, Dec. 2, 4, 5, 9, 1946, Jan. 19, 1947; *Madison Capital-Times*, Dec. 14, 15, 16, 1946; R. J. Thomas to Local Unions, Feb. 7, 1947, "Why was the Independent Union Formed?," and related exhibits sent by Thomas to locals, Nat Ganley Coll., Box 1, WSU. On the county council conflict, see *Milwaukee Journal* clippings, Oct. 6, 7, 9, 11, 16, 17, Wisconsin Industrial Union Council Coll., Wisconsin State Archives, Madison, Wisc.

16. R. J. Thomas to Local Unions, Feb. 7, 1947, and attached exhibits, Ganley Coll., Box. 1.

17. *FPEB*, Dec. 10, 1946, *FP* Coll., Butler Library, Columbia University, New York; *The Daily Picket*, Jan. 13, 1947, in Dannenberg, "Strike at Allis–Chalmers, 1946–1947;" *Milwaukee Journal*, Jan. 26, 1947; Wisconsin State Industrial Union Council press release, Jan. 3, 1947, Records of the Wisconsin Employee Relations Board, Box 40, Wisconsin State Historical Society.

18. R. J. Thomas to Local Unions, Feb. 7, 1947 and attached exhibits, Ganley Coll., Box 1; *Milwaukee Journal*, Jan. 19, 22, 23, 26, 1946; John Brophy to WPR, Jan. 31, 1947, R. J. Thomas Coll., Box 10, WSU; Minutes of the IEB, Dec. 9–18, 1946, pp. 1–11, 54–55; Mar. 17–26, 1947, p. 9.

19. R. J. Thomas to Local Unions, Feb. 7, 1947, Ganley Coll., Box 1.

20. R. J. Thomas to Local Unions, Feb. 7, 1947 and attached exhibits, Ganley Coll., Box 1; *Milwaukee Journal*, Jan. 19, 23, 26, 1946; John Brophy to WPR, Jan, 31, 1947, WPR to Thomas, Feb. 11, 1947, Thomas Coll., Box 10; *DW*, Jan. 24, 25, 1947; John Brophy, *A Miner's Life* (Madison, Wisc., 1964), pp. 292–94.

21. R. J. Thomas to Local Unions, Feb. 7, 1947 and attached exhibits, Ganley Coll., Box 1; UAW Local 248 press release, Feb. 8, 1947, Local 248 Coll., Box 3, WSU; Wisconsin Employee Relations Board, Case X, No. 1523 E–567, Decision on Challenged Ballots and Proposed Certification of Representatives, Feb. 3, 1947, Amended Decision on Challenged Ballots and Report of Recount, Feb. 11, 1947, WERB Records, Box 40. On Apr. 2, 1947, the WERB ruled that whether Local 248 had won a majority was contingent on the counting of the votes of union officers Robert Buse and Joseph Dombek, dismissed by the company prior to the election. A decision on those ballots was to be made when the NLRB disposed of their charges of discrimination. A new NLRB representation election led to the eventual dismissal of the WERB case. Temporary Certification of Results of Election Apr. 2, 1947, WERB Records, Box 40.

22. Wisconsin State Industrial Union Council, press release, Jan. 3, 1947, Closed Labor Dispute File Cases, WERB Records, Box 40; Interview with Harold Christoffel, Dec. 2, 1983.

23. R. J. Thomas to Local Unions, Feb. 7, 1947 and attached exhibits, Ganley Coll., Box 1; WPR to Thomas, Feb. 11, 1947, John Brophy to WPR, Jan. 31, 1947, Thomas Coll., Box 10; Noel Fox to Edgar L. Warren, Mar. 2, 1947, FMCS Case #466–75, FMCS Records; *Milwaukee Journal*, Jan. 27, 28, 29, 30, 1947, *DW*, Jan. 28, 1947; Joseph Mattson, Report to the Region, c. Feb. 1947, David Rothstein papers, Chicago Historical Society.

24. R. J. to Local Unions, Feb. 7, 1947, Ganley Coll., Box 1; WPR to Thomas, Feb. 11, 1947, Thomas Coll., Box 9; Minutes of the IEB, Mar. 17–26, 1947, pp. 159–61.

25. Keeran, *Communist Party and Auto Workers*, pp. 272–78; *UAW*, March 1947; *NYT*, Mar. 2, 1947; *Milwaukee Journal*, Mar. 1, 2, 1947.

26. Keeran , *Communist Party and Auto Workers*, pp. 272–78; *DW*, Mar. 24, 1947, *UAW*, April 1947; Hearing before the WERB, Case XII, No. 1634, Apr. 9, 1947, WERB Records, Box 40.

27. Local 248, "Reuther Serves Allis-Chalmers Co.," Ganley, Box 1; *DW*, June 30, July 20, 1947; Clipping, *Times Herald*, Aug. 8, 1947, Gibson Papers; Keeran, *Communist Party and Auto Workers*, pp. 272–78.

28. Minutes of the IEB, Mar. 8, 1947, pp. 3, 10–13, Mar. 17–26, p. 18.

29. Keeran, *Communist Party and Auto Workers*, pp. 272–78.

Chapter Eleven

1. *FP*CB, Aug. 9, 1946, *FP* Coll., Butler Library, Columbia University, New York; Paul R. Harvey to William Johnson, Oct. 8, 1946, UAW Ford Dept. Coll., Box 8, WSU. The quotation is from Minutes of the IEB, Aug. 5–18. 1946, p. 45, WSU.

2. "National Chrysler Conference," July 9–10, 1946, UAW Local 51 Coll., Box 30, WSU; National Chrysler Conference Minutes, July 9–10, 1946, Nat Ganley Coll., WSU.

3. Minutes of the IEB, Aug. 5–18, 1946, pp. 45–52, 64–66, 196–207.

4. *Ibid.*

5. *Ibid.*

6. Joel Seidman, *American Labor from Defense to Reconversion* (Chicago, 1953), pp. 239–40; *Labor Fact Book* (New York, 1947): 40; BLS, *Handbook of Labor Statistics*, Bull. No. 916 (Washington, 1947), p. 107; UAW press release, Oct. 6, 1946, WPR Coll., WSU.

7. The average work week was less than 40 hours due to layoffs. *Labor Statistics*, p. 62; *UAW*, Aug. 1946.

8. Nat Ganley, "Present Wage–Price Situation," Sept. 28, 1946, Ganley Coll., Box 9; Minutes of Chrysler Presidents' Meeting, Oct. 16, 1946, Local 51 Coll., Box 23.

9. Minutes of the IEB, Oct. 18–20, 1946, pp. 18–49; *NYT*, Oct. 21, 1946.

10. "Meeting Top [GM] Negotiation Committee with Walter P. Reuther," Oct. 8, 1946, WPR Coll.; George F. Addes, *Planning for Better Health* (n.p., [1946]), p.6.

11. "Notes on Chrysler–UAW Wage Negotiations," Oct. 30–31, 1946, WPR Coll.; *FP*CB, Nov. 15, 1946, *FP* Coll.

12. Minutes of the IEB, Aug. 5–18, 1946, pp. 213–30.

13. Minutes of the IEB, Oct. 18–20, 1946, pp. 39–40. Murray also emphasized his strong desire for a peaceful settlement in his public remarks at the CIO convention in November. *Proceedings of the Eighth CIO Convention* pp. 243–45.

14. *NYT*, Dec. 13, 14, 1946; Minutes of the IEB, Dec. 9–18, 1946, pp. 58–66. Reuther denied that Murray opposed the setting of a specific wage demand. The comments of Murray and his staff to journalists indicated the opposite. *NYT*, Dec. 13, 14, 16, 17, 1946; *New Republic* 114 (Dec. 30, 1946): 924, 115 (Jan. 20, 1947): 44.

15. Minutes of the IEB, Dec. 9–18, 1946, pp. 58–66.

16. *NYT*, Dec. 14, 1946, Jan. 23, 29, Feb. 27, 1947; Minutes of the IEB, Mar. 17–26, 1947.

17. *NYT*, Apr. 13, 15, 16, 1947.

18. *NYT*, Apr. 18, 192, 22, 1947; WPR to Albert Fitzgerald, Apr. 15, 1947, WPR Coll.; Minutes of the IEB, Apr. 15, 1947, pp. 1–6; *Michigan Herald*, June 22, 1947. When the president of Reuther's home local wired Murray asking if he approved the UE agreement, the CIO president waited a week before replying that the UE was an autonomous union. Edward J. Cote to Murray, Apr. 15, 1947, Murray to Cote, Apr. 22, 1947, Murray Papers, Box A4–37, Catholic University, Washington. The Greater Detroit Construction, Maintenance, and Powerhouse Workers Council called the UE settlement a "sell-out." *Maintenance News*, May 15, 1947, John Oneka Coll., Box 3, WSU.

19. *Michigan Herald*, June 22, 1947; *NYT*, Apr. 13, 19, 1947; *Business Week* #922 (Apr. 27, 1947): 80.

20. Bruce R. Morris, "Industrial Relations in the Automobile Industry," in *Labor and Postwar America*, Colston E. Warne *et al.* eds. (Brooklyn, 1949), p. 415; *NYT*, Apr. 15, 16, 22, 23, 25, 1947; Minutes of the IEB, Apr. 15, 1947, pp. 15–16; Thomas to WPR, Apr. 11, 1947, "What was the UAW–CIO Position on Wage Increases?," R. J. Thomas Coll., Box 10, WSU; WPR to Thomas, Apr. 8, 1947, WPR Coll. The quotation is from Robert M. MacDonald, *Collective Bargaining in the Automobile Industry* (New Haven, Conn., 1963), pp. 73–74.

21. MacDonald, *Collective Bargaining in the Automobile Industry*, p. 33; *Michigan Herald*, June 22, 1947; *DFP*, Apr. 25, 1947.

22. *DN*, Apr. 24, 1947; *Flint Journal*, Apr. 26, 1947.

23. *Business Week* No. 929 (June 21, 1947): 84.

24. *Labor Statistics*, 1947, p. 107.

25. *NYT*, May 6, 27, 29, 1947. Bugas is quoted in Ken Bannon to Jack Conway, Mar 25, 1948, UAW Ford Dept. Coll., Box 5. Leonard is quoted in *UAW*, June 1947.

26. *UAW*, June 1947; Tommy Thompson to WPR, June 29, 1947, WPR Coll.; Minutes of the IEB, Aug. 2, 1947, pp. 8–85.

27. Reuther denied a *New York Times* report that he engineered the meeting between Ford and Murray in New York. Minutes of the IEB, Aug. 2, 1947, pp. 27–29.

28. Minutes of the IEB, Aug. 2, 1947. The protective clause established a union-management committee that was given a year to devise a solution to the question of liability. During this period the company could not institute suits for damages. If the committee was unable to agree, the UAW was free to strike on the issue. *UAW*, Aug. 1947.

29. *NYT*, Aug. 23, 1947; *UAW*, Sept. 1947.

30. Ed Lock *et al*. "A Letter to the Ford National Bargaining Committee . . . ," WPR Coll.; Minutes of the National Ford Council, July 28, 1947, pp. 19, 29; Aug. 5, 1947, p. 26; Aug. 21, 1947, p. 25, Ganley Coll., Box 33; Minutes of the IEB, Aug. 2, 1947, pp. 32–34, 70–72; Frank Ellis to locals, Oct. 4, 1947, Local 51 Coll., Box 26; *Michigan Herald*, Sept. 21, 1947.

Chapter Twelve

1. Irving Howe and B. J. Widick, *The UAW and Walter Reuther* (New York, 1949). Bert Cochran and Harvey Levenstein also overemphasized the Reuther caucus's wartime progress on this issue. Cochran, *Labor and Communism* (Princeton, N. J., 1977), pp. 214–220; Harvey A. Levenstein, *Communism, Anticommunism, and the CIO* (Westport, Conn., 1981), pp. 196–206.

2. "Communist Part in Proposed GM Contract," Feb. 20, 1941, Class. No. 242, Labor—Strike and Disputes Folder, Policy Documentation File, Records of the War Production Board, RG 179, National Archives, Washington. The umpire system involved placing an impartial arbitrator at the last step of the grievance procedure.

3. Victor Reuther is quoted in Nelson Lichtenstein, *Labor's War at Home* (Cambridge [Cambridgeshire], 1982), p. 226. See Chapter Four herein.

4. See Chapter Four, Five, and Six herein for a detailed discussion of these issues.

5. *NYT*, Aug. 4, 1946; *UAW*, Aug. 1946.

6. *NYT*, Apr. 18, Aug. 4, 6, 1946; Victor Reuther, *The Brothers Reuther and the Story of the UAW* (Boston, 1976), p. 258; Minutes of the IEB, Apr. 16–21, 1946, pp. 10–11, WSU.

7. Hilliard Ellis to WPR, Aug. 2, 1946, WPR to Ellis, Aug. 22, 1946, WPR Coll., WSU.

8. *Milwaukee Journal*, Dec. 9, 1946; *Hartford Times*, Dec. 9, 1946.

9. Richard Gosser, "What the Labor–Management–Citizens' Committee Has Accomplished . . . ," ". . . Remarks of . . . R. J. Thomas to National Wage Conference . . . ." Jan. 18, 1947, "Report of Mayor's Labor–Management–Citizens' Committee, May 8, 1947, WPR Coll.; *UAW*, Apr. 1947; *Michigan Herald*, May 18, 1947. The WPR quotation is from a *Hartford Times* clipping, Dec. 9, 1946, WPR Coll.

10. *Michigan Herald*, May 18, 1947.

11. *UAW*, May 1946.

12. On the UAW–FE merger and Taft–Hartley affidavits issues, see below, pp. 205–09.

13. "Management–Labor Cooperation in Cutting Costs," Aug. 8, 1947, Nat Ganley Coll., Box 8, WSU; UAW Press Release, Aug. 27, 1947, WPR Coll., Box 15; *UAW*, Sept. 1947.

14. *UAW*, Oct. 1947 (Special Edition); Minutes of the IEB, Sept. 22–24, 1947, pp. 153–58.

15. *Michigan Herald*, Sept. 21, Oct. 12, 1947; Ellsworth Kramer to WPR, Sept. 8, 1947, WPR Coll.; "The Betrayal of the Production Workers . . . ," "Time to Wake Up!," Ganley Coll. Even Reuther supporters complained bitterly about the GM Board of Review's throwing out grievances and the GM Department's negotiation of supplements to the agreement without ratification by the locals. Neal Edwards to WPR, Dec. 13, 1946, Neal Edwards Coll., Box 1, WSU; Russell White to WPR, Jan. 2, 1947, Resolution of Local 652, WPR Coll., Box 25. See also Minutes of the IEB, Dec. 9–18, 1946, pp. 105–10.

16. Minutes of the IEB, Sept. 22–24, 1947, pp. 153–54; Kramer to WPR, Sept. 8, 1947, WPR Coll., Box 37. The quotation is from *UAW*, Sept. 1947.

17. Minutes of the IEB, Apr. 15, 1947, pp. 14–16.

Chapter Thirteen

1. Minutes of the IEB, Mar. 17–26, 1947, pp. 159–61, Apr. 22–28, 1947, pp. 20–22, WSU; Michigan CIO Legislative Conference Minutes, Mar. 6, 1947, ACTU Coll., WSU.

2. GM Sub–Council Number 3 to WPR, Apr. 14, 1947, WPR Coll.; R. Alton Lee, *Truman and Taft–Hartley* (Lexington, Ken., 1966), p. 67; *UAW*, Apr. 1947; *DW*, Apr. 15, 1947; Minutes of the IEB, Mar. 17–26, 1947, pp. 82–83, Apr. 15, 1947, pp. 6, 13.

3. Minutes of the IEB, Apr. 22–28, 1947, pp. 4, 20–22.

4. *UAW*, May 1947; *DFP*, Apr. 25, 1947; *DN*, Apr. 25, 1947; *Voice of Local 212*, May 16, 1947; Minutes of Local Presidents Meetings, May 12, 1947, Local 212 Coll., Box 9, WSU.

5. "Meeting of Discharged and Disciplined Workers," Apr. 30, 1947, Nat Ganley Coll., Box 8, WSU; WPR, "Notes on . . . Disciplining of GM Leaders," WPR Coll.; Minutes of Local Presidents Meeting, May 12, 1947, Local 212 Coll., Box 9; *Michigan Herald*, May 11, 1947. The quotation is from "Resolution on GM's 'Drastic Action' Penalties," WPR Coll.

6. Minutes of the IEB, Apr. 22–28, 1947, pp. 244–46; UAW–GM Memorandum of Understanding, May 8, 1947, WPR, "Notes on . . . Disciplining of GM Leaders," A. L. Zwerdling to WPR, May 6, 1947, WPR Coll.; Minutes of Local Presidents Meeting, May 12, 1947; George Addes to Tony Czerwinski, May 2, 1947, Local 212 Coll., Box 9. A number of locals sent telegrams expressing concern over the firings. See WPR Coll.

7. Minutes of Local Presidents Meeting, May 12, 1947, Local 212 Coll., Box 9; WPR, "Notes on . . . Disciplining of GM Leaders," WPR Coll.

8. On the 1947 Michigan CIO convention, see above, pp. 226–34.

9. Daniel B. Crowder, "Profile in Progress: History of Local 287, UAW–CIO" (Ph.D. thesis, Ball State University, 1969), pp. 185–87; *UAW*, May 1947; Lee, *Truman and Taft-Hartley*, pp. 80–100; *DW*, June 12, 16, 1947.

10. Resolution of Local 477, Chiakulas Coll., Box 21, WSU; "Resolution adopted by a conference of Region 2 and 2A . . . ," R. J. Thomas Coll., Box 11, WSU; *Michigan Herald*, June 29, 1947; Proceedings of the CIO Executive Board, May 16–17, 1947, pp. 6–10; June 27, 1947, pp. 132–41; WSU.

11. Susan Hartman, *Truman and the Eightieth Congress* (Columbia, Mo., 1971), pp. 87–90; *DW*, July 2, 1947; MacDougall, *Gideon's Army*, I: 178–79. Reynolds is quoted in James A. Gross, *The Reshaping of the National Labor Relations Board*, 2 vols. (Albany, N. Y., 1981), 2: 258–59.

12. Lee, *Truman and Taft-Hartley*, pp. 62–66, 110; Interview with Leonard Woodcock, Feb. 9, 1982. Some of the provisions of the law did not have the impact they were expected to have. Overwhelming rank–and–file votes in favor of the union shop in NLRB ballots helped to extend this form of union security. Closed shops continued to have a *de facto* existence, as did some forms of the secondary boycott. Clyde W. Summers, "A Summary Evaluation of the Taft-Hartley Act," *Industrial and Labor Relations Review* 11 (Apr. 1958): 405–12.

13. R. J. Thomas to Local Unions, Feb. 7, 1947 and attached exhibits, Nat Ganley Coll., WSU; *NYT*, Mar. 29, 1947.

14. Minutes of the IEB, Apr. 22–28, 1947, pp. 166–68, June 9–13, 1947, pp. 147–53; "Proposal for Merger of UAW–CIO and FE–CIO," Addes to Local Recording Secretarys, June 16, 1947, Local 51, Coll., Box 12, WSU.

15. *NYT,* July 16, 1947; "Real Purpose of the FE Political Maneuver," Michigan AFL–CIO Coll., Box 90, WSU. Reuther is quoted in *Michigan CIO News,* July 16, 1947, and in *UAW,* Aug. 1947.

16. Interview with George Addes, Jan. 23, 1982; Interview of Jack Conway by Frank Cormier and William Eaton, Oct. 13, 1967, p. 13, Cormier and Eaton Papers, John F. Kennedy Library, Boston; Oral History Interview of Leonard Woodcock, Apr. 30, 1963, pp. 37–38, Oral History Interview of Ken Morris, June 28, 1963, pp. 49–50, Michigan Historical Collections, Ann Arbor, Mich. There are conflicting figures on the precise votes in the merger referendum. See *UAW,* Aug. 1947; Addes to WPR, July 18, 1947, WPR Coll. Box 125; "Recapitulation of Vote on Merger Proposal," Art Hughes Coll., Box 3, WSU.

17. Interview with Martin Gerber, Feb. 12, 1982; Frank Emspak, "The Break-Up of the Congress of Industrial Organizations (CIO), 1945–1950, (Ph.D. thesis, University of Wisconsin, 1972), p. 169; Interview with Leonard Woodcock, Feb. 10, 1982.

18. Interview with George Addes, Jan. 23, 1982.

19. Lee, *Truman and Taft-Hartley,* pp. 185–88; *DW,* Aug. 21, 1947; Oral History Interview of Carl Haessler, pp. 194–95, Nov. 27, 1959–Oct. 24, 1960, Michigan Historical Collections; *NYT,* July 18, 1947. Some Reutherite regional directors later stated they had disagreed with the initial noncompliance decision, but no dissenting votes were recorded in the minutes. Minutes of the IEB, July 9, 1947, pp. 17–18, Sept. 8–12, 1947, pp. 37–38.

20. Minutes of the IEB, Sept. 8–12, 1947, p. 146; MacDougall, *Gideon's Army,* I: 187–88; *DW,* Sept. 2, 1947.

21. Minutes of the IEB, Sept. 8–12, 1947; pp. 28–30.

22. *Ibid.,* pp. 119–45,

23. *Ibid.,* pp. 107–15, 174–87.

24. Proceedings of the CIO Executive Board, Oct. 8–17, 1947, pp. 59–72, 84–88, 122–24, WSU; *Proceedings of the Ninth CIO Convention,* pp. 186–204.

25. Interview with George Addes, Jan. 23, 1982; Interview with Martin Gerber, Feb. 12, 1982. See Chapter Fifteen herein for a discussion of the campaigns for convention delegates.

26. *UAW,* Nov. 1947; Addes to WPR, Oct. 31, 1947, WPR Coll., Box 65.

27. Oral History Interview of Carl Haessler, Nov. 27, 1959–Oct. 24, 1960, pp. 194–95; Interview with George Addes, Jan. 23, 1982. Denham had originally set an August 22 deadline, but he extended it first to September 29 and then to October 31 because so many unions were not complying. After the CIO abandoned its united front against compliance, there were no further extensions. Proceedings of the CIO Executive Board, Oct. 8–17, 1947, pp. 84–85.

Chapter Fourteen

1. See, for example, August Meier and Elliot Rudwick, *Black Detroit and the Rise of the UAW* (New York, 1979), pp. 209–12. Bert Cochran has a somewhat modified version of this argument. *Labor and Communism* (Princeton, N. J., 1977), pp. 220–28. Roger Keeran, on the other hand, emphasizes the positive role of the Communists. *The Communist Party and the Auto Workers Unions* (Bloomington, Ind., 1980), pp. 231–35.

2. Interview with Chris Alston, Aug. 18, 1985; Dominic J. Capeci, Jr., *Race Relations in Wartime Detroit: The Sojourner Truth Housing Controversy of 1942* (Philadelphia, 1984), pp. 70–74; Meier and Rudwick, *Black Detroit*, pp. 126–130, 211–12n.

3. Ray Marshall, *The Negro and Organized Labor* (New York, 1965), pp. 34–49; John Baxter Streater, Jr., "The National Negro Congress, 1936–1947" (Ph.D. thesis, University of Cincinnati, 1981), pp. 78–79, 158–59.

4. During the factional split in the UAW, a few Black unionists sided with Homer Martin and one of these, Frank Evans, was elected to the UAW–AFL executive board at its 1939 founding convention. Given the history of the AFL's failure to open its ranks to Black workers, the action of the Martin group was surprising. Given Martin's ties to the Ford Motor Company, however, it appears that the AFL group was attempting to position itself to win the right to represent the Ford workers by taking advantage of Ford's attempt to appear as a friend of the Black community. When Black workers at the UAW–CIO convention raised the issue of Black representation on the board, their idea was given short shrift by R. J. Thomas, the moderate chosen by the CIO leaders to serve as the new UAW president. The CIO was nevertheless able to win the support of most Black workers and defeat the alliance between the Ford Motor Company and the UAW–AFL in 1941. Meier and Rudwick, *Black Detroit*, pp. 64–65; Martin Halpern, "The 1941 Strike at the Ford Motor Company," unpublished paper, 1973.

5. *Michigan Chronicle*, Sept. 18, 25, October 2, 1943 (including clippings, Vertical File, WSU). The committee minority originally proposed that the constitutional amendment specifiy a Black director who would carry votes equal to the average of other board members (about 30). In response to the criticism that this would be a "Jim Crow" office, the minority dropped the requirement that the director be Black, but remained confident that a Black would be selected if the convention accepted the minority report. To respond to Reuther caucus concerns that the Black board member would tip the factional balance to the Addes caucus, the minority reduced the number of votes to be carried to one. UAW, *Proceedings of the Eighth Constitutional Convention, October 4–10, 1943, Buffalo, N. Y.* (n.p., n.d.), pp. 370–89.

6. *Michigan Chronicle*, Aug. 8, 1942, Sept. 25, Oct. 2, 9, 16, 1943, (including clippings, Vertical File.)

7. Interview with Dave Moore, Sept. 17, 1985.

8. *Proceedings of the Eighth Convention*, pp. 373–74, 384.

9. Philip S. Foner, *American Socialism and Black Americans* (Westport, Conn., 1977), pp. 340–63.

10. *Proceedings of the Eighth Convention*, pp. 377–78, 382–83.

11. Sheffield to WPR, Oct. 7, 1948, WPR Coll., Box 249, WSU. More recently, Sheffield reaffirmed his 1943 position and maintained that the Reuther group had not used the reverse discrimination argument. Interview with Horace Sheffield, Aug. 17, 1985.

12. Interview with George Crockett, September 15, 1985, Oral History Interview with George Crockett, February 2, 1968, WSU; Clipping, *Detroit Free Press*, October 5, 1944, Vertical File, WSU.

13. See above, pp. 94–95.

14. Robert Weaver, *Negro Labor* (New York, 1946), pp. 69–74; UAW press release, April 7, 1946, Region V, FEPC, affidavit by Edward Swan, Admin. files, FEPC, FEPC Records, National Archives. Interview with George Crockett, Sept. 15, 1985; Oral History Interview with Shelton Tappes,. Feb. 10, 1968, pp. 17–20, WSU.

15. Interview with George Crockett, September 15, 1985. The second quotation is from Oral History Interview of Shelton Tappes, Feb. 10, 1968, p. 14, WSU. George Crockett to Walter Reuther, Oct. 23, 1945, George Crockett Coll., WSU; *Daily Worker*, Sept. 12, 1945, Apr. 13, 1946; Shelton Tappes to Walter Reuther, Apr. 14, 1945, Reuther to Tappes, Apr. 23, 1945, WPR Coll., Peter Friedlander, *The Emergence of a UAW Local, 1936-1939* (Pittsburgh, 1975), pp. 115–16; Oral History Interview of John Bartee, Apr. 30, 1961, Michigan Historical Coll., Ann Arbor, Mich. See also pp. 237–39 above.

16. Interview with George Crockett, Sept. 15, 1985; Keeran, *Communist Party*, pp. 231–35; Interview with Shelton Tappes, June 3, 1984; Interview with Chris Alston, Aug. 18, 1985; Interview with Dave Moore, Sept. 17, 1985; Interview with Oscar Noble, Aug. 5, 1984.

17. There was a qualitative deterioration of the Black position in the industry during reconversion as Black workers were more often downgraded into less skilled jobs than were white workers. See Chapter Three herein.

18. Minutes of the IEB, Apr. 16–26, 1946, pp. 35–43, WSU; *United Automobile Worker*, May 1946; *SW*, June 27, 1948; Saul Wellman, "The Party and the Trade Unions," *Emphasis!*, Nat Ganley Coll., Box 31; Arthur C. McPhaul, Report on a Negro in Top Office in the UAW–CIO, [c. Aug. 1947], Ganley Coll., Box 7; Typed draft of Keynote Address, 1948 Convention, Communist Party of Michigan, Nat Ganley–Saul Wellman Coll., Box 1, WSU; Interview with Shelton Tappes, June 3, 1984; Interview with Arthur McPhaul, Oct. 7, 1984.

19. Arthur C. McPhaul, Report on a Negro in Top Office in the UAW–CIO, [c. Aug. 1947], Ganley Coll., Box 7; Interview with Arthur McPhaul, Oct. 7, 1984. See pp. 230–32 above for an account of the events at the 1947 state CIO convention.

20. Clippings, *Michigan Chronicle*, July 16, 1943, *Wage Earner*, Jan. 8, Dec. 17, 1943, *CIO Councillor*, June 25, 1945, VF; Interview with Betty Yochim, Aug. 25,1985.

21. Clippings, *Michigan Chronicle*, July 16, 1943, *Wage Earner*, Dec. 17, 1943, *CIO Councillor*, June 25, 1945, VF; Interview with Betty Yochim, Aug. 25, 1985.

22. Interview with James Jackson, Oct. 23, 1983. The second quotation is from interview with Shelton Tappes, June 3, 1984.

23. *Michigan Herald*, Sept. 7, 1947; Interview with Douglas Fraser, Aug. 8, 1984.

24. Interview with Harold Shapiro, Aug. 16, 1985; Interview with Dave Moore, Sept. 17, 1985.

25. Interview with Douglas Fraser, Aug. 8, 1984; *Michigan Herald*, Aug. 3, 1947.

26. Interview with Hodges Mason, July 21, 1984; Interview with Arthur McPhaul, Oct. 7, 1984; Interview with Harold Shapiro, Aug. 16, 1985; Interview with James Jackson, Oct. 23, 1983.

27. The Young quotations are from an interview published in Studs Terkel, *American Dreams Lost and Found* (New York, 1980), pp. 355–68; Interview with Hodges Mason, July 21, 1984; Meier and Rudwick, *Black Detroit*, pp. 103n, 113; Capeci, *Race Relations in Wartime Detroit*, pp. 111–12; Interview with Harold Shapiro, August 16, 1985; Interview with James Jackson, October 23, 1983; Patrick James Ashton, "Race, Class and Black Politics: The Implications of the Election of a Black Mayor for the Police and Policing in Detroit" (Ph.D. thesis, Michigan State University, 1981), pp. 296–98; Streater, "National Negro Congress," p. 333.

28. Interview with Shelton Tappes, June 3, 1984. Harold Shapiro recalled that the coalition of non–UAW unions was one of the sources of Young's strength. Interview with Harold Shapiro, August 16, 1985. A somewhat different version of the process of selection was given by Arthur McPhaul, a leading Black leftist from Local 600. McPhaul recalled that when "things weren't going so good on the convention floor," he called the Black delegates off the floor into a caucus to report that it "had been decided" the previous night that Young would be the candidate. The Black caucus went along with a decision made elsewhere, according to McPhaul. Interview with Arthur McPhaul, Oct. 7, 1984. Another Local 600 Black leader, Dave Moore, recalls the decision as one of the Black caucus itself, with even Fuller joining in a unanimous vote. Interview with Dave Moore, Sept. 17, 1985.

29. Interview with Dave Moore, Sept. 17, 1985.

30. Interview by telephone with Stanley Nowak, Aug. 12, 1985; Interview with Harold Shapiro, Aug. 16, 1985; Interview with James Jackson, Oct. 23, 1983.

31. Election Results, Wayne County CIO Convention, July 26, 1947, Merle E. Hendrickson Coll., Box 2, WSU; *Wage Earner*, August 1, 1947; Interview with Douglas Fraser, Aug. 8, 1984; *Michigan Chronicle*, Aug. 2, 1947.

32. Martin Halpern, "The Politics of Auto Union Factionalism: The Michigan CIO in the Cold War Era," *Michigan Historical Review* 13 (Fall 1987): 51–73.

33. Interview with Arthur McPhaul, Oct. 7, 1984.

34. *Michigan Herald*, Aug. 3, 1947.

35. Interview with Douglas Fraser, Aug. 8, 1984.

36. Resolution on House Un–American Committee, July 25, 1947, Civil Rights Congress Coll., Box 41, WSU; *Michigan Herald*, Aug. 3, 1947, *Wage Earner*, Aug. 1, 1947.

37. Minutes of the Wayne CIO Executive Board, July 30, 1947, Metropolitan Detroit AFL–CIO Coll., Box 30, WSU; Minutes of the Wayne County Executive Board, July 30, Aug. 12, 1947, Minutes of the Wayne County CIO Delegate Body, Aug. 19, 1947, Report on Campaign to Repeal the Callahan Act, Aug. 19, 1947, Metropolitan Detroit AFL–CIO Coll., Box 30. See also Committee to Repeal the Callahan Act, "Put It on the Ballot Bulletin!," (Communist Party) Memorandum #2 on the Campaign for the Repeal of the Callahan Act. Civil Rights Congress Coll., Box 33. When a referendum on the Callahan Act was placed before the voters (by action of the legislature) in Nov. 1948, it was approved by a vote of 890,435 to 585,469. *Michigan Manual, 1949*, p. 306.

38. Interview with Shelton Tappes, June 3, 1984; Interview with James Jackson, Oct. 23, 1983, Interview with Harold Shapiro, Aug. 17, 1985, Interview with Arthur McPhaul, Oct. 7, 1984; Interview with Betty Yochim, Aug. 25, 1985.

39. *Michigan Chronicle*, Aug. 2, 1947; U. S. Congress, House of Representatives, 82nd Congress, 2d Session, Committee on Un–American Activities, *Hearings on Communism in the Detroit Area*, Part 1, 1952, pp. 2888–89. Davis was actually the second Black council member elected in New York City; Adam Clayton Powell, Jr., was the first.

40. *Michigan Chronicle*, Oct. 4, 1947.

41. Minutes of the Wayne County CIO Executive Board, July 30, Aug 26, 1947; *Michigan Chronicle*, Sept. 6, 1947; *Michigan Herald*, Sept. 7, 1947.

42. *Michigan Chronicle*, Aug. 30, Sept. 6, 13, 20, 27, Oct. 4, 11, 18, 25, Nov. 1, 8, 1947.

43. Interview with Harold Shapiro, Aug. 16, 1985; Terkel, *American Dreams*, p. 363.

Chapter Fifteen

1. Frank Cormier and William J. Eaton, *Reuther* (Englewood Cliffs, N. J., 1970), p. 248; Committee for UAW–CIO Progress and Unity, "Is It So Illogical?," Local 51 Coll., Box 25, WSU; "The Issues and the Answers," Bull. No. 2, Oct. 14, 1947, Local 212 Coll., Box 13, WSU; Oscar Cohen to WPR, Oct. 15, 1947, L. M. Birkhead to WPR, n.d., WPR Coll., WSU; *The Cross and the Flag*, 5 (Jan. 1947): 8888.

2. *UAW*, Sept., Oct. (Special Edition), 1947; Elizabeth Hawes, *Hurry Up Please Its (sic) Time* (New York, 1946), pp. 177–91, 199–206; Minutes of the IEB, Apr. 22–28, 1947, p. 168, WSU; *Report of the President to 12th UAW Convention, July 10, 1949* (n.p., 1949), pp. 116–17; Interview with Jack White, June 1976.

3. *UAW*, Sept., Oct. (Special Edition), 1947; Minutes of the IEB, Sept. 22–24, 1947, pp. 158–79.

4. *UAW*, Sept., Oct. (Special Edition), 1947.

5. "Open Letter to Packard Members," "The Voice of Chrysler Workers," "Support Walter Reuther, Vote for Paul Duncan," WPR to Local 142, Oct. 3, 1947, WPR Coll.

6. *Michigan Herald*, Oct. 12, 26, Nov. 2, 9, 1947; *Local 599 Headlight*, Oct. 2, 1947.

7. *DW*, Nov., 14, 26, 1947; "Had Enough Factionalism," UAW Local 212 Coll., Box 17; Interview with George Addes, Jan. 23, 1982; Interview with Martin Gerber, Feb. 12, 1982.

8. Report of the Fair Practices Department, Dec. 10, 1946, WPR Coll.; WPR to Local Unions, May 18, 1946, WPR and William Oliver to Local Union Presidents, etc., Nov. 13, 1946, Ganley Coll.

9. "A Tentative Program for Mobilizing Negro Support," WPR Coll.; William Kennedy to WPR, Apr. 6, 8, 9, 1946, WPR Coll.

10. "Draft Memorandum for Campaign for Michigan State FEPC; Committee for a State FEPC, Call to Conference, Oct. 26, 1946, Ann Shore to Friends, Oct. 3, 1946, William H. Oliver to Local Unions, Local 51 Coll. Box 12; "Tabulation of FEPC Petitions," Wayne County CIO Council to Local Unions, Jan. 2, 1947, "Call to a People's Lobby," Jan. 11, 1947, Local 212 Coll., Box 9; Newspaper Clippings, Jan. 15, 1947, Emil Mazey Coll., Box 11, WSU; William H. Adams to Kim Sigler, Dec. 23, 1946, Francis J. Haas to Sigler, July 31, 1947, Kim Sigler Papers, Box 61, State of Michigan Archives, Lansing; Henry S. Sweeney to Sigler, Mar. 7, 1947, Papers of the Attorney General, RG71–92, Box 51, State of Michigan Archives.

11. Fair Practices and Anti-Discrimination Department Report to the IEB, Dec. 10, 1946, WPR and Addes to Local Unions, Aug. 25, 1947, William Oliver to WPR, Aug. 19, 1947, Addes to Local Unions, Jan. 7, 1947, William Oliver to Ralph Young, Nov. 12, 1948, Olgar Madar and William Oliver to WPR, Oct. 3, 1947, WPR Coll.

12. "Reuther Wins High Praise," *Michigan Chronicle* reprint, Sept. 27, 1947, WPR Coll.; "Program, Award Dinner Honoring Mr. Walter P. Reuther," Detroit Urban League Coll., Box 21, Michigan Historical Collections, Ann Arbor, Mich.

13. *Michigan Herald*, Sept. 7, 1947; *DW*, Nov. 27, 1947.

14. "Program for a Third Caucus," Matthew Hammond and Helen Cross to UAW Members, July 9, 1947, Local 51 Coll., Box 18; Walter Hardin and Helen Cross to UAW members, n.d., R. J. Thomas Coll., Box 9, WSU; "Speech by . . . Lloyd Jones in Opposition to Factionalism in the UAW," n.d., ACTU Coll., Box 35, WSU.

15. *Proceedings of the Eleventh UAW Convention, Nov. 9–14, 1947, Atlantic City, N. J.* (n.p., n.d.), pp. 7–13.

16. *Ibid.*, pp. 38–39.

17. *Proceedings of the Eleventh UAW Convention, Nov. 9–14, 1947, Atlantic City, N. J.* (n.p., n.d.), pp. 76–116.

18. It is interesting to note that Truman's Secretary of Labor, Lewis Schwellenbach, had proposed the outlawing of the Communist party and the barring of Communists from holding office in local unions. *NYT*, Mar. 12, 1947.

19. *Proceedings of the Eleventh Convention*, p. 93.

20. *Ibid.*, pp. 61–67; Interview with George Addes, Jan. 23, 1982.

21. *Proceedings of the Eleventh Convention*, pp. 7–13, 128–19, 204, 269–70, 280; *Report of the President*, pp. 51–52.

22. *Proceedings of the Eleventh Convention*, pp. 7–13.

23. *Ibid.*, pp. 128–29.

24. *NYT*, Dec. 14, 1946, Oct. 3, 1947; *Michigan Herald*, Nov. 2, 1947. The analysis of the vote totals in this and the following paragraphs is based on the roll calls in the *Proceedings* of the tenth and eleventh conventions. A listing of most of the convention's Black delegates is in *Michigan Chronicle*, Nov. 22, 1947.

25. Gad Horowitz, *Canadian Labour in Politics* (Toronto, 1968), pp. 116–117.

26. Oral History Interview of James Cleveland, Oct. 3, 1961, pp. 21, 26–27, Michigan Historical Collections; WPR, "How to Beat the Communists," in Henry M. Christman, ed., *Walter P. Reuther; Selected Papers* (New York, 1961), pp. 18–30.

27. Interview with Victor Scott, Feb. 4, 1982.

28. An abstention in the presidential race was counted as a vote against Reuther.

29. Jack William Skeels, "Development of Political Stability within the United Auto Workers Union" (Ph.D. thesis, University of Wisconsin, 1957), p. 237; Notes on 1947 Convention Elections—Connecticut locals, n.d., WPR Coll.; IEB Minutes, June 9–13, 1947, pp. 153–63; Sept. 8–12, 1947, pp. 186–87; Sept. 22–24, 1947, p. 214.

30. *Michigan Chronicle*, Nov. 22, 1947.

Chapter Sixteen

1. Roger Keeran, *The Communist Party and the Auto Workers Unions* (Bloomington, Ind., 1980), pp. 283–85; *Wage Earner*, Jan. 16, 1948.

2. Reminiscences of R. J. Thomas, 1956, pp. 234–44, Columbia University Oral History Office, Butler Library; Jack William Skeels, "The Development of Political Stability within the United Auto Workers Union (Ph.D thesis, University of Wisconsin, 1957), p. 308; Interview with George Addes, Jan. 23, 1982.

3. Keeran, *Communist Party and Auto Workers*, p. 284; Jack Stieber, *Governing the UAW* (New York, 1962), pp. 14–15; Interview with Percy Llewellyn, Jan. 1, 1982;

Proceedings of the Twelfth UAW Convention, Milwaukee, Wisc. July 10-15, 1949 (n.p., n.d.), pp. 380–81.

4. *Wage Earner*, Jan. 9, 1948.

5. Emil Mazey to Local Unions, Dec. 1, 1947, Louis Ciccone Coll., Box 1, WSU; FPCB, Nov. 29, 1947, *Federated Press* Coll., Butler Libary, Columbia University, New York.

6. *UAW*, Jan., Feb. 1948; *Ford Facts*, Jan. 17, Feb. 7, 21, Apr. 24, 1948; "We Have Just Begun to Fight," Nat Ganley Coll., WSU.

7. Local 216 General Membership Meeting Minutes, Dec. 4, 1947, "Majority vs. Minority," "Why It's Phony to 'Go One Better' Than Taft-Hartley," Notes on trial of Local 216 members, Louis Ciccone Coll., WSU; "We Plead Guilty . . . to Charge of Fighting Speed-Up!," "Trial Date Set . . . ," Ganley Coll., Box 2.

8. "Who Is Protecting 'Who'??," WPR Coll., WSU; "The Case of Harold Christoffel," Ganley Coll.

9. *Proceedings of the Twelfth Convention*, pp. 245-54; "The Allis-Chalmers Story—or How to Wreck a Union," "8 percent of What?" Ganley Coll.

10. *Common Sense* (UAW Local 155), Mar. 1947; *Union Builder*, No. 3, May 20, 1948, UAW Local 212 Coll. Box 17, WSU; *Wage Earner*, Feb. 20, 27, Mar. 5, Apr. 2, 1948.

11. *Wage Earner*, Feb. 13, 20, Mar. 5, 19, May 14, 1948; *Michigan CIO News*, July 21, 1948.

12. *Union Builder*, No. 3, May 20, 1948; *DFP*, June 23, 1948.

13. *Proceedings Tenth Annual Convention, Michigan CIO Council, June 21-23,* 1948, Grand Rapids, Michigan (n.p., n.d.), pp. 123–65; *DFP*, June 22, 1948.

14. *Proceedings Tenth Michigan CIO Convention*, pp. 5-6, 41-42, 70-72, 83-88.

15. *Michigan CIO News*, Aug. 4, 1948; *NYT*, Aug. 30, 1948; Nat Ganley, Report to Communist party convention, 1948, copy in author's possession.

16. Interview with Betty Yochim, August 25, 1985.

17. *UAW*, Feb., Apr. 1948; Norman D. Markowitz, *The Rise and Fall of the People's Century* (New York, 1973), pp. 279–81; Mary Sperling McAuliffe, *Crisis on the Left* (Amherst, Mass., 1978), pp. 41-47.

18. Markowitz, *People's Century*, pp. 279–81; McAuliffe, *Crisis on the Left*, pp. 41-47; Marvin Persky, "Walter Reuther, the UAW-CIO, and Third Party Politics" (Ph.D. thesis, Michigan State University, 1974), pp. 179–81.

19. *UAW*, April 1948.

20. Fay Calkins, *The CIO and the Democratic Party* (Chicago, 1952), pp. 115–16; *DW*, Apr. 30, 1948; *Proceedings of Tenth Michigan CIO Convention*, pp. 110–15; *DFP*,

June 22, 1948; Bill Dodds to Emil Mazey, Oct. 19, 1948, WPR Coll., WSU; Persky, "Reuther and Third Party Politics," pp. 185–87; 192.

21. Persky "Reuther and Third Party Politics," pp. 48–56, 88–97, 132–38, 185–94; Fay Calkins, *CIO and Democratic Party*, pp. 112–46. See also Robert Lee Sawyer, Jr., The *Democratic State Central Committee in Michigan, 1949–1957* (Ann Arbor, Mich., 1960), pp. 201–33, 259–62.

22. W. Willard Wirtz, "Memorandum for the President," Sept. 24, 1964, File: 1964—White House—President, NN 370–108 [127], Records of the Secretary of Labor, RG 174, National Archives, Washington (emphasis in the original).

23. Ralph Urban and Dave Miller to Sir and Brother, n.d., Ganley Coll., Box 7; Call to Michigan Wallace for President Conference, Feb. 21, 1948, Local 212 Coll.; *NYT*, May 13, 1948; Persky, "Reuther and Third Party Politics," pp. 204–5.

24. Rank and File Committee for Wallace, Ford Local 406, "Read It Yourself, Brother!" Ganley Coll., Box 2; Frank Danowski and Stanley Bartnicki, "Danger," Earl Abel to WPR, Oct. 29, 1948, Local 78 to Emil Mazey, Nov. 3, 1948, Charles Reddeck *et al.*, Local 259 to WPR, Nov. 1, 1948, Hilliard Ellis to WPR, Oct. 27, 1948, UAW-PAC, "Who Wants Wallace?," WPR Coll.; Persky, "Reuther and Third Party Politics," pp. 194-97.

25. Persky "Reuther and Third Party Politics," pp. 194–202; Tracy Doll *et al.* "An Open Letter to Phil Murray," Ganley Coll., Box 1; Minutes of Greater Detroit and Wayne County Industrial Union Council, June 16, 1948, Frank Danowski to Philip Murray, June 2, 1948, UAW Local 51 Coll., WSU.

26. Persky, "Reuther and Third Party Politics," pp. 198–204; Doll *et al.*, "Open Letter," Phillip M. Connelly, Report on the Detroit and New York CIO Councils," Ganley Coll., Box 2; Diary of Adolph Germer, Sept. 7–8, 1948, Germer Coll., Wisconsin State Historical Society, Madison, Wisc.; Clipping, *Michigan CIO News, Sept. 8, 1948*, Vertical File, WSU.

27. Markowitz, *People's Century*, pp. 271–81; Alonzo Hamby, *Beyond the New Deal* (New York, 1973), pp. 258–62; *DFP*, Oct. 18, 1948; *NYT*, May 13, Oct. 18, 1948; Richard J. Walton, *Henry Wallace, Harry Truman and the Cold War* (New York, 1976), pp. 280–344; Allen Yarnell, *Democrats and Progressives* (Berkeley, Calif., 1974), pp. 87–107.

28. Persky, "Reuther and Third Party Politics," pp. 190–91; Interview with Leonard Woodcock, Feb. 10, 1982; Hamby, *Beyond New Deal*, pp. 225–43.

29. Persky, "Reuther and Third Party Politics," pp. 190–91; Clifton Brock, *Americans for Democratic Action* (Washington, 1962), pp. 88–99.

30. Irwin Ross, *The Loneliest Campaign* (New York, 1968), pp. 176–79.

31. *Michigan Manual*, 1949, pp. 230–31.

32. *UAW*, Apr. 1948; Frank Danowski to Emil Mazey, June 25, 1948, Grant W. Oakes To Danowski, May 10, 1948, Local 51 Coll., Box 7; Clyde J. Casper to Philip Murray,

July 22, 1948, Julius Emspak to Murray, Mar. 16, 1948, Ganley Coll., Box 1; William H. Johnson to WPR and Mazey, Jan. 28, 1948, WPR Coll.; Rice quoted in Ronald Lee Filippelli, "The United Electrical, Radio and Machine Workers of America, 1933–1949" (Ph.D thesis, Pennsylvania State University, 1970), pp. 175, 183–86.

33. "Prior Bargaining Status of Elections in Which UAW-CIO Was Petitioner or Intervenor," Aug. 22, 1947 to Oct. 31, 1948, WPR Coll.; Fact Sheet for Organizers, #9, Jan. 11, 1950; FPCB, Aug. 3, 1951, FP Coll.; Robert Ozanne, *A Century of Labor-Management Relations at McCormick and International Harvester* (Madison, Wisc., 1967), pp. 217–19; James J. Matles and James Higgins, *Them and Us* (Englewood Cliffs, N. J., 1974), pp. 192–94.

34. Frank Cormier and William J. Eaton, *Reuther* (Englewood Cliffs, N. J., 1970). pp. 255–75; Victor G. Reuther, *The Brothers Reuther and the Story of the UAW* (Boston, 1976), pp. 276–99; Ernest Goodman to DN (copy), Apr. 23, 1948, Local 51 Coll., Box 5; Heber Blankenhorn, "Investigation: Interim Summary of Main Clues," Jan. 25, 1950, Ralph D. Winstead, "Summary Report on the Bolton Case and Investigative Developments Up to Dec. 19, 1949," Heber Blankenhorn Coll., WSU; UAW Press Release, Apr. 21, 1948, UAW Ford Dept. Coll., Box 3, WSU; FPCB, May 1, 1948, Feb. 25, 1950, FP Coll.

35. Cormier and Eaton, *Reuther*, pp. 257–61; Oral History Interview of Carl Haessler, Nov. 27, 1959–Oct. 24, 1960, p. 220, Michigan Historical Collections, Ann Arbor, Mich.

36. DN, Jan. 8, 9, 1949, DFP, Jan. 9, 1949; Emil Mazey to Francis Danowski, Dec. 29, 1948, WPR to Danowski, Jan. 11, 1948 [*sic* 1949]; Proceedings of the IEB Trial of Local 51, p. 338, Local 51 Resolution, c. Feb. 1949, Local 51 Coll.; Stieber, *Governing the UAW*, pp. 140–41.

37. BLS, *Handbook* of *Labor Statistics*, Bulletin No. 916 (Washington, 1947), p. 107; *Michigan Herald*, Dec. 7, 1947; FPCB, Dec. 27, 1947, FP Coll.

38. FPCB, Dec. 27, 1947, FP Coll.; Kathy Groehn El-Messidi, *The Bargain: The Story Behind the 30-Year* Honeymoon of *GM and the UAW* (New York, 1980), pp. 45–48; *UAW*, Feb. 1948; Local 142, Resolution on Wages, Feb. 8, 1948, Local 51 Coll., Box 27; WPR to John Panzner, Feb. 10, 1948, WPR Coll.

39. *UAW*, Jan. 7, Apr. 18, May 13, 16, June 1948; Local 51, *Picket Line News*, May 26, 1948, Local 51 Coll., Box 3; *Dodge Main Strike News*, May 18, 20, 1948, National Chrysler Dept., *Chrysler Picket*, Bulletin #1. Art Hughes Coll., Box 2, WSU; LFB 9 (New York, 1949), pp. 146–47.

40. FPCB, May 14, 1948, FP Coll.; NYT, May 15, 18, 24, 26, 1948; Norman Matthews to Robert Condor, May 21, 1948, Hughes Coll., Box 2; Minutes of UAW National Conference on Economic Objectives, Feb. 19, 1949, p. 153, WPR Coll.; El-Messidi, *The Bargain*, pp. 59–63; *UAW*, June 1948.

41. *UAW*, June 1948; El-Messidi, *The Bargain*, pp. 59–65.

42. Cormier and Eaton, *Reuther*, pp. 292–94; Alfred P. Sloan, Jr., *My Years with General Motors* (New York, 1963), pp. 346–403; El-Messidi, *The Bargain*, pp. 29, 41, 64.

43. *UAW,* June 1948; Sloan, *My Years with General Motors*, pp. 396–98; El-Messidi, *The Bargain*, pp. 39–43. See Chapter Three herein.

44. *UAW*, June 1948.

45. *Ibid.*; *NYT,* May 29, July 23, 1948; *LFB* 9: 40–41.

46. *FP,* June 4, 1948, *FP* Coll.; Nat Ganley, Notes on GM Pact, Ganley Coll., Box 2. See Chapter One herein for discussion of profits and productivity.

47. "Operation of UAW-CIO Escalator and Improvement Factor Clauses," Neal Edwards Coll., Box 9, WSU; *UAW,* Mar., Sept., 1949; *NYT,* July 10, 1949.

48. "Operation of UAW-CIO Escalator and Improvement Factor Clauses."

49. *Proceedings Thirteenth Annual Convention Michigan CIO, June 4-6, 1951* (Detroit, n.d.), p. 171.

50. *UAW,* Mar., Sept. 1949; WPR, Memorandum to Regional Directors, July 1, 1949, WPR Coll.; Cormier and Eaton, *Reuther*, p. 296; Minutes of UAW National Conference on Economic Objectives, Feb. 19, 1949, pp. 87–94, 103–9.

51. *UAW,* Oct. 1949.

52. *FPCB,* Oct. 7, 20, 21, 28, 1949, *FP* Coll.; Contract Ratification, Oct. 27, 1949, Acc. 378 Box 13, FMC, Dearborn, Mich.; William "Bill" McKie, " . . . Bosses [*sic*] good deal, our raw deal," Ganley Coll., Box 5; Local 51, "Statement of Policy," Oct. 3, 1949, Local 742, "Resolution on Ford Pension," Local 51 Coll.

53. *UAW-Ford Agreement*, Sept. 29, 1949, Mar. 16, 1950; Sept. 4, 1950 (n.p., 1950); Malcolm L. Denise Memorandum to John Bugas and William T. Gossett, Jan. 6, 1950, Acc 354, Box 1, FMC; Interview of Ken Bannon by Cormier and Eaton, June 18, 1968, JFK.

54. *UAW-Ford Agreement* 1949–50; Edwin E. Witte, *Social Security Perspectives* (Madison, Wisc., 1962), pp. 167–70.

55. *NYT,* Nov. 1, 9, 12, 1949.

56. For discussion of the Ford speed-up strike, see below, pp. 359–61.

57. *NYT,* Nov. 23, 1949; *UAW,* Feb., May, 1950; WPR and N. Matthews to Chrysler, Jan. 23, 1950, Local 51 Coll., Box 4; Local 51 Resolution, Jan. 15, 1950, Nat Ganley telegram to *Worker,* n.d., Ganley Coll., Box 4; *FPCB,* Jan. 14, 1950, *FP* Coll.

58. Local 7 Strike Bulletin, #1, Jan. 27, 1950, Nat Ganley, Notes on Chrysler Settlement, 1950, "100-day 1950 Chrysler Strike," Ganley Coll. Box 4; Emil Mazey to John Jasinski, Feb. 23, 1950, Local 51 Coll., Box 3; *LFB* 10: 122; *UAW,* May 1950.

59. *UAW,* June 1950; *FPCB,* June 3, 1950, *FP* Coll.; Wyndham Mortimer to CIO Members, June 6, 1950, Louis Ciccone Coll., Box 1; "Comments on the GM-UAW

Five-Year Contract," May 25, 1950, Secretary Maurice J. Tobin, General Correspondence, Records of the Department of Labor, RG 174, NA; UAW Press Release, May 23, 1950, Ganley Coll., Box 3.

60. Using the concept that the contract was a "living document" that had to meet changed circumstances and applying economic pressure to the companies at a time of relatively full employment, the UAW was in fact able to secure additional wage and benefit gains in 1953. Robert MacDonald, *Collective Bargaining in the Automobile Industry*, (New Haven, Conn., 1963), pp. 35–36, 146, 178.

61. *NYT*, May 24, 27, 1950.

62. *FP*, Aug. 26, Sept. 2, 5, 15, 22, 1950, *FP* Coll.; Ford News Bureau releases and report, Aug. 29–Sept. 1, 1950, Memorandum of Ford offer, Sept. 1, 1950, Acc. 378, Box 23, FMC.

63. MacDonald, *Collective Bargaining*, pp. 29–76.

64. Interview with Leonard Woodcock, Feb. 10, 1982; *LFB* 10: 42–44; *UAW*, June 1950.

65. UAW press release, May 23, 1950, Ganley Coll., Box 3, Thomas A. Johnstone to H. W. Anderson, Sept. 13, 1948, WPR Coll.; *FPCB*, Apr. 1, May 13, June 24, 1949, Nov. 14, 1950, *FP* Coll; Minutes of GM Sub-Council #9, Sept. 16, 1948, Dec. 16, 1948, WPR Coll.; Wilson quoted in "Speed-up," 1954, Ganley Coll., Box 4.

66. Nelson W. Samp, Report for week ending Dec. 4, 1948, UAW Ford Dept. Coll., Box 6; "Chronology of the Labor Dispute which Culminated in the May 1949 Strike," Acc. 378, Box 16, FMC; John S. Bugas and D. S. Harder, Executive Communication, "Work Standards Policy," Mar. 5, 1948; Analysis of Ford Policy Regarding Work Standards for the New Model," [July 19, 1948,] Ed Lock *et al.*, "Stop the Bugas Plan," "Speed-Up," 1954, Ganley Coll.; Ken Bannon to Ford Locals, Apr. 12, 1948, WPR Coll.

67. "Speed-Up," 1954, " . . . Ford Workers Are Not Fools!," "Strike Betrayal . . . A Documented Report," Ganley Coll.; Thomas Thompson *et al*, "A Message to All Members of Local 600 . . . ," Local Executive Board Minutes, Nov. 1, 9, 1948, James Couser Coll., Box 1, WSU; "Chronology of the Labor Dispute Which Culminated in the May 1949 Strike," Acc. 378, Box 16, FMC; *NYT*, Mar. 30, 1949; Ken Bannon Memo to WPR, Dec. 9, 1948, WPR Coll.; *UAW*, Jan. 1949.

68. UAW Proposals, May 5, 13, 1949, Tommy Thompson *et al.* to Henry Ford II, May 9, 1949, UAW press release, May 15, 1949, Ganley Coll., Box 5.

69. "Strike Betrayal . . . ," Ganley Coll., Box 5; Dick Paulson memo to John Rose, c. May 8, 1949, Acc. 378, Box 16, "Report on Public Opinion Survey . . . Ford . . . May 21–22, 1949," Acc. 572, Box 38, FMC.

70. WPR statement, May 20, 1949, UAW press releases, May 19, 31, 1949, "Strike Betrayal . . . ," "Settlement Agreement," Ganley Coll., Box 5.

71. UAW press release, May 31, 1949, *UAW-Ford Agreement, 1949-1950;* "Arbitration Award," "Strike Betrayal...A Documented Report," "Why We Voted No!," Ganley Coll., Box 5.

72. *Michigan Worker* reprint, "Ford Workers Win Victory," "A Letter from Tommy Thompson," "Want Real Unity? Select the Best from Each Slate," "Walter Reuther and Joe McCusker Are Behind Carl Stellato!," "Unite to Fight the 'Company'," Ganley Coll.; William D. Andrew, "Factionalism and Anticommunism: Ford Local 600," *Labor History* 20 (Spring 1979): 239-40.

73. Andrew "Ford Local 600," pp. 240-45; *NYT,* July 10, Oct. 31, 1950, Mar. 17, 1951; Local 600 press release, July 10, 1950, Maurice Sugar Coll., WSU; "We Favor Preserving Basic American Freedoms," Pat Rice *et al.,* "We Voted to Defend Your Rights," Ganley Coll., Box 3; "The Roll Call!," Harry Ross Coll., Box 4, WSU.

74. *Proceedings Twelfth Convention,* pp. 70-72, 211.

75. *Ibid.,* pp. 304-457.

76. *Ibid.,* pp. 464-93; "The 12th UAW-CIO Convention," Ganley Coll., Box 9.

77. *Proceedings Twelfth Convention,* pp. 106, 216, 261-77; "The 12th UAW-CIO Convention," Harry Weaver and James Lindahl, "Time for a Fresh Approach," Bill to Saul, June 30, 1949, Delegates from Locals 72, 278, 364, etc. to Convention Delegates, Ganley Coll.; Edith Shepard to WPR, June 22, 1949, James B. Ellison to WPR, June 22, 1949, WPR Coll.

78. Marc J. Parsons, "Report on the UAW-CIO Convention," July 20, 1949, Acc. 378, Box 13, FMC; Interview with Leonard Woodcock, Feb. 10, 1982.

79. Clippings, DFP, Mar. 11, 1948, Ken Morris, press release, Mar. 12, 1948, Local 212 Coll., Box 9; DN, Mar. 12, 1948; FPCB, Mar. 13, 1948, FP Coll.,; Thomas Smith to WPR, May 19, 1949. See also WPR, Notes for Thirteenth Convention, WPR Coll.

80. David Caute, *The Great Fear* (New York, 1978), pp. 360-64; *FP,* July 25, 27, 28, Aug. 11, 1950, FP Coll.; Thomas W. Gavett, *Development of the Labor Movement in Milwaukee* (Madison, Wisc., 1965), p. 196.

81. Caute, *Great Fear,* pp. 360-64; B. J. Widick, *Detroit: City of Race and Class Violence* (Chicago, 1972), pp. 127-36; Andrew, "Ford Local 600," pp. 250-55; *FP,* June 20, 1952, FP Coll.; " 'Red Probers to Take Swipe at Auto Union'," Charles (Chuck) Walters Statement, Civil Rights Congress newsletter, Feb. 29, 1952, Statement of Policy, Ford Local 600, Mar. 10, 1952, Ganley Coll.; *NYT,* Feb. 29, Mar. 13, Aug. 31, 1952, May 9, 1953.

82. "We Accuse You! Mr. Clardy!," "Chevrolet Local 659 . . . Old Timers Say Stop the Violence . . . ," "Threat of the Open Shop," "General Motors: Stop Monkeying Around," Ganley Coll. Charles Shinn recalled that when GM agreed to let him return to work in exchange for dropping a suit against the corporation, the attacks against him ceased. After assuring a supervisor that he was not a Communist, Friendly Dantzler, a Chevrolet worker, was warned by the supervisor to leave the plant to avoid being

attacked. Interview with Charles Shinn, Jan. 16, 1982; *Flint Weekly Review*, May 21, 28, 1954; *FPCB*, May 29, June 19, 1954, *FP* Coll.

83. The 1954 Elections and the 1955 Contract Struggle," UAW reprint, *Flint Journal and News Advertiser*, May 31, 1954, "Labor Fact Sheet on HUAC," 1954, Ganley Coll.; *Flint Weekly Review*, May 21, 28, 1954. The union stopped processing grievances in cases in which GM gave falsification of the employment application as the grounds for the discharge. The workers concerned had not stated their full educational attainment. *FPCB*, May 29, June 19, 1954, *FP* Coll.

84. *DFP*, May 13, 1954; *Flint* Journal, May 14, 1954; "Memorandum on Flint," 1954, Ganley Coll., Box 5.

Chapter Seventeen

1. Interview with Carl Winter, June 6, 1974; Interview with Leo Fenster, October 23, 1982.

2. John Earl Haynes, "The New History of the Communist Party in State Politics: The Implications for Mainstream Political History," *Labor History* 27 (Fall 1986): 549–63.

3. Dick Meister and Anne Loftis, *A Long Time Coming: The Struggle to Unionize America's Farm Workers* (New York, 1977), pp. 138–39.

4. *Proceedings Fourteenth Constitutional Convention, Atlantic City, N. J., March 22–27, 1953*, pp. 82–89.

5. Walter P. Reuther's Report on His Trip to India, Excerpts from the President Report to the IEB, May 3, 1956, Richard G. Deverall Papers, Correspondence and Reports, Catholic University of America, Washington; Nat Ganley notes on WPR's India Policy, Ganley Coll., Box 9, WSU; WPR to John Foster Dulles, March 23, 1956, Ganley Coll., Box 7.

6. John Barnard, *Walter Reuther and the Rise of the Auto Workers* (Boston, 1983), pp. 188–99.

7. *Proceedings Twenty-Third Constitutional Convention, Atlantic City, N. J., April 23–28, 1972*, pp. 356–65.

8. Richard Thomas, "Blacks and the CIO," in Paul Buhle and Alan Dawley, *Working for Democracy: American Workers from the Revolution to the Present* (Urbana, Ill., 1985); Philip S. Foner, *Organized Labor and the Black Worker, 1619–1973* (New York, 1974), p. 296.

9. Dudley Buffa, *Union Power and American Democracy: The UAW and the Democratic Party, 1935–1972* (Ann Arbor, Mich., 1984), pp. 191–92.

10. *Where We Stand; Resolutions Adopted By the Delegates to the 26th Constitutional Convention, UAW, Anaheim Calif., June 1–6, 1980*, pp. 120–21.

11. *Proceedings Twenty-Sixth Constitutional Convention, Anaheim, Calif, June 1–6, 1980*, pp. 153–58; Interview with Douglas Fraser, August 8, 1984.

Bibliography

Manuscript Sources

The Walter P. Reuther Collection is the most important of the many manuscript collections of the auto workers in the postwar era housed in the Wayne State University Archives of Labor History and Urban Affairs, Detroit, Michigan, The collection, which contains documents on all aspects of the union's activities, is an especially good source of information on the General Motors (GM) strike and on United Auto Workers (UAW) factionalism. Among other official UAW records deposited at the Labor History Archives are Minutes of the International Executive Board (IEB) which provide valuable summaries of discussions up until mid-1947 and a verbatim record thereafter. Verbatim transcripts of the Proceedings of the CIO Executive Board are also available at the Wayne Archives, but the records of some important 1946 meetings are missing.

The Nat Ganley Collection provides considerable material on the Communist role in the auto industry, the Communist analysis of the union and industry, and on such events as the Allis-Chalmers and Ford speed-up strikes. The Detroit Association of Catholic Trade Unionists (ACTU) Collection contains important information on the ACTU and on UAW factionalism. The minutes of the Resolutions Committee of the Tenth UAW Convention, located in the Paul Silver Collection, are useful for an understanding of the differing views of the factions. The George Crockett Collection, located, like all of the above, in the Labor History Archives, provides documentation on the first UAW Fair Practices Committee. The R. J. Thomas Collection contains material on factionalism and on the GM strike, but the George Addes Collection is less useful.

Several UAW local union collections deposited at the archives provide information on strike participation, factionalism, and the functioning of the union at the grass roots. The collections of Locals 51, 212, 248, and 602 were especially valuable in this regard. The Ford and GM Department Collections are an important source for information on those sections of the union. The UAW Washington Office—Donald Montgomery Collection contains important material on the GM strike of 1945–1946. The UAW Research Department Collection includes statistical data on Black and women workers in the industry and on economic issues. The UAW War Policy Division contains information on reconversion and on Black and women workers. The Michigan AFL-CIO Collection includes material on various CIO bodies and on UAW controversies as well. The CIO Secretary-Treasurer's Collection also contains some information on the UAW, including its dispute with the United Electrical Workers (UE).

Other collections at the Labor History Archives of particular value for this study are the Charles Chiakulas Collection, which has material on social and political activities, and the Carl Haessler, Maurice Sugar, and Neal Edwards Collections, which have

information on internal union politics. The Art Hughes Collection contains information on Chrysler negotiations and strikes. The M. A. "Bill" Williams Collection contains
an interesting history and other documents on Local 560 in California, and the Louis
Ciccone Collection has some documentation on Local 216 and on the Trotskyite role
in the auto industry. The James Couser Collection contains material on Local 600.

Several collections in the Ford Motor Company Archives, Dearborn, Michigan,
including Accessions 378 and 572, contain valuable information on the 1949 speed-up
strike. There are also items of interest on pension negotiations in Accession 354 and
on the company's labor relations policy in the Frank Hill Papers.

The Records of the Federal Mediation and Conciliation Services (FMCS), Record
Group 280, National Archives and Records Service, Washington, and General Archives
Division, Suitland, Maryland are a major source for collective bargaining developments
and for strikes in the auto industry. The comments of the FMCS conciliators and their
recording of off-the-record discussions with the parties are of special interest. The
Proceedings of the GM Dispute Panel, included in the FMCS records, are a valuble source
for the GM strike. Unfortunately, some of the relevant case files in the FMCS Records
are now missing, as are the National Labor Relations Board records dealing with the
GM strike. The Records of the Department of Labor, Record Group 174, have a number
of useful items on the GM and Allis-Chalmers strikes. The Records of the President's
Fair Employment Practices Committee (FEPC), Record Group 228, document racial
incidents in war plants and discrimination against Black workers during the war and
reconversion. The Records of the Office of War Mobilization and Reconversion (OWMR),
RG 250, located, like all of the above, in the National Archives, contain material on
the evolution of the Truman Administration's wage-price policy in 1945–46.

Several collections pertinent to the subject are housed in the Harry S. Truman Library
in Independence, Missouri. There is a good deal of information on the Truman
administration's wage policy and its response to strikes in the President's Official File,
the President's Secretary's File, and the President's Personal File. The Papers of Matthew
J. Connelly contain useful summaries of cabinet meetings. The John W. Gibson Papers
include valuable material on the GM and Allis-Chalmers strikes, including transcripts
of phone conversations between Gibson and Allis-Chalmers officials. The Alfred
Schindler Papers document the controversy surrounding the 1945 Department of
Commerce study of the auto industry. The Paul Herzog Papers contain a few items of
interest on the NLRB role in the 1945–1946 GM strike.

The George Romney Papers at the Michigan Historical Collections in Ann Arbor
contain some items of interest for 1945–46, when Romney headed the Automobile
Manufacturers' Association. The Blair Moody Papers include some material on the
Reuthers and on the UAW's factional politics. The Michigan Historical Collections also
house records of two UAW-GM negotiating sessions just prior to the start of the strike
in 1945.

The daily dispatches of the *Federated Press* are available in the *Federated Press*
Collection in Columbia University's Butler Libary. The collection provides an excellent
account of collective bargaining, strike activity, problems of discrimination, and

factionalism in the auto industry. The Lewis Corey Papers, also at Columbia, are a source for the attempt of Socialists and social democrats, including figures from the Reuther caucus and the Michigan Commonwealth Federation, to found a new party in 1946.

The Philip Murray Papers at the Catholic University in Washington, D. C. contain some interesting items on the UAW. There are some items of interest on Socialists in the UAW and on Reuther in the J. B. S. Hardman Papers at the Taminent Library in New York University, New York City. The material on Socialists in the UAW in the Daniel Bell Papers in the Taminent Library pertain primarily to the pre-World War II period.

The Kim Sigler Collection at the State of Michigan Archives in Lansing contains leaflets, letters, and newspaper clippings on communism in the UAW and state labor legislation, 1947-1948. The Records of the Attorney General document some anticommunist incidents, particularly in Flint in the 1950s. The Records of the State Police, Intelligence and Security Bureau, include a daily review of the Michigan labor situation between 1944 and 1947, based largely on press accounts.

The Earl Browder Papers at Syracuse University, available on microfilm at the University of Michigan Library, Ann Arbor, Michigan, contain general material on communism in the labor movement and a few specific items about the UAW in 1944 and 1945. The Socialist Party of America Collection, Duke University, Durham, North Carolina, which I examined on microfilm, include some relevant materials on Michigan Socialists and the UAW in 1944-1946. The Henry A. Wallace Papers, University of Iowa, Iowa City, Iowa (microfilm edition) contain a small number of items about the CIO and reconversion wage-price policy.

The Americans for Democratic Action (ADA) Papers, Wisconsin State Historical Society (microfilm edition), document the development of cold war liberalism and include a number of items on the Reuthers. Many relevant collections are at the Wisconsin State Historical Society in Madison, particularly for the important Allis-Chalmers local in Milwaukee. Most useful were the Wisconsin Industrial Union Council Collection, the Records of the Wisconsin Employment Relations Board, the Fred Blair Papers, and the Adolph Germer Papers.

Interviews

Many of the oral history interviews in the UAW Oran History Project of the Institute of Labor and Industrial Relations of the University of Michigan and Wayne State University pertain to the post-World War II factional conflict in the UAW. Transcripts of interviews are at the Michigan Historical Collections in Ann Arbor and at Wayne State Archives of Labor and Urban Affairs. Among the most useful are the interviews with Carl Haessler, Leonard Woodcock, Nat Ganley, Sam Sage, William Genske, Jack Palmer, Adam Poplawski, Pat Greathouse, Ken Morris, James Cleveland, and George Addes. The Reminiscences of R. J. Thomas in the Oral History Research Office, Columbia University, are quite detailed. Unofficial transcripts of interviews conducted by Frank Cormier and William Eaton for their book *Reuther* are located in the John F. Kennedy

Library in Boston. The most valuable of these interviews are those with Kenneth Bannon, Leonard Woodcock, Richard Frankensteen, Richard Leonard, and Jack Conway. A number of interviews relevant to the Allis-Chalmers strike are available in the Wisconsin State Historical Society. Most useful were interviews with Harold Christoffel, Robert Buse, and Sigmund Eisencher.

In addition to the above, I interviewed George Addes, Chris Alston, Harold Christoffel, George Crockett, Dave Moore, Douglas Fraser, Stanley Nowak, Robert Buse, Betty Yochim, Hodges Mason, Harold Shapiro, Arthur McPhaul, Horace Sheffield, Leonard Woodcock, Percy Llewellyn, Martin Gerber, Oscar Noble, Leo Fenster, William Glenn, James Jackson, Chuck Shinn, William Allan, Jack White, Carl Winter, Frank Sykes, Shelton Tappes, Alex Wasilew, and Paul Boatin. Victor Scott and Ray Frizzell answered my questions by telephone.

Newspapers and Periodicals

The *United Automobile Worker*, a monthly, documents official international policy. Local union papers in this period were often lively in character and constitute a source of information on the various auto union factions. Among these are *Voice of Local 212, Common Sense* (Local 155), *Plymouth Beacon* (Local 51), Local 599 *Headlight, Flint Weekly Review, Dodge Main News* (Local 3), *Ford Facts* (Local 600), *Fisher Eye Opener* (Local 45), and the *Conveyor* (Local 174). The *Michigan CIO News*, the organ of the state CIO, provides good coverage of UAW matters.

The *New York Times* devoted a good deal of space to UAW affairs in the post-1945 era, particularly on the collective bargaining issue. The *Detroit Free Press, Detroit News,* and *Detroit Times* were especially concerned with UAW factionalism. The most detailed coverage of the factional conflict is contained in the *Wage Earner*, the weekly paper of the Detroit ACTU. The *Milwaukee Journal* paid close attention to the Allis-Chalmers strike. The *Daily Worker, Sunday Worker, Michigan Herald*, and *Political Affairs* report on and analyze the UAW from the Communist viewpoint. The *New Masses* has some interesting articles on the GM strike. The journals, *New Republic* and the *Nation*, are sources for liberal views on the merits and shortcomings of the two UAW factions. Relevant business-oriented publications are *Detroit Labor Trends*, which paid special attention to the UAW factional conflict, *Business Week*, and the *Commercial and Financial Chronicle*. The Luce publications, *Time, Life,* and *Fortune*, also covered the union's activities. The *Michigan Chronicle*, Detroit's leading Black newspaper, provides valuable insights on the role of Black workers in the UAW.

Government and Union Publications

Bradford C. Snell, *American Ground Transport* (Washington, 1974), is a well-documented critical analysis of the auto industry presented to the Subcommittee on Antitrust and Monopoly of the Senate Committee on the Judiciary. U. S. Congress,

Senate, Committee on the Judiciary, *Concentration in American Industry: Report of the Subcommittee on Antitrust and Monopoly*, 85th Congress, 1st Session (Washington, 1957), contains data on the structure of the auto industry. Bureau of Labor Statistics *Handbook of Labor Statistics*, provides economic data on the labor force, wages, strikes, etc. The War Manpower Commission periodical, *Labor Market*, and the Women's Bureau, *Women Workers in Ten War Production Areas and Their Postwar Employment Plans* (Washington, 1946), also contain information on the labor force.

Public Papers of the Presidents: Harry S. Truman (Washington, 1961-1) are especially valuable for understanding the GM strike. The *Congressional Record* contains a number of important documents on the UAW-GM conflict. Harvey C. Mansfield *et al.*, *A Short History of OPA* (Washington, 1947) candidly discusses the events leading to the demise of the hold-the-line price policy. Department of Labor, *The National Wage Stabilization Board, Jan. 1, 1946-Feb. 24, 1947* (Washington, n.d.); Division of Labor Standards, *President's National Labor-Management Conference*, Bulletin No. 77 ([Washington,] 1946); and U.S. Congress, Senate, Committee on Education and Labor, *Hearings on S1661: Labor Fact-Finding Boards Act*, 79 Cong., 2 Sess. (Washington, 1946), are important sources on labor relations in 1945-1946.

Amendments to the National Labor Relations Act, Hearings before the Committee on Education and Labor (Washington, 1947) is useful for an understanding of the origins of the Taft-Hartley Act. The intervention of government investigating bodies into the labor scene are recorded in U. S. Congress, House, Committee on Un-American Activities, *Hearings Regarding Communism in Labor Unions in the United States*, 80th Congress, 1st sess., 1947; *idem., Communism in the Detroit Area*, 82nd Congress, 2nd sess., 1952; and, *idem., Investigation of Communist Activity in the State of Michigan*, 83rd Congress, 2nd sess., 1954.

The *Proceedings* of the UAW, national CIO, and Michigan CIO conventions are essential sources for understanding the development of the factional conflict in the auto union. The UAW publications, *Purchasing Power for Prosperity* (Detroit, 1945), and *Wages, Prices, and Profits* (Detroit, 1947), present the union's case in favor of substantial wage increases.

Miscellaneous Unpublished Sources

Jack William Skeels, "The Development of Political Stability within the United Auto Workers Union" (Ph.D thesis, University of Wisconsin, 1957) provides a good overview of the factional fight and some insight into the role of patronage in cementing the factions but underestimates the importance of ideology. Frank Emspak, "The Break-Up of the Congress of Industrial Organizations (CIO), 1945-1950" (Ph.D. thesis, 1972), which is critical of anticommunism, focuses on the UE, UAW, and Steelworkers. Its treatment of such UAW issues as the Taft-Hartley affidavits is marred by some inaccuracies. James Robert Prickett, "Communists and the Communist Issue in the American Labor Movement, 1920-1950" (Ph.D. thesis, University of California at Los Angeles, 1975), briefly discusses the postwar period and argues that the roots of the Reuther victory lay in the failure of the Communists to remain independent of the union leadership and build a strong base. Robert Willard Ozanne, "The Effects of Communist Leadership in American Trade Unions" (Ph.D. thesis, University of Wisconsin, 1954), while unsympathetic to its subject, provides a lengthy discussion of the dynamism and militancy of the Allis-Chalmers local.

Gilbert W. Moore, "Poverty, Class Consciousness, and Racial Conflict: The Social Basis of Trade Union Politics in the UAW-CIO, 1937–1955" (Ph.D. thesis, Princeton University, 1978), is thinly researched and does not live up to its ambitious title. Sidney Kelman, "Acquisition, Consolidation and Use of Power: Walther Reuther and the UAW, 1946–1955" (Ph.D. thesis, Hebrew University, 1980), emphasizes Reuther's skills at publicity and organization and generally accepts at face value the UAW president's replies to criticisms. Kelman fails to penetrate below the surface of UAW events or sufficiently to take into account the social and political context in which the union functioned. He adopts contradictory positions when he assesses the quality of Reuther's GM strike leadership and whether there were substantive differences between the two UAW factions. Suzanne Jo Silverman, "Unionization as a Social Movement: A Case Study of the UAW, 1945–1950," (Ph.D. thesis, Columbia University, 1982), is sympathetic to the left-center caucus but is based on only a limited examination of the relevant manuscript collections.

Marvin Persky, "Walter Reuther, the UAW-CIO, and Third Party Politics" (Ph.D. thesis, Michigan State University, 1974), is a well-documented study focusing on electoral policy and factionalism. Christopher H. Johnson, "Maurice Sugar: Law, Labor and the Left in Detroit, 1912–1950," manuscript to be published by Wayne State University Press, is a sympathetic biography of a central leader of the Detroit left. Sugar's forceful role in the 1930s is well depicted. The author overstates the differences between independent leftists like Sugar and the Communist party. Michael Deveraux Whitty's "Emil Mazey: Radical as Liberal" (Ph.D. thesis, Syracuse, University, 1969), is a sympathetic but critical examination of the Socialist union leader. Nelson Lichtenstein's "Industrial Unionism under the No-Strike Pledge: A Study of the CIO during the Second World War" (Ph.D thesis, University of California at Berkeley, 1974), briefly discusses the postwar GM strike and argues that the strike raised fundamental class issues. Lloyd H. Bailer, "Negro Labor in the Automobile Industry" (Ph.D thesis, University of Michigan, 1943), is an excellent early study of the Black workers, the Black community and the automobile industry. Richard W. Thomas, "From Peasant to Proletarian: The Formation and Organization of the Black Industrial Working-Class in Detroit, 1915–1945" (Ph.D. thesis, University of Michigan, 1975), emphasizes the Black workers' role in unionization efforts.

The development of the UAW's umpire system is described in George Butler Heliker, "Grievance Arbitration in the Automobile Industry: A Comparative Analysis of Its History and Results in the Big Three" (Ph.D. thesis, University of Michigan, 1954). Richard Joseph Ward, "The Role of the Association of Catholic Trade Unionists in the American Labor Movement," (Ph.D. thesis, University of Michigan, 1958), concentrates on that organization's ideological roots, while Harold Wattel, "The Association of Catholic Trade Unionists" (M.A. thesis, Columbia University, 1947) includes some interesting comments by ACTU leaders whom the author interviewed.

Herbert Levine interviewed 48 Buffalo area shop stewards for his study "The UAW-CIO Shop Steward: A Consideration of His Role as a Force for Democracy" (M.A. thesis, University of Buffalo, 1951). William H. Friedland, "Attitude Change Toward Negroes by White Shop-Level Leaders of the United Automobile Workers Union" (M.A. thesis, Wayne State University, 1956), contains some interesting observations based on the writer's experience as a steward in the Hudson plant and an administrator of CIO Summer Schools. Daniel B. Crowder, "Profile in Progress: A History of Local 287, UAW-CIO" (Ph.D. thesis, Ball State University, 1969), emphasizes the local's independence from the international.

Marjorie Thines Stanley, "The Interrelationship of Economic Forces and Labor Relations in the Automobile Industry" (Ph.D. thesis, Indiana University, 1953) contains useful information on ecomonic matters. Lester Samuel Levy, "The Pattern of Union-Management Conflict in the Automobile Industry" (Ph.D. thesis, Cornell University, 1956), is concerned with postwar contract negotiations.

John E. Haynes, "Liberals, Communists, and the Popular Front in Minnesota: The Struggle to Control the Political Direction of the Labor Movement and Organized Liberalism, 1936–1950" (Ph.D. thesis, University of Minnesota, 1978), is a very detailed, well-researched study on the conflict between supporters and opponents of the popular front in Minnesota from an antipopular front point of view. Leslie Kerby Adler, "The Red Image: American Attitudes toward Communism in the Cold War Era (Ph.D. thesis, University of California at Berkeley, 1970), is another cold war study.

Harry Dannenberg *et al.*, "Strike at Allis-Chalmers, 1946–47" (Milwaukee Independent School, 1970–1971), gathers copies of the Local 248 strike paper, transcripts of interviews, and other material which document this important UAW defeat. The "UAW-CIO—The Auto W[or]kers Great Hope" 1954], in the Nat Ganley Collection, Box 8, WSU, is a brief history of the union and postwar collective bargaining from a Communist point of view. George Heliker, "Report on Labor, 1933–1957," Ford Motor Company Archives, Acc. 958, contains some interesting material derived from Ford company documents.

Miscellaneous Published Sources

Most early studies of the UAW's factional warfare tended to be pro-Reuther and tendentious in their characterization of his opposition as Communist, dishonest, and so forth. Max Kampelman, *The Communist Party vs. the CIO* (New York, 1957), is illustrative of this perspective. Irving Howe and B. J. Widick, in *The UAW and Walter Reuther* (New York, 1949), view the Reuther group as to the left of the Thomas-Addes-Leonard coalition, which they characterize as an alliance of conservatives and Communists. Richard O. Boyer and Herbert M. Morais, *Labor's Untold Story* (Third Edition, New York, 1970), is an early work sympathetic to the UAW left.

James R. Prickett, "Communism and Factionalism in the United Automobile Workers, 1939–1947" *Science and Society* 32 (Summer 1968): 257–77, is critical of anticommunism and the failure of some scholars to distinguish the Communists from leaders like Thomas and Addes. Prickett's "Some Aspects of the Communist Controversy in the CIO," *ibid.*, 33 (Summer-Fall, 1969); 299–321, focuses on the turn toward anticommunism of the national CIO. David M. Oshinsky, "Labor's Cold War: The CIO and the Communists," in Robert Griffiths and Athan Theoharis, ed., *The Specter: Original Essays on the Cold War and the Origins of McCarthyism* (New York, 1974), provides an overview of the conflict over communism in the CIO.

Roger Keeran, *The Communist Party and the Auto Workers Unions* (Bloomington, Ind., 1980), is a detailed study that emphasizes the positive role of Communists in building the UAW. He considers the Allis-Chalmers strike at length and concludes that Reuther's triumph was due to the red-baiting that accompanied this and other disputes. Bert Cochran, *Labor and Communism* (Princeton, N. J., 1977), sees the "Red issue" as the critical one determining the factional conflict in the UAW, but he fails to understand that the Addes group had a different response to the cold war drive than the Reuther caucus, and he makes the unwarranted assumption that in victory it too would have purged the Communists. Harvey A. Levenstein's *Communism, Anticommunism, and the CIO* (Westport, Conn., 1981), covers much the same ground as Cochran in a better-documented work and concludes that the anticommunist purge seriously weakened the CIO. In his chapter, "The UAW Falls," he mistakenly takes at face value Reuther's claim that he waged his struggle on trade unionist, not anticommunist grounds, and he sees no real differences between the two UAW factions.

Frederick H. Harbison and Robert Dubin, *Patterns of Union-Management Relations* (Chicago, 1947), presents an overview of relations between the UAW and GM and Studebaker. Nelson Lichtenstein, "Auto Worker Militancy and the Structure of Factory Life" *Journal of American History* (Sept. 1980): 335–53, notes a decline in the power of the shop stewards during the postwar years.

Joel Seidman, *American Labor from Defense to Reconversion* (Chicago, 1953), focuses on the relationship between the unions and the government. Bruce R. Morris, "Industrial Relations in the Automobile Industry," and H. M. Douty, "Review of Basic American Labor Conditions," in Colston E. Warne, *Labor in Postwar America* (Brooklyn, N. Y., 1949), are useful articles on postwar labor relations. The focus of Nelson Lichtenstein's *Labor's War at Home: The CIO in World War II* (Cambridge [Cambridge-shire], 1982) and of Martin Glaberman's *Wartime Strikes* (Detroit, 1980), is on the shop floor conflict and no strike pledge during World War II. Lichtenstein's work contains a useful epilogue on the impact of the cold war and the Taft-Hartley Act on the labor movement.

The standard studies of labor policy during the Truman administration are R. Alton Lee, *Truman and Taft-Hartley* (Lexington, Ky. 1966), and Arthur F. McClure, *The Truman Administration and the Problems of Postwar Labor, 1945-1948* (Rutherford, N. J., 1969). Barton J. Bernstein's three articles on postwar wage policy and negotiations are valuable for their analysis of the shift in the Truman administration's policy: "The Truman Administration and Its Reconversion Wage Policy," *Labor History* VI (Fall 1965): 214–31; "Walter Reuther and the General Motors Strike of 1945–1946," *Michigan History* 45

(Sept. 1965): 260–77; and "The Truman Administration and the Steel Strike of 1946," *Journal of American History* LII (Mar. 1966): 791–803. Chester Bowles considers federal wage policy in his memoir, *Promises to Keep* (New York, 1971).

The development of the split between popular front and "vital center" liberals is depicted in Alonzo L. Hamby, *Beyond the New Deal* (New York, 1973). Mary Sperling McAuliffe *Crisis on the Left* (Amherst, Mass., 1978), examines the effect of the cold war on liberalism and the CIO. David Caute, *The Great Fear* (New York, 1978), catalogues the anticommunist purges in the unions and other areas of American life in the late 1940s and early 1950s. Peter Weiler makes note of the relationship between domestic anticommunism and the anticommunist foreign policy of the CIO in "The United States, International Labor, and the Cold War: The Breakup of the World Federation of Trade Unions," *Diplomatic History* (Winter 1980): 1–22. The principal studies of Henry Wallace and the Progressive party are Curtis Macdougall, *Gideon's Army* 3 vols. (New York, 1965); Normal D. Markowitz, *The Rise and Fall of the People's Century* (New York, 1973) and Richard J. Walton, *Henry Wallace, Harry Truman, and the Cold War* (New York, 1976). Carl O. Smith and Stephen B. Sarasohn, "Hate Propaganda in Detroit," *Public Opinion Quarterly* X (Spring 1946): 24–52, includes a valuable statistical analysis of the 1945 Detroit elections. James Caldwell Foster, *The Union Politic: The CIO Political Action Committee* (Columbia, Mo., 1975), maintains that the Richard Frankensteen and other Political Action Committee (PAC) campaigns were too far to the left to win at the polls. Allen Yarnell, *Democrats and Progressives* (Berkeley, Calif., 1974), and Irwin Ross, *The Loneliest Campaign* (New York, 1968), are studies of the 1948 elections. David M. Oshinsky, *Senator Joseph McCarthy and the American Labor Movement* (Columbia, Mo., 1976), refutes the idea that the Communist-led Wisconsin CIO, in which the Allis-Chalmers local played an important role, aided McCarthy's election to the Senate in 1946. Dudley Buffa, *Union Power and American Democracy: The UAW and the Democratic Party, 1935–1972* (Ann Arbor, Mich., 1984), provides interesting anecdotes on the relationship between the UAW and the Michigan Democratic party in the 1950s and later years. It ignores the role of the left-center coalition in the UAW and the Democratic party.

Robert M. MacDonald, *Collective Bargaining in the Automobile Industry* (New Haven, Conn., 1963), provides an economic analysis of the provisions of UAW contracts. In an undocumented work based on her dissertation, Kathy Groehn El-Messidi's *The Bargain* (New York, 1980), discusses the 1948 GM-UAW contract. El-Messidi interviewed both GM and UAW personnel, but her book is marred by numerous inaccuracies. Jack Steiber, *Governing the UAW* (New York, 1962), focuses on the subject of democracy in the union under the Reuther administration. B. J. Widick, *Detroit: City of Race and Class Violence* (Chicago, 1972), is concerned with the manner in which the UAW dealt with racism, McCarthyism, and vigilantism in the p;ostwar years. C. Wright Mills, *The New Men of Power* (New York, 1948), sees the labor leader emerging as a new middle-class social type. Robert Blauner, *Alienation and Freedom: The Factory Worker and His Industry* (Chicago, 1964), includes a chapter on the working conditions of assembly line workers in the auto industry. The same subject is considered in Charles P. Walker and Robert H. Guest, *The Man on the Assembly Line* (Cambridge, Mass., 1952).

William D. Andrew, "Factionalism and Anticommunism: Ford Local 600," *Labor History* 20 (Spring 1979): 227–55, persuasively demonstrates the inaccuracy of charges that the largest UAW local was dominated or manipulated by Communists. He underestimates somewhat the Communist strength in the local and the Communist role in inspiring the 1949 speed-up strike. Nelson Lichtenstein, "Life at the Rouge: A Cycle of Workers' Control," in Charles Stephenson and Robert Asher, eds., *Life and Labor: Dimensions of American Working-Class History* (Albany, 1986), 237–59, provides an excellent overview of the sources of Communist strength at Local 600. Claude E. Hoffman, *Sit-Down in Anderson* (Detroit, 1968), a history of Local 663 sponsored by the local's education committee, contains interesting comments on the local's response to the GM strike and the Henry Wallace candidacy.

Frank Cormier and William J. Eaton's *Reuther* (Englewood Cliffs, N. J., 1970), is a sympathetic portrait based in part on interviews with the principals. The authors received significant help from UAW publicist Frank Winn. Jean Gould and Lorena Hickok, *Walter Reuther: Labor's Rugged Individualist* (New York, 1972), is also a sympathetic biography although critical of its subject for his backwardness on the "woman question." R. L. Tyler, *Walter Reuther* (Grand Rapids, Mich., 1973), is critical of Reuther. The most recent biography, John Barnard, *Walter Reuther and the Rise of the Auto Workers* (Boston, 1983), while sympathetic to its subject, is more balanced than previous works on the UAW leader.

August Meier and Elliot Rudwick, *Black Detroit and the Rise of the UAW* (New York, 1979), examines the development of the alliance between the Black community and the UAW in the 1930s and early 1940s. Dominic J. Capeci, Jr., *Race Relations in Wartime Detroit: The Sojourner Truth Housing Controversy of 1942* (Philadelphia, 1984), is a well-documented and thoughtful examination of this important precursor of the 1943 race riot. Herbert Northrup, *The Negro in the Automobile Industry* (Philadelphia, 1970), focuses on the 1960s but presents some data on employment and discrimination in the auto industry before that time. Lloyd H. Bailer, "The Automobile Unions and Negro Labor" *Political Science Quarterly* LIX (Dec. 1944): 548–77, is a detailed, broad-ranging examination of Blacks in the auto industry in the 1940s (based on Bailer's doctoral dissertation). Among other useful studies of the same subject are Robert C. Weaver, *Negro Labor* (New York, 1946); and the same author's *The Negro Ghetto* (New York, 1948), which analyzes the situation in Detroit; and Philip Foner, *Organized Labor and the Black Worker* (New York, 1974), which contains a chapter on the cold war. Donald R.McCoy, *Quest and Response: Minority Rights and the Truman Administration* (Lawrence, Kan., 1973) discusses the growing strength of the civil rights coalition and is sympathetic to Truman's civil rights policy although critical of some of its shortcomings. Other works which discuss the Black experience while Truman was president include Herbert Hill, *Black Labor and the American Legal System* (Washington, 1977); and James A. Geschwender, *Class, Race and Worker Insurgency: The League of Revolutionary Black Workers* (Cambridge, Eng., 1977), which has a chapter on the 1930s and 1940s emphasizing conflict between Black and white workers and down-playing both Black participation in the UAW and examples of Black-white unity.

Among several recent studies emphasizing the UAW's failure adequately to defend the rights of women workers in the postwar period are Nancy Gabin, "Women Workers and the UAW in the Post-World War II Period: 1945–1954," *Labor History* 21 (Winter 1979–80): 5–30; Paddy Quick, "Rosie the Riveter: Myths and Realities" *Radical America* 9 (July–Aug. 1975): 115–31; Lyn Goldfarb *et al.*, *Separated and Unequal: Discrimination against Women Workers after World War II (the U.A.W. 1944–54)* (Washington, n.d.); and Sheila Tobias and Lisa Anderson, "What Really Happened to Rosie the Riveter? Demobilization and the Female Labor Force, 1944–47," MSS Modular Publications.

The Canadian labor movement, in which the UAW was represented, was driven by the same ideological and factional conflicts as the American labor movement. Gad Horowitz, *Canadian Labour in Politics* (Toronto, 1968), is a detailed study of this subject from a strongly anticommunist viewpoint. Irving Martin Abella's *Nationalism, Communism and Canadian Labour* (Toronto, 1973), is a more balanced account. The development of anticommunism during a critical postwar Canadian strike is analyzed in David Moulton, "Ford Windsor 1945," in Irving Abella, ed., *Six Key Labour Struggles in Canada, 1919–1949* (Toronto, 1974).

Clayton W. Fountain, *Union Guy* (New York, 1949), is the memoir of a strong Reuther partisan. Elizabeth Hawes, *Hurry Up Please, Its* [sic] *Time* (New York, 1946), is an account of the UAW's wartime and postwar factionalism and the position of women in the union by an anti-Reuther left-winger who was the staff of the union's Education Department. John Williamson, *Dangerous Scot* (New York, 1969), the autobiography of the Communist party's postwar labor secretary, contains an account of the division of the CIO in the 1940s and the effects of the Taft–Hartley Act on the labor movement. Len DeCaux, *Labor Radical* (Boston, 1970), is a vibrant memoir by a Communist who was the CIO's publicity director and editor of the *CIO News* until the passage of the Taft–Hartley Act. Wyndham Mortimer's *Organize!* (Boston, 1971), includes newsletters and articles the former UAW vice president and Communist wrote about the union in the postwar years. Victor G. Reuther's memoir *The Brothers Reuther* (Boston, 1976), has an interesting discussion of the brothers' early years, but its description of the postwar struggles of the UAW simply presents the factional arguments of the Reuther caucus. Frank Marquardt, *An Autoworker's Journal* (University Park, Pa., 1975), is a memoir by a Socialist who became disillusioned with the Reuther leadership. Clancy Sigal, *Going Away* (Boston, 1962), is a fictionalized account by an individual who worked briefly on the UAW staff as a left-winger and later became disillusioned and anticommunist. John Morton Blum, ed., *The Price of Vision: The Diary of Henry A. Wallace* (Boston, 1973), includes some accounts by Wallace of conversations with Philip Murray as well as Wallace's portrayal of conflicts inside the Truman Cabinet.

Lawrence J. White, *The Automobile Industry since 1945* (Cambridge, Mass., 1971), is a useful analysis focusing on the industry as an oligopoly. Peter F. Drucker, *Concept of the Corporation* (2nd Edition, New York, 1972), is an influential work based on the author's observations of the GM management. Alfred P. Sloan, Jr., *My Years with General Motors* (New York, 1963), focuses on a variety of management functions and briefly discusses labor relations. Keith Sward, *The Legend of Henry Ford* (Toronto, 1948), and David L. Lewis, *The Public Image of Henry Ford* (Detroit, 1976), both examine Henry Ford II's takeover of the company helm and the first round of postwar labor negotiations. The changes at Ford after 1945 are also discussed in Allan Nevins and Frank Ernest Hill,

Ford: Decline and Rebirth, 1933–1962 (New York, 1962). The most thought-provoking examination of business philosophy in the period is Howell John Harris, *The Right to Manage: Industrial Relations Policies of American Business in the 1940s* (Madison, 1982). Howell's work provides important insights into the labor conflicts of the period.

Richard S. Kirkendall, ed., *The Truman Period as a Research Field: A Reappraisal, 1972* (Columbia, Mo., 1974); Barton J. Bernstein, ed., *Politics and Policies of the Truman Administration* (Chicago, 1970); and Barton J. Bernstein, *The Truman Administration: A Documentary History* (New York, 1966) are valuable studies of the Truman administration.

Sidney Fine, *Sit-down: The General Motors Strike of 1936–1937* (Ann Arbor, Mich., 1969), is the definitive account of that historic union victory. Peter Friedlander, *The Emergence of A UAW Local, 1936–1939* (Pittsburgh, 1975), focuses on the role of ethnicity but is off the mark in its assumption that the entry of large numbers of workers into the union led to an automatic deradicalization. Alan Clive, *State of War* (Ann Arbor, Mich., 1979); Lowell Julliard Carr and James Edson Stermer, *Wilow Run* (New York, 1952); and Joshua Freeman, "Delivering the Goods: Industrial Unionism during World War II" *Labor History* (Fall 1978): 570–93, all contain information on the auto workers in World War II.

Douglas P. Seaton, *Catholics and Radicals* (London, 1981), focuses on the anticommunist activities of the ACTU. James J. Matles and James Higgins, *Them and Us* (Englewood Cliffs, N. J., 1974), deals with the UE and Robert Ozanne, *Century of Labor-Management Relations at McCormick and International Harvester* (Madison, Wisc., 1973), depicts the conflict between the UAW and the FE.

Several novels are concerned with the role of workers during World War II and the cold war. Harriette Arnow, *The Dollmaker* (New York, 1954) is a moving treatment of a Southern family that migrated to Detroit when the husband took a job in a war plant. The locale of Ben Field, *Piper Tompkins* (Garden City, N. Y., 1946), is a wartime electrical plant. K. B. Gilden, *Between the Hills and the Sea* (New York, 1971), provides a vivid portrait of the effects of the cold war on left and progressive workers in a New England electrical plant.

Index

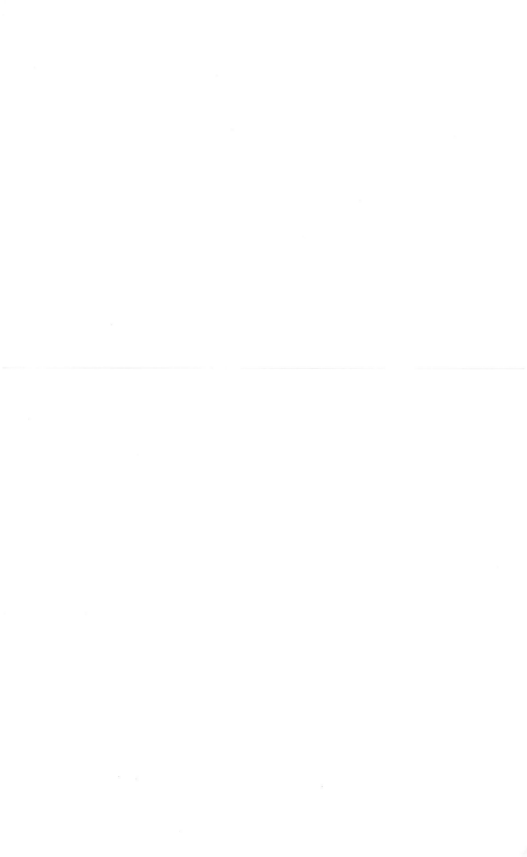